Yugoslav Folk Music

NUMBER 10 IN THE NEW YORK BARTÓK ARCHIVE

STUDIES IN MUSICOLOGY

THE NEW YORK BARTÓK ARCHIVE

Benjamin Suchoff, *Trustee*

The Béla Bartók Archives:
History and Catalogue

Rumanian Folk Music
I Instrumental Melodies
II Vocal Melodies
III Texts
IV Carols and Christmas Songs (*Colinde*)
V Maramureș County

Turkish Folk Music from Asia Minor

Béla Bartók Essays

Yugoslav Folk Music
I Serbo-Croatian Folk Songs (with Albert B. Lord)
II Tabulation of Material
III Source Melodies: Part One
IV Source Melodies: Part Two

Yugoslav Folk Music

VOLUME TWO

Yugoslav
FOLK MUSIC

Volume Two

Tabulation of Material

by BÉLA BARTÓK

Edited by BENJAMIN SUCHOFF

State University of New York Press

1978

Published by
State University of New York Press
Albany, New York 12246

Printed in the United States of America

Library of Congress Cataloging in Publication Data

Bartók, Béla, 1881–1945.
Yugoslav folk music.

(New York Bartók Archive studies in musicology; no. 9)
Vol. 1 originally published in 1951 by
Columbia University Press, New York,
which was issued as no. 7 of its
Studies in musicology.
Includes bibliographies and indexes.
CONTENTS: v. 1. Serbo-Croatian folk songs and
instrumental pieces from the Milman Parry collection.
1. Folk-songs, Yugoslav—History and criticism.
2. Folk-songs, Croatian—History and criticism.
I. Lord, Albert Bates, joint author.
II. Suchoff, Benjamin.
III. Herzog, George, 1901–
IV. Series: Béla Bartók Archives.
Studies in musicology; no. 9.
V. Series: Columbia University studies in musicology; no. 7.
VI. Title.
ML3590.B32 784.4′9497 78-8188
ISBN 0-87395-383-5

Contents

Editor's Preface

Bartók's Tabulation of [Yugoslav] Material (hereafter: "Tab. of Mat."), which he completed in New York during July, 1942, was begun "some years ago when still in Europe."[1] An innovation in Bartókian ethnomusicological methodology, its purpose as a compendium of supporting research data is perhaps best expressed in Bartók's own words which were written shortly before he completed the work:

> Only a systematically scientific examination of the morphological aspects of folk music material (consisting first of grouping the material according to certain methods, and then, of describing the typical forms and structures which will appear in a material thus grouped) will enable us to determine clearly the types and to draw various conclusions concerning the transformation, migration of the melodies, their connection with foreign materials, etc.[2]

The Yugoslav folk music material Bartók examined for tabulation is described in Volume I (pp. 22–25) but is listed here in short form as a convenience for the reader.

1. Š. Bosiljevac. Folk Songs from Bosnia and Hercegovina (50 melodies). Cited as *Bosiljevac.*
2. T. M. Bušetić. Folk Songs and Folk Dances from Levač (88 melodies). Cited as *Iz Levča.*
3. V. Đorđević. Serbian Folk Melodies; Southern Serbia (428 melodies). Cited as *Juž. Srb.*
4. —— Serbian Folk Melodies from Prewar Serbia (600 melodies). Cited as *Đorđević.*
5. —— Folk Song Book (380 melodies). Cited as *Đorđević Nar. Pev.*
6. B. Kačerovski. Round Dance (87 melodies). Cited as *Kačerovski.*
7. L. Kuba. Songs and Melodies from Bosnia and Hercegovina (965 melodies). Cited as *Kuba B.H.*

[1] Vol. I, p. 22.

[2] *Béla Bartók Essays,* comp. and ed. Benjamin Suchoff (London: Faber & Faber, 1976), essay No. 7, "On American and British Folk Material," p. 37.

8. —— The Slavs in Their Folk Songs (Vols. IX–XIV, 347 melodies). Cited as *Kuba IX . . . XIV*.
9. F. Š. Kuhač. Yugoslav Folk Songs (1,628 melodies). Cited as *Kuhač*.
10. K. P. Manojlović. The Musical Characteristics of Our South (20 melodies). Cited as *Manojlović*.
11. L. Kuba (MS collection). Songs and Melodies from Bosnia and Hercegovina (160 melodies). Cited as *Kuba B.H. Ms*.
12. B. Bartók (MS collection). Serbian Peasant Music from the Banat (21 melodies). Cited as *Bartók Ms*.

Total number of melodies tabulated (duplications excluded): 3,449.

The complete "Tab. of Mat." was constructed on transparent master sheets, in folio form, from which a set of Ozalid prints, cut apart, was made for Bartók's personal use.[3] The master sheet draft, written in india ink, contains a number of pencilled additions. The proof copy has corrections in india ink, pencil, and red crayon. Discrepancies and other editorially determined differences between the drafts, including their comparison with the source melodies in Vol. III, are given below in the Addenda and Corrigenda (p. xix).

In addition to the melodies selected from the twelve collections listed above, which make up the bulk of "Tab. of Mat." (pp. 1–135), is a smaller tabulation of the seventy-five Parry vocal melodies (including record nos.: pp. 137–38); Appendix I, melody-stanza structures based on text-line splitting (three unnumbered folios); Appendix II, other range formulas (one unnumbered page); and Appendix III, a series of concordances of "Tab. of Mat." Current Nos. and the numeric designations of the twelve tabulated collections (pp. 1–23).

The classification technique used by Bartók in the "Tab. of Mat." reveals a departure from the system of alphabetic letters in conjunction with numerals used in his other major studies of East European musical folklore (Hungary, Slovakia, Rumania). In the present case all classes are designated with roman numerals for main groups and italicized or punctulated arabic figures for subgroups. The following editorial survey of the tabulated melodies, patterned after Bartók's own format that he first implemented in his book on Rumanian folk song,[4] describes the complete material:

[3] The master sheet draft is kept in the Special Collections department of Butler Library, Columbia University, New York, N.Y. The proof copy is in the New York Bartók Archive (NYBA) of the Estate of Béla Bartók.

[4] *Rumanian Folk Music*, ed. Benjamin Suchoff, Vol. II (The Hague: Martinus Nijhoff, 1967), pp. 7–9.

Survey of the Tabulated Melodies

(Figures in Italics Indicate Syllabic Structure)

I. One-Section Melodies, Nos. 1–35; Parry 1

7, : 1–4
8, : 5–9
8b, : 10
10, : 11–26; Parry 1
11, : 27–32
12, : 33–34
13, : 35

Two-Section Melodies, Nos. 36–619; Parry 2–17

II. Isometric, Nos. 36–460	III. Heterometric, Nos. 461–619	
	First section of higher syllabic number, Nos. 461–581	Second section of higher syllabic number, Nos. 582–619
5, : 36–40	*6, (5,)* : 461–462	*5, (7, 8,)* : 582–584c.
6, : 41–78	*7, (5, 6,)* : 463–465	*6, (7, 8,)* : 584d.–586
7, : 79–110	*8, (5–7,)* : 466–526	*7, (8–11, 13, 14,)* : 587–596
8, : 111–201; Parry 2–3	*10, (4, 6–8,)* : 527–557	*8, (9–12,)* : 597–616
8b, : 202–251; Parry 4–5	*11, (6–8, 10,)* : 558–568	*9, (11,)* : 617
9, : 252–256	*12, (6–10,)* : 569–578	*10, (12,)* : 618
10, : 257–406; Parry 6–13	*14, (12,)* : 579–580	*12, (14,)* : 619
11, : 407–446 Parry 14–15	*15, (11,)* : 581	
12, : 447–459; Parry 16a., 17		
13, : 460		

Three-Section Melodies, Nos. 620–1023; Parry 18–21

IV. Isometric □ [Structure, Nos. 620–659	V. Isometric] □ Structure, Nos. 660–727
5, : 620	*5,* : 660–662
6, : 621–626	*6,* : 663–675

7, : 627–628	*7,* : 676–681
8, : 629–646; Parry 18	*8,* : 682–700; Parry 20, 21a.b.
8b, : 647–654	*8b,* : 701–711
10, : 654bis.–657; Parry 19	*9,* : 712
11, : 658	*10,* : 713–723
12, : 659	*11,* : 724–726
	13, : 727

VI. Heterometric □ ⊏ Structure, Nos. 728–919; Parry 22–24

1) With two equal sections, Nos. 728–832	2) With double sections, Nos. 833–861	3) With unequal sections, Nos. 862–919
1. : 728–738; Parry 22	2. : 833–852	2. : 862–864
3. : 739–743	3. : 852bis.	3. : 865–872
4. : 744–745	4. : 853	4. : 873
5. : 746–828; Parry 23–24	5. : 854–859	5. : 874–882
6. : 829–832	6. : 860	6. : 883–919
	11. : 861	

VII. Heterometric ⊐ □ Structure, Nos. 920–1023; Parry 25–30

1) With two equal sections, Nos. 920–993	3) With unequal sections, Nos. 994–1023
1. : 920–944	1. : 994
2. : 945–971; Parry 25	2. : 995–1013
3. : 972–992; Parry 26–28	3. : 1013bis.–1017; Parry 30
4. : 993; Parry 16b., 29	4. : 1018
	5. : 1019–1021
	6. : 1022–1023

VIII. Melodies of Special Structure, Nos. 1024–1053; Parry 31–33

Four-Section Melodies, Nos. 1024–1830; Parry 34–53

IX. Isometric, Nos. 1054–1364	X. Heterometric, Nos. 1365–1830
5, : 1054–1087	1. : 1365–1386
6, : 1088–1171	2. : 1387–1392
7, : 1172–1201	3. : 1393–1429

8, : 1202–1273, 1295–1303; Parry 34–36
8b, : 1274–1294
9, : 1304–1308
10, : 1309–1331
11, : 1332–1339
12, : 1340–1351; Parry 37
13, : 1352–1354
14, : 1355–1364

4. : 1430–1459
5. : 1460–1638; Parry 38–52
6. : 1639–1650
7. : 1651–1655
8. : 1656–1657
9. : 1658–1663
10. : 1664–1685; Parry 53
11. : 1686–1692
13. : 1693
14. : 1694–1700
15. : 1701–1719
16. : 1720–1732
16bis. : 1733
17. : 1734–1775
20. : 1776–1786
21. : 1787–1794
21bis. : 1795–1797
22. : 1798–1810
22bis. : 1811–1814
23. : 1815–1819
24. : 1820–1830

Melodies of Children's Play Type (no definite structure), Nos. 1831–1855

Melodies of Confused, Indeterminable Structure, Nos. 1856–1896; Parry 54

Bartók's first use of **Z** symbol formulas, to represent the proportion of syllabic figures in heterometric melodies (further details are on p. xv, below), occurs in his classic ethnomusicological study of Hungarian folk song.[5] The formulas are extended in his book on Slovak folk song[6] and published in a more refined tabular form in *Rumanian Folk Music*.[7] They are described, too, in Vol. I (pp. 29–30) of the

[5] The first version, *A magyar népdal,* was published by Rózsavölgyi (Budapest) in 1924; the second one, in German, by Walter de Gruyter (Berlin/Leipzig) the next year; the third one, in English, by Oxford University Press (London) in 1931. A reprint edition of the Hungarian and German versions was issued in 1965 (ed. by D. Dillę) by Editio Musica, Budapest; a revision of the English version, with annotations by Zoltán Kodály and edited by the present writer, is in preparation.

[6] *Slowakische Volkslieder,* published by Academia Scientiarum Slovaca (Bratislava). Vol. I appeared in 1959, Vol. II in 1970, and Vol. III is in preparation.

[7] *Op. cit.,* p. 11.

present publication, in which Bartók states that "the heterometric melodies will be grouped according to their formulas. The order of the formulas is to be seen in the 'Tab. of Mat.,' pp. 39–50, 56–79, 103–135."[8] As a convenience to the reader, and in conformity with Bartók's procedure in *Rumanian Folk Music,* the "Tab. of Mat." **Z** symbols have been extracted and are listed below in accordance with their placement in "Tab. of Mat." (roman numerals indicate Class; parenthetic figures, Subclass; punctulated ones, Group):

SYLLABIC PROPORTION IN THE HETEROMETRIC MELODIES

III. : **Zz,** (Nos.) 461–581; **zZ,** 582–619

VI. 1) : 1. **ZZz,** 728–738, Parry 22; 3. **ZzZ,** 739–743; 4. **zZz,** 744–745; 5. **Zzz,** 746–828, Parry 23–24; 6. **zZZ,** 829–832

2) : 2. **Zz + zZ,** 833–852; 3. **Zz + Zz,** 852bis.; 4. **Zz + Zz,** 853; 5. **Zz + zZ,** 854–859; 6. **Zz + zZ,** 860; 11. **ZZ + Zz,** 861

3) : 2. **ZzZ,** 862–864; 3. **ZzZ,** 865–872; 4. **zZZ,** 873; 5. **zZz,** 874–882; 6. **ZZz,** 883–919

VII. 1) : 1. **ZZz,** 920–944; 2. **zzZ,** 945–971, Parry 25; 3. **ZzZ,** 972–992; Parry 26–28; 4. **zZz,** 993, Parry 16b., 29

3) : 1. **zZZ,** 994; 2. **ZzZ,** 995–1013; 3. **ZzZ,** 1013bis.–1017, Parry 30; 4. **zZZ,** 1018; 5. **zZz,** 1019–1021; 6. **ZZz,** 1022–1023

X. : 1. **zzZz,** 1365–1386; 2. **ZZzZ,** 1387–1392; 3. **ZZzz,** 1393–1429; 4. **zzZZ,** 1430–1459; 5. **ZzZz,** 1460–1638, Parry 38–52; 6. **zZzZ,** 1639–1650; 7. **Zzzz,** 1651–1655; 8. **zZZZ,** 1656–1657; 9. **zzzZ,** 1658–1663; 10. **ZZZz,** 1664–1685, Parry 53; 11. **ZZZ + ZZ,** 1686–1692; 13. **zzZ + Zz,** 1693; 14. **ZZz + zZ,** 1694–1700; 15. **zzZ + Zz,** 1701, 1710; **ZZz + Zz,** 1702, 1709–1709, 1711–

[8] **Z**-formulas are not printed for three-section heterometric melodies in "Tab. of Mat." pp. 39–50 but they do appear in Vol. I, Table 3, p. 49.

1715, 1717–1719a.; **ZZZ + Zz,** 1703–1706; **ZZz + zz,** 1707, 1716; 16. **zzZ + ZZ,** 1720, **ZZz + zZ,** 1719b., 1721–1722, 1725–1730; **zzz + zZ,** 1723; **ZZz + zZ,** 1724, 1731–1732; 16bis. **ZZz + zZ,** 1733

EXPLANATION OF SIGNS USED IN THE TABULATION

The main part of "Tab. of Mat." is in eight-column format, with these headings: Current No., Original edition, Syll., Last note of sections, Range, Rhythm structure, and Remarks. After it is the Parry Tabulation, in the same format, with two changes in heading (Record No. in the second column and Referring to variants in Tab. of Mat. in the last column). Then follows the three appendices, each one with a different structure. As an aid for ready reference purposes a description of each heading or appendix and its symbolic representations is given here, for the most part in Bartók's own language as extracted from Vol. I.

Current No.—The 3,449 melodies ordered in 1,896 variant groups, each group distinguished by small letters, for example, current Nos. 123a. to 123gg.

Original edition—The number of the melody or of the page in each collection. When the same melody is published elsewhere, citation is given in parenthesis below the main entry.

For information on the various collections cited, see pp. ix–x, above or Vol. I, pp. 22–25.

Syllabic structure—The number of syllables in a given melody section is represented by an italicized arabic numeral with comma.

(1) Isometric melodies—those with melody sections of the same syllabic length—are indicated by one number.

(2) Heterometric melodies are represented by two or more numerals: *8, 5, 8, 5,* means a melody of four sections in which the first and third sections have eight syllables, the second and fourth sections, five. In addition the syllabic proportion of these melodies are symbolized by **Z** formulas. *8, 5, 8, 5,* (or *7, 6, 7, 6,* and so forth) is indicated by **ZzZz.** Exceptions: two-section melodies and four-section melodies with peculiar mixtures of syllabic length.

Subclasses are indicated by parenthetic numerals in three-section melodies: 1) contains the groups (designated 1., 2., and so on) with two sizes of **Z**; 2), the double-section groups, similarly designated; and 3), those groups with three sizes of **Z.**

The subclasses in four-section melodies are designated by punctulated numbers (there are no other subdivisions), from 1. to 11., 13. to 17., and 20. to 24.[9]

(3) In case of splitting of text lines (that is, the splitting of isometric text lines in order to make them applicable to heterometric melody stanzas) an additional italicized figure in parentheses indicates the syllabic number of the original proper text-line: *(10) 10, 6, 10, 6,* means that the text of the six-syllable melody section is a portion of the original ten-syllable text line.

(4) The figure *8b,* represents the metrical structure *3+2+3=8,* (*b* stands for "Bulgarian," since this metrical structure is very characteristic in Bulgarian folk-poem texts).

(5) When one (sometimes two) section of a melody is composed of two metrically equal ("twin") parts, these will be regarded as "double" sections, that is, virtually as one section. Double sections are indicated by a plus sign connecting (italicized) numbers which are followed by a comma.

(6) Melodies of special structure include the frequently occurring syllabic symbols *(10) 4, 6, 6, 4,* (the sign ‿ means one text-line). That is, a dekasyllable *(4 || 6)* is sung to the first half of the melody and again, in inverted order, to the second half. The sign || indicates the main metrical caesura: when, on repetition, the dekasyllable is inverted, syllables 5 to 10 precede this caesura and 1 to 4 follow it.

(7) The letter *r.* indicates the presence of a refrain.

More detailed descriptions and other illustrative matter will be found in Vol. I, pp. 15, 28–30, 45, and 51–52.

Last note of sections—Full and half-circles indicate main and secondary caesuras (converted to full and half-boxes in Vol. I) which, in the music examples (Vols. I, III, IV), are placed above that note considered to be the final note of the respective melody section (the portion of a melody corresponding to an entire text line or to its repeated fragment or fragments).

All melodies have been transposed to g^1 as the final tone. This tone

[9] The missing numbers 12., 18., and 19. can be construed as tacit reminders that certain **Z** formulas are lacking in the tabulated Yugoslav material. The complete classification of these formulas is contained in an MS draft (one leaf, NYBA files) which Bartók prepared in anticipation of a revision of his Hungarian folk song study.

is represented by the numeral 1, below it by roman numerals (VII, VI . . . I), and above it by arabic numerals (2, 3 . . . 11). Chromatic alteration is indicated by accidentals placed before the numeral.

The reader is referred to Vol. I, pp. 15–16, 27–28 for additional information on caesura designation and the labeling of scale degrees.

Range—The same degree-symbols used to designate caesuras are employed to indicate ambitus of the melody, from lowest to highest (principal) tone. See also Vol. I, pp. 16, 28, 31, 52–56.

Rhythm structure—Three types of indicators are used: music notations derived from the skeleton form (that is, stripped of embellishment tones) of the melodies, signed digits to mark syllabic subdivision of the melody section, and small letters in the case of isometric yet heterorhythmic (unequal rhythm) melodies. The same letter indicates the same rhythm; different letters, different rhythm: a b , a b a b , a b c, and so forth. See also Vol. I, pp. 29–30, 65–70.[10]

Structure—Similarity or difference in the content of sections is designated by capital letters: A A B A, A B C D, and so forth. Superscript and subscript arabic numerals (A^5, A_5) indicate repetitions (higher, lower) at a specified intervallic distance, except that the letter *s* is used to indicate a stepwise (A^s, A_s) sequence (A_{sss}=A repeated three times in downward sequence). The letter *v* as a subscript attachment indicates a slight change in content of a given section, for example, A A_v. See aso Vol. I, pp. 28–29, 47–50.

Remarks—More than a dozen types of comments are placed in the last column of "Tab. of Mat.". Genre description is the most prevalent type (see Bartók's enumeration in Vol. I, pp. 82–83), followed by variant determination in which references are made to the following folk music materials: Bulgarian, French, German, Hungarian, Italian, Moravian, Parry Collection, Rumanian, Russian, Slovak, Slovenian, Turkish, Ukraïnian, urban, and the Yugoslav collections at hand. In addition there are references to variants in art music works of Haydn, Beethoven, and other composers as well as to urban and foreign "contaminations" in certain melodies.

The wide range of analytic treatment of the collected materials is evident in Bartók's remarks on these subject areas: chromaticism; fragmented (incomplete) melodies; maccaronic, heroic, and urban poetic texts; part songs; performance peculiarities (as listed and de-

[10] In certain cases this column shows data concerning type of cadence, and variants in the Parry Collection, apparently for the sake of expediency.

scribed in Vol. I, pp. 73–81); rhymes; text-stanza structure; transposing structure; and questions on various morphological aspects of the melodies.

The following special symbols appear:[11]

3 —̓ *3*, means a line- or word-interruption. The apostrophe, appearing above the dash separating the two syllable figures, indicates that the interruption occurs between the third and fourth syllables in a six-syllable melody section.

4+[5.]+*1* means that the fifth syllable is interrupted in a six-syllable melody section.

The sign * indicates that the remark is a marginal note to an item, similarly marked, appearing in another column of the same Current No.

Cf. or Var. followed by a figure indicates the location of a variant elsewhere in "Tab. of Mat." Figures prefixed by "Parry" refer to variants among the music examples in Vol. I.

APPENDIX I

This tabulation of "melody-stanza structures based on text-line splitting, and not occurring but once" is an extension of Table 2 in Vol. I (pp. 42–43). Since Appendix I should be studied in conjunction with its counterpart in Vol. I, the reader will find a complete explanation of symbols there (pp. 43–44). Exceptions: punctulated arabic numerals indicate specific syllables of a main line; when such numerals are followed by a parenthesis, the figure refers to schema number (there are 33 schemata in Table 2).

APPENDIX II

This tabulation is an extension of Table 4 in Vol. I (p. 53), that is, the former breaks down the 332 "less important" range formulas which are condensed in the first listing of the latter (I–1 to VI–10).

APPENDIX III

In these concordances a figure followed by a long dash indicates that the melody has been omitted from the "Tab. of Mat." listings for various reasons (see Vol. I, pp. 24–25).

[11] See also Vol. I, p. 76 (note 73).

The Kuba *B.H.* 615 entry shows a question mark following the long dash. The reader should add there 317c. as "Tab. of Mat." concordance, even though Bartók (inadvertently) omitted the melody from the tabulation (see No. 317c., the source melody, in Vol. III).

The Đorđević 528 entry shows 528 = 528. The "Tab. of Mat." concordance number is 7d. (see the melody—notated with 7c.—in Vol. III).

ADDENDA AND CORRIGENDA

Both drafts of "Tab. of Mat." show identical remarks added by Bartók in pencil or, in the proof copy (of the master sheet MS), red crayon. There are many other red crayon additions and corrections in the proof copy that were subsequently overwritten with india ink, apparently at the same time the master sheet draft was emended to incorporate the new data. Since the penciled remarks on the master sheet draft are too faint to be legible for facsimile reproduction, and in view of their similarity in content and scope to the material in the Remarks column of "Tab. of Mat.," they are given below in Current No. order (editorial comments are enclosed in brackets). In addition the placement of certain melodies from the Parry Collection (Vol. I) in "Tab. of Mat.," which are indicated in "Tabulation of Parry No. 1–54" (pp. 136–138, below) but not in "Tab. of Mat." proper,[12] are listed for the convenience of the reader.

Comparative survey of the "Tab. of Mat." drafts with the Source Materials revealed various types of discrepancies; other errata turned up after analysis of content-structure had been made, in preparation for the data processing of the incipits which are indexed in Part Two (below). These editorial determinations are indicated by placing the pertinent Current No. in brackets.[13]

1a. Nos. 1a. and 1b. together would be *7*, [2].
[7d.] Omitted from "Tab. of Mat.": see the source melody, notated with No. 7c., in Vol. III.

[12] The Parry melodies as *variants* are listed in their respective places; those as *new melodies,* to be "inserted" by the reader, are not. It can thus be concluded that Bartók completed "Tab. of Mat." prior to final numbering of the Parry music examples in Vol. I.

[13] Bracketed commentaries following the author's remarks are also editorial additions. The reader will find another list in Vol. III (Source Melodies: Part One) containing remarks which were editorially extracted from the "Tab. of Mat." source melodies.

22a. *Kralj Matijaš* [Hungarian: King Mátyás (Matthias, Matthew)].
22b. *Kad se isprosi djevojka* [When the marriage proposal is accepted].
47b. = *párosító* [see Vol. I, p. 82: IV. 2.]
107. Phrygian. *Barcsai* text. Not old Hungarian?[14]
123ff. *Noć tomna noć* [= refrain: Night, dark night].
143e. *Táncrahívó* [calling to the dance].
161. Like a Rumanian *colindă* (not a variant).
165b. Arab-like.
237a. *Görög Ilona* text! [Hungarian title].
268./269. Parry 7 as new melody: its place between Nos. 268 and 269.
327c. *Terentete, Kerdigata* as Hungarian text borrowings.
369a. "*Čupava, garava* [Shaggy, raven-haired] . . ." variant? [Cf. No. 1155].
403./404. Parry 13 as new melody; its place between Nos. 403 and 404.
[441.] The range is 1–9-flat.
454a.b. This variant group is in the wrong place: it should precede No. 453.
492e. Same remark as to No. 492a.
492g. "How do we plant the pepper?" [trans. from Hung. entry].
[511a.] Missing structure designation; the respective source melody shows A B content.
517a. *Bendbašu* [Cf. Nos. 915, 1619, Parry 51].
553a. *Petrole!* [= refrain].
557. [Sultan] Sulejman; Zrinyi Miklós [Hungarian hero].
572. *go-gi-go*
592c.d. Parry [No. 14]: *Sitna trava zelena* [Tiny green grass].
617. "hm"-like [that is, the refrain *bre, bre, bre!* has a resemblance to but is not derived from a Rumanian refrain (*hm hm hm:* cf. *Rumanian Folk Music* II, melody Nos. 444j.l.)].
639./640. Parry 18 as new melody; its place between Nos. 639 and 640.
654bis./655. Parry 19 as new melody; its place between 654bis. and 655.

[14] A *Barcsai* text, whose melody is also in the Phrygian mode, will be found in Zoltán Kodály, *A magyar népzene* (ed. by Lajos Vargyas), Zeneműkiadó Vallalat, Budapest, 1960, melody No. 339 (pp. 220–221).

682./683. Parry 20 as new melody; its place between Nos. 682 and 683.
685. Rumanian?
696a. *Dva Morića?* [The source melody (Vol. IV) suggests a variant relationship with Parry 20. Compare, for instance, the last melody section in the respective music examples].
699. *Himzibeg!* [Cf. Parry 34–36].
717a. Hungarian fragment?
727./728.–729. Parry 22 as new melody; its place between Nos. 727 and 728–729.
788a. Like a [Rumanian] *colindă?*
812a.b.c. *na Bendbašu* [see editorial comment for 517a., above].
850. Text related to the Hungarian song *Elmentem én a vásárra* [I went to the fair].
858. Cf. [? The source melody points to the contamination as stemming from a Bucharest urban popular song. See, however, *Rumanian Folk Music* II, melody No. 51].
882a.b. *Neka bude proha mak* [Cf. the respective texts in Vol. IV].
883b. *Paun moj* [My peacock].
897a. Imperfect cadence.
897a.b. Going in "imaginary" thirds.
920–921. The *8, 8,* syllabic structure of the first two melody sections is Rumanian-like.
[969.] Cf. Haydn Op. 33, No. 3 ("The Bird"), IV.: first theme.
1040–1./1042. Parry 32 and 33 as new melodies; their place between Nos. 1040–1 and 1042.
1128a.–e. *Szeretnék szántani* [I would love to plough] text variant.
1136. Pirot![15]
[1137.] Cf. M. A. Balakirev, Russian Folk Songs for Voice and Piano, No. 26 ("Under the Green Apple Tree"). The same melody can be found in Tschaikovsky's Serenade for String Orchestra, Op. 48 (IV. movement), and a variant of it is Hugo Wolf's song, *Wohl kenn' ich Euren Stand.*
1155. *Čupava garava* [Cf. No. 369a.].
[1161.] The rhythm structure of *a* should read: two eighth notes, quarter note; bar line; quarter note, two eighth notes.
[1209c.] The respective melody (Vol. IV) correctly shows A A B A.

[15] The source melody of Nos. 1310l. and 1367a. shows this designation with the remark: Bulgarian? Pirot is a Serbian town near the Bulgarian border.

[1222.] The respective melody (Vol. IV) correctly shows A B C B.
1224./1225. Parry 35 as new melody; its place between Nos. 1224 and 1225.
[1246h.j.] The missing caesura symbols will be found in the respective source melodies (Vol. IV).
1256. Turkish-Hungarian-like text-beginning (a picture out of life) [see Bartók, *Turkish Folk Music* (Princeton University Press, 1976), p. 206].
1314a.b. *Patkó Pista* [Hungarian title].
1339./1340. Parry 37 as new melody; its place between Nos. 1339 and 1340.
[1347.] The respective melody (Vol. IV) correctly shows A B C D.
[1357a.b.] Haydn Symphony No. 104 ("London") in D, IV. movement: first theme.
1498./1499 Parry 40 as new melody; its place between Nos. 1498 and 1499.
1506./1507. Parry 43 as new melody; its place between Nos. 1506 and 1507.
1521./1522. Parry 45 as new melody; its place between Nos. 1521 and 1522.
1530a. The A^5 B^4 melody sections have imperfect-like cadences (??).
1534. *Dojčin Petar.*
1570d. *Smiješno čudo* (*Poskočnica*?) [Cf. Vol. I, p. 82: V. 2.].
1572./1573. Parry 47 as new melody; its place between Nos. 1572 and 1573.
[1596.] Haydn, Symphony No. 103 ("Drum Roll") in E-flat, IV. movement.
1610./1611. Parry 49 as new melody; its place between Nos. 1610 and 1611.
1615./1616. Parry 50 as new melody; its place between Nos. 1615 and 1616.
1637./1638. Parry 52 as new melody; its place between Nos. 1637 and 1638.
1638. Variant: *neću varošanka 8, 8, 6, 6,* [cf. No. 1403b.].
[1743.] Cf. *Rumanian Folk Music* II, melody No. 501.[16]
[1748–9.] Cf. *Rumanian Folk Music* II, melody No. 317.

[16] As listed by Bartók on p. 40 of that volume.

1822. Hungarian text variant: *Teríti a láng a vászonat* [The girl spreads out the linen].

* * *

Following Bartók's compendia is a lexicographical index of "Tab. of Mat." themes (that is, melody section incipits), including the seventy-five Parry Collection melodies in Vol. I, an editorial supplement constructed by means of electronic data processing.

Acknowledgement is therefore made to the American Council of Learned Societies for supporting the research and subsequent data extraction procedures, to Jack Heller for special programming assistance, and to the following students: Marilyn B. Cohen, Seth Kasten, Linda Krummel, and Michael A. Suchoff, who encoded the music notations into machine readable form.

BENJAMIN SUCHOFF

New York

I. One-section melodies

I 7, –10,

Current No.	Original edition	Syll.	Last note of sections	Range	Rhythm. structure	Structure	Remarks
1a. }	Kuba B.H. 849	7,		VII – ♭3			
b. }	" 850	7,		1 – 4			
2.	Kuhač 1026	7,		VII – 4			„Igra"
3.	Đorđević 583.	7,		1 – 4			
4.	Kuhač 1028.	7,			3+4		
5.	Đorđević 525.	8,		VI – 1			
6.	Kuhač 1076.	8,		#VII – 2			„žensko kolo"
7a. }	Đorđević 254.	8,		1 – ♭3			„lazarička"
b. }	" 255.	7,		1 – ♭3			
c. }	Kuhač 1210.	8,		1 – ♭3			„svatovska"
8.	Kuhač 1047.	8,		1 – 4			„poziv u kolo"
9.	Kuhač 1079.	8,		1 – 5			„žensko kolo"
10.	Kuhač 834.	8b,		♭VI – ♭3			
11.	Kuba B.H. 792.	10,		VII – ♭2			
12.	Kuba B.H. 486.	10,		VII – ♭3			
13.	Kuhač 1524.	10,		VII – ♭3			heroic?
14.	Kuba B.H. 860.	10,		VII – ♭3			„svatovska"
15.	Kuba B.H. 827.	10,		VII – 4			
16.	Kuba XI. 56.	10,		1 – ♭2			„uspavanka"
17a. }	Đorđević 325.	10,		1 – ♭3			„lazarička"
b. }	" 326.	10,		1 – ♭3			„lazarička"
18.	Kuhač 1049.	10,		1 – ♭3			„u kolo"
19.	Kuhač 476.	10,		1 – 4			
20.	Kuhač 327	10,		1 – 4			
21a. }	Kuba B.H. 350.	10,		1 – 4			

Current No	Original edition	Syll.	Last note of sections	Range	Rhythm structure	Structure	Remarks
b.	" 401.	10,		1–4			
22a.	Kuhač 929.	10,		1–4			
b.	" 1205.	10,		1–4			
23.	Đorđević 445.	10,		1–4			
24a.	Kuhač 197.	10,		1–4			
b.	" 448.	10,		1–4			
c.	Đorđević 247.	10,		1–4			
d.	" 586.	10,		1–4			
e.	" 588.	10,		1–4			
25.	Kuba X. 42	10,		1–5,			„Uspavanka"
26.	Bosiljevac 12.	10,		1–b6			
27.	Kuba B.H. 563.	(7)A. 11,		VII–4			
28.	Đorđević 133.	(8) * 11,		VII–4			
29.	Kuba XI. 54.	(7) 11,		VII–4			
30.	Đorđević 441.	(8) r. 11,		1–4			
31.	Kuhač 1080.	(8) r. 11,		1–5			„u ženskom kolu"
32.	Iz Levča 53.	(7) r. 11,		1–4	4+3+4		
33.	Kuhač 69	(8) r. 12,		VII–2			
34.	Đorđević 8.	(8) r. 12,		1–4		Var. Parry 17.	(two section form: AAv)
35.	Đorđević 314.	(10) r. 13,		VII–2			„Kraljička"

II. Two (equal)-section melodies

Current No	Original edition	Syll.	Last note of sections	Range	Rhythm structure	Structure	Remarks
36a.	Đorđević 418.	5,	(I)	1–4	AB		„sedeljka"
b.	Kuhač 1249a)	5,	(I)	1–4	AB		„svatovska"
c.	" 1284.	5,	(VII)	VII–b3	AB		
d.	Đorđević 224.	(5) 7, 5,	(I)	1–4	AB		„sedeljka"
37.	Kuba B.H. 759.	5,	(I)	1–4	AAv		

3

II.5,−6, (bVI)−(1)

Current №	Original edition	Syll.	Last note of section	Range	Rhythm structure	Structure	Remarks
38.	Kuhač 181.	5,	(2)	1−3		A B	
39a.	Kuhač 1267.	5,	(b3)	1−4		A B	„Svatovska"
b.	" 1266.	5,	(VII)	VII−4		A B	"
c.	" 1264a)	5,	(1)	1−4		A B	"
d.	Bartók Mk. 1712a) Ms. Sarafla	7, 5,	(1)	1−5		A B	" * from Torontal swallowing of last syll.
e.	Kuba B.H. 96.	7, 5,	(1)	1−5		A B	"
f.	" " 602.	7, 5,	(1)	1−5		A B	"
g.	" " 425.	7, 5,	(1)	1−5		A B	"
h.	Kačerovski 30a)	7, 5,	(1)	1−5		A B	"
40.	Đorđević 202.	5,	(3)	1−4		A B	„Igra"
41.	Kuhač 860.	6,	(bVI)	bVI−b2		A Av	
42.	Đorđević 228.	6,	(VII)	VII−b3		A Av	„Igra"
43a.	Kuhač 542.	6,	(VII)	VII−4		AA^s	
b.	" 170.	6,	(VII)	VII−4		AA^s	
c.	" 196.	6,	(VII)	VII−4		AA^s	
d.	" 751.	6,	(VII)	bVI−4		?	
e.	" 187.	6,	(VII)	bVI−5		A B	
f.	" 242.	6,	(VII)	VII−4		A B	
g.	" 243.	6,	(VII)	VII−4		A B	
44.	Đorđević 32	6,	(VII)	VII−4		A A	
45.	Đorđević 509. (= Đorđević Nár. Par. p.18/21)	6,	(VII)	VII−5		A Av	
46a.	Kuba B.H. 774.	6,	(1)	VII−b3		A B	„Kolo"
b.	Đorđević 465.	6,	(b2)	1−4		A B	„sadeljka"
47a.	Kuhač 441.	6,	(1)	VII−b3		A Av	
b.	" 823.	6,	(1)	1−4		A B	„Drepievka"

II. 6, ①–♭3

Current №	Original edition	Syll.	Last note of sections	Range	Rhythm. structure	Structure	Remarks
c.	Đorđević 36.	(10) 6,	①	1–♭3		A A	Syll. inkr.: 6, 4+[3]+1
48a.	Kuhač 1063.	(10) 6,	①	1–♭3		A A_v	„u ženskom kolu"
b.	" 1064.	(10) 6,	①	VII–♭2		A A_v	„u kolu"
49a.	Kuba B.H. 911.	6,	①	1–4		A B	
b.	" " 828.	6,	①	1–♭3		A A_v	„Kolo"
c.	Đorđević 471.	6,	①	1–4		A A	
50–51.	Đorđević 541.	6,	①	1–4		A A_v	
52.	Đorđević 174.	(10) 6,	①	1–4		A B	
53.	Đorđević 398.	(10) 6,	①	1–5		A B	„Žetvarska"
54.	Kuba B.H. 305.	6,	①	1–[♭]6		A B	same text (54–55)
55.	Kuba B.H. 331.	6,	(♭2)	VII–♭4		A B	
56a.	Kuhač 969.	6,	(♭2)	VII–4		A A_s	
b.	" 716.	6,	(♭2)	VII–♭3		A A_s	
c.	Kuba X. 27.	6,	(♭2)	VII–4		A A_s	
d.	" " 20.	6,	(♭2)	1–4		A A_s	
e.	Kuhač 442.	6,	②	1–4		A A_v^s	clucking tones?
f.	" 1250.	(8) 6,	(♭2)	VII–♭3		A A_{sv}	„Svatovska"
57.	Kuba X. 61.	6,	(♭2)	1–5		A A_v	
58.	Đorđević 234.	6,	②	#VII–♭3		A B	„Kad seide u branje Zdravca"
59.	Kuhač 1526.	6,	②	1–4		A B	
60a.	Kuhač 1145	6,	②	1–4		A A_v	
b.	Đorđević Nar. Pev. p. 107/2	6,	②	VII–4		A A_{sv}	
61.	Kuba X. 29.	6,	(♭3)	♭VI–4		A A_v	
62.	Đorđević 34.	6,	(♭3)	VII–♭3		A B	
63.	Kuba B.H. 332 (= Kuba XIII. 53)	6,	(♭3)	VII–♭4		A B	

II. 6, (b3)-(4)

Current No	Original Edition	Syll.	Last note of sections	Range	Rhythm. structure	Structure	Remarks
64a.	Kuba B.H. 258.	6,	(b3)	VII - 4		A B	
b.	" 868.	6,	(b3)	VII - 4		A B	
c.	" 870.	6,	(b3)	VII - 4		A B	
65.	Đorđević 235.	6,	(b3)	1 - b3		A A v	„na prelaz (bačija)“
66.	Kuhač 487.	6,	(b3)	1 - b3		A B	
67.	Đorđević 177.	6,	(b3)	1 - 4		A A s v	„Igra“
68.	Kuhač 812.*	6,	(b3)	1 - 4		A B	„pirawiti“ is sung inst. of „prawiti“ (probably porawiti!)
69.	Kuhač 329.	6;	(b3)	1 - 4		A A v	
70a.	Kuhač 300.	6,	(b3)	1 - 5		A B	Line interv.: $3^2$3, 6,
b.	" 1534	6,	(4)	1 - 5		A B	
71.	Kuhač 507.	6,	(b3)	1 - b6		A A s v	
72a.	Kuhač 354.	6,	(3)	1 - 5		A B	
b.	Kuba B.H. 355	6,					2nd line of a.
73a.	Kuba X. 18.	6,	(b3)	VII - 5	3+3,	A B	
b.	" " 32.	6,	(b3)	VII - 5	3+3,	A B	
c.	" " 53.	6,	(b3)	1 - b6	3+3,	A B	
d.	Kuhač 858.	6,	(b3)	1 - 5	3+3,	A B	moj lati' amante!
74.	Kuhač 856.	6,	(3)	1 - 4	3+3,	A B	
75a.	Kuhač 805.	(10) 6,	(1)	1 - 4	2+4,	A A s v	
b.	Đorđević 412.	(10) 6,	(1)	1 - b3	2+4,	A A	„sedeljka“
76.	Đorđević 250.	6,	(2)	VII - b3	2+4,	A A v	„Igra“
77a.	Đorđević 302.	6,	(4)	1 - 4	2+4,	A A v	„Četvorska“
b.	" 551.	6,	(4)	1 - 4	2+4,	A A v	
c.	Đorđević Nar. Pev. p. 11/1	6,	(4)	1 - 4	2+4,	A A v	
d.	Đorđević 576.	6,	(VII)	VII - b3	2+4,	A A v	

II.6–II.7, (4), (bVII)–(1)

Current No.	Original edition	Syll.	Last note of section	Range	Rhythm structure	Structure	Remarks
78a.	Kuhač 254.	6,	(4)	1–5	a b	AB	
b.	Kuba X. 57.	6,	(4)	1–5	a b	AB	
c.	Kuhač 543.	6,	(4)	1–5	3+3,	AB	
79 a.	Đorđević 348.	7,	(bVI)	bVI–b2		AAv	„lazarička" (79 a.–d.)
b.	" 312.	7,					2nd section of a. (79 b.–d.)
c.	" 313.	7,					
d.	" 372.	7,					
80a.	Đorđević 300.	7,	(VII)	VII–1		AAv	„lazarička" (80 a.–b.)
b.	" 73.	7,	(VII)	VII–b2		AAv	
81.	Kuhač 806.	7,	(VII)	VII–4		AB	
82 a.	Kuba B.H. 517.	7,	(VII)	VII–4		AB	
b.	" " 940.	7,	(VII)	VII–4		AB	
c.	" " 518.	8b,	(2)	VII–4		AAv	Line interr.: 8b, 1–2 2+2+3
d.	Đorđević 472.	7,					2nd section of a.b. (82 d.–e.)
e.	" 419.	7,					„sedeljka"
83.	Đorđević 52.	7,	(#VII)	VI–1		AAv	„lazarička"
84.	Đorđević 17.	7,	(1)	VI–b3		AAv	Syll. interr.: 7. 1+[2]+2+3 „lazarička"
85.	Đorđević 22.	7,	(1)	VII–b2		AAv	„lazarička"
86.	Đorđević 408.	7, (8b)	(1)	VII–b3		AA	Line interr.: |: 4–3 :| „sedeljka"
87.	Đorđević 30.	7,	(1)	VII–b3		AAv	Word interr.: 7, 2–2+3
88.	Đorđević 308.	7,	(1)	1–b3		AAv	„pripev"
89a.	Iz Levča 41.	7,	(1)	1–b3		AA	„sedeljka"
b.	Đorđević 539.	7,	(1)	1–b3		AA	„U oči Jeremijinoga dana"
c.	" 540.	8,	(1)	1–b3		AAv	
90a.	Đorđević 77.	7,	(1)	1–4		AAv	

II. γ_1 ①-⑤, 3+4

Current №	Original Edition	Syll.	Last note of section	Range γ	Rhythm structure	Structure	Remarks
b. }	" 220.	γ_1	(1)	VII-4		AA_v	
91.	Đorđević 188.	γ_1	(b2)	1-4		AB	„peva se putem"
92.	Kuba B.H. 380.	γ_1	(2)	III-5		AB	
93.	Kuba B.H. 772.	γ_1	(2)	VII-2		AA_v	
94a.	Kuhač 417.	γ_1	(2)	VII-4		AB	
b.	" 819.	γ_1	(2)	VI-4		AB	
c.	" 480.	γ_1	(2)	VII-b3		AB	
95a.	Kuba B.H. 675.	γ_1	(2)	VII-5		AB	
b.	" " 754.	γ_1	(2)	IV-4		AB	
96.	Đorđević 542.	γ_1	(2)	1-4		AB	
97.	Kuba B.H. 891.	γ_1	(b3)	bVII-4		AB	
98a.	Kuhač 1201.	γ_1	(b3)	VII-4		AA_v	„Svatovska (na prosidbi)"
b.	" 347.	γ_1	(b3)	VII-4		AB	
99a.	Đorđević Nar. Pev. p. 38/2	γ_1	(b3)	VII-5		AB	
b.	Bosiljevac 45.	γ_1	(b3)	VII-5		AB	
100.	Đorđević 273.	γ_1	(b3)	1-b3		AB	„lazarička"
101.	Đorđević 383.	γ_1	(b3)	1-b3		AA_v	„koleda"
102.	Đorđević 428.	γ_1	(b3)	1-4		AB	„sedeljka"
103.	Kuba B.H. 92.	γ_1	(b3)	1-b6		AB	
104.	Kuhač 992.	γ_1	(3)	V-4		AB	
105.	Kuba B.H. 384.	γ_1	(3)	VI-5		AB	„Kolo"
106.	Đorđević 245.	γ_1	(4)	1-4		AA_v	
107.	Kuba XII. 6.	γ_1	(4)	VII-7		A^5A_v	
108.	Kuba B.H. 164.	γ_1	(5)	1-7		AB	
109.	Kuba B.H. 393.	γ_1	(1)	1-b3	3+4	AA_v	Swallowing of last syll. perhaps „uspavanka"? (in text: „nina")

Current No	Original Edition	Syll.	Last note of section	Range	Rhythm structure	Structure	Remarks
110.	Đorđević 201.	7,	(2)	1–b3	3+4	AAv	„Igra"
111.	Bosiljevac 34.	8,	(bIII)	bIII–b3		AB	
112.	Kuhač 489.	8,	(IV)	I–b3		AB	
113.	Kuhač 185.	8,	(VI)	III–3	N.b. 8 = ♩.♪♪♩. | ♩.♪♪♩. |	AB	
114.	Kuhač 186.	8,	(VII)	bVI–4		AA^s_v	
⊕ 115a.}	Đorđević 213.	8, (7,)	(VII)	VII–b2		AAv	„lazarička"
116.	Kuba B.H. 1001. (Ms.)	8,	(VII)	VII–b3		AB	
117a.	Kuba B.H. 807.	8,	(VII)	VII–b3		AAv	line interr.: 8, 4 2 4, „Kolo"
b.	" " 789.	8,	(VII)	VII–b3		AAv	„Kolo"
118.	Kuba B.H. 484.	8,	(VII)	VII–b3		AB	„kolo"
119a.	Kuba B.H. 918.	8,	(VII)	VII–4		AB (B=2nd half of A+new part)	„kolo"
b.	" " 920.	8,	(VII)	VII–4		"	„kolo"
c.	" " 921.	8,	(VII)	VII–4		"	(kolo?)
d.	" " 613	8,	(1)	VII–4		"	
e.	Kuhač 1071.	8,					1st half of d. (žensko kolo?)
f.	Kuba B.H. 585.	8,					1st half of d. „kolo"
g.	Kuhač 662	8,					1st half of d.
120a.	Iz Levča 14.	8,	(VII)	VII–4		AA^s	„Naricanja"
b.	Đorđević 475.	8,					2nd half of a. „Naricanja"
121.	Đorđević 510	8,	(VII)	VII–4		AB	line interr.: 8, 4 2 4,
122a.	Đorđević Nar. Pev. p. 17/2	8,	(VII)	VII–4		AAv	
b.	Iz Levča 21.	8,					2nd half of a. „Sedeljka (na tano)"
c.	" 47.	8,					2-nd half of a. „Sedeljka"
123a.	Kuhač 1004.	8,	(VII)	VII–4		AB	„kolo"
b.	Kuba B.H. 366.	8,	(VII)	VII–5		AB	
⊕ 115b.	Kuba B.H. 1005. Ms.	8,	(VII)	VII–2		AB	two part song

Current №	Original Edition	Syll.	Last note of section	Range	Rhythm structure	Structure	Remark
(123) c.	Kuhač 1007.	8,	(VII)	VII – 4		AB	„Igra"
d.	Đorđević 421.	8,	(VII)	VII – b3		AB	„sedeljka"
e.	Kuhač 1006.	8,	(2)	VII – 4		AB	„Igra"
f.	" 1005.	8,	(b3)	VII – 4		AB	„Igra"
g.	Đorđević 96.	(10) r. 8, 7, 7,	(2) (1	VII – 4		ABB	
h.	" 187.	(10) 8, 10,	(1)	1 – 2		AAv	„krstonoška"
i.	" 479.	8,	(VII)	VII – 4		AB	„Dodola"
j.	" 384.	(8) r. 8, 6,	(2)	1 – 4		AB	„Uskršnja"
k.	" 35.	(8) r. 8, 6,	(1)	1 – 4		AB	
l.	" 173.	(8) r. 8, 9,	(VII)	VI – b3		AAv	„krstonoška" (l.–u.)
m.	" 153.	(8) r. 8, 9,	(1)	1 – b3		AAv	
n.	" 258.	(8) r. 8, 9,	(VII)	VII – b2		AB	
o.	" 301.	(8) r. 8, 9,	(#VII)	#VII – b3		AB	
p.	" 215.	(8) r. 8, 9,	(2)	1 – b3		AAv	
r.	" 164.	(8) r. 8, 9,	(2)	1 – b3		AAv	
s.	" 127.	(8) r. 8, 9,	(VII)	VII – b3		AB	
t.	" 288.	(8) r. 8, 6,	(VII)	VII – b2		AB	
u.	" 478.	(8) r. 8, 6,	(VII)	VII – 4		AB	
v.	Iz Levča 72.	(8) 8, 6,	(1)	1 – 5		AB	„Obredno"(!) [of course „krstonoška"]
x.	Đorđević 143.	8, 6,	(VII)	VII – 2		AB	„Pripev"
y.	" 23.	(8) r. 8, 6,	(2)	1 – 4		AB	„krstonoška" (y.–bb.)
z.	" 138.	(8) r. 8, 6, 6,	(1) (VII)	VII – b3		ABC	
aa.	Juž. Srb. 399.	(8) 8, 6, 6,	(VII) (VII	VII – 5		ABBv	
bb.	Đorđević 233.	(8) r. 8, 7, 6,	(b2) (b2	1 – 4		AAvAv	
cc.	" 597.	(8) (r.) 8, 9,	(VII)	1 – b3		AB	
dd.	" 139.	8,	(1)	1 – 4		AB	„Dodola"

Current №	Original Edition	Syll.	Last note of section	Range	Rhythm structure	Structure	Remarks
(123) ee.	Đorđević 489.	8,	(VII)	VI - b3		AB Cf.	„sedeljka"
ff.	" 406.	(8) r. 8, 5,	(b2)	VII - 4		AB № 1561	„sedeljka"
gg.	" 356.	(8) r. 8, 7,	(b2)	1 - b3		AB d. e.	„sedeljka"
124.	Kuhač 1479.	8,	(VII)	VII - 4		AAv	
125 a.	Kuba B.H. 846.	8,	(VII)	VII - 5		AB	
b.	" " 844.	8,	(VII)	VII - 4		AAv	„Svatovska"
c.	Kuhač 583.	8,	(VII)	VII - 4		AB	
126 a.	Kuhač 146a)	8,	(VII)	VII - 5		AB	
b.	" 146b)	8,	(I)	VII - 5		AB	
127.	Kuhač 1594.	8,	(I)	V - 4		AB	
128 a.	Kuba XI. 50.	8,	(I)	VI - 4		AAv	
b.	Kuba B.H. 382.	8,	(I)	VI - 4		AAv	
129 a.	Đorđević 21.	8,	(I)	VII - b2		AAv	Line interr.: 8, 2-6 „lazaričke"
b.	" 185.	8,	(I)	VII - 1		AA	„lazaričke"
c.	" 329.	8,	(I)	VII - b2		AAv	Line interr. 8, 4-4 „Na ranilu"
d.	" 330.	10,	(I)	1 - b3		AAv	Line interr.: 8, 2-6 „Svatovska"
e.	" 331.	8b		VII - b2			half
130 a.	Kuba B.H. 459.	8,	(I)	VII - b3		AB	Var. Parry № 2.
b.	" " 767.	8,	(I)	VII - b2		AB	
c.	"Ms." 1041.	8,	(I)	1 - b3		AA	„Kolo"
d.	Kuba B.H. 460.	8,	(VII)	VII - b3		AB	
e.	" " 461.	8,	(I)	VII - b3		AB	„Kolo"
f.	" " 458.	8,	(I)	VII - b3		AB	
g.	Kuhač 1045a)	8,		VII - b3			2nd half of e. „Poziv u kolo"
131 a.	Đorđević 170.	8,	(I)	VII - b3		AB	
b.	Kuba B.H. 470.	8,	(I)	VII - b3		AA	
132 a.	Kuba B.H. 464.	8,	(I)	VI - b3		AB* *B = 2nd half of A+4	

11

II. 8, (1)

Current №	Original Edition	Syll.	Last note of section	Range	Rhythm structure	Structure	Remarks
b.	"Ms." 986	8,	(1)	VII – 4		AB (sim.)	
c.	Kuba B.H. 465.	8,	(1)	VI – b3		AB (sim.)	
d.	" " 455.	8,	(1)	VII – b3		AB (sim.)	
e.	Đorđević 440.	8,	(1)	VII – b3		AB (sim.)	
f.	" 328.	8,	(1)	1 – b3		AB (sim.)	„kad se ide u branje zdravca"
g.	" 358	8,	(1)	1 – b3		AB (sim.)	„sedeljka"
h.	" 327.	9, (10,)	(1)	1 – b3		AA	„u oči Đurđevadana kad se ide u zdravac"
133.	Đorđević 248.	8,	(1)	VII – b3		AA_v	
134 a.	Kuhač 1074.	8,	(1)	VII – b3		AA_v	„žensko (?) kolo"
b.	" 1065.	8,	(1)	VII – b3		AB	„žensko kolo"
c.	" 1045 b)	8,	(1)	VII – b3		AB	„poziv u kolo"
d.	" 1066.	(8) 8, 5, 7. (9,)	(1)	VII – 4		AB	„žensko kolo (?)"
e.	" 1046.	8,	(1)	VII – 4		AA_v	„poziv u kolo"
f.	" 1055.	8,	(1)	1 – 4		AA	„muško kolo"
g.	" 1070.	8,	(2)	1 – 4		AA_v	žensko kolo (?)
h.	" 1044.	8,	(2)	1 – 4		AA_v	„poziv u kolo"
i.	" 1043.	8,	(b2)	VII – b3		AB	„poziv u kolo"
j.	" 1056.	8,	(b3)	VII – 4		AA_v	kolo (?)
k.	" 157.	8,	(b3)	VII – 4		AB	
l.	" 1051.	8,	(4)	VII – b5		AA_v	„muško kolo"
m.	" 1050.	8,					2nd half of previous
135 a.	Kuhač 529.	8,	(1)	VII – b3		AB	
b.	Kuba B.H. 867	8,	(1)	VII – 4		AB	
136.	Manojlović 5.	8,	(1)	VII – 4		AA	
137.	Kuba B.H. 504.	8,	(1)	VII – 4		AB	„kolo"

Current No	Original edition	Syll.	Last note of section	Range	Rhythm. structure	Structure	Remarks
⊕ 139.	Kuba B.H. 707.	8,	①	VII-5		AB	
140.	Đorđević 186.	8,	①	1-b3		AAv	„Kralja (na Spasovdan)"
141-142	Đorđević 554.	8,	①	1-b3		AA	
143 a.	Kuba B.H. 757.	8,	①	1-b3		AA	
b.	" " 453.	8,	①	1-b3		AA	
c.	" " 451.	8,					half of previous
d.	Kuba XI. 44.	8,					„poskočnica" half of previous
e.	Juž. Srb. 401.	8,					half of previous
144-145	Đorđević 152.	8,	①	1-4		AAv	
146 a.	Đorđević 183.	8,	①	1-4		AB	„Igra" Cf. Parry No 1.
b.	" 211.	8,	①	1-4		AB	„Igra"
c.	" 168.	8,	①	1-4		AB	
147.	Kuhač 1218.	8,	①	1-4		AAv	„Svatovsko"
148 a.	Đorđević 178.	8,	①	1-4		AAv	„Igra"
b.	Kuba B.H. 896.	8,					1st half of a.
↑138.	Kuba XIV. 26.	8,	①	VII-b5		AB	
149-150	Kuba B.H. 1016. Ms.	8,	①	1-6		AB	
151 a.	Đorđević 537.	8,	(b2)	VII-b3		AB	„Svatovska"
b.	Kuhač 402.	8,	①	VII-b3		AA	
152 a.	Đorđević 403.	8,	(b2)	VII-4		AB	„sedeljka"
b.	" 306.	8,					2nd half of a. „Svatovska"
153.	Kuba B.H. 115.	8,	(b2)	VII-4		AB	after last section, stuttering beginning, seemingly of the following st.
154.	Đorđević 40.	8,	(b2)	VII-b5		AB	
155 a.	Đorđević 60.	8,	(b2)	1-4		AB	
b.	" 239.	8,	(b2)	VII-4		AB	

II.8,

Current No	Original Edition	Syll.	Last note of section	Range	Rhythm. structure	Structure	Remarks (b2)-(2)
156.	Kuhač 333.	8,	(b2)	1–4		AB	
157a.	Đorđević 552.	8,	(2)	VII–b3		AAv	
b.	" 364.	8,	(2)	VII–b3		AAv	Sedeljka
c.	" 65.	8,	(2)	VII–b3		AAv	
158a.	Đorđević Nar. Pev. p. 77/2	8,	(2)	VII–4	r.b. imperfect cadence (158a–f)	AB	Cf.: Bartók, Colinde, No 45 (158a–f)
b.	Kačerovski 40a)	8,	(2)	VII–4		AB	
c.	Bosiljevac 47.	8,	(2)	VII–4		AB	
d.	Kuhač 878.	8,	(2)	VII–4		AB	
e.	Kuba B.H. 581.	8,	(2)	VII–4		AB	
f.	" " 913.	8,	(b2)	VII–4		AB	„Kolo"
g.	Kuhač 877.	8,	(3)	V–5 (1–5?)	perfect cadence	AB	
159a.	Kuba B.H. 719.	8,	(2)	VII–5		AB	Cf. Bartók, Ruman. Folkmusic II. No 15; 665. (159a–d)
b.	" " 729.	8,	(2)	VII–5		AB	
c.	Đorđević Nar. Pev. p. 15/2	8,	(2)	VII–5		AB	
d.	Kuba B. H. 654.	8,	(2)	VII–5		AB	
160 a.	Kuba B.H. 704	8,	(2)	VII–5		AAv	
b.	Kuba XI. 20.	8,	(2)	VII–5		AAv	
161.	Kuhač 550.	8,	(2)	VII–b6		AAs	
162.	Kuhač 1075	8,	(2)	#VII–4		AB	„ženske kolo"
163.	Kuhač 239.	8,	(2)	#VII–4		AB	
164 a.	Kuhač 478.	8,	(2)	1–b3		AB	
b.	Kuba B.H. 481.	8,	(2)	1–b3		AB	„svatovsko kolo"
c.	Đorđević 274a)	8,	(2)	1–b3		AAv	„lazarička"
165 a.	Đorđević 227.	8,	(2)	1–b3		AAv	„Igra"
b.	Kuba B.H. 388.	8,	(2)	1–b3		AAv	

Current №	Original edition	Syll.	Last note of section	Range	Rhythm. structure	Structure	Remarks
c.	" " 389.	8,	②	1–♭3		AAv	
d.	" " 397.	8,	②	1–4		AB	
e.	Đorđević 193.	8,	②	1–4		AAv	
f.	Iz Levča 24.	8,	②	1–4		AAv	„Sedeljka"
g.	Kuba B.H. 394.	8,	②	1–4		AAv	
h.	Đorđević 569a)	8,	②	1–4		AAv	„Kukuruza di na prelu, na komidbu Grojenice" (?)
i.	Kuhač 1068.	8,					2nd half of previous; „Kad se hvata žensko kolo"
j.	Kuba B.H. 385.	8,					2-nd half of previous
166-167	Đorđević 172.	8,	②	1–4		AB	„Koleda"
168 a.	Đorđević 42.	8,	②	1–4		AB	
b.	" 589.	8,					2-nd half of a. „Sedeljka" (b.–e.)
c.	" 581.	8,					
d.	" 413.	8,					
e.	" 516.	8,					
169.	Đorđević 26.	8,	②	1–4		AB	„Dodola"
170.	Đorđević Nar. Pev. p. 33/2	8,	②	1–4		AAv	
171.	Đorđević Nar. Pev. p. 39/1	8,	②	1–5		AB	
172.	Kuhač 1054.	8,	②	1–5		AA	Word interr.: ‖: 2?–6 :‖
⊕173a.}	Đorđević 4.	8,	②	1–5		AAv	
174a.	Đorđević 120.	8,	②	1–5		AB	„Igra"
b.	" 78.	8,	②	1–5		AB	„Igra"
c.	" 565.	8,					2-nd half of previous; „uspavanka"
d.	" 179.	8,					2-nd half of previous
175.	Kuhač 705.	8,	②	1–5		AAv	cf.: (Maramureș, № 21. Bartók)
176.	Kuhač 1453.	8,	②	1–♭6		AB	
⊕173 b.}	Kuhač 249.	9,(?)	②	1–5		AAv	

II.8, (b3)

Current №	Original edition	Syll.	Last note of section	Range	Rhythm. structure	Structure	Remarks
177 a.	Đorđević: Nar. Pev. p. 24/1	8,	(b3)	VII – 4	N.b. imperfect cadence	AB	Cf. Bartók: Colinde [illegible]
b.	Iz Levča 23.	8,	(b3)	VII – b3		AB	„sedeljka"
c.	Đorđević 449.	8,	(b3)	VII – b3		AB	
d.	Kuba B.H. 175.	8, 10,	(3)	VI – 5	perfect cadence	AB	
178.	Kuba B.H. 822.	8,	(b3)	VII – 4		AB	„Uspavanka"
179.	Kuba XII. 59.	8,	(b3)	VI – 4		AB	
180 a.	Đorđević 69.	8,	(b3)	1 – 4		AB	
b.	Iz Levča 61.	8,	(b3)	VII – 4		AB	
181.	Đorđević 380.	8,	(b3)	1 – 4		A Av	Var. Parry 3.
182.	Đorđević 409.	8,	(b3)	1 – 4		A Av	„Sedeljka"
183 a.	Kuba B.H. 91.	8,	(b3)	1 – 5		AB	
b.	Kuhač 553.	8,	(b3)	1 – 5		AB	
c.	Kuba XII. 22.	8,	(b3)	1 – 5		AB	
d.	Kuba IX. 10.	8,	(b3)	VII – 5		AB	
e.	Đorđević 63.	8,	(b3)	1 – 5		AB	
f.	Kuba XII. 50.	8,	(b3)	1 – 5		AB	
g.	Kuba B.H. 594.	8,	(b3)	1 – 5		AB	
h.	Kuhač 1058.	8,					2nd half of the previous „muško kolo"
i.	Đorđević 223.	8,					2nd half of the previous „sedeljka"
184.	Đorđević 134.	8,	(b3)	1 – 5		A Av	
185 a.	Kuba B.H. 233. (= Kuba XIII. 51.)	8,	(b3)	1 – 5		AB	
b.	Kuba XII. 4	8,	(b3)	1 – 5		AB	
c.	Kuba B.H. 195. (= Kuba XIV. 18.)	8,	(b3)	1 – 8		AB	
186 a.	Kuhač 373.	8,	(b3)	1 – b6		AB	
b.	Kuba B.H. 134.	8,	(b3)	VII – b6		AB	

Current №	Original edition	Syll.	Last note of section	Range	Rhythm structure	Structure	Remarks
187.	Kuba IX. 44.	8,	(b3)	1–b6		AB	
188.	Kuba IX. 31.	8,	(b3)	1–7		A^3A	
189.	Kuhač 4.	8,	(3)	V–5		AB	
190.	Kuba B.H. 927.	8,	(3)	VII–5		AB	
191 a.	Kuhač 1117.	8,	(3)	#VII–3		AAv	Cf. Slovakian Form. „Poskočnica"
b.	Đorđević 93.	8,					2-nd half of a. „sedeljka"
192.	Đorđević 548.	8,	(3)	1–4		AAv	
193 a.	Kuba B.H. 370.	8,	(3)	1–5		AB	„Kolo"
b.	" " 357.	8,	(3)	1–5		AB	
194 a.	Kuhač 473.	8,	(3)	1–5		AB	
b.	Iz Levča 56.	8,					2-nd half of a.
195.	Kuhač 706.	8,	(3)	1–5		AAv	
196 a.	Kuba B.H. 376.	8,	(3)	1–6		AB	
b.	" " 377.	8,	(3)	1–6		AB	
c.	" " 378.	8,	(3)	1–6		AB	
d.	" " 1123. Ms.	8,	(3)	1–6		AB	
e.	Kuhač 787.	8,	(3)	V–5		AB	
f.	Kuba B.H. 374.	10,	(3)	1–5		AB	
197 a.	Đorđević 51.	8,	(4)	VII–4		AAv	
b.	" 230	8,					2-nd half of a. „Igra"
198.	Kuhač 1087.	8,	(4)	VI–4		AB	poskočnica(?)
199 a.	Đorđević 200.	8,	(4)	1–4		AAv	
b.	" 199.	8,	(4)	1–4		AAv	„Igra"
c.	" 136.	8,	(4)	1–4		AAv	„Igra"
200 a.	Kuhač 122.	8,	(4)	1–5		AAv	

II. 8, (4)–(5) — 8b, (VII)–(1)

Current No	Original edition	Syll.	Last note of section	Range	Rhythm. structure	Structure	Remarks
b.	" 124.	8,	(4)	1–5		AB	
c.	" 125.	8,	(4)	1–5		AB	
d.	" 127	8,	(4)	1–5		AB	
e.	Kuba B. H. 953.	8,	(4)	VII–5		AA_v	
f.	Kuhač 123.	8,	(5)	1–5		AA_v	
g.	" 126.	8, 10,	(4)	1–5		AB	
201 a.	Kuba X. 8.	8,	(5)	1–b6		AB	
b.	" " 52.	8,	(5)	1–7		AB	
202.	Kuhač 451.	8b, (8)'	(V)	V–4		AA^5_v	
203.	Đorđević 256.	8b,	(VII)	VII–b3		AB	"Svatovska"
204.	Kuhač 1380.	8b,	(VII)	VII–b3		AA_v	
205.	Kuba B.H. 674.	8b,	(VII)	VII–4		AA_v	
206 a.	Kuba B.H. 573.	8b,	(VII)	VII–4		AA_v	
b.	" " 624.	8b,	(4)	1–4		AA_v	
c.	" " 625.	8b,	4) (2) (1	1–5		AA_v BB_v	
207.	Kuba B. H. 721.	8b,	(VII)	VII–5		AB	
208 a.	Đorđević 100. = Đorđević Nar. Pev. p. 70/1	8b,	(VII)	VII–5		AB	
b.	Đorđević 111. = Đorđević Nar. Pev. p. 83/1	8b,	(VII)	VII–5		AB	
209.	Đorđević 165.	8b,	(1)	VII–1		AA_v	line-interr.: 8b, 5–3 "svatovska"
210 a.	Đorđević 212.	8b,	(1)	VII–b2		AA_v	"svatovska"
b.	Đorđević 296.	8b,	(1)	VII–b2		AA_v	"sedeljka"
c.	Kuba B.H. 1116. Ms.	8b,	(1)	VII–b2		AB	"uspavanka" word interr.: 8b, 2–1+5
d.	Đorđević 395.	8b,					2-nd half of a. b. "svatovska"

Current No	Original edition	Syll.	Last note of section	Range	Rhythm structure	Structure	Remarks
211 a.	Kuhač 459.	8b,	(1)	VII - b3		AAv	
b.	" 19.	8b,	(1)	VII - b3		AAv	
c.	Kuba B. H. 795.	8b,	(VII)	VII - b3		AAv	"svatovska"
d.	Đorđević 142.	8b,	(1)	VII - b3		AB	"sedeljka"
212 a.	Kuba B. H. 450.	8b,	(1)	VII - b3		AAv	
b.	" " 790.	8b,	(1)	VII - b3		AAv	"svatovska"; word-interrupt.: 8b, 2 – 1+5
213.	Kuba B. H. 479.	8b,	(1)	VII - b3		AAv	word-interr.: 8b, 2 – 1+5
214 a.	Kuba B. H. 463.	8b,	(1)	VII - b3		AAv	
b.	" " 467.	(8b) 5+3+8, 5,	(2)	VII - b3		AB	Cf. No. 1049
c.	" " 489.	8b,	(2)	VII - 4		AB	
d.	" " 466.	8b,	(b3)	VII - b3		AAv	
e.	" " 490.	8,	(1)	VII - 4		AB	"kolo"
215.	Đorđević 289	8b,	(1)	VII - b3		AA	"svatovska"
216 a.	Kuhač 1237.	8b,	(1)	VII - b3		AAv	"svatovska"
b.	" 1236	8b,	(1)	VII - b3		AAv	"svetovska"
c.	Kuba B. H. 503.	8b,	(1)	1 - b3		AAv	line interr.: 8b, 3 – 5
d.	Kuhač 1235.	8b,	(2)	1 - b3		AAv	"svatovska"
e.	Đorđević 481.	8b,					"svatovska"; 2-nd half of previous
f.	" 463.	8b,					2-nd half of previous. "u maskarad Beloj Nedelji"
217.	Đorđević 404.	8b,	(1)	1 - b3		AA	"sedeljka"
218.	Kuba B. H. 883.	8b,	(1)	1 - 4		AAv	
219 a.	Đorđević 57.	8b,	(1)	1 - 4		AA	
b.	" 244.	9,	(1)	1 - 4		AAv	
220.	Kuba B. H. 500.	8b,	(1)	1 - 4		AAv	
221.	Kuba B. H. 703.	8b,	(1)	1 - 5		AAv	line interr.: 8b, 1 – 2+5
222.	Kuhač 1073.	8b,	(1)	1 - 5		AB	"u ženskom kolu"

II. 8b, ①–②

Current No	Original edition	Syll.	Last note of section	Range	Rhythm structure	Structure	Remarks
223.	Kuba B.H. 200.	8b,	①	1–5		AB	
224.	Kuba B.H. 959.	8b,	①	1–5		AB	
225.	Đorđević 151.	8b,	①	1–5		AA_v	„sedeljka"
226.	Kuba IX. 60.	8b,	①	1–5		AB	(Russian ?)
⊕227.	Kuba X. 24.	8b,	①	1–♭6		AA_v	three part song
229a.	Kuhač 457.	8b,	(♭2)	1–4		AA_{sv}	
b.	" 139.	8b,	(♭2)	1–5		AA^s_v	
c.	Kuba X. 33.	8b,	②	♯VII–4		AA_s	two part song
d.	Kuhač 470.	9,	(♭2)	VII–4		AA_s	
↥228.	Kuba B.H. 922.	8b,	(♭2)	VII–4		AB	
230.	Đorđević 27. (=Đorđević Nar. Pev. p.113/2)	8b,	(♭2)	1–4		AA_v	
231a.	Kuba B.H. 179.	8b,	②	IV–4		AB	
b.	" " 180.	8b,	①	IV–4		AB	
232a.	Kuba B.H. 509.	8b,	②	VII–4		AA_v	
b.	Đorđević 106	8b,	②	VII–4		AB	
c.	Kuhač 748.	8b,	②	VII–♭3		AB	
d.	Kuba XI. 69.	8b,	①	VII–♭3		AA_v	word-interr.: 8b, 2–1+5
e.	Kuba B.H. 390	8b,	①	VII–♭2		AA_v	word-interr.: 8b, 2–1+5
f.	Đorđević 58.	8b,	(♭3)	VI–4		AB	
g.	" 56	8b,	(♭3)	VI–♭3		AB	syll.-interr.: 8b, 3+[4]+1+3
h.	Kuba XIV. 13.	8b,	(♭3)	VII–4		AA_v	
i.	Kuba B.H. 570.	8b,	④	VII–4		AB	
233.	Kuba B.H. 1000 Ms.	8b,	②	1–♭3		AA_v	chromatic
234a.	Đorđević 157.	8b,	②	1–♭3		AA_v	„svatovska"
b.	" 488.	8b,	②	1–♭3		AA_v	

Current №	Original Edition	Syll.	Last note of section	Range	Rhythm structure	Structure	Remarks
c.	Đorđević Nar. Pes. p. 24/2	8b,	(2)	1–b3		AA_v	
235.	Kuhač 715.	8b,	(2)	1–4		AA_v	
236.	Đorđević 31.	8b,	(2)	1–4		AA_s	Var. Parry 4.
237a.	Đorđević 350.	8b,	(2)	1–4		AA_v	„sedeljka"
b.	" 426.	8b,	(2)	1–4		AA_v	„sedeljka"
c.	" 141.	8b,					„pri kopanju" / 2nd half of previous; syll.-interv.: 3+1+[5]+3
d.	Đorđević 122.	8b,					(d–h: second half of previous; line-interv.: 5 | 3) „žetvarska"
e.	" 166.	8b,					„žetvarska"
f.	" 219.	8b,					„kad se vlači vuna"
g.	" 130.	8b,					„žetvarska"
h.	" 226.	8b,					žetvarska, pri kopanja
i.	Kuhač 1254	8b,					2-nd half of previous „svatovska"
238.	Kuhač 1259a)	8b,	(2)	1–5		AB	„svatovska"
239.	Kuhač 1240	8b,	(2)	1–5		A^3A_v	„svatovska"
240a.	Kuba B.H. 372.	8b,	(2)	1–6		AB	
b.	" " 27.	8b,	(2)	1–6		AB	
c.	" " 381.	8b,	(2)	1–6		AB	
241.	Kuhač 1257.	8b,	(b3)	VII–b3		AA_v	„svatovska"
242.	Kuhač 616.	8b,	(b3)	VII–4		AB	
243a.	Đorđević 379.	8b,	(b3)	VII–4		AA_v	(a–e: Var. Parry 5.)
b.	" 249.	8b,	(b3)	VII–4		AA_v	
c.	" 20.	8b,	(b3)	1–4		AA_v	„lazarička"
d.	" 556.	8b,	(b3)	VII–4		AA_v	
e.	" 558.	8b,	(b3)	1–4		AA_v	
f.	" 28.	8b,	(b3)	1–4		AB	

II. 8b, (b3)-(7), — 10, (bVI)

Current №	Original edition	Syll.	Last note of section	Range	Rhythm. structure	Structure	Remarks
g.	" 394.	(5) 8b,	(b3)	VII - b3		AAv	svatovska
h.	" 44.	8b,	(4)	1 - 4		AAv	
i.	Kuba B.H. 786.	8b,					2-nd half of previous
j.	Đorđević 17 5.	8b,					2-nd half of previous & two part song (Bozm. „pozdrav devojaka na sa-)
k.	" 311.	8b,					2-nd half of previous „svatovska"
l.	" 55.	8b,					1-st half of previous
m.	" 332.	8b,					1-st half of previous „sedeljka"
244.	Kuba B.H. 133	8b,	(b3)	VII - b6		AB	
245.	Đorđević 107.	8b,	(b3)	1 - 4		AAv	
246 a.	Đorđević 92.	8b,	(b3)	1 - 5		AAv	„sedeljka"
b.	" 131.	8b,	(b3)	1 - 5		AB	„žetvarska"
247 a.	Kuba B.H. 28.	8b,	(3)	1 - 5		AB	
b.	Kuba XIII. 9.	8b,	(3)	VI - 5		AB	
248.	Kuba B.H. 686.	8b,	(4)	VII - 5		AB	
249.	Kuba X. 14.	8b,	(5)	V - 6			four part song
250.	Đorđević Nar. Pev. p. 154/2	8b,	(5)	1 - b6		AAv	
251.	Đorđević 105.	8b,	(7)	1 - 7		AB	
252 a.	Đorđević 381.	(7) 9, r.	(VII)	VII - b2		AAv	„lazarička"
b.	" 382.	(8) 10, r.	(VII)	VII - b2		AA	„lazarička"
254.	Đorđević 387.	(6) 9,	(1)	VII - b3		AA	„uskršna"
253.	Đorđević 430.	(7) 9, r.	(1)	IV - 4		AB	
255-256.	Kuba B.H. 766.	(6) 9, r.	(b3)	1 - 4		AB	line interv.: 9, 4-2+3
257.	Kuba B.H. 532.	10,	(bVI)	bVI - b2		AB	„Kolo"
258.	Kuhač 1089.	(8) 10,	(VI)	V - 2		AAv	

Current No	Original Edition	Syll.	Last note of section	Range	Rhythm. structure	Structure	Remarks
259.	Kuba B.H. 174.	10,	(VI)	VI-4		AAv	
260a.	Kuba B.H. 264.	10,	(VII)	bVI-4		AAv	
b.	" " 151.	10,	(VII)	bVI-4		AB	
261a.	Đordević 72.	10,	(VII)	VI-b2		AAv	cf. No 448 (a.–e.)
b.	" 424.	10,	(VII)	VII-b3		AB	„sedeljka"
c.	" 74.	10,	(I)	VI-2		AAv	„lazarička" line interr.: 10, 4–6
d.	" 19.	10,	(I)	VII-b2		AAv	„lazarička", line interr.: 10, 2–8
e.	" 16.	(8) r. 10,	(b2)	VII-b2		AAv	
262a.	Kuba B.H. 878.	10,	(VII)	VII-2		AAv	
b.	Kuhač 1224.	10,					2-nd half of previous (b.–f.)
c.	Đordević 274b)	10,					„lazarička"
d.	" 272	10,					
e.	Kuba B.H. 775.	10,					
f.	Kuhač 1364.	10,					
263a.	Kuba B.H. 771.	10,	(VII)	VII-2		AAv	
b.	Đordević 568.	10,					2-nd half of a. „žetvarska"
c.	" 567.	(10) r. 6,					last fourth of a. „žetvarska"
264a.	Kuba B.H. 812.	10,	(VII)	VII-b3		AB	„Uspavanka"
b.	Đordević 303.	10,					2-nd half of a. „žetvarska"
c.	" 304.	10,					2-nd half of a. „kad se vraća sa poljskih-radova"
265a.	Kuba B.H. 784. (=Kuba XIII. 19)	10,	(VII)	VII-b3		AB	Var. Parry 6. (a.–d.)
b.	Kuba B.H. 811.	10,	(VII)	VII-b3		AAv	
c.	" " 804.	10,	(VII)	VII-b3		AAv	
d.	" " 257.	10,	(VII)	VII-b5		AB	word interr. 8–2, 10 „gi-ga"

Current No	Original Edition	Syll.	Last note of section	Range	Rhythm. structure	Structure	Remarks
e.	" " 541.	10,	(VII)	VII - 4		AAv	
f.	" " 545.	10,	(VII)	VII - 4		AB	
g.	" " 533.	10,	(VII)	VII - b3		AB	
h.	" " 571.	10,	(VII)	VII - b3		AB	
i.	" " 472.	10,	(VII)	VII - b3		AB	emphatic ornam. notes
j.	" " 473.	10,	(VII)	VII - b3		AB	
k.	Kuhač 376.	10,	(VII)	VII - 4		AB	
266 a.	Đorđević 455.	10,	(VII)	VII - b3		AAv	"svatovska"
b.	Iz Levča 32.	10,	(VII)	VII - b3		AAv	
c.	Juž. Slo. 404.	10,	(VII)	VII - b3		AAv	"slavna"
267 a.	Kuba B.H. 564.	10,	(VII)	VII - 4		AAv	
b.	Kuhač 1504.	10,	(VII)	VII - 5		AAv	
c.	Kuba B.H. 842.	10,	(VII)	VII - 4		AAv	swallowing of last syll.
268.	Kuba B.H. 274. (= Kuba XII. 37)!	10,	(VII)	VII - 4		AAv	
269.	Đorđević 587.	10,	(VII)	VII - 4		AAv	
270 a.	Kuhač 692.	10,	(VII)	VII - 5		AAv	
b.	" 745.	10,	(VII)	VII - 5		AAv	
c.	" 21.	10,	(VII)	VII - 5		AB	
d.	" 25.	10,	(VII)	VII - 5		AB	
e.	" 22.	(10) (x.) 10, 9,	(VII)	VII - 4		AB	
f.	" 23.	(10) (x.) 10, 7,	(VII)	VII - 4		AB	
271 a.	Kuba B.H. 745.	10,	(VII)	VII - 5		AB	
b.	" " 746.	10,	(VII)	VII - 5		AB	
c.	" " 730.	10,					2-nd half of previous

Current No	Original Edition	Syll.	Last note of section	Range	Rhythm. structure	Structure	Remarks
d.	" " 731.	10,					2.
e.	Kuba B.H. 244. (=Kuba XIV. 9.)	10,					nd half of
f.	Kuba B.H. 952.	10,					
g.	Juž. Srb. 412.	10,					previous
272.	Kuba B.H. 670.	10,	(VII)	VII – 5		AB	swallowing of last syll.
273.	Kuba B.H. 667.	10,	(VII)	VII – 5		A Av	swallowing of last syll.
274.	Kuba B.H. 572.	10,	(VII)	VII – 5		A Av	
275.	Kuba B.H. 144.	10,	(VII)	VII – b6		AB	
276 a.	Đorđević 291.	10,	(#VII)	#VII – 2		AAv	line interr.: 10, 2 – 8, „svatovska"
b.	" 290.	10,					2-nd half of a. „svatovska"
277.	Kuhač 1059.	10,	(#VII)	#VII – b3		AAv	„U kolo"
278.	Kuba B.H. 877.	10,	(1)	bVI – b2		A Av	
279.	Kuhač 1278.	10,	(1)	bVI – 4		AB	„svatovska"
280 a.	Kuhač 514.	10,	(1)	bVI – b6		AB	
b.	Kuba IX. 59.	10,	(1)	bVI – b6		AB	
c.	" " 24.	10,	(1)	bVI – b6		AB	
d.	Kuba B.H. 159.	10,	(1)	bVI – b6		AB	
e.	" " 64.	10,	(2)	VII – 7		AB	
f.	" " 65.	10,	(2)	VII – 7		AB	
g.	" " 66. (=Kuba XIII. 4.)	10,	(2)	VII – 7		AB	
281 a.	Đorđević 371.	10,	(1)	VII – b2		AAv	
b.	Kuba B.H. 306.	10,	(1)	VI – b2		A Av	
c.	Đorđević 370.	(10) 6, 8,	(b2)	1 – b2		A Av	„svatovska"
d.	Kuhač 1067.	10,					half of a. „u ženskom kolu"
282.	Đorđević 155	10,	(1)	VII – 2		AAv	„pri bučkanu"

Current No	Original Edition	Syll.	Last note of section	Range	Rhythm. structure	Structure	Remark
283a.	Kuba B.H. 456.	10,	①	VII – b3		AB	two part song
b.	" " 497.	10,	①	VII – 4		AB	
c.	" " 798.	10,					half of previous „uspavanka"
284.	Đorđević 79.	10,	①	VII – b3	Var. Parry 8.	AAv	syll. interr. : 10, 1+[2.]+8, svatovska
285.	Kuba B.H. 1019. Ms.	10,	①	VII – b3		AAv	two part song line interr. : 10, 4 – 6,
286a.	Kuba B.H. 311.	10,	①	VII – 4		AAv	
b.	" " 544.	10,	①	VII – 4		AAv	
c.	" " 914.	10,	①	VII – 4		AAv	line interr. : 10, 4 – 6,
d.	" " 916.	10,	(b2)	VII – 4		AAv	line interr. : 10, 4 – 6,
e.	" " 915.	10,	④	VII – 4		AAv	line interr. : 10, 4 – 6,
f.	Kuba XI. 61.	10,					half of a.
g.	Kuba B.H. 1092. Ms.	10,					half of a.
287.	Kuhač 761.	10,	①	VII – 4		AB	
288a.	Kuhač 956.	10,	①	VII – 4		AAv	
b.	Kuba B.H. 310.	10,	①	VII – 4		AB	
289a.	Đorđević 37.	10,	①	VII – 4		AAv	
b.	Kuba B.H. 803.	10,					half of a.
290a.	Kuhač 1222 b)	10,	①	VII – 4		AAv	„svatovska (poziv)"
b.	Kuba B.H. 909.	10,	①	VII – 4		AAv	„uspavanka" line interr. : 10, 4 – 6,
291.	Kuhač 304.	10,	①	VII – 4		AAv	
292a.	Đorđević 86.	10,	①	VII – 4		AAv	„čilimarska"
b.	Đorđević Nar. Pev. p. 85/1	10,	①	VII – 4		AAv	
293.	Kuba B.H. 494.	10,	①	VII – 4		AAv	
294.	Kuba B.H. 628.	10,	①	VII – 4		AB	
295.	Kuba B.H. 501.	10,	①	VII – 4		AB	

Current No	Original Edition	Syll.	Last note of section	Range	Rhythm. structure	Structure	Remarks
296 a.	Kuba B. H. 923.	10,	①	VII – 4		AAv	swallowing of last syll.
b.	" " 895.	10,	①	1 – 4		AAv	
297 a.	Kuba B. H. 714.	10,	①	VII – 5		AB	
b.	Kuhač 645.	10,	①	VII – 5		AB	
c.	Kuba B. H. 610.	10,	①	VII – 5		AAv	
298.	Kuba B. H. 946.	10,	①	VII – 5		AB	Var. Parry 9.
299.	Kuba B. H. 436.	10,	①	VII – 5		AA	
300.	Juž. Srb. 419.	10,	①	VII – b6		AB	Swing Song for St. George's day
301 a.	Kuba B.H. 222.	10,	①	VII – 7		AAv	
b.	" " 129.	10,	①	VII – b6		AB	swallowing of last syll.
302 a.	Kuba B.H. 1002. Ms.	10,	①	1 – b3		AAv	chromatic „žetvarska"
b.	Kuba B. H. 999. Ms.	10,					2-nd half of a. chromatic „kolo"
303 a.	Kuba B.H. 391.	10,	①	1 – b3		AAv	Var. Parry 10. (a.–d.)
b.	Kuhač 250.	10,	①	1 – 4		AAv	
c.	" 251.	10,					2-nd half of e. (c.–f.)
d.	Kuba X. 34.	10,					
e.	Kuba B.H. 387.	10,					
f.	" " 1018. Ms.	10,				cf. also Parry 1.	two part song chromatic
304 a.	Đorđević 355.	10,	①	1–4		AAv	„sedeljka"
b.	Kuhač 792.	10,					2-nd half of a.
c.	Đorđević 494.	10,					2-nd half of a. „svatovska"
305 a.	Đorđević 359.	10,	①	1–4		AAv	line interv.: 4–3–6, 4–3–6, „sedeljka"
b.	Đorđević Nar. Pev. p. 2/2	10,	①	1–4		AAv	
c.	Kuhač 1503.	10,	①	1–4		AAv	„uz gusle"

Current No	Original Edition	Syll.	Last note of section	Range	Rhythm. structure	Structure	Remarks
d.	Đorđević 375.	10,	①	1–♭3		AAv	
e.	" 24.	10,					„na Svetog Nikolu"
f.	" 401.	10,					syll. interv.: 3+[4.]+6, „sedeljka"
g.	" 579.	10,					second half of previous
h.	" 584.	10,					
i.	" 590.	10,					
j.	" 473.	10,					
k.	" 216.	10,					„na premlaz"
l.	Manojlović 6.	10,					
306.	Đorđević 222.	10,	①	1–4		AB	„sedeljka"
307.	Đorđević 25,	10,	①	1–4		AAv	„svatovska" line interv.: 10,2–8,
308.	Kuba B.H. 1006. Ms.	10,	①	1–4		AAv	two part song chromatic
309 a.	Kuba B.H. 432.	10,	①	1–4		AAv	line interv.: 10, 1–9,
b.	Đorđević 462.	10,	①	1–4		AAv	„prilikom meskarada o Beloj Nedelji"
c.	Kuhač 495.	10,	①	1–5		AAv	
310 a.	Kuba B.H. 825.	10,	①	1–4		AAv	Var.: Ranny No 1.
b.	" " 319.	10,	①	1–4		AAv	
c.	" " 321.	10,	①	1–4		AB	
d.	Đorđević 580.	10,	①	1–4		AAv	
e.	" 578.	10,	①	1–4,		AAv	
f.	Kuba B.H. 398.	10,					half of previous
g.	" " 2.	10,					
h.	" " 318	10,					
i.	Đorđević 569b)	10,					
311 a.	Kuba B.H. 3[illegible]	10,	①	1–♭4		AAv	
b.	" " 330.	10,	(♭2)	VII–♭4		AAv	

Current No	Original edition	Syll.	Last note of section	Range	Rhythm. structure	Structure	Remarks
c.	Kuba XI. 55.	10,					2-nd half of previous
312 a.	Đorđević 342.	10,	①	1–5		AB	
b.	" 112.	10,	①	VII–5		AAv	
c.	Kuba B.H. 656.	10,	①	1–5		AB	
d.	Đorđević Nar. Pev. p. 36/2	10,	①	1–4		AAv	
e.	Kačerovski 41.	10,	①	1–5		AB	
313.	Kuhač 882.	10,	①	1–5		AB	
314.	Kuhač 968.	10,	①	1–5		AA	
315.	Kuba XIII. 21.	10,	①	1–5		AB	
316.	Kuhač 234.	10,	①	1–♭5		AAv	
317 a.	Kuba B.H. 430.	10,	①	1–5		AAv	
b.	" " 35.	10,	①	1–5		AAv	
318.	Kuba B.H. 898.	10,	①	1–5		AB	
319.	Kuhač 218.	10,	①	1–5		AB	
320 a.	Kuba B.H. 440.	10,	①	1–♭6		AB	
b.	Kuba XI. 6.	10,					half of a.
321 a.	Kuhač 53.	10,	①	1–♭6		AB	
b.	Kuba IX. 20	10,	①	1–♭6		AB	
c.	Kuba B.H. 108 (=Kuba XIII. 14.)	10,	①	1–♭6		AB	
d.	Kuba B.H. 109. (=Kuba XII. 56.)	10,	①	1–♭6		AB	
e.	Kuba B.H. 107.	10,	①	1–7		AB	
f.	" " 181.	10,	①	1–7		AB	
g.	Kuba IX. 5.	10,	①	VII–5		AB	three part song
h.	Kuba B.H. 958.	10,	①	1–♭6		AB	
322.	Kuba B. H. 33.	10,	①	1–6		AB	

Current №	Original edition	Syll.	Last note of section	Range	Rhythm. structure	Structure	Remarks
323 a.	Kuba B.H. 839.	10,	(b2)	VII – b3		AAv	line interv.: 10, 4 $\overset{2}{-}$ 6,
b.	" " 505.	10,	(2)	VII – 4		AAv	
c.	" " 1004. Ms.	10,	(b2)	VII – b3		AAv	line interv.: 10, 4 $\overset{2}{-}$ 6, chromatic
324.	Kuba XI. 23.	10,	(b2)	VII – 4		AB	
325 a.	Đorđević 68.	10,	(b2)	VII – 4		AAv	
b.	" 76.	10,	(b2)	VII – 5		AAv	„sedeljka"
326.	Kuhač 827 (Đorđević Nar. Pev. p. 32/2)	10,	(b2)	VII – 4		AB	
327 a.	Kuhač 51.	10,	(b2)	VII – 4		AAsv	
b.	" 510.	10,	(b2)	VII – 4		AAs	
c.	" 287.	10,	(b2)	VII – 4		AB	
328.	Kuba B.H. 1007. Ms.	10,	(b2)	1 – 3		AAv	chromatic
329.	Kuhač 1502.	10,	(b2)	1 – 5		AAv	„uz gusle"
330 a.	Kuba XIV. 29.	10,	(b2)	1 – 5		AB	
b.	Kuba B.H. 899.	10,					2-nd half of a.
331.	Kuhač 350.	10,	(2)	VII – b3		AAv	
332.	Kuba B.H. 514.	10,	(2)	VII – 4		AAv	
333 a.	Kuhač 262.	10,	(2)	VII – 4		AAv	
b.	" 67.	10,	(2)	VII – 4		AAv	
c.	" 1097.	10,	(2)	VII – 4		AAv	„poskočna"
d.	" 445.	10,	(2)	VII – 4		AAv	
e.	Iz Levča 62.	10,					2-nd half of previous
334 a.	Kuhač 717 a)	10,	(2)	VII – 4		AAv	
b.	" 717 b)	10,	(2)	VII – 5		AAv	„from 1828!"
c.	Đorđević 33.	10,					2-nd half of previous line interv.: 8 $\overset{2}{-}$ 2
335 a.	Kuhač 1132 a)	10,	(2)	VII – 4		AAv	„plješkavica"

II.10,②

Current №	Original Edition	Syll.	Last note of section	Range	Rhythm. structure	Structure	Remarks
b.	Iz Levča 33.	10,	②	VI – 4		AAv	„sedeljka"
c.	Kuhač 155.	10,	①	VI – 4		AB	
d.	" 1126.	10,	①	VI – 4		AB	„poskočnica"
336.	Đorđević 347.	10,	②	VII – 4		AAv	„slavska"
337–338.	Kuba B.H. 542.	10,	②	VII – 4		AAv	
339a.	Kuba B.H. 519, 520	10,	②	VII – 5		AB	
b.	" " 596.	10,	②	VII – 5		AAv	
340.	Kuba B.H. 632	10,	②	VII – 5		AB	
341.	Kuhač 1541.	10,	②	VII – 5		AB	
342.	Đorđević 39.	(8) r. 10,	②	VII – 5		AB	
343.	Kuba B.H. 62	10,	②	VII – 7		AB	
344a.	Kuba B.H. 63. (= Kuba XIII. 26.)	10,	②	VII – 7		AB	line interr.: 10, 4 ² 6,
b.	Kuba B.H. 58.	10,	②	VII – 7		AB	
c.	" " 1021. Ms.	10,	②	VII – 7		AB	line interr.: 10, 4 ² 6,
d.	Kuba B.H. 160. (= Kuba XIII. 23.)	10,	①	bVI – b6		AB	
e.	Kuba B.H. 70.	10,	⑤	1 – 7		AB	line interr.: 10, 4 ² 6,
f.	" " 1022. Ms.	10,	⑤	VII – 7		AB	line interr.: 10, 4 ² 6,
345.	Kuhač 650.	10,	②	#VII – 5		AB	
346a.	Đorđević 415.	10,	②	1 – b3		AAv	„sedeljka"
b.	" 318.	10,	②	1 – b3		AAv	„svatovska"
c.	Đorđević Nar. Pev. p. 108,	10,	②	1 – b3		AAv	
347.	Kuba B.H. 402.	10,	②	1 – b3		AB	
348.	Đorđević 417.	10,	②	1 – 4		AB	„sedeljka"
349a.	Đorđević 351.	10,	②	1 – 4		AAv	
b.	" 402.	10,	②	1 – 4		AAv	„sedeljka"

Current No	Original edition	Syll.	Last note of section	Range	Rhythm. structure	Structure	Remarks
c.	" 317.	10,	(2)	1-b3		AB	„svatovska"
350.	Kuhač 228.	10,	(2)	1-4		AAv	
351.	Đorđević 460.	10,	(2)	1-4		AAv	line interv.: 10, 4 3/– 6,
352.	Kuhač 993.	10,	(2)	1-5		AAv	
353a.	Kuhač 1497.	10,	(2)	1-5		AB	„uz gusle"
b.	" 721.	10,	(2)	1-5		AB	
c.	Kuba B.H. 617.	10,					2d half of preceding
354.	Kuhač 390.	10,	(2)	1-5		AB	
355.	Kuhač 773.	10,	(2)	1-5		AAv	
356a.	Kuhač 434.	10,	(2)	1-5		AB	
b.	" 1274.	10,	(2)	1-5		AB	„svatovska"
c.	" 698.	10,	(2)	1-5		AB	
357a.	Kuba B.H. 749.	10,	(2)	1-5		AAv	
b.	" " 750.	10,	(5)	1-5		AAv	word interv.: 10, 1 2/– 9, swallowing of last note
c.	" " 751.	(10) 10, 4,	(2)	1-5		AB	cf. No 1026 e. No 1036 h.
358.	Kuba B.H. 416.	10,	(2)	1-5		AAv	
359a.	Kuhač 1202.	10,	(2)	1-5		AAv	„svatovska"
b.	" 1052.	10,	(3)	1-4		AAv	„mužko kolo" two part song
360a.	Kuhač 1060.	10,	(2)	1-6,		AAv	kolo ?
b.	" 1061.	10,	(2)	1-6,		AAv	„žensko kolo"
361-362.	Kuhač 778.	10,	(2)	1-7,		AB	
363.	Kuba B.H. 158.	10,	(b3)	bVII-b6		AB	
364a.	Kuba B.H. 560.	10,	(b3)	VII-b3		AAv	
b.	" " 543.	10,	(b3)	VII-4		AB	
365a. (-366)	Kuba B.H. 528.	10,	(b3)	VII-4		AAv	Var. Parry II.

Current №	Original edition	Syll.	Last note of section	Range	Rhythm. structure	Structure	Remarks
b.	" " 529.	10,	(2)	VII – 4		AAv	line interr.: 10, 4–6,
c.	" " 575.	10,					2d half of preceding
d.	" " 711.	10,					
367–368	Kačerovski 75.	10,	(b3)	VII – 4		AAv	
369 a.	Kuba B.H. 587.	10,	(b3)	VII – 4		AAv	"uspavanka"
b.	Kuba IX. 26.	10,	(b3)	VII – 4		AAv	swallowing of last syll.
370.	Kuba B.H. 682.	10,	(b3)	VII – 5		AB	
371.	Kuhač 1431.	10,	(b3)	VII – b6		AAsv	
372.	Kuba B.H. 137.	10,	(b3)	VII – 7		AB	
373.	Đorđević 414.	10,	(b3)	1 – b3		AAv	line interr.: 10, 4–6 "sedeljka"
374.	Đorđević 363.	10,	(b3)	1 – 4		AAv	line interr.: 10, 4–6, "sedeljka"
375.	Đorđević 149.	10,	(b3)	1 – 4		AB	"sedeljka"
376 a.	Đorđević 71.	10,	(b3)	1 – 4		AB	
b.	" 75.	10,	(b3)	VII – 4		AB	"lazarička"
377 a.	Kuhač 33.	10,	(b3)	1 – 4		AAv	
b.	" 554.	10,	(b3)	VII – 4		?	
c.	" 730	10,	(b3)	1 – b6		AAv	
378.	Kuba B.H. 765.	10,	(b3)	1 – 4		AAv	
379 a.	Kuhač 305.	10,	(b3)	1 – 5		AAv	
b.	Kuba IX. 25.	10,	(b3)	1 – 5		AAv	
c.	" " 4.	10,	(b3)	1 – 4		AAv	
380.	Kuba B.H. 424.	10,	(b3)	1 – 5		AB	
381.	Kuba B.H. 433.	10,	(b3)	1 – 5		AAv	
382.	Đorđević Nar. Pev. p. 120/1	10,	(b3)	1 – 5		AAv	

Current No	Original Edition	Syll.	Last note of section	Range	Rhythm structure	Structure	Remarks
383a.	Kuhač 1459.	10,	(b3)	1-b6		AB	
b.	Kuba X. 54.	10,	(b3)	1-b6		AB	three part song
384a.	Kuba B.H. 1108. Ms.	10,	(3)	VII-5	Var. cf. Parry No 983/12 and Parry No 27.	AB	line interv.: 10, 6-4,
b.	Kuba B.H. 111.	10,	(b3)	VII-5		AB	"putnička" emph. ornament tones
d.	" Ms." 1013.	10,	(2)	VII-5		AB	
385.	Kuba B.H. 173.	10,	(3)	1-4		AB	
386.	Kuba B.H. 901.	10,	(3)	1-5		AAv	
387.	Kuhač 1376.	10,	(3)	1-5		AAv	
388.	Kuba B.H. 8.	10,	(3)	1-6		AB	
389.	Kuhač 1435.	10,	(4)	VII-4		AAv	
390a.	Kuba B.H. 577.	10,	(4)	VII-4		AAv	
b.	" " 565.	10,	(4)	VII-5		AAv	
c.	Kuhač 1518.	10,	(4)	VII-4		AAv	
d.	" 1092.	10,	(4)	VII-4			poskočnica?
391a.	Đorđević Nar. Pev. p. 15½	10,	(4)	VII-4		AAv	
b.	Đorđević 435.	10,	(4)	1-4		AAv	
c.	Kuhač 1244.	10,					2nd half of preceding "svatovska"
392a.	Kuba B.H. 4.	10,	(4)	VII-4		AB	line interv.: 10, 4-6,
b.	" " 930.	10,	(4)	VII-4		AAv	
c.	" " 309.	10,	(4)	VII-4		AAv	line interv.: 10, 4-6,
d.	" " 599.	10,	(4)	VII-5		AB	
393a.	Kuhač 1263.	10,	(4)	VII-5		AB	
394a.	Kuba B.H. 434.	10,	(4)	VII-5		AB	line interv.: 10, 4-6,
b.	" " 671.	10,	(4)	VII-5		AB	
395.	Kuba B.H. 212.	10,	(4)	VII-5		AB	
384c.	Kuba B.H. 821.	10,	(b3)	VII-4		AB	"uspavanka"

II. 10, (4)–(5), – 4+3+3
 " , (VII) – (1)

Current No	Original edition	Syll.	Last note of section	Range	Rhythm. structure	Structure	Remarks
396 a.	Kuhač 642.	10,	(4)	1–5		AB	
b.	Kuba B.H. 240.	10,	(4)	VII – 7		AB	
c.	Kuba XII. 33.	10,	(4)	1–7		AB	
397.	Kuhač 1492.	10,	(4)	1–5		AB	"uz gusle"
~~397 bis.~~	~~Kuba B.H. 296.~~	~~10,~~	~~(5)~~	~~VII – 7~~		~~AB~~	
398.	Kuba XII. 41.	10,	(5)	1–6		AB	
399.	Kuhač 723.	(8) r. 10,	(VII)	VII – 5	♫♫♩♩|♩♩♩♩||	AB	
400 a.	Đorđević 503.	(7) 10,	(VII)	VII – b3	♫♫|♩♫|♩♫||	AAv	"sedeljka"
b.	" 410.	(7) 10,					2-nd half of preceding "sedeljka"
c.	" 137.	(7) 10,					2-nd half of a. "lazarička"
401 a.	Kuhač 726.	(7) r. 10,	(1)	VII – 4	♫♫|♩♫|♩♫||	AB	
b.	" 579.	(7) 10,					2-nd half of a.
402 a.	Đorđević 210.	(?) 10,	(1)	1–4	♩♩♩♩|♫♩|♫♩||	AB	"igra"
b.	" 231.	(7) 10,	(1)	1–4	♩♩♩♩|♫♩|♫♩||	AB	"igra"
c.	" 474.	(7) 10,	(1)	1–4	♩♩♩♩|♫♩|♫♩||	AB	
d.	" 340.	(7) 10,			"		2-nd half of preceding
~~e.~~	~~" 518.~~	~~"~~			"		"dečja igra"
403.	Đorđević 159.	(7) 10,	(1)	1–4	♫♫|♫♩|♫♩||	AAv	~~"u oči Jeremijinog dana"~~
404 a.	Iz Levča 74.	(7) 10	(b2)	VII – 4	♩♩♩♩|♩♩𝅗𝅥|♩♩𝅗𝅥||	AAv	"obredno"(!)
b.	" " 75.	?					fragments of a. "obredno"(!)
405.	Kuhač 738.	(7) 10,	(b3)	bVI – 4	♫♫|♩♫|♫♩||	AB	
406.	Kuhač 766.	(7) 10,	(4)	V – 5	♫♫|♫♩|♫♩♩||	AB	< Hungar. type?
407 a.	Đorđević 505.	(8) r. 11,	(VII)	VI – b3		AAv	
b.	" 405.	(8) r. 11,	(VII)	1 – b3		AAv	"sedeljka"
408.	Kuhač 505.	11,	(VII)	VII – 4		AB	
409.	Đorđević Nar. Pev. p. 19½	(8) r. 11,	(VII)	VII – b6		AAv	
410.	Đorđević 257.	11,	(1)	VII – b2		AAv	"svatovska"

II.11, ① – ②

Current №	Original edition	Syll.	Last note of section	Range	Rhythm. structure	Structure	Remarks
411.	Đorđević 454.	11,	①	VII – b3		AAv	„svatovska"
412.	Kuhač 585.	11,	①	VII – 4		A Av	line interr.: 11, 4 ? 7,
413.	Kuba B.H. 438.	11,	①	VII – 4		AB	
414 a.	Kuhač 912.	11,	①	VII – 4		AAv	
b.	" 911.	11,	①	VII – 4		AAv	
c.	" 68.	11,	①	VII – 4		AAv	
d.	" 910.	11,	①	bVII – 4		AAv	
415.	Kuba B.H. 568.	11,	①	VII – 4		A Av	
416.	Kuba B.H. 322.	11,	①	VII – b5		AB	
417.	Kuba B.H. 813. (= " " " 1121. inc.)	11,	①	1 – 4		AAv	word interr.: 11, 1 ? 10,
418.	Đorđević 181.	(8) r. 11,	①	1 – 4		AA	Var. Parry № 14. Cf. № 592, 679
419.	Kuba B.H. 764.	11,	①	1 – 4		AAv	
420 a.	Iz Levča 45.	(8) r. 11,	②	VII – b3		AAv	„sedeljka"
b.	Bosiljevac 14.	11,					2-nd half of a.
421 a.	Iz Levča 35.	11,	②	VII – b3		AAv	„sedeljka"
b	Đorđević 29.	11,					2-nd half of a.
c.	" 444.	11,					2-nd half of a.
422 a.	Iz Levča 44.	11,	②	VII – 4		AAv	„sedeljka"
b.	" " 63.	11,	②	VII – 4		AAv	
c.	" " 71.	(8) 11,	②	VII – 4		A Av	
423 a.	Kuhač 60.	(10) 11,	②	VII – 4		AAv	
b.	" 61.	(10) 10, 11,	②	VII – 4		AAv	
424 a.	Kuhač 637.	11,	②	VII – 5		AB	
b.	Kuba B.H. 595.	11,	②	VII – 5		AB	
c.	Kuba XII. 57.	11,	②	1 – 5		AB	

Current No.	Original edition	Syll.	Last note of section	Range	Rhythm. structure	Structure	Remarks
d.)	Đorđević Nar. Pev. p. 155/2	11,	(2)	VII–5		AB	
425.	Đorđević Nar. Pev. p. 7/1	11,	(2)	VII–5		AB	
426a.)	Kuba B.H. 735.	11,	(2)	VII–5		AB	
b.)	" " 736.	11,	(2)	VII–5		AB	
427.	Đorđević Nar. Pev. p. 42/1	11,	(2)	1–4		AAv	
428.	Kuba B.H. 701.	11,	(2)	1–5		AAv	
429a.)	Kuba B.H. 413.	11,	(2)	1–5		AB	
b.	" " 218.	11,	(2)	VII–5		AB	
c.)	" " 219.	11,	(2)	1–5		AB	
430a.)	Đorđević 14.	11,	(b3)	VII–b3		AAv	
⊕ b.)	Kuba B.H. 452.	11,					2-nd half of a.
432a.)	Kuhač 578.	11,	(b3)	1–4		AAv	Var. Parry 15.
b.	Kuba B.H. 184. (= Kuba XIII. 31.)	11,	(b3)	1–7		AB	
c.	Kuhač 508.	11,					2-nd half of a.
d.)	Kuba B.H. 315.	11,					2-nd half of a.
433 a.)	Kuba B.H. 90.	11,	(b3)	1–5		AAv	
b.	" " 122.	11,	(b3)	1–5		AAv	
c.	" " 121. (= Kuba XIII. 20.)	11,	(b3)	1–5		AAv	
d.	Kuba B.H. 597.	11,	(b3)	1–5		AAv	line interr.: 11, 4 $\underline{2}$ 7,
e.)	Kuhač 1531.	(8) 7. 11,	(b3)	1–5		AB	
434.	Kuba B.H. 673.	11,	(b3)	1–5		AB	
435a.)	Kuba B.H. 444.	11,	(b3)	1–b6		AAv	
b.	" " 604.	11,	(b3)	VII–5		AAv	
c.	" " 966. Ms.	11,	(b3)	1–b6		AAv	
d.)	Kuba B.H. 418.	11,					2-nd half of a.
⊕431.	Kuba B.H. 228.	11,	(b3)	VII–7		AB	

II.11, ③-⑧; 6+5, 5+3+3,

Current No	Original edition	Syll.	Last note of section	Range	Rhythm. structure	Structure	Remarks
e.	" " 354.	11,					2nd half of a.
436.	Kuhač 1216.	11,	③	V – 4		AB	Slovak. var.
437.	Kuba B.H. 947.	11,	④	1 – 4		AAv	
438.	Kuba B.H. 280.	11,	⑤	1 – b6		AB	
439 a.	Kuba B.H. 752.	11,	⑤	1 – 7		AAv	
b.	Kuba IX. 14.	11,	⑤	1 – 7		AAv	
c.	Đorđević 59.	11,	⑦	1 – 7		AAv	
440 a.	Kuba B.H. 191.	11,	⑤	1 – 7		AB	
b.	" " 192.	13,*	⑤	1 – 7		AB	* new Hungar. syllable-doubling ?
441.	Đorđević 109.	11,	⑧	1 – 9		AB	half of a Hungar. Turkish-type ne[illegible]. ?
442.	Kuhač 562.	11,	③	1 – 6	[rhythm notation]	AB	Slovak. ?
443 a.	Đorđević 225.	(8b) 11,	①	1 – 4	[rhythm notation]	AB	
b.	" 217.	(8b) 11,			"		2-nd half of a.
444.	Đorđević Nar. Pev. p. 130/2	(8b) 11, +	①	1 – 5	[rhythm notation]	AB	
445 a	Kuba B.H. 840.	(8b) 11,	b3	VII – 4	[rhythm notation]	AAv	line interr. : 11, 5?6,
b.	" " 887.	(8b) 11,	b3	bVII – b3	"	AB	"svatovska"
c.	" " 776.	(8b) 11,	b3	VII – b3	"	AB	
d.	" " 778.	(8b) 11,	b3	VII – b3	"	AAv	
e.	" " 779.	(8b) 11,	b3	VII – b3	"	AB	line interr. : 11, 5?6
f.	" " 782.	(8b) 11,	b3	VII – b3	"	AAv	
g.	Bosiljevac 33.	(8b) 11,	b3	VII – b3	"	AAv	
h.	Kuba B.H. 773.	(8b) 11,	②	VII – 2	"	AAv	
i.	" " 780.	8b,	②	VII – b3		AAv	
j.	" " 777.	8b,					2-nd half of i.

38

II. 11, 3+4+4
12, (VII) — (2)

Current №	Original Edition	Syll.	Last note of section	Range	Rhythm structure	Structure	Remarks
446a.	Kuba XI. 11.	(8) 11,	(1)	VII - b3	♫♩|♬♬|♬♬| *	AAv	line interr.: 11, 2–9
b.	Đorđević 251.	(8) 11,	(1)	VII - b3	"	AAv	* cf. № 1396. (similar break)
c.	Kuba XI. 5.	(8) 11,			"		half of a.
d.	Đorđević 207.	(8) 11,			"		half of a.
447.	Đorđević 550.	(10) 12,	(VII)	VII - 4	4+4+4	AAv	
448a.	Đorđević 262.	(8) r. 12,	(1)	VII - b2	"	AA	„kraljička"
b.	Kuba B.H. 308.	(8) 12,	(1)	1 - b2	"	AA	
c.	" " 267.	"	"	1 - b3	"	"	
d.	Đorđević 184.	(8) 12, r. (10)	(VII)	VII - b2	"	AA	„kraljička"
e.	" 283.	(8) r. 12,	(VII)	VII - b2	"	AA	„kraljička"
f.	" 373.	(8) 12, r. (10,)	(VII)	VII - b2	"	AAv	
g.	" 53.	(8) 12, r. (10,)	(b2)	VII - b2	"	AAv	„kraljička", word interr.: 12, 1–9,
h.	" 284.	(8) r. 12,	(2)	1 - b3	"	AAv	„kraljička"
i.	" 374.	(8) r. 12,	(2)	1 - 4	"	AAv	
j.	" 349.	(10) r. 14, 12,	(# VII)	VI - 1		AAv	„lazarička"
k.	" 282.	(10) r. 13,					„kraljička" 2nd half of precedings
l.	" 287.	(10) r. 13,					„kraljička" 2nd half of precedings
m.	Kuba B.H. 386.	(8) 12,			4+4+4		2-nd half of precedings
n.	Đorđević 232	(8) r. 12,			"		" " " „lazarička"
449.	Kuba B.H. 485.	(8) r. 12,	(1)	VI - b3	"	AAv	
450-451.	Kuba B.H. 830.	12,	(1)	VI - 4	"	AAv	
452a.	Đorđević 486.	(8) r. 12,	(1)	1 - 4	"	AA	„sedeljka" Var. Tamo/6a. ([illegible] form)
b.	" 497.	"	"	VII - 4	"	"	
c.	" 485.	(8) r. 12,			"		„sedeljka" half of a.
d.	Kuhač 1245.	(8) 12,			"		half of a. „svatovska"
e.	" 1042	"			"		half of a. „oro"
453a.	Iz Levča 64.	(8) 12,	(2)	VII - b3	"	AAv	

II. 12, (2)–(b3), –13; III. Z2, 6/5, –8/5,

Current No	Original edition	Syll.	Last note of section	Range	Rhythm structure	Structure	Remarks
b.	" " 65.	(8) 12,	(2)	VII–4	4+4+4	AAv	
c.	" " 67.	(8) 12,	(2)	VII–b3	"	AAv	
454a.	Đorđević 470.	(8) r. 12,	(b2)	VII–4	"	AAv	„sedeljka"
b.	Iz Levča 43.	(8) r. 12,	(VII)	VII–4	"	AAv	„sedeljka"
455a.	Bosiljevac 10.	(8) 12,	(2)	VII–5	"	AB	
b.	Đorđević Nar. Pev. p. 37/1	(8) (r.) 12,	?	VII–5	"	AB	
c.	Kuba B.H. 162. (= Kuba XIV. 2.)	(8) 12,	(2)	VII–5	"	AB	
d.	Kuba X. 47.	(8) 12, 8,	(2)	VII–5		AB	
e.	Kuba B.H. 793.	(8) (r.) 8, 12,	(1)	VII–b3		AAv	
⊕ 456.	Đorđević 396.	(8) r. 12,	(2)	1–4	4+4+4	AAv	„svatovska"
458.	Kuhač 591.	(8) r. 12,	(b3)	1–b6	"	AAv	
459.	Đorđević 9. (= Đorđević Nar. Pev.) p. 83/1	12, (!)	(b3)	1–b6	"	AAv*	*Av = 1–4 syl. A + 5–12 syl. A_3
↕ 457.	Kuba B.H. 678.	(8) 12,	(b3)	VII–5		AB	
460.	Kuba XI. 41.	(8) r.* 13,	(VII)	VII–b3		AAv	* refr.: Dangubo moja

III. Heterometric two-section melodies

Current No	Original edition	Syll.	Last note of section	Range	Rhythm structure	Structure	Remarks
461.	Kuba B.H. 998. Ms.	(8b) 6, 5,	(1)	1–2		AB	„kolo"
462.	Kuba B.H. 395.	(8b) 6, 5,	(2)	1–4		AB	
463.	Kuhač 438.	7, 5,	(VII)	VII–4		AAv	
464.	Kuba B.H. 477.	7, 6,	(1)	VII–2		AB	„Kolo"
465.	Kuba B.H. 294.	7, 6,	(4)	1–b6		AB	
466.	Bosiljevac 8.	8, 5,	(VII)	IV–2		AB	
467a.	Kuba IX. 29.	8, 5,	(VII)	VII–5		AB	
b.	Kuba B.H. 113.	8, 5,	(VII)	VII–5		AB	
468.	Kuba B.H. 989. Ms.	8, 5,	(1)	1–3		AAv	
⊕ 469–470.	Kuhač 1072.	8, 5,	(2)	VII–4		AAv	
472a.	Đorđević 461.	8, 5,	(2)	1–4		AAv	„žetvarska"

III. 8,5, – 8,6,(VII) – Zz

Current No	Original edition	Syll.	Last note of section	Range	Rhythm. structure	Structure	Remarks
b.	Đorđević 390.	8, 5,	(2)	1 – 4		AAv	„slavska"
c.	Iz Levča 1.	8, 5,	(b2)	VII – 4		AB	„slavska"
473 a.	Kuhač 343.	8, 5,	(2)	1 – 4		AB	
b.	Kuba IX. 21.	8, 5,	(2)	1 – 5		AB	three part song
c.	Đorđević 457.	8, 5,	(1)	1 – 4		AB	
471. ↑	Bosiljevac 9.	8, 5,	(2)	VII – 5		AB	
474.	Bosiljevac 19.	8, 5,	(4)	VII – 5		AB	
475.	Iz Levča 6.	(8b) 8b, 5,	(1)	VII – b2		AAv	„svatovska"
476.	Đorđević 577.	(8b) 8b, 5,	(b3)	1 – 4		AB	
477.	Đorđević 64	(5) r. 8b, 5,	(b3)	1 – 5		AB	
478.	Juž. Srb. 418.	(5) r. 8, 5,	(1)	1 – 4	3+3+2, 5,	AB	„igra"
479 a.	Kuba B.H. 823.	(10) 8, 6,	(VII)	VII – b2		AB	„uspavanka" word interr.: 8, 2 – 4,
b.	" " 809.	(10) 8, 6,	(VII)	VII – b2		AB	„svatovska" word interr.: 8, 2 – 4,
c.	" " 770.	(10) 8, 6,	(VII)	VII – b2		AB	„uspavanka" line interr.: 8, 2 – 4,
d.	Đorđević 352.	(10) 8, 6,	(VII)	VII – b2		AB	„sedeljka"
e.	Kuba B.H. 307.	(10) 8, 6,	(VII)	VII – b2		AB	line interr.: 8, 2 – 4,
f.	" " 879.	(10) 8, 6,	(VII)	VII – b2		AB	„svatovska" word interr.: 8, 2 – 4,
g.	Juž. Srb. 427.	(10) 8, 6,	(VII)	VII – b2		AB	
h.	Kuba B.H. 449.	(10) 8, 6,	(2)	VII – b3		AB	word interr.: 8, 2 – 4
i.	" " 718	(11) sic! 8, 6,	(2)	VII – 5		AB	
480 a.	Kuhač 1219.	(8) r. 8, 6,	(VII)	VII – b3		AB	„svatovska"
b.	" 1217.	(8) r. 8, 6,	(VII)	VII – b3		AB	„svatovska"
c.	" 1209.	(10) 8, 6,	(VII)	VII – b3		AB	„svatovska"
481 a.	Kuba B.H. 881.	8, 6,	(VII)	VII – 4		AB	
b.	" " 833.	8, 6,	(VII)	VII – 4		AB	

III. 8, 6, (VII) – (1)
Ž2

Current №	Original edition	Syll.	Last note of section	Range	Rhythm structure	Structure	Remarks
c.	" " 834.	(10) 8, 6,	(VII)	VII – 4		AB	
482.	Kačerovski 13.	8, 6,	(VII)	VII – 7		AB	urban text?
483.	Kuhač 458.	(10) 8, 6,	(1)	bVI – 4		AB	
484.	Kuba B. H. 892.	8, 6,	(1)	VII – 4		AB	
485a.	Kuhač 1470.	8, 6,	(1)	1 – b3		AB	also: two part song
b.	" 958.	8, 6,	(1)	1 – b4		AB	
486.	Kuba B. H. 335.	(10) 8, 6,	(1)	1 – b4		AB	
487.	Kuhač 370	8, 6,	(1)	1 – 4		AB	two part song
488a.	Kuba B. H. 516.	(10) 8, 6,	(1)	1 – 4		AB	
b.	" " 515.	(10) 8, 6,	(1)	1 – 4		AB	
489a.	Đorđević 214.	(10) 8, 6,	(1)	1 – 4		AAv	„žetvarska"
b.	" 129.	(10) 8, 6,	(1)	1 – 4		AAv	„žetvarska"
c.	" 206.	(10) 8, 6,	(1)	1 – 4		AAv	
d.	" 593.	(10) 8, 6,	(1)	1 – 4		AAv	
e.	Iz Leveča 52.	(10) 8, 6,	(1)	1 – 4		AAv	„sedeljka"
f.	" " 66.	(10) 8, 6,	(1)	1 – 4		AAv	„sedeljka"
490.	Kuba B. H. 685.	(10) 8, 6,	(1)	1 – 5		AB	
491.	Đorđević Nar. Pev. p. 1/2	8, 6,	(1)	1 – 5		AB	
492a.	Kuhač 1255.	8, 6,	(1)	1 – 5		AB	sim. to Beeth. VI. symph. beginning. „svatovska"
b.	Kuba B. H. 579.	8, 6,	(1)	1 – 4		AB	
c.	Kuba XIII. 35.	8, 6,	(1)	1 – 5		AB	
d.	Kuba B. H. 114.	8, 6,	(1)	VII – 4		AB	
e.	Kuhač 1269.	(11) 8, 6,	(1)	1 – 5	6, = ♩♩|𝅗𝅥|♩♩|𝅗𝅥|	AB	„svatovska"
f.	Kuba B. H. 948.	(11) 8, 6,	(1)	1 – 5	"	AB	
g.	" " 399.	(11) 8, 6,	(1)	1 – 4	"	AB	

III. 8,6, (b2) – (b6)
Z = 8, 3+3, 8, 7,

Current №	Original edition	Syll.	Last note of section	Range	Rhythm. structure	Structure	Remarks
493.	Kuhač 199.	(10) 8, 6,	(b2)	1–4		AB	
494.	Đorđević 66.	(6?) 8, 6,	(2)	VII–4		AB	
495.	Kuba XI. 29.	(10) 8, 6,	(2)	1–5		AB	Word interr.: 1 2 7, 6, (in each st., except the 1st one.)
496 a.	Kuba B. H. 722.	(10) 8, 6,	(b3)	VII–5		AB	
b.	Đorđević Nar. Po. p. 35 (= Bosiljevac 41)[2]	(10) 8, 6,	(b3)	VII–5		AB	
497.	Kuba B. H. 607.	8, 6,	(b3)	VII–5		AB	
498.	Đorđević 218.	(10) 8, 6,	(b3)	1–4		AB	"Kad se vraća sa rada" two part song
499.	Kuhač 893.	8, 6,	(b3)	1–b6		AB	
500 a.	Kuba B. H. 337.	(10) 8, 6,	(b4)	1–b4		AB	two part song
b.	" " 338.	(10) (4.) 7, 8, 6,	(b4) (b2)	1–b4		ABC	two part song
501.	Juž. Srb. 413.	(10) 8, 6,	(4)	VII–4		AB	
502.	Kuhač 1096.	(10) 4. 8, 6,	(4)	1–4		AB	"poskočnica"
503 a.	Kuba B. H. 98. (= Kuba XIII. 27.)	(10) 8, 6,	(4)	1–5		AB	
b.	Kuba X. 50.	(10) 8, 6,	(4)	1–4		AB	
c.	Kuba B. H. 125.	(10) 8, 6,	(4)	1–5		AB	line interr.: 6 2 2, 6,
504.	Đorđević 180.	(8) (4.) 8, 6,	(4)	1–5		AB	"sedeljka"
505.	Kuba IX. 35	(10) 8, 6,	(#4)	1–5		AB	
506.	Kuba XII. 12.	(10) 8, 6,	(b5)	IV–b5		AAv	
507.	Kuhač 841.	(10) 8, 6,	(b6)	1–b6		AB	
508.	Đorđević 570.	(8) 4. 8, 6,	(1)	1–b3	6, = ♫♩|♩♩𝅗𝅥||	AB	"sedeljka" two part song
509.	Đorđević 158.	(8) 4. 8, 6,	(b2)	1–b3	6, = ♫♩|♫♩||	AB	
510 a.	Juž. Srb. 408.	(11) 8, 6,	(2)	VII–4	"	AB	"igra"
511 a.	Kuba B. H. 313. (= Kuba XII. 24.)	8, 7,	(VII)	IV–5			
b.	Kuhač 106. (= Đorđević Nar. Po. p. 8/1)	(7) 8, 7,	(b3)	IV–4		AB	
512.	Kuba B. H. 713.	(8) 4. 8, 7,	(VII)	VII–4		AB	
510 b.	Kuba B. H. 712.	(11) 8, 6,	(VII)	VII–5		AB	

III. 8, 7, — 10, 6
Z₂ (VII)

Current No	Original edition	Syll.	Last note of section	Range	Rhythm structure	Structure	Remarks
513 a.	Kuhač 233.	(11) 8, 7,	(VII)	VII – 4		AB	
b.	" 486.	(10) r. 8, 6,	(VII)	VI – 5		AB	
c.	Kuba B.H. 705.	8, 7,	(VII)	VII – 5		AB	text-stanzas, rimes (urban t.)
514.	Kuhač 1354.	8, 7,	(1)	bVI – b6		AB	
515.	Kuba B.H. 785.	8, 7,	(1)	VII – b2		A Av	
516 a.	Kuhač 1456.	8, 7,	(1)	VII – b3		AB	
b.	" 143.	8, 7,	(1)	VII – b3		A Av	
517 a.	Kuba B.H. 889.	(11) 8, 7,	(1)	VII – 4		A Av	
b.	" " 888.	(11) 8, 7,	(1)	bVI – b3		AB	
518.	Kuhač 479.	8, 7,	(1)	VII – 4		AB	
519 a.	Kuba XI. 63.	8, 7,	(1)	1 – 4		AB	
b.	Kuba B.H. 871.	8, 7,	(1)	1 – 5		AB	
520.	Kuba B.H. 172.	(11) 8, 7,	(1)	1 – 4		AB	
521.	Kuba B.H. 426.	(7?) 8, 7,	(1)	1 – 5		A Av	
522.	Kuba XI. 34.	8, 7,	(b2)	VI – 4		AB	
523.	Đorđević 369.	(8) r. 8, 7,	(b2)	VII – 4		AB	„na ranila"
524.	Kuhač 88.	8, 7,	(b3)	VII – 4		AB	
525.	Kuhač 572.	8, 7,	(b3)	VII – b6		AB	
526 a.	Kuba B.H. 996. Ms.	8, 7,	(4)	1 – 7		AB	urban text.
b.	Kuba B.H. 79.	(11) 8, 7,	(4)	1 – 7		AB	
527.	Kuhač 665.	(10) r. 10, 4	(2)	1 – 5		AB	
528 a.	Iz Levča 11.	(10) 10, 6,	(VII)	VII – b3		A Av	„svatovska"
b.	" " 40.	(10) 10, 6,	(VII)	VII – b3		A Av	„sedeljka"
c.	Đorđević 536.	(10) 10, 6,	(VII)	VII – b3		A Av	„svatovska"
d.	" 544.	(10) 10, 6,	(VII)	VII – b2		A Av	

III. 10,6,(VII) – (1)
Z=

Current №	Original edition	Syll.	Last note of section	Range	Rhythm structure	Structure	Remarks
529 a.	Iz Levča 3a.b.	(10) 10, 6,	(VII)	VII - b3		AAv	„slavska"
b.	" " 13.	(10) 10, 6,	(VII)	VII - b3		AAv	„svatovska"
c.	" " 26.	(10) 10, 6,	(VII)	VII - b3		AAv	„sedeljka"
d.	" " 37.	(10) 10, 6,	(VII)	VII - b3		AAv	„sedeljka"
e.	Đorđević 362.	(10) 10, 6,	(VII)	VII - b3		AAv	„sedeljka"
⊕530 a.	Kuhač 908.	(10) 10, 6,	(VII)	VII - 4		AAv	
531.	Kuhač 666.	(10) 10, 6,	(1)	bVII - b3		AB	
532 a.	Iz Levča 7.	(10) 10, 6,	(1)	VII - b2		AAv	„svatovska"
b.	" " 5.	10,					„svatovska" 1st half of a.
c.	" " 12.	7,					„svatovska" 2nd half of a.
533 a.	Kuba B.H. 496	(10) 10, 6,	(1)	VII - b3		AAv	
b.	Đorđević 377.	(10) 10, 6,	(1)	VII - b3		AAv	„sedeljka"
c.	" 433.	(10) 10, 6,	(1)	VII - b3		AAv	
d.	Juž. Srb. 426.	(10) 10, 6,	(1)	VII - b3		AAv	„svatovska"
534 a.	Đorđević 480.	(10) 10, 6,	(1)	VII - b3		AAv	„svatovska"
b.	" 482.	(10) 10, 6,	(1)	1 - b3		AAv	„svatovska"
c.	Kuba B.H. 884.	(10) 10, 6,	(1)	VII - b3		AAv	line interr.: 10, 1 $\frac{2}{}$ 5
535 a.	Đorđević 458.	(10) 10, 6,	(1)	VII - b3		AAv	„sedeljka"
b.	" 487.	(10) 10, 6,	(1)	VII - b3		AAv	„sedeljka"
536.	Đorđević 397.	(10) 10, 6,	(1)	#VII - 1		AAv	„svatovska"
537.	Đorđević 316.	(10) 10, 6,	(1)	1 - 2		AAv	„svatovska"
538 a.	Kuba B.H. 760.	(10) 10, 6,	(1)	1 - b3		AAv	
b.	" " 762.	10,					1st half of a.
539.	Kuba XI. 45.	(10) 10, 6,	(1)	1 - b3		AAv	
540.	Đorđević 559.	(10) 10, 6,	(1)	1 - b3		AAv	
⊕530 b.	Kuhač 831.	(10) 10, 6	(VII)	VII - 4		AAv	

III. 10,6,①–⑤
Zz 4+3+3

Current No	Original edition	Syll.	Last note of section	Range	Rhythm. structure	Structure	Remarks
541.	Đorđević 389.	(10) 10, 6,	①	1–b3		AAv	„slavska"
542.	Đorđević 205.	(10) 10, 6,	①	1–4		AAv	
543a.	Đorđević 476.	(10) 10, 6,	①	1–4		AAv	„žetvarska"
b.	" 238.	(10) 10, 6,	①	1–4		AB	
544a.	Đorđević 553.	(10) 10, 6,	(b2)	VII–b3		AAv	
b.	" 555.	(10) 10, 6,	(b2)	VII–b3		AAv	
c.	" 543.	(10) 10, 6,	(b2)	VII–b3		AAv	
d.	Iz Levča 59.	(10) 10, 6,	(b2)	VII–b3		AAv	
e.	" " 68.	(10) 10, 6,	(b2)	VII–b3		AAv	
f.	Đorđević 190.	(10) 10, 6,	(b2)	1–b2		AAv	„Kad se ide u branje zdravca"
g.	Iz Levča 39.	(10) 10, 6,	②	VII–b3		AAv	„sedeljka"
i.	Đorđević 253.	(10) 10, 6,	②	1–b3		AAv	
h.	" 499.	(10) 10, 6,	②	VII–b3		AAv	
545a.	Đorđević 160.	(10) 10, 6,	(b2)	1–4		AB	
b.	" 154	(10) 10, 6,	(b3)	1–4		AB	„kad se bere seno"
546.	Kuba B.H. 1.	(10) 10, 6,	②	#VII–3		AAv	
547a.	Kuba B.H. 761.	(10) 10, 6,	②	1–4		AAv	line interv.: 6–4, 2–4,
b.	Đorđević 422.	(10) 10, 6,	②	1–4		AAsv	„sedeljka"
548.	Kuhač 214.	(10) 10, 6,	②	1–4		AAv	
549a.	Iz Levča 25.	(10) 10, 6,	(b3)	VII–4		AAv	„sedeljka"
b.	Đorđević 456.	(10) 10, 6,	(b3)	1–4		AAv	„sedeljka"
550a.	Kuba B.H. 420. (= Kuba XIII. 6.)	(10) 10, 6,	④	1–4		AAv	
b.	Kuba B.H. 582.	(10) 10, 6,	④	VII–4		AAv	swallowing of last syll.
551.	Kuba B.H. 368.	(10) (+) 10, 6,	⑤	1–6.		AB	
552.	Iz Levča 48.	(10) +. 10, 6,	①	1–4	10,: ♩♩ | ♩♩ | ♫♩ | ♫	AB	„sedeljka"

III. ^{Zz} 10, 7, — 11, 10,

Current No.	Original edition	Syll.	Last note of section	Range	Rhythm structure	Structure	Remarks
553 a.	Đorđević 399.	(7) r. 10, 7,	(VII)	VII – b3		AAv	„sedeljka“
b.	" 452.	(7) r. 11, 7	(VII)	VII – b3		AAv	„sedeljka“
c.	" 466.	(7) r. 11, 7,	(VII)	VII – b3		A Av	„sedeljka“
d.	" 484.	(8b) r. 12, 8,	"	"		"	"
554.	Đorđević 15.	(7) r. 10, 7,	(1)	VII – 2		AB	„lazarička“
555 a.	Đorđević 446.	(7) 10, 7,	(2)	VII – b3		AB	
b.	Kuhač 1251.	(7) 10, 7,	(2)	VII – 4		AB	„svatovska“
556.	Kuba B. H. 943.	10, 8,	(1)	VII – 4		AB	
557.	Kuba XIII. 36.	(10) (r.) 10, 8,	(4)	1 – b6		AB	swallowing of last syll.
558-559.	Đorđević 439.	(10) r. 11, 6,	(VII)	VII – 4		AB	
560.	Iz Levča 10.	(11) 11, 7,	(1)	VII – b2		A Av	„svatovska“
561.	Kuba B. H. 826.	(11) (r.) 11, 7,	(b3)	VII – 4		AB	
562.	Kuba B. H. 356.	(11) r. 11, 8,	(1)	1 – 4		AB	
563 a.	Kuhač 82. (= Đorđević Nar. Pev. p. 46/2)	(8b) 11, 8,	(VII)	VII – 5		AB	Cf. Bartók, Colinde No. 45 (a.–c.)
b.	Kuba XI. 49.	(8b) 11, 8,	(VII)	VII – 4		AB	
c.	" " 314.	(8b) r. 11, 8,	(VII)	VII – 5		AB	
d.	Bosiljevac 6 a)	8b,	(4)	VII – 5		AB	
564.	Đorđević 117.	(8b) r. 11, 8,	(1)	VII – 4		A Av	
565.	Kuba X. 31.	(8b) 11, 8,	(1)	VII – 5		AAv	
566 a.	Kuba B. H. 215.	(7) r. 11, 10	(VII)	VII – b6		AAv	
b.	" " 407.	(7) r. 11, 10	(1)	1 – 5		AAv	
c.	Đorđević Nar. Pev. p. 7/2	(7) r. 11, 10	(b3)	1 – 5		A Av	
567 a.	Kuhač 1460.	(7) r. 11, 10,	(2)	VII – 5		AB	
b.	Kuba B. H. 536.	(7) 11, 10,	(4)	VII – 4		AAv	
568.	Iz Levča 73.	11, 10,	(1)	1 – 5	11,: [illegible] 10,: [illegible]	AAv	„obredno“ (!)

III. Zz, 12,6 – 15,11; – zZ 5,7 – 7,9,

Current №	Original edition	Syll.	Last note of section	Range	Rhythm. structure	Structure	Remarks
569.	Kuhač 344.	(10) (r.) 12, 6,	(2)	1–5		AB	
570.	Kuba B. H. 814.	(11) r. 12, 7,	(VII)	VII – b3		AAv	
571.	Kuhač 769.	(8) (r.) 12, 7,	(VII)	VII – b3		A Av	
572.	Kuba B. H. 152.	(8) r. 12, 8,	(bVI)	bVI – 5		AB	
573 a.	Đorđević 547.	(8) 12, 8,	(VII)	VII – b3		AAv	
b.	" 378.	(8) 12, 8,	(VII)	VII – b3		AAv	„sedeljka"
574.	Kuba B. H. 483.	(8) 12, 8,	(VII)	VII – b3		AAv	
575.	Kuba B. H. 974. Ms.	(8) 12, 8,	(VII)	VII – 5		AB	
576.	Kuba B. H. 359.	(8) r. 12, 8,	(3)	1–5		AB	
577 a.	Kuba B. H. 272.	(9) r. 12, 9,	(1)	IV – 4		AB	perhaps: < new Hungar. mel.? (ref. „Čahajka")
b.	" " 81.	(9) r. 12, 9,	(1)	IV – 4		AB	
578.	Kuba B. H. 72. (= Kuba XIII. 18)	(10) (r.) 12, 10	(VII)	VI – 4		AB	> Hung.? „kolo
579–580.	Kuhač 405.	(10) r. 14, 12,	(VII)	VII – 4		AAv	
581.	Kuba B. H. 629.	(11) r. 15, 11,	(1)	VI – 4		AB	
582.	Kuba B. H. 882.	5, 7,	(VII)	bVI – b3		AB	
583.	Kuba B. H. 991. Ms.	5, 7,	(b2)	VII – 4		AB	
584 a.	Đorđević 492.	(8b) 5, 8,	(VII)	VII – b3		AAv	„sedeljka"
b.	" 464.	(8b) 5, 8,	(VII)	VII – b3		AAv	„sedeljka"
c.	" 169.	(8b) 5, 8,	(1)	VII – b3		AAv	syll. interr.: 5, [1] + 7,
d.	Iz Levča 18.	(8) 6, 8,	(VII)	VII – b3		AAv	„sedeljka"
e.	" " 16	8b,					2nd half of a. „sedeljka"
585.	Đorđević 386.	(7) r. 6, 7,	(1)	VII – b3		AB	„Uskrsna"
586.	Kuhač 77.	(8) 6, 8,	(1)	1–4		AAv	
587.	Kuba B. H. 645.	7, 8,	(b3)	VII – 5		AB	
588.	Kuba IX. 16.	(7) r. 7, 9,	(b3)	VII – 4		AB	two part song

III. zZ 7,10,– 8,10,

Current No	Original edition	Syll.	Last note of section	Range	Rhythm. structure	Structure	Remarks
589.	Đorđević 388.	(10) 7, 10,	(b2)	1–4		AAv	slavska
590a.	Kuba B.H. 605.	(10) 7, 10,	(4)	VII–5		AAv	
b.	" " 832.	(10) 7, 10,	(4)	1–5		AAv	
c.	" " 960.	(10) 7, 10,	(3)	1–4		AAv	
591a.	Kuba B.H. 155.	(7) r. 7, 11,	(VII)	bVI–b6		AB	
b.	Kuhač 942.	(7) r. 7, 11,	(VII)	bVI–b6		AB	
592a.	Kuba B.H. 805. (= Kuba XIII. 13.)	(7) 7, 11,	(VII)	VII–b3		AB	"Kolo" Var. (?) Cf. Parry 4. No 679. No 418 a.–d.
b.	Kuba B.H. 799.	(7) 7, 11,	(VII)	VII–b3		AB	"kolo"
c.	" " 478.	(7) 7, 11,	(1)	VII–b3		AB	"kolo"
d.	" " 457.	(7) 7, 11,	(2)	VII–b3		AB	line interr.: 7, 6–5
593a.	Kuhač 939.	(7) r. 7, 11,	(1)	#VI–5		AAv	
b.	" 940.	(7) r. 7, 11,	(2)	1–5		AB	
c.	" 941.	(7) r. 7, 11,	(2)	1–5		AB	
d.	" 943.	(7) r. 7, 11,	(2)	1–6		AB	
594.	Đorđević 434.	(8) r. 7, 11,	(1)	1–4	11, : [rhythm notation]	AAv	
595.	Kuhač 276.	(10) (r.) 7, 13,	(1)	1–5		AB	
596.	Kuba B.H. 410.	(10) 7, 14,	(4)	1–5		AAv	< new Hungar. mel.?
597a.	Đorđević 189.	(8) r. 8, 9,	(2)	1–5		AB	"dodole"
b.	" 400.	(8) r. 8, 10,	(VII)	VII–4		AB	"sedeljka"
598.	Kuba XI. 18.	(10) 8, 10,	(VII)	VII–4		AB	
599.	Kuhač 118.	(10) (r.) 8, 10,	(VII)	VII–5		AB	
600.	Kuba B.H. 9.	(10) 8, 10,	(1)	V–5		AB	
601.	Kuhač 306.	(8) r. 8, 10,	(1)	VI–5		AB	
602.	Kuba B.H. 694.	(10) (r.) 8, 10,	(1)	VII–5		AB	
603a.	Kuhač 668.	(10) (r.) 8, 10,	(1)	1–4		AB	

III. = Z 8,10, – 8,12,

Current №	Original edition	Syll.	Last note of section	Range	Rhythm. structure	Structure	Remarks
b.	Kuba B.H. 323.	(10) 8, 10,	(1)	VII – 4		AB	
604 a.	Dordević 566.	(10) r. 8, 10,	(1)	1 – 4		AAv	„uz kopanje"
b.	" 571.	(10) r. 8, 10,	(1)	1 – 4		AAv	
c.	" 572.	(10) r. 8, 10,	(1)	1 – 4		AAv	
d.	" 573.	(10) r. 8, 10,	(1)	1 – 4		AAv	
⊕ e.	" 574.	(10) r. 8, 10,	(1)	1 – 4		AAv	
606.	Dordević 135.	(8) (r.) 8, 10,	(b2)	VII – 4		AB	
607 a.	Dordević 315.	(10) 8, 10,	(b2)	1 – b4		AB	„žetvarska" syll. interr.: 7+[8], 10,
b.	Kuba B.H. 328.	(10) (r.) 8, 10,	(1)	VII – b4		AAv	
608.	Kuba B.H. 897.	(10) (r.) 8, 10,	(b2)	1 – 5		AAv	
609 a.	Kuhač 1536. (= Dordević Nar. Pes. 166/1)	(10) 8, 10,	(2)	VII – 4		AB	
b.	Kuhač 1306.	(10) 8, 10,	(1)	VII – 4		AB	
610 a.	Kuba B.H. 856.	(10) 8, 10,	(2)	1 – 5		AB	
b.	Kuhač 722.	(10) (r.) 8, 10,	(2)	1 – 5		AB	
c.	Kuba XI. 43.	(10) 8, 10,	(2)	1 – 5		AB	
d.	Kuhač 488.	(10) (r.) 8, 10,	(1)	1 – 5		AB	
e.	Kuba IX. 46.	(10) (r.) 8, 10,	(1)	VII – 4		AB	two part song
611.	Dordević 391.	(10) (r.) 8, 10,	(b3)	1 – 4		AAv	„slavska"
612.	Juž. Srb. 420.	(11) 8, 10,	(1)	VII – b3	10,: ♩♩♩♩/♩♩𝅗𝅥/♩♩𝅗𝅥//	AAv	
613 a.	Dordević 366.	(8b) r. 8, 11,	(b2)	1 – 4		AAv	„slavska"
b.	" 502	(8b) 8, 11,	(b3)	1 – 4		AAv	„sedeljka"
614.	Juž. Srb. 406.	(8) 8, 12,	(1)	VII – 4		AB	„igra"
↕ 605.	Juž. Srb. 422.	(8) r. 8, 10,	(1)	1 – 5		AAv	word interr.: 8, 1–2–9
615 a.	Kuba B.H. 320.	(8) 8, 12,	(b2)	1 – 5		AB	„kolo"
b.	" " 353.	(8) 8, 12,	(2)	1 – 5		AB	

Current No.	Original edition	Syll.	Last note of sections	Range	Rhythm. structure	Structure	III. z Z 8,12,–12,14, IV. 5–8, Remarks
615 c.	Kuba B. H. 343.	(8) 8, 12,	(b2)	bVII – 4		AB	
616 a.	Kuhač 1014.	(8) 8, 12,	(2)	VII – 5		AB	„igra" > Slovak. horvát song a.
b.	" 770.	8, 12,	(2)	VII – 5		AB	Slovak. var. (for text too)
617.	Kuba XII. 42.	(8) +. 9, 11,	(V)	IV – b6		AB	"
618.	Kuba IX. 12.	(10) +. 10, 12,	(1)	VII – b6		AB	swallowing of last syll.
619.	Kuhač 1019.	12, 14,	(b3)	1 – 5		AAv	„igra" [accord. to Kuh., Turkish!]
IV. Isometric three-section melodies, O C structure							
620.	Đorđević 427. (= Đorđević Nar. Pev. p. 58)	5,	(1) (2	1 – b3		AAvA	„sedeljka"
621.	Kuhač 821.	6,	(VII) (bVI	bVII – b6		ABC	
622.	Kuba B. H. 929.	(10) 6,	(VII) (1	VII – 4		ABBv	„kolo"
623 a.	Kuba B. H. 97.	6,	(1) (b3	1 – 5		ABC	
b.	Kuhač 822.	6,	(1) [C]	1 – 5		A[ ]C	
624.	Kuba X. 12.	6,	(2) (4	1 – 5		ABC	two part song
625.	Đorđević 229.	6,	(b3) (2	1 – 4		AAv1Av2	„igra"
626.	Đorđević 12.	6,	(5) (b3	1 – 7		ABBv	
627.	Đorđević 360.	(10) (+.) 7,	(b3) (1	VII – 4		ABBv	„sedeljka" text with „stuttering" parts
628.	Kuba B. H. 1008. Ms.	7,	(8) (7 (!)	1 – b10		ABC	Hungar.-Turkish type?
629.	Đorđević 208.	8,	(VII) (bVI	bVII – b3		ABBv	
630.	Kuba B. H. 550.	8,	(VII) (VII	VII – 4		ABBv	
631.	Kuba B. H. 932.	8,	(VII) (1	VII – 5		ABB	Rumanian?
632.	Kuba B. H. 753.	8,	(1) (1	IV – 5		ABA	
633.	Kuba XI. 25.	8,	(1) (1	bVII – 4		ABB	
634.	Kuba B. H. 618.	8,	(1) (1	1 – 4		ABB	
635.	Kuhač 1454.	8,	(1) (1	1 – b6		ABC	
636.	Kuba B. H. 348. (= Kuba XIII. 24.)	8,	(1) (1	1 – b6		ABB	
637.	Kuba B. H. 619.	8,	(2) (1	VII – 5		ABBv	

Current No	Original edition	Syll	Last note of sections	Range	Rhythm. structure	Structure	Remarks
638a.	Kuba B.H. 1113. Ms.	8,	(b3) (VII	VII–b3		ABC	
638b.	" " 1051. Ms.	8,	(b3) (1	VI–4		ABC	
c.	Kuba B.H. 820.	8,	(b3) (1	VI–4		ABC	„uz tepsiju"
639–640	Kuba B.H. 326.	8,	(b3) (1	VII–4		ABBv	
641.	Kuhač 99.	8,	(b3) (1	1–5		ABB	
642.	Kuba X. 35.	8,	(b3) (b3	1–b6		ABAv	
643.	Kuhač 521.	8,	(b3) (4	1–7		ABC	cf. No 1439.
644.	Đorđević 46.	8,	(4) (1	1–5		ABB	
645.	Kuhač 771.	8,	(4) (b6	1–b6		ABBv	
646.	Đorđević Nar. Pev. p. 185/1	8,	(5) (4	VI–7		ABBv	Ruman. Hungar. var.?
647.	Kuba B.H. 531.	8, 8b, 8b,	(VII) (2	VII–4		ABC	
648a.	Kuhač 710.	8, 8b, 8b,	(1) (1	VI–4		ABBv	
b.	Kuba XII. 10.	8, 8b, 8b,	(1) (1	VI–5		ABB	
c.	Kuba B.H. 89. (= Kuba XII. 9.)	"	(b3) (1	1–5		ABBv	
d.	Kuba B.H. 1035. Ms.	"	"	"		"	
649.	Đorđević 156.	8, 8b, 8b,	(1) (1	1–b3		ABBv	„svatovska"
650.	Đorđević 561.	8, 8b, 8b,	(1) (1	1–5		ABB	
651.	Kuhač 876.	8b,	(V) (1	V–4		ABB	> Slovak. mel.
652a.	Kuba XII. 14.	8b,	(1) (1	1–5		ABBv	
b.	Kuhač 651.	"	(b2) (1	VII–4		ABB	
653.	Kuba B.H. 251.	8b (8b, 9, 9, ?)	(b3) (1*	VII–5		ABBv	* perhaps > (1)?
654.	Đorđević 94.	8b,	(4) (4	1–5		ABBv	
654bis a.	Kuba XIII. 49.	10,	(1) (1	1–7		ABBv	
b.	Kuba B.H. 837.	"	(1) (2	1–5		ABC	
c.	" " 229.	"	(b3) (1	1–b6		ABC	
655a.	Kuba IX. 13.	10,	(b3) (b3	1–8		ABC	
b.	Kuhač 7.	"	(b3) (5	"		"	
c.	" 8a)	"	(b3) (b6	"		"	
d.	" 8b)	"	(b3) (b6	"		"	

Current No	Original edition	Syll.	Last note of sections	Range	Rhythm. structure	Structure	Remarks
e.	Đorđević Nar. Pev. p.16/1	10,	(b3) (5	1-8		ABC	
f.	Bosiljevac 32.	10,	[0] (4	1-8		[ ]BC	
g.	Kuhač 667,	10,	(V) [C]	III-2		A[ ]C	
656a.	Kuba B.H. 59.	10,	(5) (4	VII-7		ABB$_v$	
c.	" " 190.	10,	(7) (b3	1-7		ABB$_v$	
b.	" " 187.	10,	(5) (4	1-7		ABB$_v$	
d.	" " 230.	10,					fragment of the preceding
657.	Kuba B.H. 194.	10,	(5) (5	1-8		ABB$_v$	pentaton.
658.	Kuba B.H. 236.	11,	(4) (1	1-7		AA$_v$A$_v$	
659.	Kuba B.H. 949. (= Kuba XIII. 29)	12,	(1) (1	VI-5		ABA$_v$	

V. Isometric three-section melodies, ⊃ O structure

Current No	Original edition	Syll.	Last note of sections	Range	Rhythm. structure	Structure	Remarks
660a.	Kuhač 635.	5,	VII) (VII)	VII-4		ABC	
b.	" 547.	5,	VII) (2)	VII-5		ABC	
661a.	Đorđević 128.	5,	1) (1)	VII-b3		ABC	
b.	" 123.	5,	1) (1)	1-b3		ABC	„kad se kopa lojze"
662.	Đorđević 118.	5,	2) (2)	1-3		AAB	
663.	Kuhač 169.	6,	VII) (VII)	VII-b3		AAA$_v$	
664a.	Đorđević 61.	6, (?)	b3) (VII)	VII-5		AA$_v$B	syll. inter.: 6, 6, 4+[5]+1
b.	" 62.	6, (?)	b3) (VII)	VII-5		AA$_v$B	
665a.	Kuba B.H. 31.	6,	1) (1)	V-5		AAB	
b.	" " 32.	6,	1) (1)	V-5		AAB	
666a.	Đorđević 436.	(10) (r.) 6,	1) (1)	VII-b3		AAB	
b.	" 294.	(r.) 6, 8b, 6,	1) (1)	1-b3		BAB !	„žetvarska"
667.	Đorđević 10.	6,	1) (1)	1-4		AAB	
668.	Kačerovski 77.	6,	2) (1)	1-7		ABC	
669.	Đorđević 564.	6,	b3) (1)	VII-b3		AA$_v$B	

Current No	Original edition	Syll.	Last note of section	Range	Rhythm. structure	Structure	Remarks
670.	Đorđević 431.	(10) (5.) 6,	2) (2)	1–4		AA_vB	
671 a.	Đorđević 43.	6,	b3) (b3)	1–5		AAA_v	
b.	" 45.	6,	4) (4)	1–4		AAA_v	
672 a.	Kuhač 464.	6,	2) (4)	1–4		ABC	
b.	" 466.	6,	2) (4)	1–5		ABC	
673.	Iz Levča 69.	6,	b3) (b3)	VII–b3	♩♩ / ♫♫ ‖	AAA_v	
674.	Kuhač 340.	6,	5) (3)	1–8,	a b c	ABC	
675.	Đorđević 97.	6,	1) (bV)	bV–b5		ABC	
676.	Kuhač 130.	7,	1) (1)	VII–4		AAB	
677.	Đorđević 11.	7,	4) (1)	VII–5		ABC	
678.	Kuhač 675.	7,	2) (2)	1–5		AAB	
679 a.	Kuba B.H. 523.	7,	b3) (b3)	VII–4		AA_vB	Cf. Garry 14. Var. (?): No 592 a.–d. No 418. Line interr.: 7,4–3,7,
b.	" " 524.	7,	b3) (b3)	VII–4		AA_vB	
c.	" " 525.	7,	b3) (b3)	VII–4		AA_vB	
d.	Kuba B.H. 262. (= Kuba XIV. 3)	7,	b3) (b3)	VII–4		AA_vB	
680.	Kuhač 767.	7,	b6) (b3)	VII–7		ABC	Slovak. var.: b3) (VII)
681.	Đorđević Nar. Pev. p170/1	7,	6) (b3)	VII–7		ABC	
682.	Juž. Slb. 423	8,	VII) (VII)	VII–4		ABA_v	Var.: (Rum. Col. No 74a.b. Bartók)
683.	Kuhač 1105.	8,	VII) (VII)	VII–5		AAA_v	„poskočnica"
684 a.	Kuba B.H. 341. (= Kuba XIII. 11)	8,	b3) (VII)	VII–b4		ABC	
b.	Kuba B.H. 334.	8,	b3) (VII)	VII–b4		ABC	
c.	" " 859.	8,	b3) (VII)	VII–b4		ABC	
685.	Kuba B.H. 209.	8,	b3) (VII)	VII–b6		ABC	
686.	Kuba XII. 7.	8,	1) (1)	IV–5		AAB	
687.	Kuba B.H. 950.	8,	1) (1)	VII–4		$AA_{v_1}A_{v_2}$	

Current №	Original edition	Syll.	Last note of section	Range	Rhythm structure	Structure	Remarks
688.	Kuba B.H. 409.	8,	1) (1)	1–5		AA_vB	
689a.	Kuba B.H. 188.	8,	1) (1)	1–b6		AAB	
b.	" " 964.	8,	1) (1)	1–b6		AAB	
690a.	Kuba IX. 8	8,	b2) (b2)	VII–4		AAA_v	three part song (of gipsies?)
b.	Kuba B.H. 510.	8,	2) (2)	VII–4		AA_vB	
c.	" " 903.	8,	3) (3)	VII–4		AA_vB	
691a.	Đorđević 504.	8,	2) (2)	1–4		AAA_v	„sedeljka"
b.	Iz Levča 20.	8,	2) (2)	VII–4		AAA_v	„sedeljka"
692.	Kuba B.H. 861.	8,	4) (2)	1–5		ABC	
693.	Kuba XIV. 30a)	8,	1) (b3)	V–5		ABA_v	Var. Rumanian Folkmusic I. Vol. № 730, II. Vol. № 352. (a.–c.)
694.	Kuba B. H. 189.	8,	b3) (b3)	1–7		AAB	
695.	Kuba B.H. 1040. Ms.	8,	b3) (b3)	1–7		AAB	Rumanian var.?
696a.	Kuba B.H. 249.	8,	5) (b3)	1–8		ABC	Hungar.-Turkish
b.	" " 250.	8,	5) (b3)	1–8		ABC	
697a.	Kuba B.H. 970. (=Kuba XIII. Ms. 43)	8,	3) (3)	1–b6		AAB	
b.	Kuba B.H. 972. Ms.	8,	3) (3)	1–b6		AAB	
698.	Đorđević Nar. Pev. p. 147/2	8,	4) (4)	VII–5		ABC	
699.	Kuba B.H. 291. (=Kuba XIII. 33)	8,	4) (4)	VII–b6		AA_vB	
700.	Kuba B.H. 284.	8,	5) (5)	1–b6		AAB	
701a.	Đorđević 495.	8, 8, 8b,	VII) (VII)	VII–b3		AAB	
b.	" 507.	8, 8, 8b,	VII) (VII)	VII–b3		AAB	
c.	" 508.	8, 8, 5,	VII) (VII)	VII–b3		AAB	
702.	Kuba B.H. 611.	8b,	1) (1)	1–4		AA_{v_1}, A_{v_2}	„svatovska"
703.	Kuba B.H. 962.	8b,	1) (1)	1–b6		AAB	

V. 8b,—10,

Current №	Original edition	Syll.	Last note of sections	Range	Rhythm. structure	Structure	Remarks
704–705.	Đorđević 490.	8b,	2) (2)	1–b3		AAAv	
706 a.	Bosiljevac 27.	8b,	2) (2)	1–5		AAB	
b.	Kačerovski 12.	8b,	2) (2)	1–5		AAB	
707.	Kuba B.H. 437.	8b,	2) (2)	1–5		AAB	
708 a.	Đorđević 240.	8b,	b3) (b3)	VII–4		AAAv	
b.	" 522.	8b,	b3) (b3)	1–4		AAAv	
c.	Kuba B.H. 845.	8b,	b3) (b3)	VII–4		AAB	
d.	" " 612.	8b,	b3) (b3)	VII–4		AAB	
e.	Đorđević 496.	8b,	b3) (b3)	1–4		AAvB	
709 a.	Kuba B.H. 893.	8b,	b3) (b3)	1–5		AAvB	
b.	Kuhač 246.	8b,	b3) (b3)	1–5		AAvB	
c.	Kuba B.H. 412.	8b,	b3) (b3)	1–5		AAvB	
710.	Kuba B.H. 57.	8b,	b3) (b3)	1–7		AAB	
711 a.	Kuhač 643.	8b,	4) (4)	VII–5		AAvB	
b.	" 644.	8b,	4) (4)	1–5		AAB	
c.	Kuba B.H. 411.	8b,	4) (4)	1–5		AAB	
d.	" " 39.	8b,	4) (4)	1–7		AAB	
712.	Kuba B.H. 633.	9,	b3) (VII)	V–5		ABC	
713 a.	Kuba B.H. 592.	10,	2) (VII)	VII–5		ABC	
b.	" " 216.	10,	b3) (1)	VII–b6		ABC	
c.	" " 417.	10,	b3) (b3)	1–5		AAC	
d.	Kuhač 1277.	10,	2) (2)	1–5		AAC	„svatovska"
e.	" 741.	10,	2) [○]	1–5		A[ ]C	
f.	Kuba B.H. 593.	10,	b3) (VII) (1)	VII–1		ABDC	
714.	Kuhač 764.	10,	D (1)	VII–4		ABC	

Current No	Original edition	Syll.	Last note of section	Range	Rhythm. structure	Structure	Remarks
⊕715-716.	Kuba B.H. 211. (= Kuba XIII. 50.)	10,	2) (1)	VII-5		AA$_v$B	
718.	Kuba B.H. 52.	10,	2) (2)	VII-7		AAB	
719.	Đorđević 88,	10	2) (2)	1-b6		AA$_v$B	„Ćilimarska"
720.	Bosiljevac 7.	10,	3) (3)	VII-b6		AAB	
721 a.	Kuhač 1098.	10,	5) (4)	1-b6		ABC	„poskočnica"
b.	" 740.	10,	5) (4)	1-5		ABC	
c.	" 522.	10,	5) (4)	1-b6		ABC	
d.	" 619.	10,	b3) (4)	1-b6		ABC	
e.	" 1116.	10,	2) (1)	V-4		ABC	„čarušanke" (igra?)
717 a.	Kuhač 1288.	10,	1) (2)	VII-5		ABA	[illegible]ka magyar?
b.	" 1289.	10,	[ )] (2)			[ ] BA	
722-723.	Kuba XII. 16.	10,	1) (1)	1-5	a a b b: [illegible]	AAB	
724 a.	Kuba B.H. 653.	11,	1) (1)	VII-5		AAB	
b.	" " 614.	11,	1) (1)	VII-5		AAB	
c.	" " 652.	11,	) (2)			[ ] AB	
d.	" " 254.	13,	1) (1) (1)	VII-5		AABB	
726.	Kuba B.H. 283.	11,	3) (1)	VII-b6	a a b b: [illegible]	AAB	
725.	Kuba B.H. 67.	(9) r. 11,	4) (4)	1-8	[illegible]	AAB	
727 a.	Kuba B.H. 286.	13,	4) (1)	VII-b6		AA$_v$B	
b.	" " 287.	13,					last section of a.

VI. Heterometric three-section melodies, ○(structure

Current No	Original edition	Syll.	Last note of section	Range	Rhythm. structure	Structure	Remarks
728-729.	Kuhač 600.	(8) ZZz 1)1. r. 8,8,7,	(3) (1	1-6		ABB$_v$	

VI. ZZz 1)1. — Zzz 1)5.

Current No	Original edition	Syll.	Last note of section	Range	Rhythm structure	Structure	Remarks 7,5,5–8,5,5 (VI) 63
730–731.	Kuhač 1410.	(10) ZZz 1)1. r. 10, 10, 4,	(1) (1	bVI–b2		AAvB	line interr.: 10, 4 ? 6, 4,
732.	Kuba B.H. 415.	(10) ZZz 1)1. r. 10, 10, 4,	(2) (2	1–5		AAB	
733.	Kuba B.H. 468.	(10) ZZz 1)1. 10, 10, 6,	(2) (2	VII–b3		AAvB	
734 a.	Kuba B.H. 588.	(10) ZZz 1)1. 10, 10, 6,	(4) (4	VII–4		AAv1Av2	
b.	Kuba B.H. 912.	"	(3) (1	VII–4		AAv1Av2	
735.	Kuba B.H. 665.	(10) ZZz 1)1. r. 10, 10, 8,	(2) (VII	VII–5		ABC	
736.	Kuba B.H. 300.	(11) ZZz 1)1. (r.) 11, 11, 5,	(5) (4	1–7		ABC	
737.	Kuba B.H. 788.	(11) ZZz 1)1. 11, 11, 5,	(1) (1	VII–4	11, = 6+5	AAvB	line interr.: 11, 6 ? 5, 5,
738 a.	Kuba B.H. 43.	(11) ZZz 1)1. (r.) 11, 11, 10	(5) (1	1–8		ABC	
b.	" " 44.	(11) (r.) 11, 9, 10,	(4) (1	1–8		ABC	
739 a.	Đorđević 18.	(5) ZzZ 1)3. r. 6, 5, 6,	(1) (1	1–b2		ABA	„lazarička" syll. interr.: 6, 2+[5]+2, 6,
b.	" 3.	"	(1) (1	1–b2		ABA	„lazarička" syll. interr.: 6, 2+[3.]+2, 6,
740.	Kuhač 957.	(8b) ZzZ 1)3. r. 8b, 5, 8b,	(3) (1	1–4		ABAv	
741.	Kuba B.H. 796.	(8) ZzZ 1)3. r. 8, 7, 8b	(2) (1	VII–b3		ABC	
⊕ 742.	Kuhač 855.	(9) ZzZ 1)3. r. 9, 8b, 9,	(b3) (VII	VII–5		ABC	
744.	Đorđević 194.	(5) zZz 1)4. r. 5, 7, 5,	(1) (1	1–4		ABC	
745.	Kuba XII. 31.	(7) zZz 1)4. r. 7, 8, 7,	(4) (VII	VII–5		ABC	
743.	Kuba X. 22.	ZzZ 1)3. 14, 10, 14	(VII) –(1	IV–b3		ABC	two part song
746.	Đorđević Nar. Pev. p. 14/2	(7) Zzz 1)5. r. 7, 5, 5,	(1) (1	VII–4		ABBv	
747.	Kuba IX. 32.	Zzz 1)5. 7, 5, 5,	(b3) (b3	1–b6		ABC	
748.	Kuhač 71.	(8) Zzz 1)5. r. 8, 4, 4,	(VII) (1	VII–4		ABB	
749 a.	Kuba B.H. 802.	Zzz 1)5. 8, 5, 5,	(VII) (b3	VII–b3		ABC	
b.	" 801.	"	(VII) (b3	VII–b3		ABC	„svatovska"
c.	" 800.	"	(VII) (b3	VII–b3		ABC	„kolo"
750 a.	Kuhač 1095.	Zzz 1)5. 8, 5, 5,	(VII) (b3	VII–4		ABBv	„poskočnica" (?)

VI. Zzz, 8,5,5, 1)5. (VII) (b3 — (2) (2

Current No	Original Edition	Syll.	Last note of section	Range	Rhythm. structure	Structure	Remarks
750 b.	Kuba B. H. 539.	Zzz 1)5. 8, 5, 5,	(VII) (b3	VII - 4		ABB_v	
751.	Kuba B. H. 720.	Zzz 1)5. 8, 5, 5,	(VII) (b3	VII - 5		ABC	
752 a.	Kuba B. H. 810.	Zzz 1)5. 8, 5, 5,	(1) (VII	VII - b3		AA_{v1}, A_{v2}	„svatovska"
b.	" 808.	" "	(VII) (VII	VII - b3		AA_{v1}, A_{v2}	„svatovska" word interr.: 8, 5, 1 ? 4,
c.	" 474.	Zzz 1)5. 8, 5, 5,	(2) (1	VII - b3		ABB_v	two part song line interr.: 8, 5, 2 ? 3,
753 a.	Kuba XI. 28.	Zzz 1)5. 8, 5, 5,	(1) (1	VII - b3		ABB	
b.	Kuhač 1239.	"	(1) (1	VII - b3		ABB_v	„svatovska"
754.	Kuba B. H. 327.	Zzz 1)5. 8, 5, 5,	(1) (1	VII - b4		ABB	
755 a.	Kuba XI. 10.	Zzz 1)5. 8, 5, 5,	(1) (1	VII - 4		ABB_v	
b.	Kuhač 1225.	"	(1) (1	VII - b3		ABB	„svatovska"
c.	" 492.	"	(1) (1	VII - 4		ABB_v	
d.	Kuba 317.	"	(1) (1	1 - 4		ABB	
e.	Kuhač 1027.	"	(1) (VII	VII - b3		ABB	„igra"
f.	" 70.	"	(1) (b3	VII - b3		ABB_v	
g.	" 1273.	"	(1) (b3	VII - 4		ABC	„svatovska"
h.	Kuba XI. 7.	"	(1) (b3	VII - b3		ABB_v	
i.	Đorđević 500.	"	(VII) (1	VII - 4		ABB	„sedeljka"
j.	" 453.	"	(VII) (1	VII - b3		ABB	„svatovska"
k.	" 538.	"	(1) (1	VII - 4		ABB	„žetvarska"
l.	Kuhač 491.	8, 5,	(1) [C]			AB[ ]	
756.	Kuba B. H. 603.	Zzz 1)5. 8, 5, 5,	(1) (2	V - 5		ABC	
757.	Kuba XI. 38.	Zzz 1)5. 8, 5, 5,	(1) (b3	1 - 5		ABB_v	
758 a.	Kuhač 1270.	Zzz 1)5. 8, 5, 5,	(1) (4	1 - 5		ABB_v	„svatovska"
⊕ b.	" 808.	Zzz 1)5. 8, 5, 5,	(2) (2	1 - 5		ABB_v	
760 a.	Đorđević 353.	Zzz 1)5. 8, 5, 5,	(2) (2	1 - 4		ABB_v	„sedeljka"

Current №	Original edition	Syll.	Last note of sections	Range	Rhythm. structure	Structure	Remarks
b.	Kuhač 1268.	Zzz 1) 5. 8,5,5,	(b2) (b2	1–4		ABB$_v$	„svatovska"
759.	Južn. Srb. 424.	Zzz 1) 5. 8,5,5,	② (1	1–5		ABB$_v$	
761.	Kuba B. H. 1053. Ms.	Zzz 1) 5. 8,5,5,	(b3) (1	1–b6		ABB	
762.	Kuba B. H. 118.	Zzz 1) 5. 8,5,5,	(b3) (4	1–5		ABC	
763.	Kuhač 1379.	Zzz 1) 5. 8,5,5,	④ (1	1–5		ABB$_v$	
764a.	Kuhač 868.	Zzz 1) 5. 8,5,5,	(VII) (1	IV–4	5, < d d | ♩♩d ‖	ABC	
c.	" 869.	"	(VII) (b3	IV–4	"	ABC	
b.	Kuba B. H. 301.	"	(VII) (1	IV–4	"	ABC	
d.	Đorđević Nar. Pev. p. 100/1	"	(VII) b3	IV–4	"	ABC	
765.	Đorđević Nar. Pev. p. 21/2	Zzz 1) 5. 8,5,5,	① (1	1–4	5, = d d | ♩♩d ‖	ABB	
766a.	Đorđević 252.	Zzz 1) 5. 8,5,5,	① (b3	1–4	5, = ♩♩ | ♫♩ ‖	ABB$_v$	
b.	" 345.	(8) + Zzz 1) 5. 8,5,5,	② (2	1–4	"	ABB$_v$	„pripev"
767.	Kuhač 887.	Zzz 1) 5. 8,6,6,	(bVI) (VII	bVI–4		ABB$_v$	
768–769.	Kuba XII. 39.	(10) Zzz 1) 5. 8,6,6,	(VII) (VII	VII–4		ABB$_v$	
770 a.	Kuba B. H. 569.	(10) Zzz 1) 5. 8,6,6,	(VII) (1	VII–4		ABB	
b.	Đorđević Nar. Pev. p. 47/1	(10) Zzz 1) 5. 8,6,6,	(VII) (1	VII–4		ABB$_v$	
c.	Kuba B. H. 743.	(10) Zzz 1) 5. 8,6,6,	① (1	1–4		ABB$_v$	
d.	Iz Levča 4.	"	(VII) (1	VII–b3		ABB	„slavska"
e.	Kuba B. H. 982. Ms.	(10) 8,6,	(VII) [C]			AB[ ]	
771.	Kuba B. H. 744.	(10) Zzz 1) 5. 8,6,6,	(VII) (1	VII–5		ABB$_v$	
772.	Kuba B. H. 620.	(10) Zzz 1) 5. 8,6,6,	(VII) (4	VII–5		ABC	swallowing of last syll.
773a.	Kuba B. H. 279.	Zzz 1) 5. 8,6,6,	(VII) (4	VII–b6		ABC	Var.: (Rum. Col. N°10. Bartók)
b.	Kuba B. H. 978. Ms.	"	(VII) (4	VII–b6		ABB$_v$	
c.	" 980. Ms.	"	① (4	1–b6		ABB$_v$	
774.	Južn. Srb. 402.	(10) Zzz 1) 5. 8,6,6,	① (VII	VII–4		ABB$_v$	

VI. Zzz 8,6,6, ① (1

Current №	Original edition	Syll.	Last note of sections	Range	Rhythm structure	Structure	Remarks
775 a.	Kuba B.H. 530.	(10) Zzz [1])5. 8,6,6,	① (1	VII-4		ABBv	
b.	" " 534.	"	① (1	VII-4		ABC	line inter.: 8,6,3 2 3 emphat. perf. of orn.
776 a.	Kuba B.H. 938.	(10) Zzz [1])5. 8,6,6,	① (1	VII-5		ABBv	
b.	" " 894.	"	① (1	1-4		ABBv	
d.	" " 924.	"	(b2) (b2	VII-4		ABBv	
c.	" " 906.	"	① (1	VII-4		ABBv	
e.	" " 905.	Zz,z [1])5. 8,6,6,	④ (b2	VII-4		ABBv	
777.	Kuba XI. 40.	(10) Zzz [1])5. 8,6,6,	① (1	VII-5		ABB	
778 a.	Kuba B.H. 447.	(10) Zzz [1])5. 8,6,6,	① (1	1-b3		ABB	
b.	" " 758.	"	"	"		"	
c.	" " 768.	"	"	VI-2		"	
d.	Đorđević 468.	(10) 8,6,	① [C]			AB[ ]	„sedeljka
779 a.	Đorđević 491.	(10) Zzz [1])5. 8,6,6,	① (1	1-4		ABB	
b.	Kuba B.H. 1037. Ms.	"	"	1-b4		"	
c.	" " 983. Ms.	"	① (b2	"		ABBv	
780 a.	Đorđević 361.	(10) Zzz [1])5. 8,6,6,	① (1	1-4		ABB	„sedeljka"
b.	" 90.	(10) 8,6,	① [C]			AB[ ]	„ćilimarska"
781 a.	Đorđević 582.	(10) Zzz [1])5. 8,6,6,	① (1	1-4		ABB	Cf. № 1655.
b.	" 515.	(10) (+) " "	"	1-5		"	„sedeljka
782 a.	Kuba B.H. 1027. Ms.	(10) Zzz [1])5. 8,6,6,	① (1	1-5		ABB	
b.	Kuba B.H. 95. (= Kuba B.H. 1025.!!)	"	"	1-b6		"	
c.	Kuba B.H. 1029. Ms.	"	① (1	"		"	
d.	" " 1028. Ms.	"	"	1-7		"	
e.	" " 1024.	"	"	VII-b5		"	
f.	" " 1026. Ms.	"	(VII) (1	VII-4		"	

VI. Zzz 8,6,6, (1) (b2 — (b4) (1

Current No	Original edition	Syll.	Last note of sections	Range	Rhythm. structure	Structure	Remarks
783.	(10) Kuhač 259. 8, 6, 6,	(10) Zzz ¹)5. 8, 6, 6,	(1) (b2	VII – 4		ABB v	
784a.	Kuba B. H. 1058. Ms.	(10) Zzz ¹)5. 8, 6, 6,	(1) (b3	VII – b3		ABC	
b.	" " 1055. Ms.	Zzz ¹)5. 8, 5, 5	(4) (1	VI – 4		ABB v	
785.	Đorđević 132.	(10) Zzz ¹)5. 8, 6, 6,	(1) (3	1 – 5		ABB v	„sedeljka" syll. interr.: 8, 4+[5.]+1, 6
786.	Kuba B. H. 316.	(10) Zzz ¹)5. 8, 6, 6,	(1) (b4	1 – b4		ABC	Var. Parry 23.
787.	Kuba B. H. 954.	(10) Zzz ¹)5. 8, 6, 6,	(1) (4	VII – 4		ABB v	
788a.	Đorđević 124.	(10) Zzz ¹)5. 8, 6, 6,	(1) (4	1 – 4		ABB v	„sedeljka"
b.	" 140.	"	(1) (4	1 – 4		ABB v	„pri kopanje kukuruza"
c.	" 167.	"	(1) (4	1 – 4		ABB v	„sedeljka" syll. interr.: 8, 4+[5.]+1, 6,
d.	" 192.	"	(1) (4	1 – 4		ABB v	„sedeljka" word interr.: 8, 5–³1, 6,
e.	" 126.	Zzz ¹)5. 8, 6, 6,	(1) (4	1 – 5		ABB v	„svatovska" syll. interr.: 8, 4+[5.]+1, 6,
f.	Kuba B. H. 910.	"	(1) (4	1 – 4		ABB v	
g.	" " 931.	"	(1) (4	1 – 5		ABB v	word interr.: 8, 5–³1, 6,
h.	" " 102.	"	(1) (4	1 – 5		ABB v	" " " "
i.	Đorđević 125.	(10) 8, 6,	(1) [C]			A[ ]B	
789.	Kuba XI. 39.	(10) Zzz ¹)5. 8, 6, 6,	(2) (1	1 – 5		ABB v	
790a.	Kuba B. H. 1038. Ms.	(10) Zzz ¹)5. 8, 6, 6,	(2) (2	VII – 4		ABB v	Belong perhaps into one var. group (790a–791b)
b.	" " 1039. Ms.	"	(b2) (b2	VII – 4		ABB v	
c.	" " 1036. Ms.	"	(2) (2	1 – 4		ABB v	
791a.	Đorđević Nar. Pev. p. 105/1	(10) Zzz ¹)5. 8, 6, 6,	(2) (2	1 – 4		ABB v	
b.	Bosiljevac 43.	"	(2) (2	1 – 4		ABB v	
792a.	Đorđević 432.	(10) Zzz ¹)5. 8, 6, 6,	(2) (4	VII – 4		ABB v	
b.	Đorđević Nar. Pev. p. 2/1	"	(2) (4	VII – 4		ABB v	
793.	Đorđević 524.	(10) Zzz ¹)5. 8, 6, 6,	(b3) (b3	1 – 4		ABB v	
794.	Kuba B. H. 336.	(10) Zzz ¹)5. 8, 6, 6,	(b4) (1	1 – b4		ABB v	

Current No	Original edition	Syll.	Last note of section	Range	Rhythm structure	Structure	Remarks
795.	Kuba XI. 32.	(10) Zzz [1)] 5. 8,6,6,	(4) (VII	VII − 5		ABC	
796 a.	Kuba B.H. 590.	(10) Zzz [1)] 5. 8,6,6,	(4) (4	IV − 4		ABB$_v$	swallowing of last syll.
b.	" " 87.	(10) Zzz [1)] 5. 8,6,6,	(4) (4	IV − 4		ABB$_v$	
c.	" " 756.	"	(2) (2	IV − b3		ABB$_v$	swallowing of last syll.
797.	Kuba B.H. 1023. Ms. (= Kuba XIII. 28)	(10) Zzz [1)] 5. 8,6,6,	(4) (4	1 − 7		ABB$_v$	
798.	Kuhač 704.	(10) Zzz [1)] 5. 8,6,6,	(5) (1	1 − 5		ABB$_v$	
799.	Juž. Srb. 428.	(10) Zzz [1)] 5. 8,6,6,	(5) (1)	1 − 7		ABB$_v$	
800 a.	Kuhač 742.	(10) Zzz [1)] 5. (+) 8,6,6,	(2) (2	VII − 4	8, 6, 6, = ♩♩♩ | ♩♩♩ ‖	ABC	
b.	" 772	"	(b2) (b2	VII − 4	"	ABC	
801.	Kuba X. 41.	(8) Zzz [1)] 5. + 8,6,6,	(1) (1	VII − 4	6, = ♩♫ | ♫♩ ‖	ABB$_v$	„koleda" (Cf. No 814.)
802 a.	Đorđević 549.	Zzz [1)] 5. 8,6,6,	(VII) (VII	VII − b3	6, = 𝅗𝅥𝅗𝅥 | ♩♩♩♩ ‖	ABB$_v$	(Cf. No 814.)
b.	" 535.	"	(VII) (VII	VII − 4	"	ABB$_v$	(Cf. No 814.)
c.	" 438.	"	(VII) (b3	VII − b3	"	ABB$_v$	(Cf. No 814.)
d.	" 236.	(8) Zzz [1)] 5. + 8,6,6,	(VII) (1	VII − b4	"	ABB$_v$	„sedeljka" (Cf. No 814.)
e.	" 148.	(10) Zzz [1)] 5. 8,6,6,	(1) (1	1 − b3	6, = 𝅗𝅥𝅗𝅥 | ♩♩♩♩ ‖	ABB$_v$	„svatovska" (Cf. No 814.)
803 a.	Kuba XI. 42.	Zzz [1)] 5. 8,6,6,	(1) (1	VII − 4	6, = 𝅗𝅥𝅗𝅥 | ♩♩♩♩ ‖	ABB	
b.	Kuba B.H. 608.	"	(VII) (1	VII − 4	"	ABB$_v$	
804 a.	Kuba B.H. 285.	(10) Zzz [1)] 5. (+) 8,6,6,	(1) (1	VII − 5	6, = 𝅗𝅥𝅗𝅥 | ♩♩♩♩ ‖	ABB$_v$	
b.	" " 902.	Zzz [1)] 5. 8,6,6,	(1) (1	1 − 4	"	ABB$_v$	
805.	Đorđević 562.	Zzz [1)] 5. 8,6,6,	(1) (1	1 − 5	6, = 𝅗𝅥𝅗𝅥 | ♩♩♩♩ ‖	ABB	
806.	Đorđević 145.	(10) Zzz [1)] 5. 8,6,6,	(2) (1	1 − 5	6, = 𝅗𝅥𝅗𝅥 | ♩♩♩♩ ‖	ABB$_v$	
807.	Đorđević 221.	(8) Zzz [1)] 5. + 8,6,6,	(b3) (b3	1 − 4	6, = 𝅗𝅥𝅗𝅥 | ♩♩♩♩ ‖	ABB$_v$	
808.	Kuba B.H. 787.	Zzz [1)] 5. 8,6,6,	(1) (1	VII − b3	8, 6, = 𝅗𝅥𝅗𝅥 | ♩♩♩♩ ‖ 6, = 𝅗𝅥𝅗𝅥 | ♩♩𝅗𝅥 | 𝅝 ‖	ABC	„kolo"
809.	Kuba B.H. 969. Ms.	Zzz [1)] 5. 8,6,6,	(1) (1	VII − 5	8, 6, = 𝅗𝅥𝅗𝅥 | ♩♩♩♩ ‖ 6, = 𝅗𝅥𝅗𝅥 | ♩♩𝅗𝅥 | 𝅝 ‖	ABC	gigaga

Current №	Original edition	Syll.	Last note of section	Range	Rhythm structure	Structure	Remarks
810 a.	Kuba B.H. 818.	Zzz [1])5. 8, 7, 7,	(VII) (VII	VII–4	incomplete cadence	ABB	
b.	" " 817.	"	(VII) (VII	VII–4		ABB$_v$	
c.	" " 439.	"	(1) (1	1–5	complete cadence	ABB	
811.	Đorđević 501.	Zzz [1])5. 8, 7, 7,	(1) (1	1–3		ABB	„sedeljka"
812 a.	Kuba B.H. 935.	(11) Zzz [1])5. 8, 7, 7,	(4) (VII	VII–4		ABC	
b.	" " 627.	"	(4) (1	VII–4		ABB$_v$	
⊕ c.	" " 101	"	(b3) (b3	1–b6		ABB	
814.	Kuba XI. 16.	Zzz [1])5. 8, 7, 7,	(1) (1	VII–b2	7, = ♫♩|♬♬||	ABB	
815 a.	Đorđević 310.	(8) Zzz [1])5. r. 8, 7, 7,	(1) (1	1–b4	7, = ♩♫|♬♬||	ABB$_v$	„pripev" (Cf. № 802.)
b.	" 237.	"	(VIII) (VII	VII–4	"	ABB$_v$	„pripev"
c.	" 376.	"	(2) (2	1–b3	"	ABB$_v$	„sedeljka"
d.	" 425.	"	(2) (4	1–4	"	ABB$_v$	„sedeljka"
e.	" 309.	(8) r. 11,					„pripev" one section
813.	Kuba B.H. 141.	(11) Zzz [1])5. (r.) 8, 7, 7,	(5) (1	1–7		ABB	
816.	" " 769.	Zzz [1])5. 8, 7, 7,	(VII) (VII	VII–b2	7, = ♩♩|♩♫|♩♩|	ABB$_v$	
817.	Kuba XI. 35.	(10) Zzz [1])5. r. 10, 5, 5,	(1) (4	bVII–b6		ABC	
818 a.	Kuba B.H. 944.	(10) Zzz [1])5. r. 10, 6, 6,	(1) (1	VII–5		ABB$_v$	Belong perhaps to one var. group
b.	" " 945.	"	(1) (1	VII–5		ABB	
819 a.	Kuba B.H. 269.	(10) Zzz [1])5. r. 10, 6, 6,	(1) (1	1–5		ABB$_v$	
b.	Bosiljevac 38	"	(1) (1	1–5		AA$_{v_1}$A$_{v_1}$	
c.	Kuba B.H. 210.	"	(1) (2	1–5		AA$_{v_1}$A$_{v_1}$	
d.	" " 270.	"	(1) (4	1–5		ABB$_v$	
e.	Đorđević 70.	10, 6,	(1) [C]			AA$_v$[ ]	
820.	Đorđević 560.	(10) Zzz [1])5. (r.) 10, 6, 6,	(1) (2	1–5	10, 6, = ♩♫|♫♩|| 6,	ABA$_v$	
821.	Đorđević 506.	Zzz [1])5. * 10, 6, 6,	(VII) (VII	VII–4	6, = ♩♫|♫♩||	ABC	

* 1st st. only, the others are different (of various structure)

VI. Zzz 1)5. – Zz+zZ 2)2.

Current №	Original edition	Syll.	Last note of sections	Range	Rhythm. structure	Structure	Remark
822.	Kuhač 427.	(10) Zzz 1)5. r. 10, 8, 8,	(1) (VII	VII – 4		ABC	
823.	Kuba B. H. 74.	(8) Zzz 1)5. (r.) 10, 8, 8,	(1) (1	VII – 4		ABB_v	
824.	Kuba B. H. 469.	(11) Zzz 1)5. 11, 6, 6	(2) (1	VII – b3		ABC	
825.	Kuhač 820.	(11) Zzz 1)5. (r.) 11, 6, 6,	(b3) (VII	VII – b3	11, 6, 6, : ♩♩ | ♫♫ ‖	ABC	
826.	Kuba B. H. 874.	(11) Zzz 1)5. (r.) 11, 7, 7,	(1) (1	VII – 4		AA_vB	
827a.	Đorđević Nar. Pev. p. 106/1	(8b) Zzz 1)5. 11, 8, 8,	(b3) (4	VII – 5		$AA_{v1}A_{v2}$	Cf. Parry 24.
b.	Kačerovski 54.	"	(b3) (4	VII – 5		$AA_{v1}A_{v2}$	
c.	Kuba XII. 20.	(8b) 11,					fragment of preceding
828.	Kuba XII. 18.	(8) Zzz 1)5. r. 12, 8, 8,	(5) (1	1 – b10!		ABB	Turko-Hungar. swallowing of last syll.
829.	Kuba XI. 17.	(8) zZZ 1)6. r. 8, 9, 9,	(1) (1	1 – 5		ABB	
830.	Kuhač 638.	(11) zZZ 1)6. (r.) 8, 9, 9,	(3) (1	1 – 5		ABB_v	
831.	Đorđević 203.	(8) zZŻ 1)6. r. 8, 11, 11,	(1) VII	VII – 4		ABB_v	"igra"
832.	Kuba B. H. 917.	(10)? zZZ 1)6. r. 10, 11, 11,	(1) (1	VII – 4		ABB_v	
833a.	Kuba B. H. 741.	(8b) Zz+zZ 2)2. r. 8b, 5+5, 8b,	(1) (VII	VII – 5		$A_{B+B_v}A_v$	
b.	" " 742.	(8b) Zz+zZ 2)2. r. 8b, 6+5, 8b,	(1) (VII	VII – 5		$A_{B+B}A_v$	
c.	" " 739.	(8b) Zz+zZ 2)2. r. 8b, 5+6, 10,	(1) (2	1 – 5		$A_{B+B_v}A_v$	
d.	" " 740.	"	(1) (2	1 – 5		$A_{B+B}A_v$	
e.	Đorđević Nar. Pev. p. 150/1	(8b) Zz+zZ 2)2. r. 8b, 5+5, 8b,	(1) (VII	VII – 4		$A_{B+B}A$	
f.	Bosiljevac 31.	"	(1) (2	1 – 4		$A_{B+B}A$	
g.	Đorđević 467.	"	(1) (VII	VII – b3		$A_{B+B}A_v$	"sedeljka"
h.	" 557.	(7) Zz+zZ 2)2. r. 7, 6+6, 7,	(1) (VII	VII – b3		$A_{B+B}A$	
834a.	Kuba XI. 52.	(8b) Zz+zZ 2)2. r. 8b, 6+6, 8b,	(1) (VII	VII – 4		$A_{B+B}A$	
b.	Kuba B. H. 622.	"	(1) (VII	VII – 5		$A_{B+B_v}A$	
835a.	Kuba X. 40.	Zz+zZ 2)2. 9, 8+8, 9	(1) (V	V – 5		$A_{B+B}A$	
b.	Kuhač 977.	"	(1) (b2	1 – b6		$A_{B+C}A$	

VI. Z z+z Z 2)2.

Current №	Original edition	Syll.	Last note of section	Range	Rhythm structure	Structure	Remarks
c.	Kuhač 980.	"	① (5	1–8		A B+Bv A	Slovak. Hungar. var. (also text var.) [Ej travo, travo]
d.	" 981.	Z z+z Z 2)2. 9, 8+8, 9,	(V) (4	V–5		A B+Bsv C	
e.	" 978.	7, 8+8, 7,	① (2	1–5		A B+B A	
f.	" 979.	7, 8+8, 5,	(VII) (1	VII–b3		A B+B C	
g.	Kuba B.H. 556.	5+5, 8+8, 5,	② (1	IV–4		A B+B3 C	
h.	" 557.	"	① (VII	VII–4		A B+B A	
836.	Kuhač 1346.	Z z+z Z 2)2. 9, 8+8, 9 (4+5) (4+5)	① (b2)	1–b3		A B+B A	
837.	Kuhač 1316.	Z z+z Z 2)2. 10 (5+5), 6+6, 10 (5+5),	① (2	V–5		A B+Bv C	Slovak.?
838a.	Kuhač 1440.	Z z+z Z 2)2. 10, 7+7, 10,	① (3	1–5		A B+Bs A	
b.	" 1334.	Z z+z Z 2)2. 10, 8+8, 10,	① (VII	VII–b3		A B+B A	a b c = song-text
839.	Kuba B.H. 405.	(10) Z z+z Z 2)2. t. 10, 8+8, 10,	④ (2	1–4		A B+Bv Av	
840.	Kuba B.H. 143.	Z z+z Z 2)2. 10 (5+5), 10+10, 10 (5+5)	① (1	VII–4		A B+Bv Av	
841a.	Kuhač 976.	Z z+z Z 2)2. 11 (5+6), 8+8, 11 (5+6)	① (1	VII–4		A B+B A	
b.	" 975.	10, 12, 13, 13,	2) ② (2	VII–4		AABBv	contamination: 2nd half from a different mel. Text: Ej travo, travo
842.	Kuba XIV. 7.	(13) Z z+z Z 2)2. t. 13, 6+6, 13,	① (VII	IV–4		A B+C A	
843.	Kuhač 337.	Z [z+z] Z 2)2. 13, [8+8] 13,	① [C]	1–6		A [ ] Av	„Erben № 316" (?) German mel.: Einmal hin, einmal her
844.	Kuhač 1358.	Z [z+z Z] 2)2. t. 14 (7+7), [7+7] [14 (7+7)]	① [C]	1–6		A [ ] [ ]	German–French children song (Mozart var.)
845.	Kuhač 1452.	Z z+z Z 2)2. 15, 8+8, 15,	① (III	I–1		A B+B A	German urban?
846–847.	Kuhač 58.	Z z+z Z 2)2. 16, 6+6, 16,	① (2	1–6		A B+B A	„varoška" German?
848a.	Kuhač 160.	Z z+z Z 2)2. 16, 8+8, 16,	① (VII	VII–b6		A B+B A	German?
b.	" 161.						fragments of a.
c.	" 219.						
849a.	Kuhač 802.	Z z+z Z 2)2. 16, 8+8, 16,	① (1	VII–4		A B+B A (A+A) – (A+A)	urban?
b.	" 803.	"	"	"		"	

VI: Z z+z Z — z z Z

Current No	Original edition	Syll.	Last note of sections	Range	Rhythm. structure	Structure	Remarks
850.	Kuhač 1025.	Z z+z Z 2)2. 18, 8+8, 18,	① (1	♭VI-♭6		A B+B A	"igra" "German orig.?"
851.	Kuhač 1282.	Z z+z Z 2)2. 18, 8+8, 18,	③ (1	1-9		A B+B C	
852a.	Kuhač 116.	Z z+z Z 2)2. 20, 6+6, 20,	① (♭3	VII-♭6		A B+Bv Av	
b.	" 117.	?	?	VII-♭6		?	
852 bis.	Kuhač 1038.	Z z+z z 2)3. 10, 5+5, 5,	(VII) (VII	VII-5		A B+B C	„Oro"(?)
853a.	Kuhač 601.	(8) Z z+z z 2)4. r. 9, 8+8, 5	③ (4	1-6		A B+B♭ C	< German: Es klappert die Mühle (also) Hung. and Rum. var. Bartók, Rum. Folk Music, II. 394
b.	Đorđević Nar. Pev. p. 177/2	"	③ (4	1-6		"	
c.	Kuhač 602.	"	③ (5	1-6		"	
d.	Kačerovski 60.	"	③ (5	1-6		"	
e.	Kuhač 603.	(8) Z z+z z 2)4. r. 9, 8+8, 7,	① (♭3	♭VII-4		"	
f.	Kuba IX. 36.	(8) r. 9, 8+8, 1(!)	① (♭2	♭VI-4		A B+B♭[ ]	
854a.	Đorđević Nar. Pev. p. 44/1	(8) Z z+z Z 2)5. r. 8, 5+5, 6,	② (2	VII-4		A B+B C	
b.	Bosiljevac 48.	"	① (1	VII-4		"	
855a.	Kuba B.H. 547.	(8) Z z+z Z 2)5. r. 8, 6+8, 7,	(VII) (VII	VII-5		A B+C D	
b.	Đorđević 84.	"	③ (3	1-6		A B+B Bv	„Ćilimarska"
856.	Kuba B.H. 710.	(10) Z z+z Z 2)5. (r.) 10, 5+7, 6,	② (VII	VII-5		A B+Bv C	
857.	Iz Levča 51.	(10) Z z+z Z 2)5. (r.) 10, 6+5, 6,	② (2	1-5		A Av+Av B	„sedeljka"
858.	Bosiljevac 29.	(7) Z z+z Z 2)5. r. 11, 7+7, 10,	④ (VII	VII-7		A B+C D	contamination? cf.
859.	Bosiljevac 36.	Z z+z Z 2)5. 16, 6+6, 14,	② (5	1-8		?	last note misprint, major third too high. < new Hung. mel.?
860a.	Kuba B.H. 661.	(10) z z+z Z 2)6. r. 10, 7+7, 11,	④ (VII	VII-5		A B+B C	
b.	" " 664.	"	④ (VII	VII-5		A B+Bv C	
c.	Kuhač 743.	(10) z z+z Z 2)6. r. 10, 6+6, 11,	④ (1	VII-5		A B+B C	
861a.	Đorđević Nar. Pev. p. 151/1	(8) Z Z+Z z 3)11. r. 8, 8+8, 6,	② (1	1-4		A B+B C	word inter.: 8, 8+8, 1-5,
b.	" " " p. 139/1	8, 5+5, 10,	① (VII	VII-♭3		"	
862.	Kuba XI. 48.	(8) Z z Z 3)2. r. 8, 5, 10,	① (1	VII-♭3		A B Bv	

VI. z z Z — z Z z 3)2. v5.

Current No	Original edition	Syll.	Last note of section	Range	Rythm. structure	Structure	Remarks
863.	Kuhač 35.	(8) z z Z 3)2. r. 8, 6, 9,	② (2	1–5		ABC	
864.	Kuhač 739.	(10) z z Z 3)2. r. 10, 8, 17,	② (2	VII–5		ABC	
865.	Iz Levča 38.	(8) Z z z 3)3. r. 8, 6, 7,	(b2) (VII	VII–4		ABAv	„sedeljka"
866.	Kuhač 702.	(8) Z z z 3)3. r. 8, 6, 7,	(b3) (b3	VII–b6		ABC	
867.	Đorđević Nar. Pev. p. 86/1	(10) Z z z 3)3. (r.) 10, 5, 6,	② (2	VII–5		AAvB	gigaga
868a.	Kuhač 744.	(10) Z z z 3)3. r. 10, 6, 7,	④ (b3	1–b6		ABC	
b.	" 198.	"	(b3) (2	1–b6		ABC	
c.	" 756.	"	(b3) (1	1–5		ABBv	
869.	Kuba B.H. 3.	(10) Z z Z 3)3. (r.) 13, 6, 7,	③ (4	1–6	In the wrong place! Correct place after No. 872 b.	ABC	gigaga Cf. Parry 54.
870.	Kuba B.H. 794.	(10) Z z z 3)3. (r.) 10, 8, 9,	(b3) (b3	VII–b3		AAv1Av2	
871.	Kuhač 754.	(10) Z z Z 3)3. r. 11, 6, 7,	(VII) (2	VII–4		ABC	
872a.	Kuba B.H. 246.	(11) Z z Z 3)3. (r.) 11, 9, 10,	⑤ (1	1'–8		ABC	
b.	" " 344.	"	④ (1	1–8	Here should follow No. 869.	ABBv	
873.	Kuhač 569.	(10) z Z z 3)4. (r.) 7, 10, 9,	② (5	1–b6		ABC	
874.	Iz Levča 46.	(10) z Z z 3)5. (r.) 7, 8, 6,	④ (VII	VII–5		ABC	„sedeljka"
875a.	Kuhač 986.	(7) z Z z 3)5. 7, 8, 6,	(b3) (1	1–b5		ABC	
b.	" 987.	(7) z Z z 3)5. 7, 8, 3,	⑤ (1	1–5		ABC	
876.	Kuhač 302.	(10) z Z z 3)5. (r.) 7, 10, 4,	④ (2	1–7		AAvB	
877a.	Kuba B.H. 737.	(10) z Z z 3)5. (r.) 8, 10, 6,	② (2	VII–4		ABBv	
b.	" " 738.	(10) r. 8, 10, [ ]	② (1			AB[ ]	
878a.	Kuhač 294.	z Z z 3)5. 8, 11, 7,	(VII) (VII	VII–5		ABBv	
b.	" 293.	"	(VII) (VII	VII–5		ABBv	
879.	Kuba B.H. 693.	(10) z Z z 3)5. (r.) 9, 10, 4,	④ (VII	VII–5		AAvB	
880a.	Kuba B.H. 182. (= Kuba XIII. 39.)	(10) z Z z 3)5. (r.) 10, 11, 6,	④ (1	1–7		ABC	
b.	Kuba B.H. 53.	"	④ (1	1–7		ABC	

VI. zZ_z 3)5. — ZZ_z 3)6.

Current №	Original edition	Syll.	Last note of sections	Range	Rhythm. structure	Structure	Remarks
881a.	(10) zZ_z 3)5. r. 10, 12, 8,	Kuhač 374.	① (1	1–4		ABC	
b.	Kuba B.H. 169.	(10) r. 10, 13, 11	① (1	VII–4		ABC	
882a.	Kuba B.H. 890.	(11) zZ_z 3)5. (r.) 13, 14, 12	① (♭VI	♭VI–4		ABB_v	Ukrainian var.: Bartók 12, 11, 7, ① ② [44 Duos]
b.	Bosiljevac 13.	"	① (1	VII–4		"	
883a.	Đorđević 293.	(8) ZZ_z 3)6. r. 8, 6, 5,	(VII) (VII	VII–♭3		ABB_v	"na kopanju"
b.	" 292.	(8) r. 8, 6, [ ]	① (1			AB[ ]	"na kopanju"
884.	Đorđević 243. (=Đorđević Nar. Pev. p. 158/2)	(8) ZZ_z 3)6. r. 8, 7, 5,	(VII) (VII	VII–4			(no indication!) probably žetvarska
885.	Kuba B.H. 984. Ms.	(8) ZZ_z 3)6. r. 8, 7, 6,	① (1	VII–4		ABB_v	
886a.	Kuba B.H. 120.	(8) ZZ_z 3)6. r. 9, 8, 3,	① (♭3	VII–5		ABC	Var.: Bartók, Rumanian Folkmusic II. No 444 (a–l)
b.	Đorđević 448.	"	① (♭3)	VII–5		"	
c.	Đorđević 344 (=Đorđević Nar. Pev. p. 11/2)	"	(IV) (4	IV–5		"	
d.	Kačerovski 22.	(8) ZZ_z 3)6. r. 9, 8, 7,	① (♭3)	VII–5		"	
887.	Kuhač 59.	ZZ_z 3)6. 9, 8, 6,	② (4	1–5		ABC	
888a.	Kuba B.H. 1020. Ms.	(8) ZZ_z 3)6. r. 9, 8, 7,	② (2	VII–4		AA_vB	
b.	Đorđević Nar. Pev. p. 121/1	(8) ZZ_z 3)6. r. 11, 8, 7,	② (2	VII–5		"	
889.	Kuhač 1103.	(10) ZZ_z 3)6. r. 10, 7, 5,	① (4	VII–4		ABC	"poskočnica"
890.	Kuba B.H. 824.	(10) ZZ_z 3)6. r. 10, 7, 5,	(♭3) (♭3	VII–4		ABC	gigaga
891a.	Iz Levča 55.	(10) ZZ_z 3)6. (r.) 10, 7, 6,	① (1	1–5		ABB_v	
b.	" 57.	"	① (1	1–5		"	
c.	Kuba B.H. 88.	(10) ZZ_z 3)6. r. 10, 7, 6,	① (1	1–5		ABC	
892a.	Kuhač 363a)	(10) ZZ_z 3)6. r. 10, 7, 6,	① (♭2	VII–4		ABC	Belong probably to one var. group
b.	" 363b)	"	① (♭2	1–5		ABC	
c.	Kuba XI. 62a)	(10) ZZ_z 3)6. (r.) 10, 7, 6,	① (2	VII–5		ABC	
d.	Kuhač 422.	(10) ZZ_z 3)6. r. 10, 7, 6,	① (VII	VII–♭6		ABC	
893.	Kuhač 460.	(10) ZZ_z 3)6. (r.) 10, 7, 6,	② (VII	VII–4		ABC	

VI. Zz₂ 3)6.

Current №	Original edition	Syll.	Last note of section	Range	Rhythm. structure	Structure	Remarks
894.	Kuba B.H. 706.	(10) Zz₂ 3)6. r.? 10, 8, 5,	(1) (VII	VII-5		ABBv	
895.	Đorđević 337.	(10) Zz₂ 3)6. r. 10, 8, 6,	(IV) (b2	IV-4		ABC	
896.	Kuhač 318.	(10) Zz₂ 3)6. 10, 8, 6,	(VII) (VII	VII-4		ABC	
897 a.	Kuba IX. 6.	(10) Zz₂ 3)6. r. 10, 8, 6,	(VII) (VII	VII-4		ABBv	
b.	(= Kuhač 391. Đorđević Nar. Rev. p. 30/2)	(10) Zz₂ 3)6. 10, 8, 6,	(bVI)-(b2	bVI-b3		ABC	
898 a.	Kuhač 606. (= Đorđević Nar. Rev. p. 116/1)	(10) Zz₂ 3)6. r. 10, 8, 6,	(1) (VII	VII-4		ABAv	
b.	Kuhač 608.	"	(1) (VII	VII-4		"	
c.	Kuba B.H. 848.	"	(VII) (VII	VII-4		"	
d.	Kuhač 607.	"	(2) (VII	VII-4		"	
e.	" 605.	"	(b2) (VII	VII-4		"	
899.	Kuba B.H. 797.	(10) Zz₂ 3)6. 10, 8, 6,	(1) (1	VII-b3		ABBv	
900.	Kačerovski 10.	(10) Zz₂ 3)6. 10, 8, 6,	(1) (1	1-4		ABC	
901.	Đorđević 368.	(10) Zz₂ 3)6. r. 10, 8, 6,	(1) (1	1-4		ABAv	
902.	Kuba B.H. 586.	(10) Zz₂ 3)6. r. 10, 8, 6,	(1) (2	V-6		ABAv	urban! (national text!)
903.	Kuhač 1220.	(10) Zz₂ 3)6. 10, 8, 6,	(1) (2	VII-4		ABC	"svatovska"
904 a.	Kuhač 545a)	(10) Zz₂ 3)6. (r.) 10, 8, 6,	(1) (b3	VII-4		ABBv	
b.	" 545b)	" 3)6.	(2) (1	1-5		"	
c.	" 546.	(10) 3)6. r. 10, 6, 8,	(1) (VII	VII-5		"	
905 a.	Kuhač 284.	(10) Zz₂ 3)6. r. 10, 8, 6,	(1) (b3	1-4		ABAv	
b.	" 677.	(10) Zz₂ 3)6. 10, 8, 6,	(1) (4	1-4		"	
c.	Kuba XI. 47.	(10) 10, 6, 6,	(1) (1	VII-4	Perhaps do not belong to this group	AAvB	li-gili va-vade ("stuttering" text)
d.	Kuba B.H. 583.	"	(1) (1	VII-4		"	gigiga
e.	Kuhač 1101.	(10) 10, 6, 6,	(1) (1	VII-4		"	"poskočnica" gi go
f.	Kuba XII. 3.	(10) 10, 6, 6,	(VII) (4	VII-4		"	
g.	Kuba X. 11.	"	(4) (4	VII-4		"	

Current No	Original edition	Syll.	Last note of section	Range	Rhythm. structure	Structure	Remarks
906a.}	Kuhač 920.	(10) ZZz 3)6. 10,8,6,	(1)(b3)	1-5		ABAv (B+Av = A!)	
b.}	Kuba B.H. 40.	(10) ZZz 3)6. 10,8,6,	(1)(2	1-7		ABC	
907.	Kuba B.H. 292.	(10) ZZz 3)6. r. 10,8,6,	(b2)(1	VI-b6		ABC	
908.	Kuba B.H. 728.	(10) ZZz 3)6. r. 10,8,6,	(2)(VII	VII-5		ABC	
909.	Kuba B.H. 207.	(10) ZZz 3)6. r. 10,8,6,	(b3)(1	1-5		AAvB	
⊕910.	Kuba B.H. 508.	(7) ZZz 3)6. 10,8,6,	(1)(4	VII-4	10,=♩♩♩♩/♩♪♪/♩♩♩//	ABC	
912.	Kuhač 164.	(7) ZZz 3)6. r. 11,7,6,	(VII)(1	VII-4		AAvB	
913.	Juž. Srb. 410.	(8) ZZz 3)6. r. 11,8,5,	(2)(2	1-4		AAvB	
914.	Kuhač 595.	(8) ZZz 3)6. r. 11,8,5,	(8)(5	1-9		ABC	
915.	Kuba B.H. 237.	(11) ZZz 3)6. 11,8,7,	(5)(2	VII-8		ABC	Cf. No 1619., 1622.
916.	Kuba B.H. 38.	(8) ZZz 3)6. r. 12,8,5,	(2)(b3	1-5		ABC	
917.	Kuhač 321.	(10) ZZz 3)6. (r.) 12,8,6,	(VII)(1	VII-4		AAvB	
918.	Kuba B.H. 487.	(10) ZZz 3)6. 12,8,6,	(VII)(b3	VII-b3		AAvB	
919.	Kuba B.H. 936. (=Kuba XII. 44.)	(10) ZZz 3)6. (r.) 13,10,5,	(VII)(VII	VII-5		AAvB	„uspavanka"(!?)
♂911.	Kuhač 909.	(11) ZZz 3)6. (r.) 11,7,5,	(1)(2	VII-4		ABC	

VII. Heterometric three section melodies, ⊃◯ structure

Current No	Original edition	Syll.	Last note of section	Range	Rhythm. structure	Structure	Remarks
920-921.	Kuba XIV. 23	(8) ZZz ')1. r. 8,8,4,	5)(VII)	VII-b6		ABC	
922.	Đorđević 82.	(8b) ZZz ')1. 8b,8b,4	b3)(b3)	1-4		AAB	„pr radu"
923.	Iz Levča 49.	ZZz ')1. 8,8,5,	VII)(VII)	VII-b3		ABBv	„sedeljka"
924.	Kuba B.H. 655.	ZZz ')1. 8,8,5,	4)(1)	VII-4		AAvB	
925a.}	Kuba B.H. 1015. Ms.	(8b) ZZz ')1. (r.) 8b,8b,5	b3)(b3)	VII-4		AAvB	

VII. ZZz 8,8,6, – 11,11,8,

Current No.	Original edition	Syll.	Last note of section	Range	Rhythm. structure	Structure	Remarks
b.	Kuba B.H. 551.	"	b3) (b3)	VII – 4		AAvB	
c.	" " 552.	"	b3) (b3)	VII – 4		"	
d.	" " 553.	"	b3) (b3)	VII – 4		"	
e.	" " 562.	(8b) ZZz ¹)₁. 8b, 8b, 3,	b3) (b3)	VII – 4		"	
926.	Kuba B.H. 448.	(8) ZZz ¹)₁. (r.) 8, 8, 6,	1) (1)	VII – b3		ABC	
927.	Kuba B.H. 128.	(8) ZZz ¹)₁. (r.) 8, 8, 6,	1) (1)	1 – b6		AAB	
928.	Đorđević 144.	(10) ZZz ¹)₁. (r.) 8, 8, 6,	b3) (b3)	1 – 4		ABC	
929.	Kuba IX. 41.	(10) ZZz ¹)₁. (r.) 8, 8, 6,	5) (b3)	1 – 6		ABC	
930a.	Kuhač 983.	(8b) ZZz ¹)₁. 8, 8, 6,	bIII) (VII)	bIII – b3		ABC	
b.	" 984.	"	bIII) (VII)	bIII – b3		"	
c.	Đorđević 334 (= Đorđević Nar. Pev. p. 63/1)	"	bIII) (VII)	bIII – b3		"	
d.	Kuhač 985	7,	V) (3)	V – 5		"	
931.	Kuhač 261.	ZZz ¹)₁. 8, 8, 7,	bVI) (bVI)	bVI – b3		AAB	
932a.	Đorđević Nar. Pev. p. 177/1.	ZZz ¹)₁. 8, 8, 7,	VII) (VII)	VII – 4		AAAv	
b.	Kuba B.H. 273. (= Kuba XII. 55.)	"	VII) (VII)	VII – 4		"	Ruman. ?
933.	Kuhač 954.	ZZz ¹)₁. 8, 8, 7,	1) (1)	VII – b2		AAAv	
934.	Kuhač 1252.	ZZz ¹)₁. 8, 8, 7,	1) (1)	VII – 4		AAAv	„svatovska"
935.	Kuba B.H. 955.	ZZz ¹)₁. 8, 8, 7,	1) (1)	VII – 5		AAB	
936.	Kuhač 1021.	ZZz ¹)₁. 8, 8, 7,	2) (2)	1 – 4		AAAv	„pleti-kolo"
937.	Kuba B.H. 365.	(11) ZZz ¹)₁. 8, 8, 7,	2) (5)	1 – 5		ABC	
938a.	Kuba B.H. 428.	(10) ZZz ¹)₁. r. 10, 10, 6,	2) (2)	1 – 5		AAB	
b.	Kuba XI. 14.	"	2) (2)	1 – 5		"	
939.	Kuhač 541.	(10) ZZz ¹)₁. (r.) 10, 10, 6,	4) (4)	VII – 4		AAB	
940.	Kuba B.H. 838.	ZZz ¹)₁. 11, 11, 5,	1) (1)	VII – 4		AAB	
941.	Kuba B.H. 606.	(11) ZZz ¹)₁. (r.) 11, 11, 8,	b3) (1)	VII – 5		AAvB	

VII. ZZz 11,11,8, ¹)1. — zzZ 7,7,10, ¹)2.

Current No	Original edition	Syll.	Last note of section	Range	Rhythm. structure	Structure	Remarks
942a.	Kuhač 236.	(10) ZZz ¹)1. r. 11, 11, 8,	2) (2)	1–♭6		AAA$_v$	
b.	" 394.	"	2) (2)	1–♭6		"	
943.	Kuhač 379.	(12) ZZz ¹)1. 12, 12, 6,	1) (1)	1–5		AA$_v$B	line interr.: 12, 2–10, 6,
944.	Kuhač 1353.	ZZz ¹)1. 12, 12, 7,	3) (3)	1–8		AA$_v$B	urban german?
945.	Kuhač 14.	zzZ ¹)2. 5, 5, 6,	♭2) (♭2)	VII–4		ABA$_v$	probably half of a 5+5, 6, 5+5, 6, mel.
946.	Kačerovski 82.	zzZ ¹)2. 5, 5, 7,	4) (VII)	VII–♭6		ABC	probably half of a 5+5, 7, 5+5, 7, mel.
947.	Đorđević 182.	(8♭?) zzZ ¹)2. 5, 5, 8♭,	♭3) (VII)	VII–4		ABA$_v$	
948.	Đorđević 83.	(5) zzZ ¹)2. r. 5, 5, 8♭,	6) (♭3)	1–7		ABC	„ćilimarska"
949.	Đorđević 246.	(5) zzZ ¹)2. r. 5, 5, 9,	#VII) (#VII)	#VII–3		AAB	
950.	Đorđević 68)	zzZ ¹)2. 5, 5, 9,	4) (4)	1–7		ABC	
951a.	Kuba B.H. 29.	zzZ ¹)2. 5, 5, 9,	1) (5)	VI–5		ABC	>german?
b.	" " 30.	8♭, 9,	(5)	1–6		AB	
952.	Kuba B.H. 37.	(10? 6?) zzZ ¹)2. 6, 6, 8,	1) (1)	1–7		AAB	
953.	Kuhač 955.	(6) zzZ· ¹)2. r. 6, 6, 9,	♭2) (1)	VII–♭3		ABC	emphat. perform. of one embellishment tone
954a.	Đorđević Nar. Pev. p. 23/1	(9) zzZ ¹)2. r. 6, 6, 9,	IV) (1)	IV–4	6, 6, 9, ♩♩𝅗𝅥 | ♩♩𝅗𝅥 ‖	ABC	
b.	" p. 23/2	"	IV) (1)	IV–5	"	"	
c.	Kuba B.H. 866.	"	1) (2)	VII–5	"	"	
d.	Kačerovski 49.	(9) zzZ ¹)2. 6, 6, 9,	2) (VII)	VII–4	"	"	
955.	Kuba B.H. 660.	(10) zzZ ¹)2. (r.) 6, 6, 10	VII) (VII)	VII–4		AAB	
956.	Kuhač 346.	(10) zzZ ¹)2. (r.) 6, 6, 10,	1) (1)	1–5		AAB	Var. Parry 25. Cf. No 1778.
957a.	Kuba B.H. 368.	(10) zzZ ¹)2. (r.) 6, 6, 10,	4) (5)	1–6		AA$_{v1}$ A$_{v2}$	
b.	" " 93.	"	5) (5)	1–♭6		"	
958a.	Bosiljevac 15.	(10) zzZ ¹)2. (r.) 7, 7, 10,	VII) (VII)	VII–4		AAB	
b.	Kuba XII. 40.	"	VII) (VII)	VII–4		"	
c.	Kuba B.H. 907.	"	VII) (VII)	VII–4		"	
d.	" " 639.	"	♭3) (VII)	VII–3		ABC	

VII. zzZ 7,7,10, — ZzZ
1)2. 1)3.
8b, 5,8b,

Current №	Original edition	Syll.	Last note of sections	Range	Rhythm. structure	Structure	Remarks
↓ g.	" " 640.	"	5) ①	1-5		ABC	
e.	" " 50.	"	5) (VII)	VII-7		ABC	swallowing of last syll.
⊕ f.	Đorđević 336 (=Đorđević Nar. Pev. p. 173/1)	"	4) ①	VII-5		ABB_v	
959a.	Kuba B.H. 446.	(10) zzZ 1)2. (+.) 7, 7, 10	1) ①	VII-2		ABB_v	
b.	Đorđević 357.	"	2) (VII)	VII-4		"	„sedeljka"
⊕961 a.	Kuhač 838.	(7) zzZ 1)2. +. 7, 7, 10,	1) (b3)	VII-4	10; [illegible]	ABA_v	
b.	" 839.	(7) zzZ 1)2. 7, 7, 10,	1) (b3)	VII-b6	"	ABA_v	
c.	" 840.	"	(bVI) ①	bVII-4	"	AA^3B	
↕960.	Kuhač 94.	(7) zzZ 1)2. +. 7, 7, 10,	b2) (b3)	VII-b3	10; [illegible]	AA^5A_v	
962a.	Kuhač 1142.	(10) zzZ 1)2. (+.) 7, 7, 13,	b3) ①	VII-b6		$AA_{5v}B$	
b.	Kuba B.H. 869.	"	5) ②	1-6		$AA_{5v}B$	
963.	Kuba B.H. 243. (=Kuba XIII. 5)	(10) zzZ 1)2. (+.) 7, 7, 13,	5) (b3)	#VI-7		ABC	
964.	Đorđević 385.	(8) zzZ 1)2. +. 8, 8, 9,	VII) (VII)	VII-4		AAB	
965.	Kuba B.H. 908.	(10) zzZ 1)2. (+.) 8, 8, 10,	1) ①	VII-4		AAB	
966a.	Juž. Srb. 409.	(8) zzZ 1)2. +. 8, 8, 10,	4) (b2)	VII-5		AA_vB	
b.	Kuba XIV. 10.	(8) zzZ 1)2. 8, 8, 12,	4) (b2)	VII-4		AA_vB	
967.	Kuhač 447.	(10) zzZ 1)2. (+.) 8, 8, 10,	2) ②	VII-5		AAB	
968.	Đorđević Nar. Pev. p. 22/1	(8) zzZ 1)2. +. 8, 8, 11,	VII) (VII)	VII-5		AAB	
969.	Kuhač 1009.	(8) zzZ 1)2. 8, 8, 12,	2) ②	VII-5		AAB	„kolo" " (Haydn string quartet)
970.	Kuba XI. 26.	zzZ 1)2. 8, 8, 14,	VII) (VII)	VII-b3		AAB	„kolo"
971a.	Kuhač 371.	zzZ 1)2. ‡13, 13, 14	b2) (b2)	VII-4		AAB	
b.	" 372.	"	1) ①	VI-4		AAB	
972.	Iz Levča 17.	(7) ZzZ 1)3. +. 7, 6, 7,	1) (b2)	VII-4		ABA	„sedeljka"
973a.	Kačerovski 31.	(8) ZzZ 1)3. +. 8, 5, 8,	2) ②	VII-4		ABC	
b.	Đorđević Nar. Pev. p. 76/1	"	2) ②	VII-4		ABC	
974.	Đorđević 101. (=Đorđević Nar. Pev. p. 79/1)	(8b.) ZzZ 1)3. +. 8b, 5, 8b,	2) ①	VII-5		ABC	

VII. Z z Z 1)3. 8,7,8, — 10,6,10

Current №	Original edition	Syll.	Last note of sections	Range	Rhythm. structure	Structure	Remarks
975.	Đorđević Nar. Pev. p. 78/1	(8) Z z Z 1)3. r. 8, 7, 8,	b2) (b2)	VII-4		AAv1, Av2	
976a.	Kuba B.H. 498.	(10) Z z Z 1)3. r. 10, 6, 10,	VII) (1)	VII-4		AAv1, Av2	
b.	Bosiljevac 39.	"	4) (1)	VII-4		"	
977.	Đorđević Nar. Pev. p. 40/1	(10) Z z Z 1)3. 10, 6, 10,	b3) (1)	VII-4		AAvB	
978.	Kuba B.H. 471.	(10) Z z Z 1)3. 10, 6, 10,	4) (1)	VII-4		ABC	
979.	Bosiljevac 35.	(10) Z z Z 1)3. 10, 6, 10,	2) (2)	VII-4		AAvB	
980.	Kuba B.H. 700.	(10) Z z Z 1)3. 10, 6, 10,	2) (2)	VII-4		AAv1, Av2	Var. Parry 26.
981.	Đorđević 335	(10) Z z Z 1)3. 10, 6, 10,	2) (2)	VII-5		AAvB	
982.	Bosiljevac 4.	(10) Z z Z 1)3. (r.) 10, 6, 10,	2) (2)	VII-5		AAv1, Av2	
983a.	Kuba B.H. 1097. Ms.	(10) Z z Z 1)3. 10, 6, 10,	b3) (b3)	VII-4		AAvB	Var. Parry 27. Cf. № 384 and Parry № 12 (a–j)
b.	" " 1098. Ms.	"	b3) (b3)	VII-4		"	
c.	" " 1099. Ms.	"	b3) (b3)	VII-4		"	
d.	" " 1100. Ms.	"	b3) (b3)	VII-4		"	
e.	" " 1101. Ms.	"	b3) (b3)	VII-4		"	
f.	" " 1102. Ms.	"	b3) (1)	VII-4		"	
g.	" " 1103. Ms.	"	3) (3)	VII-4		"	
h.	" " 1104. Ms.	"	3) (3)	VII-4		"	
i.	" " 1105. Ms.	"	3) (3)	VII-5		"	
j.	" " 1106. Ms.	"	b3) (b3)	VII-4		"	
k.	Đorđević Nar. Pev. p. 132/1.	"	b3) (b3)	VII-4		"	
l.	Kuhač 1510.	"	b3) (b3)	VII-4		"	
m.	Kuba B.H. 340.	"	b3) (b3)	VII-4		"	
n.	" " 537.	"	b3) (b3)	VII-4		"	
o.	" " 956.	"	3) (3)	VII-4		"	
p.	Kuba XI. 46	"	b3) (b3)	VII-4		"	„uspavanka" (!)
r.	Đorđević Nar. Pev. p. 138/1	"	b3) (b3)	VII-4		"	

VII. Z z Z ')3. 10, 6, 10,

Current No.	Original edition	Syll.	Last note of sections	Range	Rhythm. structure	Structure	Remarks
983 s.	Kuba B. H. 783.	"	b3) (b3)	VII - b3		"	
t.	" " 1107. Ms.	"	3) (3)	1 - 4		"	
u.	" " 126.	"	b3) (b3)	VII - 5		"	
v.	" " 289.	"	3) (3)	VII - 5		"	
x.	" " 623.	"	b3) (b3)	VII - 5		"	
y.	Kuhač 830.	"	b3) (b3)	VII - 5		"	
z.	Kuhač 1511. (= Đorđević Nar. Pev. p. 51/1)	"	b3) (b3)	VII - 5		"	
aa.	Bosiljevac 1.	"	b3) (b3)	VII - 5		"	
bb.	Kuba B. H. 408.	"	b3) (b3)	1 - 5		"	word inter.: 10, 4-2, 2, 10,
cc.	" " 214. (= Kuba XIII. 55)	"	b3) (b3)	VII - b6		"	
dd.	Bosiljevac 46.	"	b3) (b3)	VII - 7		"	
ee.	Kuhač 1508.	"	b3) (b3)	VII - 7		"	
ff.	Kuba B. H. 880.	"	1) (1)	VII - 4		"	
gg.	Kuhač 108.	"	1) (1)	VII - 4		"	
hh.	" 703.	"	1) (1)	VII - 5		"	
ii.	" 1509.	"	1) (1)	VII - 5		"	
jj	" 241.	"	1) (VII)	VII - 4		"	like Slovakian "Valašska"-mel.?
kk.	" 1467.	"	2) (2)	VII - 4		"	
ll.	Kuba B. H. 1109. Ms.	10,	VII) [0]				
984 a.	Kuba B. H. 1110. Ms.	(10) Z z Z ')3. 10, 6, 10,	b3) (b3)	VII - 7		$AA_{v_1}A_{v_2}$	Var. Pamy 28.
b.	" " 1111. Ms.	"	b3) (b3)	VII - 7		"	
c.	" " 1115. Ms.	"	b3) (b3)	VII - 7		"	
d.	Kuba B. H. 234.	"	b3) (b3)	VII - 7		"	
e.	" " 1112. Ms.	"	b3) (b3)	VII - 8		"	
f.	Kuhač 1522.	"	b3) (b3)	VII - 8		"	
g.	Đorđević Nar. Pev. p. 161/2	"	b3) (b3)	VII - 8			"a-a" interpolated!

VII. Z z Z 1)3. 10,6,10,–11,6,4, — Z z Z 3)2.

Current No.	Original edition	Syll.	Last note of sections	Range	Rhythm. structure	Structure	Remarks
h.	Đorđević Nar. Pev. p. 147/1	"	b3) (b3)	1–8		"	
i.	Kuba B.H. 1114. Ms (= Kuba XIII 47)	"	4) (b3)	VII–7		"	
j.	Kuhač 361.	"	b3) (4)	1–7		"	
k.	Kuba B.H. 245. (= Kuba XIII. 41.)	"	VII) (VII)	VII–8		"	
985.	Kuba B.H. 223.	(10) Z z Z 1)3. 10, 6, 10,	b3) (b3)	1–7		ABC	In near relation to the previous groups
986a.	Kuba B.H. 865.	(10) Z z Z 1)3. 10, 6, 10,	4) (b3)	VII–4		AAv B	
b.	" " 221.	"	5) (4)	VII–7		"	
987.	Kuba B.H. 171.	(10) Z z Z 1)3. 10, 6, 10,	2) (3)	1–6		AAv B	
988.	Kuba B.H. 139.	(10) Z z Z 1)3. 10, 6, 10,	5) (4)	VII–7		AAv B	In near relation to the previous groups
989a.	Đorđević Nar. Pev. p. 180/1	(10) Z z Z 1)3. 10, 6, 10,	4) (4)	VII–5		AAv B	
b.	Kuba B.H. 1069. Ms.	"	4) (4)	VII–5		"	
c.	" " 1070. Ms	"	"	VII–7		"	
d.	" " 1071. Ms.	"	"	"		"	
e.	" " 1073. Ms.	"	"	"		"	
f.	Bosiljevac 3.	"	"	"		"	
g.	Kuba B.H. 1074. Ms.	"	"	VII–8		"	
h.	" Ms. " 1072	10,	4) [0]			A[ ]B	
990.	Kuhač 359.	(10) Z z Z 1)3. 7. 10, 7, 10, (5+5)	2) (2)	1–5		AAv B	
991.	Kuhač 626.	(10) Z z Z 1)3. 7. 10, 9, 10, (5+5)	VII) (VII)	VII–4		AAv B	
992.	Đorđević 99.	(11) Z z Z 1)3. 7. 11, 6, 11,	b3) (1)	VII–b6		ABC	
993a.	Kuba XI. 22.	(8) z Z z 1)4. 8, 12, 8,	1) (1)	VII–b2	Var. Parry 16b. (2nd form); 29.	AAv1, Av2	"kolo"
b.	" B.H. 454.	(8) 12,	(1)			AAv	"kolo"
c.	Kuba X. 39.	"					fragment of a.
d.	Kuhač 1041.	"					" " "oro"
e.	" 1037.	"					" " "oro"
f.	" 963.	"					" "
994.	Kuhač 360.	z Z Z 3)1. 5, 6, 7,	5) (2)	1–6		ABC	
995.	Kuba B.H. 657.	Z z Z 3)2. 6, 5, 8,	2) (2)	VII–4		ABC	
996.	Kuhač 235.	Z z Z 3)2. 7, 6, 10,	2) (2)	1–7		AAv B	
997.	Kuba B.H. 42	Z z Z 3)2. 8, 5, 9,	2) (2)	1–7		ABC	

VII. $z_z Z^{3)}_{2.}$ 8,5,11,— 8,6,10,

Current №	Original edition	Syll.	Last note of sections	Range	Rhythm. structure	Structure	Remarks
998.	Kuba B.H. 157.	z z Z 3)2. 8, 5, 11,	1) (b3)	bVI – b6		ABAv	
999a.	Kuhač 718.	(10) Z z Z 3)2. 8, 6, 10,	bVI) (VII)	bVI – b3	going in "imaginary" thirds	ABC	
b.	" 720.	"	VII) (1)	VII – 4	Imperfect cadence	"	
c.	" 719.	"	2) (2)	1 – 5	Perfect cadence	"	
1000a.	Đorđević 407.	(10) z z Z 3)2. 8, 6, 10,	VII) (VII)	VII – b2		ABC	"sedeljka"
b.	" 354.	"	2) (VII)	VII – b3		ABBv	"sedeljka"
1001a.	Kuhač 781.	(10) z z Z 3)2. 8, 6, 10	b3) (VII)	VII – 4		‖ A (=4,) B (=10) B (=10) ‖	
b.	" 782.	"	"	"		"	"from 1828! (Ljetopis)"
c.	" 783.	"	"	"		"	
d.	" 1053.	"	"	"		"	"kolo"
e.	" 1248.	"	"	"		"	"poskočnica (gajdaš...?)"
f.	" 592.	"	1) (VII)	"		"	
g.	" 593.	"	"	"		"	
h.	Kuba B.H. 260. (= Đorđević Nar. Pev. p. 117)	"	b3) (1)	"		"	
i.	Kuba XI. 53.	"	"	"		"	
j.	Kuhač 636.	"	2) (1)	"		"	
1002a.	Kuba IX. 3	(10) z z Z 3)2. 8, 6, 10,	b3) (1)	1 – 5	Imperfect cadence	ABBv	two part song
b.	Kuhač 653 b)	"	"	VII – 4		"	
c.	" 653 a)	"	b3) (VII)	"		"	
d.	" 1083.	"	1) (b3)	1 – 4		"	"poskočnica"
e.	Đorđević Nar. Pev. p. 69/2	"	2) (2)	1 – 5	Perfect cadence	"	
f.	Kuhač 1099.	"	4) (2)	1 – 5		"	"poskočnica"
g.	" 1039.	"	4) (2)	1 – 5		"	"oro (na Božić?)"
h.	" 1040.	(10) 8, 6, 6,	4) (VII)	VII – 4		"	"oro (na Božić?)" "swallowing of last syll."
1003.	Kuba B.H. 876.	(10) z z Z 3)2. 8, 6, 10,	b2) (b2)	1 – 4		AAv1 Av2	

VII. zzZ 8,6,10,–9,5,10,–zZz 3)5.

Current №	Original edition	Syll.	Last note of sections	Range	Rhythm. structure	Structure	Remarks
1004.	Kuhač 811.	(10) zzZ 3)2. (+) 8, 6, 10,	VII) (b3)	VII – 4		!A B B_v ! (=4,)(=10)(=10)	
1005a.	Kuhač 691.	(10) zzZ 3)2. 8, 6, 10,	b2) (b3)	VII – 4		ABC	
b.	Kuba X. 58.	"	b2) (b3)	1 – b6		"	
c.	" IX. 30.	"	b3) (b3)	1 – b6		"	
⊕ d.	Kuhač 132	"	1) (b3)	1 – b6		AA_vB	
1006 a.	Kuba IX. 22.	zzZ 3)2. 8, 6, 10,	b3) (b3)	VI – b6		ABC	
b.	Kuhač 13.	"	"	"		"	
1007.	Kuhač 649.	(10) zzZ 3)2. 8, 6, 10,	4) (4)	1 – 5		ABC	
1008.	Đorđević Nar. Pev. p. 84/1	(11) zzZ 3)2. 8, 6, 14,	4) (2)	VII – 5		ABC	
1009.	Kuhač 159.	(11) zzZ 3)2. 8, 6, 11,	4) (b3)	#VII – 7		ABA_v	
1010 a.	Kuba B. H. 507.	(11) zzZ 3)2. (+) 8, 7, 9,	VII) (1)	VII – 4		ABB_v	Imperfect cadence
b.	" " 688.	"	2) (VII)	VII – 5		"	
c.	Kuhač 178.	"	3) (1)	1 – 5		"	Perfect cadence
1011.	Kuhač 266.	zzZ 3)2. 8, 7, 11,	2) (1)	1 – 7		ABB_v	
1012.	Đorđević 493.	? zzZ 3)2. 8, 7, 11,	b3) (b3)	VI – b3		not clear, confused	
1013.	Kuba B. H. 476.	(10) zzZ 3)2. (+) 9, 5, 10,	2) (1)	VII – b3		AA_vB	
1013 bis.	Kuba B.H. 352.	(10) ZzZ 3)3. (+) 8, 6, 7,	1) (1)	1 – 4		$AA_{v1}A_{v2}$	
1014.	Đorđević Nar. Pev. p. 188/1	(11) ZzZ 3)3. (+) 8, 6, 7,	VII) (4)	VII – 5		ABA_v	Var. Parry 30.
1015.	Kuba B. H. 755.	(10) ZzZ 3)3. (+) 10, 5, 6,	VII) (VII)	IV – 5		ABA_v	
1016 a.	Kuba B.H. 68.	(11) ZzZ 3)3. (+) 11, 8, 10,	5) (1)	VII – 8		ABC	
b.	" " 69.	"	4) (VII)	VII – 8		"	
1017 a.	Kuhač 237.	(10) ZzZ 3)3. (+) 12, 6, 10,	VII) (1)	VII – 5		$AA_{v1}A_{v2}$	
b.	" {432. 433.	(10) (+) 12, 6, 12,	VII) (VII)	VI – 5		"	
1018 a.	Kuba B.H. 554.	(10) zZz 3)4. (+) 9, 11, 10,	1) (VII)	VII – 4		$AA_{v1}A_{v2}$	
b.	" " 555.	"	1) (1)	VII – 4		AA_vB	
1019.	Kuba B. H. 140.	(10) zZz 3)5. (+) 7, 10, 4,	4) (VII)	VII – 7		ABC	
↑1005 e.	Kuhač 133.	"	VII) (4)	VII – 4		AA_vB	

VII. zZ_z $^{3)}5.$ – Zz_z $^{3)}6.$; VIII. (special)

Current №	Original edition	Syll.	Last note of sections	Range	Rhythm. structure	Structure	Remarks
1020 a.	Bartók M.F. 2029a) Ms., Temešmoštor	(10) zZ_z $^{3)}5.$ 8, 10, 6,	7) (4)	1–7		ABB_v	three part song
b.	Kuba XII. 34.	"	2) (4)	VII–5		"	swallowing of last syll
c.	Đorđević 512.	6,	4) (4)				fragment of previous
1021 a.	Kuba B.H. 16.	(7) zZ_z $^{3)}5.$ (t.) 10, 20, 5,	5) (I)	I–3		?	Var.: Bartók, Maramureş and, № 36.
b.	Đorđević 333. (= Đorđević Nar. Pev. p. 118/1)	(7) zZ_z $^{3)}5.$ (t.) 10, 18, 5,	♭III) (♭III)	I–1		?	Bartók, Rumanian Folk-music II. vol. № 397.
c.	Kuhač 1446.	(8) t. 14, 11, 11, 11,	1) (1) (♭3	VII–4		?	this is the oldest form; a. b. are derivations
1022 a.	Kuhač 727.	(10) Zz_z $^{3)}6.$ (t.) 8, 6, 5,	2) (2)	VII–4		ABC	
b.	" 728.	"	2) (2)	VII–4		ABC	
c.	" 836.	"	2) (2)	VII–4		"	
1023.	Kuba B.H. 475.	(7) Zz_z $^{3)}6.$ t. 8, 7, 5,	VII) (VII)	VII–♭3		AA_vB	Turkish text (at least the 1. st.) gigiga

VIII. Melodies of special structure

Current №	Original edition	Syll.	Last note of sections	Range	Rhythm. structure	Structure	Remarks
1024 a.	Kuba IX. 52.	(10) 4, 6, 6, 4,	VII) (VII) (1	VII–5		ABB_vA_v	twopart song
b.	Kuba B.H. 928.	"	VII) (VII) (VII	VII–4		ABBC	
c.	Kuhač 795.	"	4) (VII) (1	VII–4		ABCD	
1025 a.	Kuba XI. 51.	(10) 4, 6, 6, 4,	VII) (VII) (♭3	VII–♭3		ABB_vC	"poskočnica"
b.	" B.H. 873.	(10) 4, [ ], 6, 4,	VII) [0] (♭3	VII–4		A[ ]BA⁺	
1026 a.	Đorđević 365.	(10) 4, 6, 6, 4,	1) (VII) (VII	VII–♭3		ABBA	"sedeljka"
b.	Iz Levča 36.	"	"	VII–4		$ABBA_v$	
c.	Đorđević Nar. Pev. p. 108/2	"	1) (VII) (♭2	VII–4		ABB_vA	
d.	Đorđević 450.	"	1) (2) (2	VII–4		ABBA	
e.	" 483.	(10) 4, [ ], 6, 4,	1) [0] (VII			A[ ]BA	"sedeljka"
f.	Kuba XI. 31.	"	VII) [0] (VII			$A[\,]BA_v$	
1027 a.	Kuba B.H. 702.	(10) 4, 6, 6, 4	1) (VII) (VII	VII–5		$ABBA_v$	
b.	" " 499.	(10) 4, [ ], 6, 4,	1) [0] (1	1–4		A[ ]BA	
c.	" " 493.	"	1) [0] (2	VII–4		$A[\,]BA_v$	
1028–9.	Kuba B.H. 872.	(10) 4, 6, 6, 4,	VII) (1) (4	VII–4		ABB_vA^+	

Current No.	Original edition	Syll.	Last note of sections	Range	Rhythm. structure	Structure	Remarks
1030 a.	Iz Levča 15.	(10) 4, 6, 6, 4,	D (1) 1	VII–b3		A Av Av A	„sedeljka"
b.	" " 8.	"	D (VII) VII	"		"	„svatovska"
c.	" " 60.	"	"	VII–4		A B B A	
d.	" " 28.	"	D (VII) 2	VII–4		"	„sedeljka"
e.	" " 34.	"	"	"		"	„sedeljka"
1031–2.	Kuba B. H. 360.	(10) 4, 6, 6, 4,	D (1) 2	1–5		A Av B C	
1034–5.	Kuba B. H. 716.	(10) 4, 6, 6, 4,	2 (1) 2	1–5		A B C Av	
1036 a.	Kuba B. H. 724.	(10) 4, 6, 6, 4,	2 (2) 1	VII–4		A B Bv C	
b.	" " 723.	"	2 (2) 2	VI–4		A B B C	
c.	" " 429.	"	"	1–4		"	
d.	Kuhač 540.	"	D (2) 2	VII–3		A B B A	
e.	Kuba XI. 1.	(10) 4, 6, [ ], 4,	2 (2) [C]			A B [ ] C	
1033 a.	Kuba XI. 30.	(10) 4, 6, 6, 4,	D (1) b3	1–4	Var. Parry 31.	A B Bv Av	„svatovska"
b.	Đorđević Nar. Pev. p. 186/2	"	D (1) 1	1–4		A B B A	
c.	Kuhač 892.	"	D (2) 2	1–4		"	
d.	Bosiljevac 16.	"	2 (2) 4	1–4		A B Bv Av	
e.	Kuba B. H. 406.	"	3 (3) 5	1–5		"	
f.	" " 193.	"	4 (4) b6	1–7		A B Bv A4v	
g.	Kuhač 736.	(10) 4, 6, [ ], 4,	D (1) [C]			A B [ ] A	
h.	" 1208.	"	"			A B [ ] Av	„svatovska"
i.	Kuba B.H. 208.	"	"			"	
1037–8.	Kuba B.H. 339.	(10) 4, 6, 6, 4,	b5 (b5) b3	1–b5		A B Bv C	
1039 a.	Kuba B. H. 1095. Ms. (= Kuba XIII. 3.)	(10) 4, 6, 6, 4,*	8 (8) 5	1–8		A B Bv C	two syll. interr.: 2+[3.]+1, 4+[5.]+1, 6, 4,
b.	Kuba XI. 36.	"	"	"		"	
c.	Kuba B. H. 1094. Ms.	"	"	"		"	

* anticipation of the four first syllables of the following line!

Current No	Original edition	Syll.	Last note of sections	Range	Rhythm. structure	Structure	Remarks
d.	Đorđević Nar. Pev. p. 29/2	(10) 4, 6, 6, 4,	8) (8) (4	1–8		ABB_vC	syll. interr.: 4, 6, 4+[5.]+1, 4,
e.	Kuba B.H. 1096. Ms.	(10) 4, 6, 6, 4,*	8) (8) (b6	1–8		ABB_vC	(two syll. interr.: 2+[3.]+1,)
f.	Bosiljevac 37.	(10) 4, 6, 6, 4,	8) (8) (b6	"		ABB_vC	(4+[5.]+1, 6, 4,
g.	Kuba B.H. 1093. Ms.	(10) 4, 6, 6, 4,*	7) (7) (4	1–7		ABB_vC	syll. interr. 4, 4+[5.]+1, 6, 4,
h.	Kuba B.H. 295.	(10) 4, 6, 6, 4,	5) (5) (b6	1–7		ABB_vC	
1040–1.	Kuba B.H. 875.	(10) |: 4, :| 6, [ ], 4,	(VII) (VII) (8,) (6,) (4,)	VII–b3		|: A :| B [ ] A_v	
1042.	Kuba B.H. 349.	(10) |: 4, :| 6, [ ], 4,	(2) (3 (8,) (6,) (4,)	1–3	Should be inverted	|: A :| B [ ] A_v	
1043.	Kuba B.H. 1003. Ms.	(10) |: 4, :| 6, [ ], 4,	(1) (b2 (8,) (6,) (4,)	1–b3		|: A :| B [ ] C	chromat. mel.
1046.	Đorđević 546.	(8) 4+4, 4+4, 4,	(1) (1 (8,) (8,) (4,)	1–b3		A+A, A+A, A	
1047a.	Kuhač 879.	(8) 4+4, 4+4, 4,	(b3) (b3 (8,) (8,) (4,)	1–5		A A B (8,) (8,) (4,)	
b.	" 880.	"	"	1–4		"	
c.	" 881.	"	"	VII–4		A A_v B (8,) (8,) (4,)	
1048.	Đorđević 307.	(8b) 5+3, 5,	(b2)	VII–b3		AB	kad se vraćaju sa rada
1049.	Kuhač 660.	(8b) 5+3+3, 5,	(1)	VII–b3		AB	Cf. No. 2148.
1044.	Kuba B.H. 392.	(11) 4+4+3+3, 4	(1) (1 (8,) (6,) (4,)	1–b3		ABC	
1045.	Kuba B.H. 480.	(13) 4+4+5, 4,	(1) (VII (8,) (5,) (4)	VII–b3		ABC	svatovska
1050.	Kuhač 1069.	(8) 2+2+4, 2,		1–b3			kolo
1051–2.	Kuhač 1271.	(8b) 3+5, 3,		1–4			svatovska
1053.	Đorđević 305.	(10) 2+8, 2		1–b3			svatovska

IX. Four-section isometric melodies

Current No	Original edition	Syll.	Last note of sections	Range	Rhythm. structure	Structure	Remarks
1054a.	Kuba B.H. 995. Ms.	5,	VII) (VII) (VII	VII–4		AABC	
b.	Kuba B.H. 546.	5,	"	"		"	
c.	" " 1124. Ms.	5,	"	"		"	
d.	Đorđević Nar. Pev. p. 28/1	5,	VII) (VII) (1	VII–4		$AABB_v$	
e.	Kuhač 519.	5,	"	VII–5		AA_vBB	
f.	Kuhač 758. (= Đorđević Nar. Pev. p. 113/1)	5,	VII) (VII) (4	VII–4		AA_vBB_v	

* anticipation of the four first syllables of the next line.

Current №	Original edition	Syll.	Last note of sections	Range	Rhythm. structure	Structure	Remarks
1055.	Đorđević Nar. Rev. p. 75/1	5,	VI)(VII)(VII	VII-4		$ABAB_v$	
1056.	Kuba B.H. 781.	5,	1)(VII)(1	VII-2		$ABAB_v$	
1057a.	Đorđević 447.	5,	1)(VII)(b3	VII-4		$ABCB_v$	text in 4-line stanzas
b.	" 498.	5,	b2)(VII)(b2	VII-4		$AA_{sv}A_vA_s$	„slavska"
c.	Kuhač 66.	5,	1)(1)(VII	VII-4		ABCB	
d.	" 65.	5,<	1)(1)(1	VII-4		"	
1058a.	Kuhač 865.	5,	b3)(VII)(b6	VII-7		$ABCB^s$	
b.	" 864.	5,	b3)(VII)(7	VII-7		"	
c.	" 866.	5,	b3)(VII)(4	VII-5		ABCD	
d.	" 863.	5,	4)(VII)(b3	VII-5		$ABCB^s$	
1059.	Đorđević Nar. Rev. p. 138/3	5,	4)(VII)(1	VII-4		ABCD	
1060.	Đorđević 67.	5,	VII)(1)(VII	VII-5		ABA_vB	
1061.	Kuhač 568.	5,	1)(1)(1	bVII-b6		ABCD	
1062.	Kuhač 759.	5,	1)(1)(1	1-4		$AABB_v$	
1063.	Kuhač 1283.	5,	1)(1)(4	1-5		AA_vBA_v	
1064.	Kuhač 1246.	5,	1)(1)(4	1-5		$AA_{v1}A_{v2}B$	„svatoška"
1065.	Đorđević 114	5,	b3)(1)(VII	VII-5		AA_vBB_v	
1066.	Kuba B.H. 708.	5,	b3)(1)(b3	VII-5		ABBB	
1067.	Đorđević 146.	5,	4)(1)(b3	1-4		$AA_{v1}A_{v2}B$	„krstonoška"
1068.	Đorđević Nar. Rev. p. 179/1	5,	VII)(b2)(b2	VII-5		$AABB_v$	
1069.	Iz Levča 2.	5,	b2)(b2)(b2	VII-4		ABAB	„slavska"
1070.	Đorđević 242.	5,	b2)(b2)(b2	1-4		AAAB	
1071.	Kuba B.H. 589.	5,	VII)(2)(VII	VII-4		ABA_vB_v	
1072a.	Đorđević Nar. Rev. p. 26/1	5,	2)(2)(2	VII-5		AA_vAA_{sv}	
b.	Kačerovski 42.	5,	"	"		"	

IX. 5, 4) ② (– VII) ④ (VII; abab

Current No	Original edition	Syll.	Last note of sections	Range	Rhythm structure	Structure	Remarks
c.	Bosiljevac 18.	5,	"	"		AA_vAB	
d.	Đorđević Nar.Pev. p. 188/2	5,	"	"		AAA_vB	
1073 a.	Kuba XIV. 8.	5,	4) ② (	1–4		ABB_vC	"svatovska"
b.	Juž. Srb. 416.	5,	4) ② (2	1–4		ABB_vC	
1074.	Kuhač 586.	5,	4) ② (4	1–6		$ABAB_v$	
1075.	Kuba XII. 48.	5,	1) (b3) (	1–5		AA_vAB	
1076.	Kuhač 757.	5,	1) (b3) (5	1–b6		ABCD	
1077 a.	Kuba XI. 8.	5,	b3) (b3) (	VII – b6		$ABBB_3$	
b.	Kuba B.H. 156. (= Kuba XIII. 44.)	5,	b3) (b3) (b2	bVII – b6		ABB_vB_{3v}	
c.	Kuba B.H. 119.	5,	b3) (b3) (b3	VII – 5		AABC	
d.	" " 185.	5,	5) ④ (b3?	1 – 7?		2	final tone perhaps a misprint?
1078.	Juž. Srb. 407.	5,	b3) (b3) (b3	VII – b3		$ABAB_v$	igra
1079 a.	Đorđević 241.	5,	b3) (b3) (b3	1–5		AAA_vB	
b.	Kuhač 255.	5,	"	VII – 4		AAAB	
c.	Kuba B.H. 75.	5,	"	"		ABBC	
1080.	Kuba IX. 43.	5,	4) (b3) (b2	1–b6		$AA_sA_{ss}A_{sss v}$	
1081.	Kuhač 1319.	5,	4) (b3) (2	1–5		$A_vA_sA_{ss}A_{sss}$	
1082.	Kuba XII. 25.	5,	5) (b3) (	1–7	N.b.: ♫♩♫ ‖ (Kiš)	ABCD	pent.
1083.	Kuba B.H. 819.	5,	VII) ④ (	VII – 4		$ABCB_v$	
1084.	Kuhač 590.	5,	b3) ④ (b3	1–5		$ABAB_v$	agigo
1085 a.	Đorđević 98.	5,	5) (b3) (b3	1–5		AA_vBB_v	pent.
b.	Kuba XII. 17.	5,	4) (b3) (b3)	1–5		"	pent.
1086.	Kuhač 1221.	5,	2) ③ (2	1–5	a b a b; a = ♪♫|♩.♪‖; b = ♬|♩‖	$ABAB_v$	"svatovska"
1087 a.	Đorđević 95.	5,	VII) ④ (VII	VII – 5	a b a b; a = ♪♫|♩♩‖; b = ♬|♩‖	ABAC	
b.	Kuba XIV. 27.	5,	"	VII – 4	"	ABA_vC	

Current No	Original edition	Syll.	Last note of sections	Range	Rhythm. structure	Structure	Remarks
1088.	Đorđević Nar. Pev. p. 90/1	6,	1)(VII)(♭VII	♭VII–♭6		ABA_vC	
1089a.	Kuhač 711 a)	6,	2)(VII)(2	VII–5		$ABCB_v$	„from 1828" (the year)
b.	" 712.	6,	1)(VII)(1	VII–5		"	
1090.	Kuhač 582.	6,	2)(VII)(♭3	VII–4		ABB_vC	
1091.	Kuhač 749. 750.	6,	♭3)(VII)(♭3	VII–8		ABA_vB_v	Hung. pentat.
1092.	Juž. Sob. 400	6,	4)(VII)(4	VII–4		$ABAB_v$	
1093.	Kuba X. 45.	6,	♭VII)(1)(VII	V–♭3		ABA^s_vC	three part song
1094a.	Kuhač 951.	6,	VII)(1)(4	VI–4		$AA^sA_vA^s_v$	
b.	" 962.	6,	♭3)(1)(♭3	VII–♭6		$AA_{sv_1}AA_{sv_2}$	
c.	" 964.	6,	1)(VII)(1	♭VII–4		AA_sAA_{sv}	
d.	" 279.	6,	4)(♭3)(♭6	1–♭6		$AA^s_vA_vB$	
e.	" 966.	6,	♭3)(1)[ ]			$AB[\,]B$	
f.	" 965.	6,	4)(1)[ ]			"	
g.	" 248.	6,	[ )( ](VII				
h.	" 114.	6,	"				
i.	" 952.	6,	[ )( ](2				
j.	" 953.	6,	[ )( ](♭3				
k.	" 967.	6,	"				
l.	" 972.	8 b,	VII)(1)[ ]				
1095a.	Kuhač 1297.	6,	1)(1)(VII	VII–4		$AA\langle A_sB$	
⊕ b.	" 453. (= Đorđević Nar. Pev. p. 149)	6,	"	VII–♭3		$AABA$	
d.	Kuhač 454.	7, 7, 7, 6,	"	VII–4		$AABA_v$	
1096.	Kuba B.H. 951. (= Kuba XII. 28.)	6,	1)(1)(VII	VII–5		$ABB_{v_1}B_{v_2}$	
1097a.	Đorđević 469.	(10) 6,	1)(1)(1	VII–♭2			„sedeljka"
b.	Kuhač 52.	(10) 6,	VII)(VII)(VII	VII–♭3		$ABAB_v$	
↕ 1095c.	Kuhač 1326.	6,	1)(1)(VII	♭VII–4		$AABC$	

IX. 6, 1)①(1 – 2)②(2

Current №	Original edition	Syll.	Last note of sections	Range	Rhythm structure	Structure	Remarks
1098a.	Kuba XII. 27.	6,	1)①(1	V–5		AABB	
b.	Kuba B.H. 177.	6,	"	"		"	
1099.	Kuhač 364.	6,	1)①(1	VII–b5		ABA_vC	
1100.	Kuhač 1078.	6,	1)①(1	1–5		ABAB	„kolo"
1101.	Kuhač 1260.	6,	1)①(b3	VII–b3		ABCD	„svatovska"
1102a.	Kuba XI. 60.	6,	1)①(b3	1–b6		AA_vBB 3)	
b.	Juž. Srb. 415.	6,	"	1–5		$AABB_{5,v}$	
c.	Kuba B.H. 235.	6,	"	1–5		AABC	
d.	" " 683.	6,	1)①(1	VII–5		AA_vAB	
1103.	Kuba X. 46.	6,	b2)①(VII	VII–b6		$>AA_sA_{ss}A_{sss}$	
1104.	Kuhač 446.	6,	b2)①(b2	1–4		$AA^s_{v_1}AA^s_{v_2}$	
1105a.	Kuhač 463.	6,	b2)①(b3	VII–5		AA_sBC	
b.	" 435.	6,	b3)①(VII	VII–5		$ABCB_v$	
1106.	Đorđević 91.	6,	b3)①(b3	VII–4		ABAB	
1107a.	Kuhač 950.	6,	3)①(3	1–5		ABB_vC	
b.	Bosiljevac 21.	6,	"	V–6		$ABCC_{4v}$	
c.	Kuhač 1262.	6,	3)①(4	1–5		ABCD	„svatovska"
d.	" 1275.	6,	2)①(2	1–5		"	„svatovska"
1108.	Kuhač 894.	6,	3)①(4	1–6		$ABCC_v$	
1109.	Kuba B.H. 282.	6,	4)①(4	1–b6		ABCD	
1110.	Kuhač 339.	(10) 6,	5)①(4	1–6	r.6. ♪♩ ⋮ ♫ ⋮ ♩♪ ‖	ABCD	Slovakian – Hungar. ?
1111.	Kuba X. 4.	6,	b6)①(1	VII–b6		ABCD	
1112.	Kuba XI. 68.	6,	b2)(b2)(b2	VII–b3		ABA_vB_v	
1113.	Kuhač 581.	6,	1)②(1	1–5		ABAC	
1114.	Kuhač 384.	6,	2)②(2	1–4		$AA_{v_1}AA_{v_2}$	

Current No	Original edition	Syll.	Last note of sections	Range	Rhythm structure	Structure	Remarks
1115.	Kuhač 56.	6,	3)②(3	#VI–5		ABCD	Hung. var.
1116.	Kuhač 735.	6,	3)②(3	1–5		ABAB$_v$	
1117.	Kuhač 142.	6,	4)②(2	1–5		ABA$_v$B$_v$	
1118.	Kuhač 555.	6,	5)②(2	1–b6		ABCD	
1119.	Kuhač 1359.	6,	5)②(4	#VII–6		ABA$_s$B$_{sv}$	
1120.	Kuhač 734.	6,	b3)(b3)(VII	VII–b6	N.b. ♪♩ ⁞ ♫ ⁞ ♪♩ ‖	ABB$_{3v}$B$_3$	Hung. var. (many)
1121.	Kuhač 314.	6,	b3)(b3)(1	V–7		AA$_v$BC	Hung. var.?
1122.	Kuba B.H. 855.	6,	b3)(b3)(1	VI–4		AABC	
1123.	Kuhač 714.	6,	b3)(b3)(b2	bVI–b6		ABCD	
1124a.	Kuhač 462.	6,	4)(b3)(b2	VII–b6		<AA$_s$A$_{ss}$A$_{sss}$	
b.	" 247.	6,	"	1–b6		"	
c.	" 179.	6,	[5○](b2				
1125a.	Kuba X. 17.	6,	5)(b3)(1	1–7		<AA$_s$A$_{ss}$A$_{sss}$	
b.	" " 44.	6,	4)(b3)(b2	1–b6		"	
c.	Bosiljevac 30.	6,	5)(b3)(b2	VII–8		"	
1126.	Kuba XII. 26.	6,	5)(b3)(b3	1–5		ABB$_v$C	Hung. var.
1127.	Kuhač 556.	6,	1)③(1	1–5		AA^{3}A^3_vA	Hung. Slovak. var.
1128a.	Kuhač 456.	6,	4)③(2	#VII–4		<AA$_s$A$_{ss}$A$_{sss}$	Hung., Slovak, Polish var. (a–e); Text: trans. of the Hung. text
b.	" 195.	6,	"	1–5		"	
c.	" 609.	6,	1)③(2	#VII–4		"	
d.	" 610.	6,	4)③(2	VI–5		"	
e.	" 1143.	6,	4)③(4	1–5		AA$_s$AA$_{sv}$	
1129.	Kuhač 385.	6,	5)③(3	1–5		ABB$_v$C	Slovak., Hung. var.?
1130.	Kuhač 1256.	6,	1)④(1	1–7		ABCD	Slovak. Hung. var.?
1131.	Kačerovski 5.	6,	4)④(4	VII–7		ABCC$_v$	

IX. 6, 7)④(5–8)⑤③; 3+3; a a b a

Current No	Original edition	Syll.	Last note of sections	Range	Rhythm. structure	Structure	Remarks
1132.	Kuba IX. 50.	6,	7)④(5	1–8		ABCD	German?
1133.	Kuhač 690.	6,	b3)⑤(b3	1–5		$ABAB_v$	
1134.	Kuhač 949.	6,	5)⑤(5	1–8		$ABAB_v$	
1135a.	Kuhač 285.	6,	6)⑤(5	V–6		$<AA_sA_{ss}A_{sss}$	
b.	" 286.	6,	"	VII–8		"	
1136.	Đorđević 102 (=Đorđević Nar. Pes. p. 169/1)	6,	8)⑤(b3	1–b9		$AB^5A_vB_v$	pentat., s.e. „transposing" structure
1137.	Kuba B.H. 176.	6,	1)①(1	V–4	♫♩|♪♩♪||	AABB	Russian? (cf. Balakirev)
1138.	Kuhač 425.	6,	5)②(5	1–6	♫♩|♩♫||	ABB_vB_s	Hung. var.?
1139a.	Kuhač 330.	6,	1)(b3)(5	1–8	♫♩|♪♩♪||	$AA^3A^5_vB$	Hung. var.
b.	" 497.	6,	1)(b3)(b3	1–b6	"	ABBC	
c.	" 775.	6,	1)④(5	1–5	"	AA^3BC	
1140.	Kuhač 1119.	6,	4)(b3)(b3	1–5	♩♫|♩♫||	$<ABA_sB_s$	„poskočnica"
1141.	Kuhač 663.	6,	1)④(1	1–5	♫♩|♩♫||	$AA^3_vAA_v$	Slovak. Hung. var.?
1142a.	Kuhač 209.	6,	4)④(4	#VII–8	♫♩|♫♩||	ABA_vB_v	Var.: Bartók, Colinde No. 12 (d.e. and s.–v.)
b.	" 944.	6,	2)(VII)(2	VII.–5	♫♩♪♪♯♫||	ABCB	
1143a.	Kuhač 397.	6,	2)⑤(2	V–5	♫♩|♪♩♪||	$<AA^4AB$	Hung. var.
b.	" 625.	6,	"	"	"	"	
1144a.	Kuhač 1212.	6,	b3)①(b3	VII–b6	♩♩♩|𝅗𝅥♩|𝅗𝅥.	$<A^4A_vAB$	„svatovska"
b.	" 1213.	6,	"	"	"	"	„svatovska"
d.	" 1214.	6,	[)O](VII		"		„svatovska"
c.	" 1215.	6,	b3)①(b3	VI–4	a a b a; a = [illegible]; b = [illegible]		
1145a.	Kuhač 1324.	6,	V)①(3	V–5	a a b a; a = [illegible]; b = [illegible]	AA^3_vBC	Slovak. German var.
b.	Kuba IX. 55.	6,	"	"	"	"	
c.	Kuhač 1323.	6,	III)(V)(1	III–6	"	"	
1146.	Kuhač 549.	6,	1)③(1	1–6	a a b a; a = [illegible]; b = [illegible]	AA^3BA	< new Hung. mel.
1144bis.	Kuhač 927.*	6,	7)(b3)(b3	1–7	♩♫|♩♩|𝅗𝅥	$<A^5B^5AB$	old Hungar. mel. From Fr. Sušil's collect.!!

Current No	Original edition	Syll.	Last note of sections	Range	Rhythm. structure	Structure	Remarks
1147.	Kuhač 538	6,	4)③V	V–5	aaba	AA_5BC	
1148a.	Kuhač 1469.	6,	3)③1	1–5	aaba	ABCD	
b.	Đorđević Nar. Pes. p. 102/1	6,	"	"	"	"	
1149a.	Kuhač 713.	6,	1)④1	VII–4	aaab	$ABAB_v$	
b.	Kuba XIII. 48.	6,	b3)b3 1	VII–4	"	AAA_vB	
1150a.	Kuhač 258.	(10) 6,	1)b2 b6	1–b6	aaab	AA^5A_vB	
b.	" 701a)	(10) 6,	1)b2 1	bVII–4	"	AA^5AB	
c.	Kuba X. 30.	(10) 6,	VII)b2 b6	VII–b6	"	AA^5A_vB	
d.	Kuhač 700.	(10) 6,	bVII)VII bVII	bVII–b3	"	AA^5AB	
e.	" 431.	(10) 6,	1)VII bVII	bVII–4	"	$AA_5A_{55}B$	
f.	" 701b)	6,					confused
1151.	Kuhač 896.	6,	3)③3	VII–5	aabb	AABB	
1152.	Kuba B.H. 663.	6,	VII)VII 2	VII–b3	aabb	$AABB_v$	
1153.	Kuhač 824.	6,	8)⑤2	1–b10	abab	ABCD	two last notes: evidently a misprint (should be a maj. sixth lower)
1154.	Kuba X. 48.	6,	?	?	abab	?	three part song; not clear which one is the main part.
1155.	Kuba IX. 51.	6,	VII)①VII	VII–4	abab	$ABAB_v$	
1155bis a.	Kuhač 308.	6,	1)b2 VII	VII–4	abab	ABA_5B_5	
1156a.	Kuhač 1381.	6,	1)b3 1	VII–4	abab	ABA_vC	
b.	Kuba IX. 58.	6,	"	1–4	"	ABAC	
1157.	Kuhač 1261.	6,	3)③3	1–5	"	$ABAB_v$	"svatovska"
1158a.	Kuhač 419.	6,	b3)④b3	1–4	"	$ABAB_v$	
b.	" 420.	6,					fragment
1159.	Kuhač 252.	6,	7)⑤b3	1–8	"	$A^5B^5AB_v$	> Hung. urban mel., 2nd half! (Simonffy)
1160a.	Kuhač 367.	6,	1)⑤1	1–6	abab	ABCD	Slovakian ?
b.	" 518.	6,	"	1–6	"	"	
1155bis b.	Kuhač 1347.	6, 7, 6, 7,	b3)b2 b2	VII–4		ABA_5B_{5v}	

Current No	Original edition	Syll.	Last note of section	Range	Rhythm structure	Structure	Remarks
⊕1161.	Kuhač 1276.	6,	3) (2) (1	1–5	a b a b; a = [illegible]; b = [illegible]	ABB_sC	"svatovska" "Slovak. Hung. ?
1163 a.	Kuba B.H. 941.	6,	1) (1) (1	1–5	a b a b; a = [illegible]; b = [illegible]	$ABAB_v$	
b.	" " 123.	6,	"	1–5	"	ABA_vB_v	word interr.: 6,6, 1 2 5,6,
c.	" " 431.	6,	"	1–5	"	$ABAB_v$	
d.	" " 904.	(10) ↖! 6,	"	VII–4	"	$ABAB_v$	swallowing of last syll.
e.	" " 124.	6,	VII) (1) (1	VII–5	"	ABA_vC	word interr.: 6,6, 1 2 5,6,
f.	Kuhač 412.	6,	1) (VII) (1	VII–4	"	$ABAB_v$	
g.	Kuba B.H. 942.	(10) ↖! 6,	"	VII–4	"	"	word interr.: 6,6, 1 2 5, 6,
↕1162.	Kuba IX. 7.	6,	1) (1) (1	1–4	"	$ABAB_v$	three part song
1164.	Kuhač 842.	6,	#VII) (2) (V	V–5	"	ABCD	
1165 a.	Kuhač 316.	6,	3) (2) (2	1–b6	"	ABCD	
b.	Dorđević 343. (=Dorđević Nar. Pev. p. 103/2)	(10) ↖! 6,	2) (b3) (2	1–5	"	$ABAB_v$	
c.	Bosiljevac 22.	6,	4) (4) (4	1–5	"	"	
1166 a.	Kuhač 413.	6,	3) (2) (3	1–5	"	$ABAB_v$	
b.	" 131.	6,	"	1–8	"	"	
1167 a.	Kuba B.H. 851.	6,	b3) (b3) (b3	1–4	"	$ABAB_v$	
b.	" " 852.	6,	"	1–4	"	"	
1168 a.	Kuba B.H. 15.	6,	1) (3) (2	V–5	a b b a; a = [illegible]; b = [illegible]	ABB_sA	Slovakian mel.
b.	" " 17.	6,	"	V–6	"	"	
c.	Dorđević Nar. Pev. p. 107/1	6,	"	V–5	"	"	
d.	Kuhač 381.	6,	"	"	"	"	
e.	" 113.	6,	1) (3) (4	V–6	"	ABB^sC	
f.	Kuba B.H. 18.	6,	1) (2) (1	V–5	"	ABB_sC	
g.	Kuhač 799.	6,	1) (5) (3	1–5	"	ABA_sA	
1169.	Kuba B.H. 375.	6,	5) (1) (5	1–5	a b a c; a = [illegible]; b = [illegible]; c = [illegible]	$ABAB_v$	Slovak. ?

Current №	Original edition	Syll.	Last note of section	Range	Rhythm. structure	Structure	Remarks
1170.	Kuhač 91.	6,	1)④(3	V–6	a b a c; a: [illegible] b: [illegible] c: [illegible]	ABCD	Slovak. Hung.?
1171.	Kuhač 206.	6,	b6)④(4	1–b9	a b a c; a: [illegible] b: [illegible] c: [illegible]	ABCD	Slovak. Hung.
1172–3	Kuhač 1486.	7,	VII)(VII)(VII	VII–4		AABC	
1174.	Kuba XIV. 30b)	7,	b2)(VII)(4	VII–4		ABA_vB_v	"pripjev to XIV 30a)!
1175.	Kuba B.H. 168.	7,	1)①(1	1–4		$ABBB_v$	
1176.	Kuba XII. 51.	7,	1)①(3	IV–5		AABC	
1177.	Kuba B.H. 502.	7,	2)①(2	VII–4		ABA_vB	
1178.	Kuba B.H. 692.	7,	2)①(2	VII–5		ABA_vB	
1179a.	Kuhač 724.	7,	b3)①(b3	VII–b3		$ABAB_v$	
b.	" 725.	(7) 7, 7, 11,	VII)①	VII–b3		ABB_v	
1180.	Kuhač 1131.	7,	b3)①(4	VII–4		AA_vBB_v	"pljeskavica"
1181a.	Kuhač 1482.	7,	b3)①(4	1–4		ABB_vA_v	
b.	Kuba B.H. 435.	7,	4)①(4	1–5		$ABAB_v$	
c.	Đorđević 279.	7,	b3)①(b3	1–4		ABAB	igra
1182a.	Kačerovski 4a)	7,	3)①(8	1–8	going in "imaginary" thirds	AA_vBC	
b.	Kuba B.H. 11.	7,	1)①(b6	VII–b6		AABC	kolo
1183.	Iz Levča 42.	7,	2)②(1	VII–4		ABA_vB_s	cf.: Bartók, Rumanian Folkmusic II. N° 492.
1184.	Kuba B.H. 54.	7,	4)②(4	VII–7		ABCD	line interv.: 7, 7, 4–3, 7,
1185.	Kuhač 988.	7,	5)②(5	1–5		$ABAB_v$	
1186.	Kuhač 353.	7,	2)(b3)(1	1–5		AA_vBB	
1187.	Kuba B.H. 127.	7,	b3)(b3)(1	1–b6		AA_vBB	
1188a.	Kuhač 1407.	7,	5)(b3)(b2	VII–b6		$< AA_sA_{ss}A_{sss}$	
b.	Kuba B.H. 99.	7,	4)①(b3	1–b6		ABCD	
1189a.	Kuhač 268.	7,	1)③(3	V–6		$< AA^3A^3B$	Hung. var.? Tertia 4line-stanzas,
b.	" 267.	7,	VII)①(4	bVI–4	going in "imaginary" thirds	$AA^3A^3_vA^3_v$	with rimes.

IX. 7, 1)(5)(6 – 6)(5)(4; 3+4; aaba–abba
8, 1)(V)(1 — VII)(VII)(VII

Current No	Original edition	Syll.	Last note of sections	Range	Rhythm. structure	Structure	Remarks
c.	" 1018.	7,	1)(3)[C]	V – 4		$AA^3[\,]B$	„igra"
1190.	Kuhač 1310.	7,	1)(5?)(6	1 – 10(?)		AA^5BA_v	N.B. 2nd section prob. in faulty transcription
1191.	Kuba B.H. 198.	7,	1)(5)(5	1 – 8		AA_v^5BC	
1192.	Kuhač 290.	7,	2)(5)(5	1 – b6		AA^4A_vB	< Hung. urban mel.
1193.	Kuhač 29.	7,	5)(5)(2	VII – 6		AABC	Hung. mel.
1194.	Kuhač 1287.	7,	5)(5)(3	1 – 6		ABCD	
1195a.	Kuba B.H. 165.	7,	6)(5)(2	1 – 8		AA_5BC	
b.	" " 167.	7,	6)(5)(3	1 – 8		"	
c.	" " 166.	7,	6)(5)(4	1 – 9		AA_vBC	
1196.	Kuhač 1132 b)	7,	6)(5)(4	1 – 6		< $AA_5A_{55}A_{555}$	
1197a.	Kuba XI. 59.	7,	1)(1)(1	VII – b4	𝅗𝅥 ♩♩ | ♩♩♩♩ ‖		
b.	Kuba B.H. 666	7,	"	1 – 4	"		„kolo"
1198–9.	Kuhač 685.	7,	5)(5)(1	1 – 6	aaba; a = ♫♫ | ♩♩ | 𝅗𝅥 ‖; b = ♩♩ | ♩♩ | ♫♩ ‖	AABC	Hung. var.
1200.	Kuhač 674.	7,	1)(5)(2	V – 6	aabb; a = ♫♫ | ♫♩ ‖; b = ♫♫ | ♩♩ | 𝅗𝅥 ‖	ABCD	Hung. var.
1201a.	Kuhač 1298.	7,	1)(5)(4	#VII – 6	abba; a = ♫♫ | ♩♩ | 𝅗𝅥 ‖; b = ♫♫ | ♩♫ ‖	$AA_v^3A_v^2A$	< Slovakian mel.
b.	" 938.	7,	"	"	"	"	„svatovska"
c.	" 1299.	7,	1)(5)(3	#VII – 8	"	"	
1202.	Kuhač 1463.	8,	1)(V)(1	V – 3		$ABAB_v$	1st half of a Hung. var. (16, 16, 14, 13) (urban)
1203a.	Kuba XIII. 40.	8,	bVI)(bVI)(1	bVI – b6		AABC	
b.	Kuba B.H. 1050. Ms.	8,	bVI)(bVI)[C]			AA[ ]B	
1204.	Kuhač 409.	8,	1)(bVI)(bIII	bIII – 4		ABCD	
1205.	Đorđević 443.	8,	VI)(VI)(1	VI – b3		AABB	
1206a.	Iv. Levča 31.	8,	VII)(VII)(VII	VII – 4		$ABAB_v$	„sedeljka"
b.	Kuhač 777.	8,	"	"		"	
1207.	Kuba B.H. 217.	8,	VII)(VII)(VII	VII – b6		$AAAA_v$	Rumanian ?

Current No	Original edition	Syll.	Last note of sections	Range	Rhythm. structure	Structure	Remarks
1208.	Kuhač 801.	8,	<VII)(VII)(1	VII-4		<AABB$_v$	free stanza structure Var.: Parry 34.
1209a.	Kuhač 1480.	8,	VII)(VII)(1	VII-4		AAA^{5}B	"beggar's song"
b.	" 1484.	8,	VII)(VII)(2	"		AABC	
c.	" 1485.	8,	1)(1)(4	1-5		AABC	
d.	" 1487.	7, 7, 8, 8, < 8,	1)(1)(b3	VII-4		AAA$_v$B	
1210.	Kuba B.H. 967. Ms.	8,	1)(VII)(1	VII-b6		ABAB$_v$	
1211.	Kuhač 921.	8,	VII)(1)(VII	bVI-4	[Kb. ♪♪♪♪ | ♫♪𝅗𝅥 ‖]	AA^{5}AB	Hung. var.? (2)(3)(2)
1212a.	Bosiljevac 42.	8,	VII)(1)(VII	VI-4		ABCB	
b.	Kuba B.H. 591.	8,	"	VII-5		"	
c.	~~Đorđević~~ Nar. Pev. p. 25/1	8,	VII)(1)[C]			AB[ ][ ]	
1213.	Kuhač 604.	8,	1)(1)(VII	VI-b6		AABA$_v$	
1214a.	Kuhač 1211.	8,	1)(1)(1	VII-4		ABAB	"from 1836"
b.	" 32.	8,	b3)(b2)(b3	VII-5		ABAC	
1215.	Kuba B.H. 672.	8,	1)(1)(1	VII-5		AABB	
1216.	Kuba B.H. 170.	8,	1)(1)(1	VII-5		AABB	
1217.	Kuba B.H. 196.	8,	1)(1)(1	1-8	[Kb. parlando]	ABBC	old Turkish-Hungarian md.? (free stanza str.?)
1218.	Kuba X.1.	8,	b2)(1)(b2	VII-b3		AA$_v$AA$_v$	
1219.	Kuhač 98.	8,	b2)(1)(b2	1-4		ABAB	
1220.	Kuba IX. 37.	8,	2)(1)(1	1-7		ABCC	old Hung.? (free stanza str.?)
1221.	Kuhač 1471.	8,	2)(1)(b3	1-4		ABCC$_v$	
1222.	~~Đorđević~~ 171.	8,	b3)(1)(2	1-5		ABC~~D~~	"igra"
1223.	Bartók M.F. 3690 Ms. Temesmonostor	8,	b3)(1)(b3	IV-4		AA$_5$BA$_v$	two part song
1224.	Kuhač 311.	8,	b3)(1)(b3	VII-b6		ABAB$_v$	
1225.	Kuhač 410.	8,	b3)(1)(b3	1-4		ABAB	
1226.	Kuhač 283.	8,	b3)(1)(4	VII-b6		ABCB	
1216 bis.	Kuhač 5a)	8,	1)(1)(1	VI-b6		AABC	

Current №	Original edition	Syll.	Last note of sections	Range	Rhythm. structure	Structure	Remarks
1227.	Kuhač 1481.	8,	3)①(1	1–5		ABBC	„beggar's song"
1228.	Kuhač 1477.	8,	3)①(8	1–8		ABCB	Hung. var.
1229a.	Kuba B.H. 299. (= Kuba XII. 56.)	8,	4)①(VII	VII–7		ABBC	Ruman. var.?
b.	Kuba B.H. 297.	8,	[>]①[C]			A[][]C	
1230a.	Kuba B.H. 256.	8,	4)①(1	1–5		ABCC	
b.	Đorđević Nar. Pev. p. 175,	8,	4)① [C]			AB[][]	
1231.	Đorđević 116.	8,	4)①(1	1–7	[Nb. parlando;? Pirot	ABCD	old Hungar. mel.
1232.	Đorđević 204.	8,	4)①(4	VII–5		AA$_v$BB$_v$ (=A+B, A+B$_v$, C+BC+B$_v$]	igra
1233.	Kuhač 810.	8,	4)(♭2)(4	1–♭6		ABAB$_v$	Beethoven Pastorale, last mov.
1234.	Kuba X. 9.	8,	1)②(1	1–6		ABAC	„koleda" (not a real one!)
1235.	Kuhač 1549.	8,	2)②(2	1–5		AABB$_{3v}$	Hung. var.
1236.	Kuhač 1468.	8,	2)②(3	1–5		AABB$_3$	
1237.	Kuhač 1416.	8,	♭3)②(♭3	1–♭6		ABAB$_v$	
1238.	Kuba B.H. 677.	8,	4)②(4	VII–5		ABA$_v$B$_v$	line interr.: 8, 8, 4+4, 8,
1239.	Kuba B.H. 990. Ms.	8,	5)②(2	1–5		ABB$_{v1}$B$_{v2}$	
1240.	Kuhač 524.	8,	5)②(5	1–8		ABB$_v$C	urban Hungar. var.
1241a.	Kuba B.H. 644.	8,	♭3)(♭3)(1	VII–5		AABC	
b.	" " 643	8,	♭3)[ ](1			A[]B[]	
1242.	Kuba B.H. 100. (=Kuba XIII. 2.)	8,	♭3)(♭3)(1	1–♭6		AAA$_3$B	
1243a.	Kuba B.H. 1044. Ms.	8,	♭3)(♭3)(1	1–7		AABB	
b.	" " 1052. Ms.	8,	"	"		"	
c.	" " 1048. Ms.	8,	"	VII–7		"	
d.	Kuba B.H. 1046. Ms.	8,	"	1–♭6		"	
e.	" " 1045. Ms.	8,	"	VII–5		"	
f.	" " 1047. Ms.	8,	♭6)(♭6)(1	VII–♭9		AABB$_v$	confused

Current No	Original edition	Syll.	Last note of section	Range	Rhythm. structure	Structure	Remarks
1244.	Kuhač 204.	8,	♭3)(♭3)(2	VII – 5		ABAB$_v$	
1245a.	Đorđević Nar. Pev. p. 52/1	8,	♭3)(♭3)(♭3	V – 8		AA$_v$BC	urban text in stanza structure
b.	Kačerovski 7.	8,	♭3)(♭3)(5	"		AABC	
1246a. ⊕	Kuba IX. 56.	8,	♭3)(♭3)(♭3	♭VI – ♭6		ABCD	
d.	Kuhač 686.	8,	1)(1)(1	♭VI – 4		AB AB$_v$	
e.	Kuhač 688.	8,	1)(1)[ ]			AB[ ][ ]	
f.	" 687.	8,	"			"	
g.	" 406.	8,	"			"	
h.	" 407.	8,					confused.
b.	" 297.	8,	1)(♭3)(1	VII – 4		ABAB$_v$	
c.	" 74.	8,	♭2)(♭3)(♭2	VI – 5		"	
i.	" 784.	8,	1)(1)[ ]			AB[ ][ ]	
j.	" 559.	8,					confused
k.	" 189.	8,	♭3)(1)[ ]			AB[ ][ ]	
l.	" 557.	8,	♭2)(1)[ ]			"	
⊕ m.	" 785.	8,	♭3)(1)[ ]			"	
o.	" 567.	8, 7,	1)(1)[ ]			"	
p.	" 786.	10,	"			"	
1247a.	Kuba B.H. 1010. Ms.	8,	♭3)(♭3)(♭3	VII – 7		ABBC	free stanza structure? < Turkish-Hungar. type; Var. Rang 36. Cf. No 1268.
b.	" " 1014. Ms.	8,	♭3)(VII)(VII	VII – 7		"	
c.	Đorđević Nar. Pev. p. 10/1	8,	♭3)(1)(♭3	1 – 8		ABCB	
1248.	Kuhač 925.	8,	5)(♭3)(5	1 – 8		ABCD	Turkish Hungar. type. From Fr. Šušil's collect.!!
1249.	Kuba B.H. 975. Ms.	8,	3)(3)(1	sic! #VII – ♭6		AABB	
1250.	Kuhač 400.	8,	2)(3)(2	1 – 6		AA^{3}AB	1-st half of an urban Hungar. mel.
1251.	Đorđević 115. (= Đorđević Nar. Pev. p. 27/1)	8,	3)(3)(3	1 – 6		AABB$_v$	Hungar. var.?
1246n.	Bosiljevac 20.	8,	1)(1)[ ]			AB[ ][ ]	

Current No	Original edition	Syll.	Last note of sections	Range	Rhythm. structure	Structure	Remark
1252.	Kuhač 800.	8,	3)③(3	1–8		AABC	< Hungar. mel.
1253.	Kuhač 924.	8,	3)③(5	1–5		AABB$_v$	< Hungar. mel.
1254a.	Kuba B.H. 1043. Ms.	8,	3)③(5	1–8		AABC	
b.	" " 1042. Ms.	8,	3)③(1	1–8		AA$_v$BB	inverted: the two halfs ought to be exchanged
1255a.	Kuhač 1442.	8,	5)③(2	V–6		AA$_{5v}$BB$_v$	< Hungar. mel.
b.	" 63b)	8,					fragment
c.	" 63a)	8,					fragment
d.	" 471.	8,					confused fragments
1256.	Kuba B.H. 934.	8,	4)④(VII	VII–5		AA$_v$BC	
1257.	Kuhač 1130.	8,	4)④(VII	VII–5		AABC	pljeskavica
1258.	Kuba B.H. 46.	8,	4)④(1	1–7		AABB	
1259a.	Kuba XI. 15.	8,	4)④(4	#VII–b6		AABB$_v$	Hungar. Ruman. var.?
b.	Bartók M.F. 1712b) Ms, Sarafdo	8,	4)④(2	1–b6		AA$_v$BC	swallowing of last syll.
1260.	Kuhač 1057.	8,	4)④(5	1–7		AABC	kolo Hungar. var.?
1261.	Kuhač 1488.	8,	5)④(1	1–b6		AA$_5$BB$_v$	"beggar's song" < Hungar. mel.
1262.	Kuhač 281.	8,	1)⑤(5	1–8		AA^{5}A^5_vA	new Hungar. mel.
1263.	Kuba B.H. 163. (= Kuba XIV. 19.)	8,	?5)⑤(1?	1–7?		AA$_v$BB$_v$	three last notes perhaps wrong.
1264.	Đorđević Nar. Pev. p. 123/1	8,	5)⑤(1	1–8		ABCD	Hungar. var.?
1265.	Manojlović 3.	8,	5)⑤(2	VII–8		AABC	
1266a.	Kuba B.H. 94.	8,	5)⑤(b3	1–b6		AAA$_{v1}$A$_{v2}$	
b.	" " 442.	8,	5)⑤(5	"		AABB$_v$	
1267.	Kuba B.H. 1078. Ms.	8,	5)⑤(4	1–8		AABC	
1268.	Đorđević 113.	8,	7)⑤(b3	1–8	Cf. No 1247 and Parry No 36.	ABCD	Turkish-Hungarian style
1269a.	Kuba B.H. 110.	8,	8)⑤(b3	1–b9		AA$_v$BC	Turkish-Hungarian style
b.	Kuba B.H. 1049. Ms. (= Kuba XII. 58.)	8,	8)(b3)(b3	"		"	

IX, 8, 8)⑤(4; ♫♫|♩♩|♩♩|
8b, 1)(VII)(1 – 1)①(·)

Current №	Original edition	Syll.	Last note of sections	Range	Rhythm. structure	Structure	Remarks
1270.	~~Đorđević Nar. Pev.~~ p. 153/1	8,	8)⑤(4	1–8		$A^5B^5A_vB_v$	old Hungar. type
1271a.	Kuhač 671.	8,	3)①(3	1–6	♫♫|♩♩|♩♩|	AA_vBB_v	Hungar. var.
b.	" 128.	8,	"	"	"	AA_vBA_v	
c.	" 1369.	8,	2)①(2	"	"	AA_vBB_v	
d.	" 1368.	8,	5)①(5	"	"	AA_vBA_v	
e.	" 1427.	8,			"		fragment
f.	" 707.	8,			"		fragment
1272.	Kuhač 814.	8,	b3)(b3)(1	VII–5	"	AABB	pentat. (accord. to Kuh. „Bulgarian"
1273a.	Kuhač 1371.	8,	5)③(3	1–8	"	AA_vBB_v	Hungar.-Croatian var.
b.	" 1115b)	8,	"	1–6	"	"	
c.	" 1107.	8,	"	1–8	"	"	„poskočnica"
d.	" 399.	8,	"	1–8	"	"	
e.	" 1001b)	8,	5)③(5	1–8	"	AA_{v1},AA_{v2}	„kolo"
f.	Kuba X. 2.	8, 8, 8+8, 7	5)③(3	1–8			contamination
1274.	Kuba B. H. 325.	8b,	1)(VII)(1	VII–4		ABCC	
⊗1275.	~~Đorđević~~ 6a)	8b,	4)(VII)(VII	VII–7		$ABBB_v$	Ruman. (Hungar.?) pentat. type
1277a.	Kuhač 158a)	8b,	VI)①(VII	VII–b6		ABAB	
b.	" 158b)	8b,	" .	"		"	
c.	Kuba IX. 57.	8b,	"	"		"	
1278.	Kuba XII. 23.	8b,	VII)①(VII	VII–7		ABA_vB	
↑1276.	Kuhač 299.	8b,	bVI)①(1	bVI–b6		ABCB	
1279a.	~~Đorđevic Nar. Pev.~~ p. 139/1	8b,	1)①(b2	1–5		AABC	
b.	" " " p. 163/2	8b,	b2)①(VII	VII–8		?	3.+4. section of preceding + new section + 4. sect. of prec.
1280a.	Kačerovski 66.	8b,	1)①(b3	VII–b6		$AABB_s$	
b.	Kuba IX. 9.	8b,	"	bVI–b6		AABC	

Current №	Original edition	Syll.	Last note of sections	Range	Rhythm. structure	Structure	Remarks
c.	Kuhač 535.	<8b,	"	"		"	
d.	Đorđević Nar. Pev. p. 141/1	<8b,	"	1–b6		"	
e.	Kačerovski 50.	<8b,	"	1–b6		"	
f.	Kuhač 533.	<8b,	"	1–4		AABA$_v$	
g.	" 534.	<8b,	1)①(5	1–8		AABA	
1281 a.	Kuba B.H. 732.	8b,	2)①(2	1–5		ABAB	word interr.: 8b, 8b, 1 ? 7, 8b,
b.	" " 681.	8b,	"	VII–5		"	word interr.: 8b, 8b, 1 ? 7, 8b,
c.	" " 684.	8b,	2)②(1	VII–4		"	line interr.: 8b, 5 ? 3, 8b, 8b,
d.	" " 676.	8b,	"	VII–5		AA$_v$BB	
1282.	Kuhač 485.	8b,	b3)①(b3	VII–4		ABAB	
1283 a.	Đorđević Nar. Pev. p. 164/1	8b,	4)①(4	1–9		ABCB	Slovakian var.
b.	Kuhač 1547.	9,	5)①(5	1–9		ABCC$_v$	
c.	" 1313 a)	9,	V)Ⓘⓘⓘ(1	I–2		ABCD	
d.	" 1313 b)	9,	"	"		"	
1284 a.	Kuba B.H. 422.	8b,	2)②(1	1–5		AABB	
b.	" " 421.	8b,	"	"		"	
c.	" " 205.	8b,	"	"		"	
1285 a.	Đorđević 420.	8b,	2)②(2	VII–4		AABB$_v$	„sedeljka"
b.	" 163. (=Đorđević Nar. Pev. p. 18/1)	8b,	"	VII–7		"	
c.	Đorđević 108.	8b,	2)②(4	VII–5		"	
d.	" 563.	8b,	"	1–b6		"	
e.	Bosiljevac 23.	8b,	"	1–7		"	
f.	Kuhač 659. (=Đorđević Nar. Pev. p. 68/1)	8b,	b3)(b3)(b3	1–5		AABB$_v$	
g.	Kuhač 657. 658.	8b,	"	VII–4		"	
h.	Iz Levča 58.	8b,	"	VII–4		AABB$_v$	
i.	" 70.	8b,	b3)(b3)[ ]			AA[ ]B	

Current No	Original edition	Syll.	Last note of section	Range	Rhythm. structure	Structure	Remarks
j.	Kuhač 18.	8♭,	♭3)(♭3)(♭3	♯VI–4		AABC	
1286.	Đorđević 150.	8♭,	♭3)(♭3)(1	1–♭6		$AABB_v$	„sedeljka"
1287.	Kuba B.H. 36.	8♭,	♭3)(♭3)(1	1–7		AABB	
1288.	Đorđević 38.	8♭,	♭3)(♭3)(♭3	1–♭6		$AABB_v$	
1289a.	Kuhač 1377.	8♭,	♭3)(♭3)(5	♯VII–5		$AABB_v$	Hungar. var. (1289a–b)
b.	" 913.	9,	1)(1)(♭3	♭VI–4	going in „imaginary" thirds	"	
1290.	Đorđević Nar. Pev. p. 142/1	8♭,	4)(♭3)(VII	VII–5		AA_vBB_v	
1291.	Đorđević 176	8♭,	♭3)(4)(♭3	1–8		AA_vBC	Transylv. Hungar. type
1292a.	Kuhač 525.	8♭,	4)(4)(1	1–5		AABB	
b.	Kuba B.H. 47. (= Kuba XIII. 16.)	8♭,	"	VI–6		"	
c.	Kuhač 526. (= Đorđević Nar. Pev. 91/1)	8♭,	"	VII–5		"	
1293.	Đorđević Nar. Pev. p. 110/1	8♭,	5)(5)(♭3	VII–7		AAB^4B_v	
1294.	Đorđević Nar. Pev. p. 46/1	8♭,	6)(6)(5	1–8		$AABB_v$	
1295.	Kuhač 884.	8,	1)(3)(3	V–5	aaba	AA^3BB_v	Hungar. Slovak. var.?
1296.	Kuba IX. 15.	8,	1)(1)(♭3	IV–5	aaba	AABA	two part song
1297.	Kuhač 560.	8,	1)(1)(3	1–9	aaba*	AABA	* prob. corrupt. of abba! then it would be: 1)(6)(5, ABB_5A Slovak. var.
1298a.	Kuhač 945. 946.*	8,	2)(2)(5	1–6	abab	ABCD	* with a slight change. Slovak var.?
c.	" 947.	8,	1)(2)(5	"	"	"	
b.	" 1031.	8,	2)(2)(5	"	"	"	„kolo" („from 1818")(?)
1299.	Kuba X. 21.	8,	VII)(♭3)(1	VII–♭6	abab	$ABCB_v$	
1300.	Kuhač 923.	8,	3)(3)(2	V–6	<abba	ABB_5C	Slovak. mel.
1301a.	Kuba B.H. 268.	8,	2)(2)(1	♯VII–5	aabc	AABC	Hungar. var. (1301a–b)
b.	Kuhač 180.	(10) 7. 10, 10, 8, 7,	2)(2)(2	1 "		"	
1302.	Kuhač 5b)	8,	3)(3)(3	V–6	aabc	AABC	Contamination, 1st half = 1st half of a Hung. mel.
1303a.	Kuhač 818.	8,	1)(2)(1	VII–5	abcc	AA_vBB	

IX. 9, —10, VII)(VII)(IV—VII)(VII)(VII

Current №	Original edition	Syll.	Last note of sections	Range	Rhythm. structure	Structure	Remarks
b.	" 850.	8,	4)②(4	VII-b6	aabb!	AAvBB	
c.	" 817.	(8) 8, 8, 11,	VII)(VII)(1	VII-4			fragments
d.	" 816.	8,					
1304.	Kuba B.H. 178.	9,	2)②(VII	IV-5		AABB	
1305.	Kuhač 1329.	9,	5)②(5	#VII-8		ABABv	
1306.	Kuhač 469.	9,	7)⑤(3	1-8		ABCCv	old-Hungar. mel.
1307.	Kuhač 163	(10)<9,	[ ) O](b3				2nd half of an old-Hungar. mel.
1308.	Kuba XII. 47.	9,	2)②(1	1-7	♩♭♩𝅗𝅥|♫♫♩♩|𝅗𝅥	AABB	
1309.	Đorđević Nar. Pe. p. 89/1	10,	VII)(VII)(IV	IV-b6		AABBv	
1310a.	Kuhač 1496.	10,	VII)(VII)(VII	VII-4			Motifs of the "heroic-poem" mel., wrongly squeezed into a 4 or more section structure
b.	" 1498.	10,	"	VII-b3			
c.	" 1499.	10,	"	VII-b5			
d.	" 1512.	10,	"	VII-4			
e.	" 1520.	10,	VII)(VII)(2	VII-4			
f.	" 1491.	10,	1)(VII)(VII	VII-5			
g.	Kuba B.H. 298 (= Kuba XIII. 15)	10,	1)(VII)(1	1-7			
h.	Kuhač 1500.	10,	1)①(1	1-4			
i.	" 1483.	10,	"	V-5			
j.	Kuba X. 36.	10,	"	1-5			
k.	Kuba B.H. 900.	10,	"	1-5			
l.	Kuba XII. 32.	10,	"	1-b6			
m.	Kuhač 1495.	10,	2)①(1	1-4			
n.	" 1519.	10,	b3)①(1	1-b5			
o.	Kuba IX. 39.	10,	2)②(1	1-5			
p.	Kuhač 1494.	10,	2)②(2	IV-5			

Current №	Original edition	Syll.	Last note of sections	Range	Rhythm. structure	Structure	Remarks
r.	" 1493.	10,					the same motifs, in 2 or 3 section struct.
s.	" 1501.	10,					
t.	" 1507.	10,					
u.	" 1550.	10,					
1311.	Kuba B.H. 153. (= Kuba XIII. 32)	10,	VII)(VII)(b3	VII–b6		$AABB_v$	
1312.	Đorđević Nar. Pev. p. 19/2	10,	2)(VII)(VII	VII–7		ABB_vC	
1314a.	Kuba B.H. 161. (= Kuba XII. 37.)	10,	1)(1)(b3	bVI–b6		AABC	Hungar. var. [3)(3)(5]
b.	Đorđević Nar. Pev. p. 158/1	10,	"	"		"	
1313a.	Kuba B.H. 225.	10,	b3)(VII)(2	VII–7		$ABCB_v$	"old" Hungarian?
b.	" " 226,	10,					fragments of a.
c.	" " 224.	10,					
d.	" " 227. (= Kuba XIII. 57.)	10,					
e.	Kuba B.H. 186.	10,					
f.	" " 220.	10,					
⊗1315.	Kuhač 1242.	10,	1)(1)(b3	VI–6		$AABB_v$	"svatovska"
1316.	Bosiljevac 24.	10,	2)(1)(2	VII–5		$ABAA_v$	
1317.	Kuba B.H. 197.	10,	5)(2)(4	1–8		ABB_vC	Hungar. var. ?
1318.	Kuba B.H. 48.	10,	b3)(b3)(1	VII–7		AABB	
1319a.	Kuba B.H.* 146.	10,	3)(3)(1	#VII–5		$AABB_v$	* perhaps a wrong figure: 164.? (cf. № 1537a.)
b.	" " 302.	10,	3)(3)(bVI	bVI–5		"	
c.	" " 985. Ms.	10,	b3)(b3)(1	1–5		"	
1320.	Kuba XI. 3.	10,	1)(1)(VII	VII–4	♩♩♩♩|♫♫♩♩‖	$AABB_v$	
1321.	Kuhač 1123.	10,	1)(1)(1	1–5	♩♩♩♩|♫♫♩♩‖	AAA_vA_v	"poskočnica"
1322.	Đorđević Nar. Pev. p. 186/1	10,	4)(3)(3	1–7	♩♩♩♩|♫♫♩♩‖	$AABB_v$	
1323.	Kuhač 1532.	10,	1)(7)(4	1–7	♩♩♩♩|♫♫♩.♪‖	AA^3A^3A	< Hungar. ?

IX. 10,(5+5); 10, aaba

Current №	Original edition	Syll.	Last note of sections	Range	Rhythm. structure	Structure	Remarks
1324a.	Đorđević 162. (= Đorđević Nar. Pev. p. 182/2)	10,	VII)(VII)(4	VII – 7	5+5	$AABB_v$	
b.	Đorđević 161.	"	b3)(b3)(b3	1 – 8	"	AABC	
c.	Đorđević 147. (= Đorđević Nar. Pev. p. 185/2)	"	4)(4)(b3	1 – b10	"	"	
1325a.	Kuba B.H. 304. (= Kuba XIII. 45.*)	10,	1)(1)(1	IV – b6	5+5	AABB	* some slight deviations
b.	Kuba B.H. 1083. Ms.	"	"	1 – 5	"	"	
c.	" " 1087. Ms.	"	5)(5)(1	1 – b6	"	"	
d.	" " 1090. Ms.	"	VII)(VII)[C]		"	AA [ ]B	
e.	" " 1085. Ms.	"	[ ](2)[C]		"	$[\,]A[\,]A_v$	
f.	" " 1086. Ms.	"	"		"	"	word interv.: 10, 1 2 9,
1326.	Kuba B.H. 1009.	10,	b2)(1)(b2	VI – 5	5+5	$AABB_v$	
1327a	Kuba B.H. 1081. Ms. (= Kuba XIII. 60)	10,	b3)(b3)(1	1 – #7	5+5,	AABB	
b.	Kuba B.H. 1082. Ms. (= Kuba XII. 59.)	10,	"	1 – 7	"	"	
c.	Kuba B.H. 1084. Ms.	10,	"	"	"	"	
d.	" " 1088. Ms.	10,	b3)(b3)(b3	1 – b6	"	"	
e.	" " 1089. Ms.	10,	[b3](b3)(1	1 – 7	"	"	
f.	Đorđević Nar. Pev. p. 36/1	10,	VII)(VII)(1	VII – 8	"	$AABB_v$	
g.	Kuba B.H. 1079. Ms. (= Kuba XIII. 58.)	10,	1)(VII)(VII	VII – b6	"	AA_vBB_v	
h.	Kuba B.H. 1080. Ms	(10 or 5?) 10, 10, 10, 5,	1)(1)(1	1 – b6	10 = 5+5	$AAAA_{2*}$	* 2nd half
1328.	Kuba XI. 62b)	10,	5)(3)(1	#VII – #7	5+5	ABCC	
1329a.	Kuba B.H. 1075. Ms.	10,	5)(5)(3	1 – 8	5+5	$AABB_v$	
b.	" " 1076. Ms.	10,	#4)(#4)(1	VI – 8	"	AABB	
1330a.	Kuba B.H. 56.	10,	2)(1)(VII	VII – 7	a a b a; a = [illegible]; b = [illegible]	$ABCB_v$	
b.	Kuhač 184.	10,	"	VII – 5	a a b a; a = [illegible]; b = [illegible]	ABCB	
c.	Kuba B.H. 55.	10,	2)(2)(2	VII – 7	"	AA_vBA_v	
d.	Kuhač 1024.	10,	4)(VII)(1	VII – 4	"	$ABCC_v$	

IX. 10, aabb; 11, — 12,

Current №	Original edition	Syll.	Last note of section	Range	Rhythm. structure	Structure	Remarks
1331.	Kuba B.H. 5. (= Kuba XII. 21.)	10,	VI) (VI) (1	VI – 5	a a b b; a = ♪♪♪♪ ; b = ♪♪♪	AABB	
1332 a.	Kuba B.H. 76. (= Kuba XIII. 23.)	11,	1) (1) (1	VII – 5		AABB	
b.	Kuba B.H. 77.	11,	"	"		"	
c.	Đorđević Nar. Rev. p. 122/1	11,	"	VII – b6		"	
1333.	Kuba XIII. 12.	11,	[>0] (1 ?	1 – 8		[ ] [ ] BA	< new Hungar. ? (1) (5) (1, ABBA ?)
1334.	Kuba XII. 5.	11,	3) (1) (1	VII – b6		AA$_v$BB	
1335–6.	Kuhač 780.	11,	1) (5) (5*	1 – 11		ABBA*	* however, the order of sections is here: B B A A ! (1)(5 D. new Hung. mel.
1337 a.	Kuhač 1405.	11,	5) (5) (1	V – 7	♪♪♪	AABA	Hungar. urban mel. var.
b.	" 165.	12,	1) [0] (5	V – 8	"		
1339 a.	Kuhač 1551.	[< 11] 13,	2) (1) [C]		a a b b; a = ♪♪♪; [b = ♪♪♪]	AA$_s$ [ ] [ ]	1st half of a Hungar. urban melody (Cselogár)
b.	" 1553.	"	4) (3) [?]		"	"	
1338 a.	Kuba B.H. 968. Ms.	11,	b3) (b3) (1	1 – 7	♪♪♪	AA BB	
b.	" " 1119. Ms.	11,	"	"	"	"	
c.	Kuba B.H. 247.	11,	"	"	"	"	
1340.	Kuhač 1233.	12,	2) (1) (2	1 – 6		AA$_v$BA$_v$	„svatovska": not a real old one, it has text st.-s and rymes! urban!!
1341.	Đorđević Nar. Rev. p. 101/1	12,	4) (1) (2	VII – 7		AA$_v$BB$_v$	
1342.	Kuba XII. 45.	(10) +. 12,	1) (2) (2*	1 – 6		ABBA*	order of sections here: AABB (1)(2)(2 ! New Hungar. mel.
1343.	Kuhač 832.	12,	5) (4) [C]			AA$_s$ [ ] [ ]	contamination; 1st half < Hungar. mel.
1344.	Kuhač 1109.	12,	6) (4) (3	1 – 9		A^{4}A^4_vAA$_v$	„poskočnica"
1345.	Kuhač 1315.	12,	1) (1) (5	VI – 6		AABB	German mel. (accord. to Kuhač, too: „nosi biljeg Njemstva")
1346.	Kuba XIV. 16.	12,	#7) (1) (1	1 – 8		AA$_v$BB	
1347.	Kuhač 1546.	12,	2) (1) (V	V – 6		ABCB	probably contamination: two differ. 6, melodies!
1348.	Kuhač 512.	12,	1) (5) (5	1 – b10		AA^{5}BA	Hungar. urban mel.
1349.	Kuba XII. 52.	12,	1) (1) (5	VII – 7	♪♪♪	AABC	
1350.	Kuhač 1552.	(10) 12,	1) (1) (1	VII – 4	a a b a; a = ♪♪♪; b = ♪♪♪	AABA	

IX. 12, – 14; X. zzZz (1.)

Current No	Original edition	Syll.	Last note of section	Range	Rhythm. structure	Structure	Remarks
1351.	Đorđević 89.	12,	1)①(4	VII – 4	a a b b a = [illegible] b = [illegible]	AABB$_v$	„čilimarska"
1352a.	Kuhač 1308.	(7) +. 13,	1)①(1	V – 4	[illegible]	AABB	German and Hungar. var.
b.	" 1307.	"	"	"	"	"	urban!
1353.	Kuba B.H. 12.	13,	1)①(5	#VI – 8	"	ABCC$_v$	
1354.	Kuba IX. 2.	13,	4)①(5	VII – 7	[illegible]	ABA$_v$B$_v$	
1355.	Kuhač 1122.	14,	VII)①(b3	VII – 4		AA$_{v_1}$A$_{v_2}$A$_{v_3}$	„poskočnica"
1356.	Kuhač 1385.	14,	1)①(VII)	bVI – 4		AABA	
1357a.	Kuhač 906.	(10) 14,	2)①(5	1 – #7		AA$_v$BB$_v$	Haydn symphony
b.	" 905.	(10) <14,	"	V – 6		"	
1358a.	Iz Levoča 22	14,	4)①[(]	VII – 5		AA$_v$[ ][ ]	„sedeljka"
b.	Kuba B.H. 404.	(10) 14,	"	1 – 4		"	
c.	Đorđević 209.	* 2	1)①(1	VII – 5		AA$_{v_1}$A$_{v_2}$A$_{v_3}$	* instrumental piece „igra"
1359.	Đorđević Nar. Pev. p. 191/1	(8) +. 14,	4) ①(4	VII – b6		AA$_{v_1}$A$_{v_2}$A$_{v_3}$	
1360.	Kuhač 1102.	(10) 14,	5)①(5	V – 5		AA$_v$BB$_v$	„poskočnica"
1361.	Kačerovski 6.	14,	5)①(5	1 – 8		AA$_{v_1}$A$_{v_2}$A$_{v_3}$	Hungar. Ruman. var.
1362.	Đorđević 1.	(10) +. 14,	b3)(b3)(1	VII – 7		AABC	„igra"
1363.	Kuhač 86.*	14,	3)③(3	1 – 6		AABB$_v$	* K. published it inverted: 2nd half + 1st half!
1364.	Kuba B.H. 199. (= Kuba XIV. 17.)	14,	[1)○](2	1 – 8		[ ][ ]BA	new Hungar. mel.: A B B A 1) ⑤(2

X. Heterometric four-section melodies

Current No	Original edition	Syll.	Last note of section	Range	Rhythm. structure	Structure	Remarks
1365.	Kuba B.H. 363.	(8) zzZz 1. 4, 4, 8, 4,	2)①(1	1 – 5		AA$_{5v}$BC	„kolo" Slovakian var.?
1366.	Kuba B.H. 60	(5) zzZz 1. +. 5, 5, 6, 5,	5)(VII)(4	VII – 8	6, = [illegible]	ABCB$_v$	
1367a.	Kuba XII. 1.	(5) zzZz 1. +. 5, 5, 6, 5,	2)②(b2	1 – b6	6 = [illegible]	AABA$_v$	
b.	Đorđević 85.	"	b2)(b2)(b2	"	6, = [illegible]	"	„čilimarska"
1368.	Đorđević 54.	zzZz 1. 5, 5, 8, 5	b3)(b3)(1	1 – 5		AABC	
1369.	Kuhač 322.	zzZz 1. 5, 5, 8, 5,	5)③(3	#VI – 6		ABCD	

Current No	Original edition	Syll.	Last note of section	Range	Rhythm. structure	Structure	Remarks
1370a.	Kuhač 280.	zzZz 1. 5, 5, 8, 5,	5) (3) (6	1–8		AA_3BC	Slovakian var. text-stanza structure with rimes
b.	" 78. *	"	b3) (1) (1	VI–b6		"	* text in Czech language?
1371a.	Kuba B.H. 132.	(5) zzZz 1. r. 5, 5, 9, 5,	4) (b3) (1	VI–b6		ABCD	
b.	" " 148. (= "Kuba" XIII. 42.)	"	"	"		"	
1372-3	Kuba IX. 23.	zzZz 1. 6, 6, 7, 6,	1) (1) (1	VII–5		$AABA_v$	two part song
1374.	Kuhač 1141.	(6) zzZz 1. 6, 6, 8, 6,	VII) (VII) (b3	VI–b3		AABC	„balkanka" (igra?)
1375.	Kuba B.H. 511.	(10) zzZz 1. 6, 6, 8, 6,	VII) (1) (VII	VII–4		ABCD	
1376.	Kuhač 145.	zzZz 1. 6, 6, 8, 6,	1) (1) (b3	1–4		AABC	maccaronico (i.e. mixed language, in this case Hung. and S.Croat.)
1377.	Kuhač 570.	zzZz 1. 6, 6, 8, 6,	2) (2) (1	VII–5		AABC	text-stanza struct, rimes
1378.	Kuba B.H. 242.	zzZz 1. 6, 6, 8, 6,	5) (b3) (1	VII–7		ABCD	
1379.	Kuba B.H. 441.	zzZz 1. 6, 6, 8, 6,	5) (b3) (1	1–b6		ABB_vC	
1380.	Kuhač 804.	zzZz 1. 6, 6, 8, 6,	1) (4) (2	1–5		ABCD	
1381a.	Kuhač 1421.	zzZz 1. 7, 7, 8, 7,	1) (1) (VII	VII–4		AAA_vB	text-stanza struct. with rimes
b.	Kuba IX. 18.	"	1) (1) (1	1–4		AABA	
c.	" X. 23.	"	"	"		"	three part song
1382.	Kuhač 1124.	zzZz 1. 7, 7, 8, 7,	1) (1) (2	VII–4		AABA	poskočnica
1383.	Kuba B.H. 843.	(7) zzZz 1. (r.) 7, 7, 8, 7,	b3) (b3) (1	VII–4		$AABB_v$	
1384a.	Kuhač 1330.	zzZz 1. 7, 7, 8, 7,	1) (3) (5	1–6		AA^3BC	German mel.
b.	" 904. *	8, 8, 6, 7	bIII) (1) (b3	bIII–4		"	* iz Jitra u gornoj Lužici u kralj. Saskoj!!!
1385a.	Kuba B.H. 25.	(10) zzZz 1. (r.) 7, 7, 10, 7,	1) (1) (5	1–5		$AABA_v$	
b.	" " 26 (= Kuba XIV. 15.)	"	"	"		"	
1386.	Kuhač 231.	(8) zzZz 1. r. 8, 8, 10, 8,	VII) (VII) (VII	VI–5		$AABB_v$	
1387.	Kuhač 153.	(7) ZZzZ 2. r. 7, 7, 4, 7,	5) (4) (1	1–8		ABCD	rimes
1388a.	Kuba XIV. 28.	(7) ZZzZ 2. r. 7, 7, 5, 7,	1) (1) (1	VII–5		ABCD	Bulgarian var. inverted: two halves of mel. exchanged.
b.	Kuba B.H. 638.	"	"	"		$ABCB_v$	

Current No.	Original edition	Syll.	Last note of sections	Range	Rhythm. structure	Structure	Remarks
1388 c.	Kuba B.H. 637.	"	"	VII–4		ABCB	
d.	" " 491.	"	1)④(1	"		ABCBv	
1389.	Kuhač 377.	(8) ZZzZ 2. r. 11, 11, 8, 11,	2)②(4	V–5		AABC	Hungar., Ruman. var.
1390.	Kuhač 482.	ZZzZ 2. 13, 13, 11, 13	3)③(5	V–8		AABC	text-stanza struct. with rimes Hungar. var.
1391.	Kuhač 1328.	ZZzZ 2. 16, 16, 14, 16,	1)①(2	1–5		AABA	text-stanza struct., rimes < German
1392 a.	Kuba B.H. 23.	(11) ZZzZ 2. 17, [ ][ ][3+7]	1)[○(]			A[ ][ ][ ]	fragment (1st section) of a new Hungar. mel.
b.	" " 24. (= Kuba XIII. 7.)	?	?			?	fragment of the preceding fragment
1393.	Kuhač 571.	ZZzz 3. 7, 7, 5, 5,	V)①(5	V–5		AAvBC	text-stanzas, rimes Slovak. text-var.
1394.	Kuhač 175.	ZZzz 3. 7, 7, 6, 6,	VII)①(VII	VII–4		AA5AB	urban text, stanzas, rimes
1395.	Kuba XI. 21.	ZZzz 3. 7, 7, 6, 6,	5)♭3(♭3	1–7		ABCD	stanzas, rimes
1396 a.	Kuba XI. 19.	(10) ZZzz 3. 7, 7, 6, 6,	VII)VII(♭3	VII–4	*7, = ♫♩ | ♩♫♩ Po-še-ta-, po-še-ta-la	AAvBC	* Cf. No. 446. (similar break)
b.	Kuba B.H. 853.	"	VII)①(1	VII–4	"	AAvBB	
c.	" " 854.	"	1)①(1	"	"	AABB	
1397.	Kuhač 1264 b)	(8) ZZzz 3. r. 8, 8, 5, 5,	VII)VII(1	VII–♭6		AABB	„svatovska"
1398 a.	Đorđević 519.	ZZzz 3. 8, 8, 5, 5,	♭2)①(1	1–4		AABB	„žetvarska"
b.	" 520.	(8) 8, 8, 4, 7, r.	♭2)♭2(1	VII–4		"	„pripjev"
1399 a.	Kuhač 901.	ZZzz 3. 8, 8, 5, 5,	VII)②(1	VII–5		AA3BB	
b.	" 900.	"	"	"		"	
c.	" 903.	"	"	"		"	
d.	Kuba X. 19.	"	"	"		"	
e.	" XI. 13.	"	"	"		AA3vBB	
f.	Kuhač 695	(5) ZZzz 3. r. 7, 7, 5, 5,	1)②(1	"		AA3BB	
g.	Kuba B.H. 725.	ZZzz 3. 8, 8, 5, 5,	"	1–5		AA3v BB	
h.	" " 726.	"	2)②(1	"		AABB	
i.	Kuhač 902.	"	VII)①(1	VII–5		AA3BB	

Current №	Original edition	Syll.	Last note of section	Range	Rhythm. structure	Structure	Remarks
j.	Kuba XII. 11.	"	1)(1)(1	1–4		AABB	
k.	Kuba B. H. 727.	"	IV)(4)(1	IV–5		ABCC	
l.	Kuhač 694.	5, 7, 5, 5,	VII)(2)(1	VII–5		AA^3BB	
m.	" 693.	"	b VII)(1)(VII	V–4		AA^3BB_v	
n.	" 697.	7, 7, 5, [],	VII)(VII)[(]			AAB[ ]	
o.	" 696.	[], 8, 5, 5,	[ ])(2)(1			$[\,]A^3BB$	
1400.	Iz Levča 50.	(8) ZZzz 3. r. 8, 8, 5, 5,	2)(2)(b3	VII–b3		$AABB_v$	„sedeljka"
1401.	Kuhač 1401.	ZZzz 3. 8, 8, 6, 6,	VI)(VII)(VII	VI–4		AA^3BB_v	urban (text-stanzas, rime)
1402.	Kuba B. H. 13.	ZZzz 3. 8, 8, 6, 6,	4)(2)(2	V–6		A^3A_vBC	text-stanzas, rime
1403a.	Kuhač 1094.	ZZzz 3. 8, 8, 6, 6,	4)(4)(1	1–5		AABC	„poskočnica"
b.	" 1093.	"	4)(4)(4	"		"	" "
c.	" 1081.	?	?			?	free var. of a. b. „poskočnica"
1404a.	Đorđević 103. (= Đorđević Nar. Pev. p. 134/1)	(10) ZZzz 3. (r.) 8, 8, 6, 6,	5)(4)(4	1–5		$ABCC_v$	
b.	Đorđević 104.	?	?			?	free var. of a.
1405.	Đorđevic Nar. Pev. p. 6/1	(8b) ZZzz 3. r. 8b, 8b, 6, 6,	4)(b3)(1	VII–7		ABCD	
1406.	Kuba B. H. 631.	(11) ZZzz 3. 8, 8, 7, 7,	4)(VII)(VII	VII–5		ABCC	
1407.	Kuba B. H. 863.	ZZzz 3. 8, 8, 7, 7,	1)(1)(1	VII–4		AABB	
1408.	Kuhač 345.	ZZzz 3. 8, 8, 7, 7,	1)(1)(1	VII–5		AABB	urban; text-stanzas, rime
1409.	Kuhač 207.	ZZzz 3. 8, 8, 7, 7,	1)(1)(b3	1–b6		AABC	" "
1410.	Kuhač 323.	ZZzz 3. 8, 8, 7, 7,	b3)(1)(b3	VII–b6		ABA_vB_v	" "
1411.	Juž. Srb. 403.	ZZzz 3. 8, 8, 7, 7,	b2)(b2)(1	1–4		$AA_v, A_{v_2}A_{v_3}$	„slavska"
1412.	Kačerovski 40b)	ZZzz 3. 8, 8, 7, 7,	2)(2)(1	1–4		AA_vBB_v	
1413.	Kuba XIV. 1.	ZZzz 3. 8, 8, 7, 7,	5)(4)(1	1–7		ABCC	
1414.	Kuba B. H. 367.	ZZzz 3. 10, 10, 6, 6,	3)(3)(1	1–6		AABB	
1415	Kuhač 174.	(10) ZZzz 3. (r.) 10, 10, 6, 6,	1)(1)(1	1–5		AABC	

X. ZZzz (3.) 10,10,7,7,–15,15,10,10,
zzZZ (4.) 6,6,7,7,–8,8,10,10,

Current No	Original edition	Syll.	Last note of section	Range	Rhythm. structure	Structure	Remarks
1416 a.	Đorđević 285.	ZZzz 3. 10, 10, 7, 7,	2) ② (VII	VII – b3		AA$_v$BB$_v$	„lazarička"
b.	" 286.						" 2nd half of a.
1417 a.	Kuba B.H. 414.	(10) ZZzz 3. +. 10, 10, 8, 8,	5) ⑤ (1	1 – 5		AABB	
b.	" " 443.	"	"	"		AABB$_v$	
c.	Kuba XI. 70.	(10) ZZzz 3. 14, 14, 10, 10,	4) ① (1	VII – 5		AA$_v$BB	
1418.	Kuhač 1140.	ZZzz 3. 10, 10, 8, 8,	2) ② (1	VII – 4	10 = ♫♫|♫♩|♫♩||	AABB	
1419.	Kačerovski 72.	ZZzz 3. 10, 10, 9, 9,	4) ④ (1	VII – 4		AABB	
1420.	Kuba XIV. 14.	ZZzz 3. 11, 11, 10, 10,	5) ⑤ (1	1 – 8		AABB	
1421.	Kuba B.H. 206.	(6) ZZzz 3. +. 12, 12, 7, 7,	VII) (VII) (4	VII – 5	12 = ♩♩♩♩|𝅗𝅥𝅗𝅥|♩♩♩♩|𝅗𝅥||	AABB$_v$	
1422.	Kuhač 1331.	ZZzz 3. 12, 12, 7, 7,	1) ① (1	VII – 4	12 = ♩♩|♫♩|♫♫|♫♩||	AABB	
1423.	Kuba B.H. 937.	(10) ZZzz 3. +. 12, 12, 9, 9,	3) ③ (1	1 – 5		AABB	
1424.	Kuhač 1341.	ZZzz 3. 13, 13, 12, 12,	VII) (VII) (b3	bVII – 4		AABB$_v$	urban; text-stanzas, rimes
1425.	Kuhač 621.	ZZzz 3. 14, 14, 8, 8,	2) ② (2	#VII – b6		AABB$_v$	urban Slovakian
1426.	Kuhač 1374.	(10) ZZzz 3. +. 14, 14, 9, 9,	3) ③ (3	1 – 5		AABB$_v$	urban
1427.	Kuba XII. 54.	(8) ZZzz 3. +. 14, 14, 10, 10,	4) ④ (4	VII – 7		AABB	Hung. Rum. var.? (4× 14,?)
1428.	Bosiljevac 28.	(7) ZZzz 3. +. 14, 14, 12, 12,	3) ③ (1	1 – 8		AABB$_v$	
1429.	Kuba XII. 46.	(10) ZZzz 3. 15, 15, 10, 10,	2) ② (b3	V – b6		AABB$_v$	
1430.	Kuhač 926.*	zzZZ 4. 6, 6, 7, 7,	b3) (VII) (2	VII – b6		ABCB$_v$	Moravian-Slovak. type! * taken from Fr. Sušil's published collection
1431.	Kuba B.H. 961.	zzZZ 4. 6, 6, 8, 8,	4) ④ (4	1 – b6		AABB$_v$	
1432 a.	Đorđević 261.	zzZZ 4. 7, 7, 8, 8,	1) ① (VII	VII – b2		AABC	„lazarička"
b.	" 260.	"	"	"		"	"
1433.	Kuhač 1249 b)	zzZZ 4. 7, 7, 8, 8,	5) ⑤ (1	VII – b6		AAA$_v$B	„svatovska"
1434.	Kuba B.H. 241.	zzZZ 4. 8b, 8b, 9, 9,	4) ④ (1	VII – 7		AABB$_v$	
1435 a.	Kuhač 1114.	(8) zzZZ 4. (+.) 8, 8, 10, 10,	1) ① (1	1 – 6		AABB	„poskočnica"
b.	" 270.	10,	3) ③ (1	"		"	

X. zzZZ(4.) 8,8,12,12, — 10,10,14,14,

Current №	Original edition	Syll.	Last note of section	Range	Rhythm. structure	Structure	Remarks
1436.	Kuba B.H. 275 (= Kuba XII. 43.)	zzZZ 4. 8, 8, 12, 12,	1)④(4	1–7		$AABB_v$	text-stanzas? rimes?
1437.	Kuhač 1247.	(8) zzZZ 4. r. <8, 8, 12, 12,	4)(b3)(4	VII–b6		AA_vBB_v	"svatovska"
1438.	Kačerovski 30b)	zzZZ 4. 8, 8, 13, 13,	4)④(1	VII–7	13, = 𝅗𝅥.|𝅗𝅥.|♩♩|♫♩||	$AABB_v$	
1439a.)	Kuhač 520.	(8) zzZZ 4. r. 8, 8, 13, 13,	5)②(V	V–8	13, = 𝅗𝅥.|♫♩|𝅗𝅥.|♩♩||	$ABCC_v$	2-nd half is identic with the 2-nd half of a Ukrainian mel.
b.)	Kuba B.H. 14. (= Kuba XII. 8.)	"	5)①(V	"	"	"	swallowing of last syll.
1440a.)	Kuhač 1129.	zzZZ 4. 8, 8, 14, 14,	1)①(3	V–5	Perfect cadence	$AABB_v$	"paračinka"
b.)	Kuba B.H. 578.	"	VII)(VII)(4	VII–4	Imperfect cadence	"	"kolo"
1441.	Kuba B.H. 662.	(8) zzZZ 4. r. 8, 8, 16, 16,	1)①(VII	VII–5		AABC	"kolo"
1442.	Đorđević 5.	(10) zzZZ 4. r. 10,10, 11, 11,	1)①(4	1–7		$AABB_v$	
1443.	Kuba B.H. 252.	(10) zzZZ 4. r. 10, 10, 12, 12,	V)(V)(VII	V–b3		$AABB_v$	Ruman. var.: (2nd half of Bartók, Ruman Folk music II. № 605.)
1444a.)	Kuhač 1437.	(10) zzZZ 4. r. 10, 10, 12, 12,	4)①(1	VII–4		AA_vBB	
b.)	Kuba B.H. 83. (= Kuba XIII. 22.)	"	4)(IV)(b3	VII–5		$ABCC_v$	
c.)	Kuba B.H. 82.	(10) zzZZ 4. r. 10,10, 14, 14,	"	IV–4		"	
d.)	" " 106.	(5) r. 10, 10, 10, 12,	b3)(b3)(b3	1–b6		$AABB_v$	only 2-nd half common with a.–c.; contamination?
1445.	Kuhač 1425.	zzZZ 4. 10, 10, 12, 12,	2)④(5	1–7	10, = ♪♫♫|♫♩|♩♩|𝅗𝅥||	AA^3BB_v	< Hungar. melod. (ies?) contamination?
1446a.) ⊕	Kuba B.H. 925.	(10) zzZZ 4. (r.) 10, 10, 13, 13,	1)①(1	IV–4		AABB	swallowing of last syll.
c.	" " 957.	"	b2)(b2)(4	IV–5		$AABB_v$	
♂ b.)	" " 1125. Ms.	"	1)①(1	IV–5		AABB	
1447a.)	Kuba XI. 12.	(10) zzZZ 4. r. 10, 10, 13, 13,	1)①(1	VII–b6		AA_vBB_v	igra?
b.	Kuhač 1293.	(10) zzZZ 4. 10, 10, 14, 14,	1)①(b3	VI–4		$AABB_v$	"varoška" from 1852"
c.	" 1082.	(10) zzZZ 4. r. 10, 10, 13, 13,	4)③(1	1–6		AA_vBB_v	"poskočnica"
d.)	" 1091.	(10) zzZZ 4. r. 10, 10, 16, 16,	4)③(3	1–6		"	"poskočnica"
1448a.	Đorđević Nar. Pev. p. 114 (= Kuba XIV. 20)	(10) zzZZ 4. (r.) 10, 10, 13, 13,	1)①(4	IV–5		$AABB_v$	
b.	Kuba XIV. 21. *	(10) zzZZ 4. (r.) 10, 10, 12, 12,	1)①(1	1–5		AABB	"kolo" * taken from Manojlović "Sveta Cecilia" publ.
1449–50.	Kačerovski 61.	(10) zzZZ 4. (r.) 10, 10, 14, 14,	4)①(4	IV–4		AA_vBB_v	"kolo"

X. zzZZ (4.) 10,10,14,14, — 13,13,15,15,
ZzZz (5.) 6,5,6,5,

Current №	Original edition	Syll.	Last note of section	Range	Rhythm. structure	Structure	Remarks
1451.	Đorđević 437.	(10) zzZZ 4. 5. 10,10,14,14,	1) (1) (1	1–5	14, = [illegible]	AABB	
1452.	Kuhač 1348.	zzZZ 4. 10,10,14,14,	1) (1) (5	#VI–8	10, = [illegible]	AABB$_v$	text-stanzas, rimes Hungar. Slovak var.?
1453.	Kuhač 1404.	zzZZ 4. 11,11,12,12,	1) (1) (1	bVI–4		AABB$_v$	
1454.	Đorđević Nar. Pev. p. 130/1	zzZZ 4. 11,11,13,13,	4) (1) (4	VII–7		AA$_{v_1}$A$_{v_2}$A$_{v_3}$	urban?
1455.	Đorđević Nar. Pev. p. 183/2	zzZZ 4. 11,11,14,14,	1) (1) (1	IV–4		AABB	
1456.	Đorđević Nar. Pev. p. 32/1	zzZZ 4. 12,12,13,13,	2) (2) (1	IV–7	the texts of both are variants	AABC	urban?
1457.	Đorđević Nar. Pev. p. 38/1	zzZZ 4. 12,12,14,14,	1) (1) (4	1–5		AABB$_v$	cf. № 1480b. (same text)
1458a.	Kuba IX. 42.	zzZZ 4. 12,12,14,14,	2) (1) (1	1–6		AA$_5$BB$_v$	text-stanzas, rimes. Hungar. var.?
b.	Kuhač 112.	— 〃	2) (3) (1	1–6		〃	„varoska"
1459.	Đorđević Nar. Pev. p. 127.	zzZZ 4. 13,13,15,15,	5) (5) (2	1–b6		AABB$_v$	urban?
1460a.	Kuhač 1333.	ZzZz 5. 6,5,6,5,	V) (5) (V	V–5		ABAC	
b.	〃 1332	〃	〃	V–6		〃	
1461.	Kuhač 1325.	ZzZz 5. 6,5,6,5,	1) (VII) (VII	VII–b3	6, = [illegible] 5, [illegible]	ABB$_v$C	
1462.	Kuhač 676.	(8b) ZzZz 5. 6,5,6,5,	3) (3) (3	1–5	〃	ABAB$_v$	
1463.	Đorđević 341.	(8b) ZzZz 5. 6,5,6,5,	VII) (4) (VII	VII–4	〃	ABAC	„prigev"
1464.	Kuhač 513.	ZzZz 5. 6,5,6,5,	1) (5) (3	1–6	〃	AA^3_vB^{3}B	
1465.	Kuba B.H. 488.	(8b) ZzZz 5. 6,5,6,5,	1) (1) (1	VII–b3	6, = [illegible] 5, = [illegible]	ABAB	
1466.	Kuhač 1203.	(8b) ZzZz 5. 6,5,6,5,	b2) (1) (1	VII–4	〃	ABA$_5$C	„svatovska"
1467a.	Kuba B.H. 734.	(8b) ZzZz 5. 6,5,6,5,	2) (1) (2	1–5	〃	ABAB	word interv.: 6, 5, 1 2 5, 5,
b.	〃 〃 733.	〃	〃	VII–5	〃	〃	
c.	〃 〃 679.	〃	2) (1) (1	〃	〃	ABCB	
1468a.	Đorđević Nar. Pev. p. 95/2	(8b) ZzZz 5. 6,5,6,5,	b2) (b2) (b2	1–4	〃	ABAB$_v$	
b.	Đorđević 575.	(8b) 6,5,[ ],	b3) (b3) [C]		〃	AB[ ]B	
c.	〃 191.	(8b) 6,[ ],[ ],5,	b2) [O C]		〃	A[ ][ ]B	„žetvarska"
1469a.	Đorđević 41.	(8b) ZzZz 5. 6,5,6,5,	1) (2) (1	1–4	〃	ABAB$_v$	Var. Parry 38.

Current №	Original edition	Syll.	Last note of section	Range	Rhythm. structure	Structure	Remarks
b.	Kuba B.H. 492.	(8b) [ ][ ], 6, 5,	[ ) O] (2		"	[ ][ ]AB	
c.	" " 400.	"	[ ) O] (b3		"	"	
d.	Kuba XI. 37.	"	"		"	"	
1470 a.	Kuba B. H. 104.	(8b) Zz Zz 5. 6, 5, 6, 5,	b6) (b3) (b6	1–b6	"	ABAB	
b.	" 136.	"	"	"	"	"	
1471.	Đorđević 110.	(8b) Zz Zz 5. 6, 5, 6, 5,	b3) (b6) (4	1–7	"	ABCD	
1472.	Kuhač 355.	Zz Zz 5. 7, 5, 7, 5,	b3) (VII) (1	VII–4		ABCD	
1472 bis.	Đorđević 545.	(10) Zz Zz 5. r. 7, 6, 7, 6,	1) (1) (1	1–b3		ABAB	
1473.	Kuhač 684.	Zz Zz 5. 7, 6, 7, 6,	b3) (1) (b3	VII–4		ABAB	
1474.	Kuhač 92.	Zz Zz 5. 7, 6, 7, 6,	V) (2) (1	V–5		ABCD	
1475.	Kačerovski 44.	Zz Zz 5. 7, 6, 7, 6,	2) (2) (2	VII–4		$AA_v AB$	
1476.	Kačerovski 9.	Zz Zz 5. 7, 6, 7, 6,	4) (2) (b3	VII–b6		ABCD	text-stanza, rimes
1477.	Kuhač 1411.	Zz Zz 5. 7, 6, 7, 6,	4) (2) (4	1–5		$ABAB_v$	" " "
1478.	Kuhač 429.	Zz Zz 5. 7, 6, 7, 6,	5) (2) (5	1–6		ABCD	
1480.	Kuhač 1222 a)	Zz Zz 5. 7, 6, 7, 6,	b3) (b3) (b3	1–5		ABAC	"svatovska" "text-st., rimes
1479 a.	Kuhač 680.	Zz Zz 5. 7, 6, 7, 6,	1) (b3) (1	VII–b6		$AA_v^s AB$	text-stanzas rimes
b.	" 678. (2nd half)	"	"	"		ABA_vC	cf. N°1457 (same text)
c.	" 679. (1st half)	5, 6, 7, 6,	"	1–b6		"	
d.	" 681. (1st half)	Zz Zz 5. 7, 6, 7, 6,	VII) (bVI) (VII	V–b3		AA_sAB	
e.	" 682.	7, 7, 7, 6,	VII) (VII) (VII	VII–5		AAAB	
1481 a.	Kuhač 1340.	Zz Zz 5. 7, 6, 7, 6,	4) (b3) (b2	VII–b6		ABCD	text-stanzas, rimes
b.	" 50.	"	b3) (b3) (4	bIII–b6		"	" " "
1482.	Kuhač 1118.	Zz Zz 5. 7, 6, 7, 6,	VII) (4) (VII	VI–4		$ABAB_v$	"poskočnica"
1483 a.	Kuhač 737.	Zz Zz 5. 7, 6, 7, 6,	VII) (4) (4	VII–b6		ABCD	text-stanzas, rimes
b.	Kačerovski 46.	"	"	"		"	" " "

X. ZzZz (5.) 7,6,7,6, – 8,5,8,5, VI) (VII) (1 – 1) (1) (1

Current No	Original edition	Syll.	Last note of sections	Range	Rhythm. structure	Structure	Remark
c.	Kuba XI. 58.	"	VII) (4) (b3	bVI – b5		"	" " "
d.	Kuhač 1303.	"	VII) (4) (1	VII – b6		"	" " "
e.	" 1304.	"	VII) (1) (1	"		"	" " "
f.	" 474.	"	b3) (1) (VII	VII – 5		"	" " "
1484 a.	Đorđević 411.	(10) ZzZz 5. r. 7,6,7,6,	2) (4) (2	VII – 4		$ABAB_v$	„sedeljka"
b.	Đorđević Nar. Pev. p. 109/2	ZzZz 5. 7,6,7,6,	"	1 – 4		"	
c.	Kuhač 1100.	(10) ZzZz 5. (r.) 7,6,7,6,	VII) (2) (VII	VII – 5		"	„poskočnica"
1485.	Kuba B.H. 630.	ZzZz 5. 7,6,7,6,	1) (1) (1	VII – 5	6, = ♩♩𝅗𝅥 | ♩♩𝅗𝅥 ‖	$ABAB_v$	
1486.	Kuba X. 43.	ZzZz 5. 8,5,8,5,	VII) (VII) (1	VII – 4		ABCD	three part song
1487.	Manojlović 4.	ZzZz 5. 8,5,8,5,	1) (VII) (VII	VII – 4		AA_vBC	
1488.	Kuba B.H. 616.	ZzZz 5. 8,5,8,5	1) (VII) (VII	1 – 4		ABAB	
1489.	Đorđević Nar. Pev. p. 1/1	ZzZz 5. 8,5,8,5,	4) (VII) (4	VI – b6		ABA_vB_v	
1490 a.	Kuhač 1015.	ZzZz 5. 8,5,8,5,	IV) (1) (VII	IV – 5		ABCD	„igra" 1st theme of Beeth. VIth symph.
b.	" 1016.	10,14,13,	(VII) (1	bIII – 4		ABB_{sv}	" " " " " "
c.	" 1156.	8,7,7,	(1) (4	VII – 5		ABB_v	
d.	Bosiljevac 25.						fragment of b.
1491.	Kuba B.H. 85.	ZzZz 5. 8,5,8,5,	V) (1) (IV	IV – 5		ABA_vC	belongs perhaps to the preceding group
1492.	Kuba B.H. 993. Ms.	ZzZz 5. 8,5,8,5,	VII) (1) (IV	IV – 4		$ABCB_v$	
1493 a.	Kuba B.H. 232.	ZzZz 5. 8,5,8,5,	VII) (1) (VII	VII – 7		ABCB	
b.	" " 61.	ZzZz 5. 8,5,8,5,	VII) (1) (VII	VII – 7		"	
c.	" " 379.	"	"	IV – 7		"	
d.	" " 78.	"	2) (VII) (VII	VII – 7		ABCD	
1494 a.	Kuba B.H. 506.	ZzZz 5. 8,5,8,5,	1) (1) (1	IV – b6		ABCB	
b.	Kuba IX. 33.	"	bVI) (VII) (bVII	bIII – b3		ABAC	
1495.	Kuba B.H. 695.	ZzZz 5. 8,5,8,5,	1) (1) (1	VII – 5		ABAB	Var. Parry 39.

Current No	Original edition	Syll.	Last note of sections	Range	Rhythm. structure	Structure	Remarks
1496.	Kuhač 851. 871. }*	ZzZz 5. 8, 5, 8, 5,	1)①(1	1–5		ABABv	* Kuhač published the same song twice, without perceiving it!!
1497.	Kuba 574.	ZzZz 5. 8, 5, 8, 5,	1)①(4	VII–4		ABAvC	
1498a.	Đorđević 346.	ZzZz 5. 8, 5, 8, 5,	b2)①(b2	1–4		ABAvB	„slavska"
b.	" 367.	"	"	"		"	"
c.	Kuba B.H. 495.	ZzZz 5. 8, 5, 8, 5,	b3)①(b3	"		"	
1499a.	Kuhač 1472.	ZzZz 5. 8, 5, 8, 5,	2)①(2	VII–5		ABCB	
b.	" 17.	"	2)②(2	VII–4		ABABv	
1500.	Kuhač 342.	ZzZz 5. 8, 5, 8, 5,	2)①(2	1–4		ABCB	
1501.	Kuba B.H. 791.	ZzZz 5. 8, 5, 8, 5,	b3)①(b3	VII–b3		ABAvBv	line interr.: 8, 5, 4?4, 5,
1502a.	Kuba B.H. 522.	ZzZz 5. 8, 5, 8, 5,	4)①(4	VII–5		ABAvBv	} Var. Parry 41.
b.	" " 535.	ZzZz 5. 8, 5, 8, 5,	"	VII–4		"	„svatovska"
c.	" " 621.	"	"	"		ABAB	
d.	" " 598.	"	4)(b3)(4	"		ABAvBv	„svatovska"
1503–4.	Đorđević Nar. Pev. p. 184/1	ZzZz 5. 8, 5, 8, 5,	b2)(b2)(b2	VII–5		ABAB	
1505a.	Kuba B.H. 576.	ZzZz 5. 8, 5, 8, 5,	VII)②(VII	VII–4		ABAC	} Var. Parry 42. Cf. No 1557.
b.	Đorđević Nar. Pev. p. 131/1	ZzZz 5. 8, 5, 8, 5,	"	"		"	
c.	Kuba B.H. 698.	"	"	VII–5		"	
d.	Bosiljevac 49.	"	2)②(2	1–5		ABAC	
1506a.	Kuhač 897.	ZzZz 5. 8, 5, 8, 5,	1)②(V	V–6		ABCD	
b.	" 899.	"	1)②(1	1–6		ABCBs	
c.	" 149.	"	4)②(5	"		ABCD	
d.	" 358.	"	b2)(VII)(1	bVI–4		ABCD	
e.	Kuba X. 51.	"	1)(VII)(1	"		ABCB^s	
f.	" " 13.	"	bIII)(b3)(1	bIII–4		ABCD	two part song
g.	Kuhač 898.	8, 5, [ ], 5,	1)②[C]			AB[ ]D	

Current No	Original edition	Syll.	Last note of section	Range	Rhythm. structure	Structure	Remarks
1507.	~~Đorđević 477.~~	ZzZz 5. 8, 5, 8, 5,	1)②(	1–5		ABAB$_v$	„Žetvarska"
1508.	Kuhač 334. (=Đorđević Nar. Pev. p. 81/1)	ZzZz 5. 8, 5, 8, 5,	1)②(	1–6		ABAB$_v$	
1509.	Kuhač 807.	ZzZz 5. 8, 5, 8, 5,	3)②(2	#VII–6		ABA$_5$B$_v$	Hungar. var.
1510.	Kuhač 853.	ZzZz 5. 8, 5, 8, 5,	bVI)(b3)(b2	bVI–4		ABCD	
1511 a.	Kuba X. 55.	ZzZz 5. 8, 5, 8, 5,	VII)(b3)(b3	VII–5		ABCD	
b.	" XI. 24.	"	b3)(b3)(	1–5		AA$_v$BC	
1512 a.	Kuba B.H. 1122. Ms.	ZzZz 5. 8, 5, 8, 5,	VII)(b3)(4	VII–4		ABCD	
~~" b.~~	~~Kuhač 341.~~	~~"~~	~~VII)(b3)(VII~~	~~VII–5~~		~~ABA$_v$B$_{5v}$~~	
1513 a.	Kuhač 843 a)	ZzZz 5. 8, 5, 8, 5,	VII)(b3)(4	VII–5		ABCD	
b.	" 843 b)	"	"	"		"	
c.	" 844.	8, 5, [ ], 5,	2)②[(]			AB[ ]B	
d.	" 846.	"	bIII)①[(]			"	
e.	" 845.	[ ][ ]8, 5,	[ ) ○](VII			[ ][ ]AB	
f.	" 870.	"	"			"	
1514 a.	Kuba B.H. 1059. Ms.	ZzZz 5. 8, 5, 8, 5,	VII)(b3)(4	VII–5		ABAC	Var. Party 44.
b.	" " 1056. Ms.	ZzZz 5. 8, 5, 8, 5,	VII)(b3)(5	"		"	
c.	" " 213.	"	"	"		ABA$_v$C	
d.	" " 1054. Ms.	"	VII)(b3)(b6	VII–b6		ABAC	
e.	" " 1057. Ms.	"	4)①(VII	1–b6		ABA$_v$B$_v$	
1515 a.	Kuba XIV. 6.	ZzZz 5. 8, 5, 8, 5,	1)(b3)(	1–5		ABA$_v$B$_v$	
b.	Kuhač 309.	"	"	"		ABAC	
c.	Kuba B.H. 939.	"	1)③(	"		"	
d.	" " 345.	"	"	"		"	
e.	" " 857.	"	1)(b3)(2	VII–4		"	
f	" " 690.	"	1)(b3)(4	1–5		ABCD	
g.	Kuhač 310.	"	b3)④(	1–b6		ABA$_v$C	
h.	" 789.	"	2)④(2	1–5		"	

Current No	Original edition	Syll.	Last note of section	Range	Rhythm. structure	Structure	Remarks
1516 a.	Kuba IX. 45.	ZzZz 5. 8, 5, 8, 5,	1)(b3)(b3	bVI–b6		ABCD	urban (German?)
b.	Kuba B.H. 135.	"	bVI)(b3)(1	"		"	
1517.	Kuba B.H. 396.	ZzZz 5. 8, 5, 8, 5,	1)(b3)(b3	1–4		$AA_{v1}A_{v2}A_{v3}$	
1518.	Kuba XIV. 22.	ZzZz 5. 8, 5, 8, 5,	1)(b3)(4	bVI–b6		ABA_vC	
1519 a.	Kuba B.H. 263.	ZzZz 5. 8, 5, 8, 5,	b3)(b3)(VII	VII–7		$A^4B^4AB_v$	
b.	" " 971. Ms.	"	"	"		A^4BA_vC	
1520.	Kuhač 383.	ZzZz 5. 8, 5, 8, 5,	5)(b3)(1	1–b6		$A^3B^3A_vB_v$	
1521 a.	Đorđević 513.	ZzZz 5. 8, 5, 8, 5,	5)(b3)(4	1–b6		ABA_vC	
b.	Kuba B.H. 1117. Ms.	"	4)(b3)(1	1–5		ABCD	
c.	Kuba XIV. 4.	"	b3)(b3)(VII	VII–5		ABA_vC	
1522.	Kuhač 1473.	ZzZz 5. 8, 5, 8, 5,	2)(3)(2	1–5		$ABAB_v$	Slovenian var.: Kuhač 809.
1523.	Kuba B.H. 259.	ZzZz 5. 8, 5, 8, 5,	IV)(4)(1	IV–b5		AB^4CB_v	
1524.	Kuba B.H. 248.	ZzZz 5. 8, 5, 8, 5,	1)(4)(1	VII–8		ABCD	
1525.	Kuba B.H. 105.	ZzZz 5. 8, 5, 8, 5,	1)(4)(b3	1–7		ABA_vC	
1526 a.	Đorđević Nar. Pev. p. 35/1	ZzZz 5. 8, 5, 8, 5,	2)(4)(VII	VII–b6		AA_vBC	
b.	Kuba XIV. 24.	"	"	"		ABCD	
1527.	Kuba XII. 15.	ZzZz 5. 8, 5, 8, 5,	b3)(4)(1	1–8		AB^3CB_v	
1528.	Kačerovski 81.	ZzZz 5. 8, 5, 8, 5,	4)(4)(VII	VII–b6		AB^4CB	
1529.	Kačerovski 21.	ZzZz 5. 8, 5, 8, 5,	4)(4)(VII	VII–b6		ABCD	
1530 a.	Kačerovski 76.	ZzZz 5. 8, 5, 8, 5,	4)(4)(VII	VII–8		A^5B^4AB	
b.	Đorđević Nar. Pev. p. 169/2	"	4)(4)(3	"		$A^5B^5A_vB_v$	
1531 a.	Đorđević Nar. Pev. p. 53/1	ZzZz 5. 8, 5, 8, 5,	V)(5)(1	V–6		ABA^4C	Var.: Bartók, Rumanian Folk Music, II. 414. (a.–d.)
b.	Kačerovski 56.	"	"	"		"	
c.	Kuhač 148.	"	V)(5)(3	"		"	
d.	Kuba B.H. 383.	"	V)(2)(3	"		ABA^4_vC	
e.	Kačerovski 3.	"	V)(2)(1	"		"	

115

X. 8,5,8,5, 4)⑤(VII – VII)⑦②; ♩♫|♩♩||; ♩♩|♫♩||; 1. and 2. half different in rhythm

Current №	Original edition	Syll.	Last note of sections	Range	Rhythm. structure	Structure	Remarks
1532 a.	Bosiljevac 44.	(8) ZzZz 5. r. 8,5,8,5,	4)⑤(VII	VII – 8		$A^5B^5A_vB$	
b.	~~Đorđević Nar. Pes.~~ p. 42/2	"	"	"		"	
c.	Kuba B.H. 1061. Ms.	ZzZz 5. 8,5,8,5,	4)⑤②	1 – 8		AB^5CB	
d.	" " 976. Ms.	"	4)⑤④	"		AB^5A_vB	
e.	Kuba XIII. 10.	(8) ZzZz 5. r. 8,5,8,5,	6)⑤(VII	VII – 8		AB^5CB	
f.	Kuba B. H. 1118. Ms.	"	"	"		"	
g.	Kuba B.H. 1066. Ms.	ZzZz 5. 8,5,8,5,	5)(b3)(5	1 – 7		$AB^5A_vB_v$	word-interr.: 8, 1 2 4, 8, 5,
h.	" " 1062. Ms.	"	b3)(b3)(1	VII – 5		ABCD	
i.	" " 1060. Ms.	8,5,[ ],5,	4)(b3)[C]			$AB^3[\,]B_v$	
j.	" " 1067. Ms.	"	1)(b3)[C]			"	
k.	" " 1063. Ms.	"	"			"	
l.	" " 1065. Ms.	[ ],[ ],8,5,	[ ][ ](1			[ ][ ]AB	
m.	" " 1064. Ms.	8,5,8,5,*	4)①④	VII – 4		ABAB*	line-interr.: 8,5, 4 2 4, 5, ; * in fact 2 sect. are repeated.
1533.	Kuba XIV. 25.	ZzZz 5. 8,5,8,5,	5)⑤(1	1 – 7		ABCD	
1534.	Kuhač 1474. (= Đorđević, Nar. Pes. p. 97)	ZzZz 5. 8,5,8,5,	7)⑤(b3	1 – 8		A^5B^5AB	Hungar. type
1535.	Kuba B.H. 49.	ZzZz 5. 8,5,8,5,	VII)⑦②	VII – 7		ABCD	
1536.	Kuhač 1223.	(8) ZzZz 5. 8, 5, 8, 5,	b3)④(b3	1 – 5	5, = ♩♫|♩♩||	$ABAB_v$	"svatovska"
1537 a.	Kuba B.H. 146.*	ZzZz 5. 8, 5, 8, 5,	b6)(b2)(VII	VII – b6	5, = ♩♩|♫♩||	$<ABA_sB_s$	* perhaps a wrong figure instead of 164. (cf. № 1319 a.)
b.	Kuhač 1451.	"	VII)(VII)(VII	V – 4	"	ABA_sB_v	
1538.	Kuhač 1426.	ZzZz 5. 8, 5, 8, 5,	4)⑤(1	1 – 8	"	AB^5CB	Hungar. var.
1539.	~~Đorđević~~ 594.	(8b) ZzZz 5. r. 8,5,8,5,	3)①③	1 – 4		ABAB	
1540 a.	Kuhač 848. (= ~~Đorđević~~ Nar. Pes. p. 104/1)	ZzZz 5. 8,5,8,5,	1)(b3)(b2	VII – 4	1. 8,5, = ♩|♩♩|♩♩|♩||; 2. 8,5, = ♩.♪|♩|♩♩|♩|♩	ABCD	
b.	Kuhač 849.	"	"	"	"	"	
c.	" 847.	"	"	"	"	"	
d.	" 1206.	"	"	"	"	"	"svatovska"
e.	" 380.	"	"	"	"	AA_vBB_v	

X. 8,6,8,6,(5.) ♭VI) ♭III I — I) I (I

Current №	Original edition	Syll.	Last note of sections	Range	Rhythm. structure	Structure	Remarks.
f.	Kačerovski 69.	"	"	♭VI – 4	"	ABCD	
g.	Kuhač 348.	"	"	VII – ♭6	"	"	
h.	Kuba B.H. 103. (= Kuba XIII. 34.)	"	I) ♭3 ♭3	VII – 4	"	"	
i.	Kuba B.H. 145. (= Kuba XIV. 12)	"	"	"	"	"	
j.	Kuhač 854.	"	♭3) ♭3 ♭2	"	"	"	
k.	" 418.	"	"	VII – ♭6	"	AA$_v$BC	
l.	" 1207.	[ ] [ ] 8, 5,	[ ) O] (I			[ ] [ ] A B	
1541.	Kuhač 147.	Z z Z z 5. 8, 6, 8, 6,	♭VI) ♭III (I	I – ♭3		ABCD	
1542.	Đorđević 416.	(10) Z z Z z 5. 8, 6, 8, 6,	VII) VII (VII	VII – ♭2		ABAB$_v$	„sedeljka"
1543.	Kuhač 107.	Z z Z z 5. 8, 6, 8, 6,	I) VII (VII	VII – ♭3		ABA$_s$B^5	
1544.	Đorđević 585.	(10) Z z Z z 5. 8, 6, 8, 6,	♭3) VII (♭3	VII – 4		ABAB$_v$	
1545a.	Kuhač 20.	(10) Z z Z z 5. 8, 6, 8, 6,	4) VII (4	VII – 5		ABAB$_v$	
b.	" 617.	"	♭3) VII (4	VII – 4		ABA$_v$C	
c.	" 752.	Z z Z z 5. 8, 6, 8, 6,	♭3) I (♭3	I – 5		ABAB$_v$	
d.	" 729.	(10) Z z Z z 5. 8, 6, 8, 6,	♭2) I (♭2	VII – 4		ABAB	
e.	" 731.	"	"	I – 4		"	
f.	" 615.	(10) 8, 6, 8, 10, *	♭3) VII (♭3	VII – 4		ABAB$_v$	Peculiar repeat of 4 previous syll.
g.	" 614.	" *	4) 2 (4	"		"	
h.	" 528.	(10) 8, 6, [ ], [ ],	4) VII [C]			AB[ ][ ]	
1546a.	Kuba IX 19.	Z z Z z 5. 8, 6, 8, 6,	I) I (I	♭VI – ♭6		ABA$_v$B	text-st., rimes
b.	Kuhač 307.	(10) Z z Z z 5. 8, 6, 8, 6,	"	♭VI – 4		"	
c.	" 140.	"	"	VII – 4		ABAB	
d.	Kuba B.H. 130.	Z z Z z 5. 8, 6, 8, 6,	♭2) I (I	♭VI – ♭6		ABA$_v$B	text-st. rimes
1547.	Kuhač 141.	(10) Z z Z z 5. 8, 6, 8, 6,	I) I (I	VII – 4		ABAB	
1548.	Đorđević Nar. Pev. p. 3/1	Z z Z z 5. 8, 6, 8, 6,	I) I (I	VII – 5		ABA$_v$B	

Current No	Original edition	Syll.	Last note of sections	Range	Rhythm. structure	Structure	Remarks
1549.	Kuba B.H. 351.	(10) ZzZz 5. 8,6,8,6,	1)①(1	1–4		ABAB	
1550 a.	Kuba B.H. 748.	(10) ZzZz 5. 8,6,8,6,	1)①(1	1–5		ABAB	line interr.: 8,6,1?7,6,
b.	" " 324.	"	VII)①(VII	VII–4		"	
c.	" " 601.	"	1)②(1	1–5		"	
d.	" " 600. (= Kuba XII. 53.)	"	1)②(4	1–5		ABA_vB_v var.	"uspavanka" interr.: 8,6,1?7,6, emphat. embellishment [illegible]
1551.	Kuba B.H. 747.	(10) ZzZz 5. 8,6,8,6,	2)①(2	1–5		ABA_vB	line-interr.: 8,6,1?7,6,
1552.	Đorđević 87.	ZzZz 5. 8,6,8,6,	b3)①(1	1–b6		$ABA_{sv}B$	"čilimarska"
1553.	Kuba B.H. 829.	(10) ZzZz 5. (+) 8,6,8,6,	b3)①(b3	1–4		ABAB	swallowing of last syll. two part song!!!
1554.	Kuba B.H. 154.	(10) ZzZz 5. 8,6,8,6,	4)①(b2	bVII–b6		ABCD	German mel. (Fuchs du hast die Gans gestohlen)
1555 a.	Kuhač 1030.	(10) ZzZz 5. 8,6,8,6,	4)①(4	VII–4		$ABAB_v$	"knjaževsko oro"
b.	Iz Levča 30.	"	b3)②(b3	"		"	"sedeljka"
c.	Kuhač 55.	(10) 8,6,10,	b3)①	"		?	
d.	" 1029.	(10) 6,	4)①(4	"		$ABAB_v$	"knjaževsko oro
1556 a.	Đorđević 13.	(10) ZzZz 5. 8,6,8,6,	4)①(4	VII–4		ABAB	
b.	Kuba B.H. 680.	"	"	VII–5		"	
1557 a.	Kačerovski 18.	ZzZz 5. 8,6,8,6,	VII)(b2)(VII	VII–4		ABA_vC	text-st., rimes Cf. No 1505. and Parry 42.
b.	Đorđević Nar. Pev. p. 146.	"	"	VII–5		ABA_vB_v	
1558 a.	Kuhač 930.	(10) ZzZz 5. 8,6,8,6,	b3)(b2)(b3	VI–4		$ABAB_v$	Slovak. text var.
b.	Kuba B.H. 112.	(10) 8,6,10,	b3)(b2)	VII–5		ABA_v	two line interrupt.: 6?2,6,4?6,
c.	Kuhač 931.	(10) 10,8,6,	(VII)(1	VII–b3		$AA_{v1}A_{v2}$	
1559.	Kuhač 596.	ZzZz 5. 8,6,8,6,	4)(b2)(VII	bVII–b6		ABCD	urban
1560.	Kuba B.H. 84.	ZzZz 5. 8,6,8,6,	IV)②(VII	IV–5		ABCD	text-st. ~~rimes~~
1561 a.	Iz Levča 19.	(10) ZzZz 5. 8,6,8,6,	VII)②(VII	VII–b3	Var. Parry 46.	$AA_{v1}AA_{v2}$	"sedeljka"
b.	" " 27.	"	"	"		"	"
c.	" " 29.	(8) +. 8,4,8,4,	"	"		"	Cf. No 123 ee. ff. gg.
d.	Đorđević 259.	(8) +. 4,11,					"

Current №	Original edition	Syll.	Last note of sections	Range	Rhythm. structure	Structure	Remarks
1562.	Đorđević 511.	(10) ZzZz 5. 8,6,8,6,	1)②(1	VII–5		$ABAB_v$	
1563a.	Đorđević 299.	(10) ZzZz 5. 8,6,8,6,	2)②(2	VII–b3		$ABAB_v$	„sedeljka" nord.inter.: 8,6,6 $\frac{3}{-}$2,6,
b.	" 429.	ZzZz 5. 8,6,8,6,	"	1–b3		"	„sedeljka"
c.	" 298.	(10) [][] 8,6,	[)O](b3			[][]AB	"
d.	" 297.	"	"			"	"
e.	" 295.	"	[)O](1			"	„četvarska"
1564.	Kuba XI. 4.	(10) ZzZz 5. 8,6,8,6,	2)②(2	1–b3		$ABAB_v$	
1565.	Kuhač 200.	(10) ZzZz 5. r. 8,6,8,6,	2)②(2	1–4		$AA_{v_1}AA_{v_2}$	
1566.	Kuhač 232.	(10) ZzZz 5. 8,6,8,6,	4)②(4	1–5		$ABAB_v$	
1567a.	Kuhač 1127.	(10) ZzZz 5. (r.) 8,6,8,6,	4)②(4	1–6		$ABAB_v$	„poskočnica"
b.	" 1387.	(10) ZzZz 5. 8,6,8,6,	2)③(2	1–5		"	
1568a.	Kačerovski 29.	ZzZz 5. 8,6,8,6,	bIII)(b3)(4	bIII–b6		ABCD	urban; text-st., rimes 8,6,8,6, ! a a b b !
b.	Kuhač 387.	6+8,6, 8,6+6,	b2)(b3)(1	VII–b6		"	urban; " " ": aabcb!!
1569a.	Kuba B.H. 669.	ZzZz 5. 8,6,8,6,	VII)(b3)(VII	VII–5		$ABCB_v$	text-st., rimes
b.	" " 841.	"	"	VII–4		ABA_vB_v	" "
c.	Kačerovski 71.	"	VII)②(VII	VII–5		"	" "
1570a.	Kuhač 888.	ZzZz 5. 8,6,8,6,	1)(b3)(1	VII–5		$ABAB_v$	
b.	" 597.	(10) ZzZz 5. 8,6,8,6,	"	VII–4		$ABAB_v$	
c.	Kuba X. 7.	ZzZz 5. 8,6,8,6	"	"		"	text-st., rimes
d.	Kuhač 1121.	(10) ZzZz 5. 8,6,8,6,	"	VII–b3		AA_vAB	„poskočnica"
e.	" 815.	"	1)④(1	VII–4		$ABAB_v$	
f.	" 134.	"	"	"		" fra	„Temišvar"!!
g.	Kuba B.H. 864.	"	1)(b2)(1	"		ABA_vB_v	
h.	Kuhač 15.	ZzZz 5. 8,6,8,6,	3)⑤(3	1–5		$ABAB_v$	„vagoška" text-st., rimes
i.	" 135.	6,	1)④(1	1–4		$AA_{v_1}AA_{v_2}$	

Current No	Original edition	Syll.	Last note of sections	Range	Rhythm. structure	Structure	Remarks
1571a	Kuhač 1234.	ZzZz 5. 8,6,8,6,	1)(b3)(1	VII–b6		ABCD	„svatovska" text-st., rimes
b.	Kuba B.H. 147.	"	"	"		"	text-st., rimes
c.	Kuhač 1466.	"	b3)(b3)(1	"		"	" "
1572.	Kuhač 1458.	(10) ZzZz 5. 8,6,8,6,	b3)(b3)(1	VII–b6		A^3BAC	
1573a.	Kuhač 886.	ZzZz 5. 8,6,8,6,	2)(3)(2	1–5		AA_vAB	text-st.; rimes
b.	Kuhač 1259 b)	"	4)(3)(4	"		$ABAB_v$	„svatovska"
c.	" 1111 a)	"	3)(3)(3	"		"	„poskočnica" = t.st., rimes → Slovenian var.: Kuhač 889.
1574.	Kuhač 1449.	(10) ZzZz 5. 8,6,8,6,	4)(3)(4	1–#7		$ABAB_v$	
1575.	Kuhač 1108.	ZzZz 5. 8,6,8,6,	VII)(4)(VII	VII–4		ABAC	„poskočnica"
1576a.	Đorđević 119.	(10) ZzZz 5. 8,6,8,6,	VII)(4)(VII	VII–4		$ABAB_v$	
b.	" 392.	"	"	"		"	„slavska"
c.	Kuhač 1002.	"	"	VII–5		ABAC	„igra"
d.	" 1003.	"	"	"		"	
e.	Đorđević 121.	(10) 8,6,[ ],6,	1)(4)[C]			AB[ ]B_v	„svatovska"
1577a.	Đorđević Nar. Pev. p. 5/1	ZzZz 5. 8,6,8,6,	VII)(4)(VII	VII–7		$AA_{v1}A_{v2}B$	text-st.; rimes
b.	Kuba B.H. 45.	(10) ZzZz 5. 8,6,8,6,	1)(5)(1	1–8		ABAC	macaronic text (Turk. + S.Cr.)
1578.	Bosiljevac 17.	(10) ZzZz 5. 8,6,8,6,	1)(4)(1	VII–5		ABCD	
1579a.	Kačerovski 36.	(10) ZzZz 5. 8,6,8,6,	1)(4)(1	1–5		$ABAB_v$	
b.	Kuba B.H. 636.	r. "	2)(4)(1	1–5		"	
1580.	Kuhač 1433.	ZzZz 5. 8,6,8,6,	1)(4)(1	1–5	Var. Parry 48.	ABAC	„napjev (!!) i text od P. Kolarića", prob. not true, as to the mel.!!
1581.	Kuhač 1455.	ZzZz 5. 8,6,8,6,	1)(4)(b3	VII–4		ABCD	
1582a.	Kuba B.H. 763.	(10) ZzZz 5. 8,6,8,6,	2)(4)(2	VII–4	Imperfect cadence	ABAC	
b.	Kuhač 1362.	r. "	3)(3)(3	1–5	Perfect cadence	"	
1583a.	Kuba B.H. 419.	ZzZz 5. 8,6,8,6,	2)(4)(2	1–5		$ABCB_v$	
b.	" " 715.	(10) " "	"	VII–5		"	

X. 8,6,8,6,(5.) ♭3) ④ (♭3 — 2) ⑤ (3

Current No	Original edition	Syll.	Last note of sections	Range	Rhythm. structure	Structure	Remarks
1584a.	Kuhač 654.	(10) ZzZz 5. 8,6,8,6,	♭3) ④ (♭3	VII–4		ABABv	
b.	" 652a) (= Đorđević Nar. Pev. p. 160/1)	"	"	"		"	
c.	Kuhač 536.	"	"	1–4		"	
d.	" 655.	(8) r. 8,4,8,4,	4) ② (2	1–5		ABAvC	
e.	" 656	[ ],[ ], 8,6,	[⊃○] (3			[ ][ ]AB	
f.	Kuba B.H. 482	"	[⊃○] (♭3			"	
1585a.	Kuhač 273.	(10) ZzZz 5. 8,6,8,6,	♭3) ④ (♭3	1–5		ABABv	
b.	" 1443.	ZzZz 5. 8,6,8,6,	"	"		"	tekst-st., rimes
c.	Đorđević Nar. Pev. p. 4/2	(10) ZzZz 5. r. 8,6,8,6,	2) ④ (2	1–7		"	
d.	Kuba XII. 13.	(10) ZzZz 5. 8,6,8,6,	1) ④ (1	VII–5		"	
e.	" " 35.	"	"	1–5		"	
f.	Kuhač 215.	6,	4) ④ (4	1–5		ABAvBv	
g.	" 317.	8,8+6,8,6,	"	1–5			
1586a.	Kuhač 1363.	ZzZz 5. 8,6,8,6,	V) ⑤ (1	V–6		ABCD	text-st.; rimes
b.	Kuba B.H. 364.	(10) ZzZz 5. 8,6,8,6,	"	V–5		"	„kolo"
c.	Kačerovski 58.	"	V) ⑤ (3	V–6		"	("pillow-danse") „vanjkušac"
d.	Kuhač 1086.	(10) (r.) 8,6,6,6,	"	"		"	„poskočnica"
e.	Kuba X. 25.	ZzZz 5. 8,5,8,5,	1) ⑤ (1	1–6		"	text-st.; rimes
1587a.	Kuhač 1085.	(10) ZzZz 5. 8,6,8,6,	1) ⑤ (1	1–5		ABAC	
b.	" 1084.	"	V) ⑤ (V	V–5		"	„poskočnica"
1588a.	Kuhač 1001a)	(10) ZzZz 5. 8,6,8,6,	1) ⑤ (1	1–6		ABAC	„vanjkušac"
b.	" 1001c)	"	3) ⑤ (3	"		"	
1589a.	Kuba B.H. 362.	(10) ZzZz 5. 8,6,8,6,	2) ⑤ (3	1–5		ABCD	
b.	Kuba XI. 27.	"	2) ⑤ (2	"		ABAvC	
c.	Kuba B.H. 361.	"	4) ⑤ (1	"		ABCD	„kolo"

Current No	Original edition	Syll.	Last note of sections	Range	Rhythm. structure	Structure	Remarks.
d.	Kuhač 1448.	(10) 8,6,10,	1)⑤	VII–6		ABC	
e.	" 1527.	"	6)⑤	1–8		"	
1590.	~~Đorđević~~ Nar. Pev. p. 173/2	(10) Z z Z z 5. 8,6,8,6,	b3)⑤(b3	1–5	Perfect cadence	ABAB$_v$	
1591 a.	Kačerovski 4b)	Z z Z z 5. 8,6,8,6,	3)⑤(3	1–6		AB^{5}AB	Slovak.; Hungar. var.; text-st.; rimes
b.	Kuhač 408.	Z z Z z 5. < 8,7,8,7,	5)⑤(3	"		ABCD	
c.	" 1111b)	8,6,7,6,	4)④(1	1–5	Imperfect cadence	"	„poskočnica"; text-st.; rimes
1592 a.	Kuhač 375.	(10) Z z Z z 5. 8,6,8,6,	4)⑤(b3	1–5		ABCB$_v$	
b.	" 101.	Z z Z z 5. 8,6,8,6,	1)⑤(1	VII–5		ABCD	text-st.; rimes
1593 a.	Kuba 979. (= Kuba B.H. MS XIII. 46.)	(10) Z z Z z 5. 8,6,8,6,	4)⑤(4	1–8		AB^{5}AB$_v$	related to Hungar. types, 2
b.	Kuba B.H. 149.	"	"	"		"	
c.	Kuba XII. 29.	Z z Z z 5. 8,6,8,6,	"	"		AB^{5}A$_v$B	
1594.	~~Đorđević~~ Nar. Pev. p. 125/1	(10) Z z Z z 5. 8,6,8,6,	5)⑤(b3	VII–8		AB^{5}CB$_v$	"
1595.	Kuhač 1523.	(10) Z z Z z 5. 8,6,8,6,	5)⑤(3	1–8		AB^{5}CB	
1596.	Kuhač 891.	Z z Z z 5. 8,6,8,6,	2)⑥(5	1–7		ABA^{4}C	
1597.	Kačerovski 24.	Z z Z z 5. 8,6,8,6,	5)⑦(4	1–8		ABCD	text-st.; rimes
1598.	Kuhač 1008.	(8) Z z Z z 5. T. 8,6,8,6,	VI)①(VI	V–5	6, = ♩♩𝅗𝅥/♩♩𝅗𝅥//	ABAB$_v$	Kolo = "(paan než")"
1599 a.	~~Đorđević~~ Nar. Pev. p. 154/1	(8) Z z Z z 5. T. 8,6,8,6,	4)①(4	VI–5	6, = ♩♩𝅗𝅥/♩♩𝅗𝅥//	ABA$_v$B	
b.	p. 74/1 " "	"	b2)(VII)(VII	VII–b5	"	ABCD	
1600.	~~Đorđević~~ 459.	(11) Z z Z z 5. 8,6,8,6,	b3)(b2)(b3	VII–b3	6, = ♫♩/♫♩//	ABAB$_v$	
1601 a.	Juž. Srb. 417.	(11) Z z Z z 5. 8,6,8,6,	VII)(b3)(VII	VII–5	6, = ♩♩𝅗𝅥/♩♩𝅗𝅥//	ABA$_v$C	
b.	Kuba B. H. 649.	"	"	"	"	"	
c.	Juž. Srb. 425.	"	"	"	"	ABA$_v$C	
1602 a.	Kuhač 916.	(11) Z z Z z 5. 8,6,8,6,	b2)(b3)(1	VII–4	6, = ♩♩𝅗𝅥/♩♩𝅗𝅥//	ABCD	
b.	Bartók MF. 2060a) MS., Garafda	"	2)(b3)(2	1–5	"	"	
c.	~~Đorđević~~ 7.	"	2)(b3)(VII	VII–5	"	"	
d.	Kuhač 440.	"	b3)(b3)(1	VII–4	"	"	

X. 8,6,8,6,(5.) 3+3; — 1. and 2. half in different rhythm
8,7,8,7,(5.) #VII)(X)(3 – 1)(1)(1

Current No	Original edition	Syll.	Last note of sections	Range	Rhythm structure	Structure	Remarks
e.	Kuhač 1010.	(11) ZzZz 5. 8,6,8,6,	b3)(b3)(b3	VII–b6	"	"	„(biberja-) igra"
f.	Kuba IX. 40.	"	4)(4)(2	1–6	"	"	
g.	Kuhač 915.	"	4)(2)(4	"	"	ABAB$_v$	
h.	" 918.	"	b3)(1)(1	bVI–4	"	ABCB$_v$	
i.	" 917.	"	1)(1)(b3	bVI–b6	"	ABA$_v$B	
j.	" 914.	(11) 8,6,11,	4)(1)			ABA$_v$	
k.	" 919.	11,	(b3)			AA$_v$	
1603.	Kuba B.H. 347. (=Kuba XIII. 1.)	(11) ZzZz 5. 8,6,8,6,	1)(4)(1	#VII–b6	6, = ♩♩𝅗𝅥/♩♩𝅗𝅥/	ABAC	
1604.	Kuba B.H. 977. Ms.	(11) ZzZz 5. 8,6,8,6,	1)(5)(1	VII–b6	"	AB^{5}CB$_v$	
1605.	Đorđević 338 (=Đorđević Nar. Pev. p. 13/1)	(11) ZzZz 5. 8,6,8,6,	3)(5)(2	1–8	"	AB^{5}CB$_v$	Slovak., Hungar. (Ruman.?) var.-s (text var.-s also)
1606 a.	Đorđević Nar. Pev. p. 168/1	(11) ZzZz 5. 8,6,8,6,	4)(5)(4	1–9	"	AB^{5}A$_v$B$_v$	
b.	Kuba B.H. 988. Ms. (=Kuba XIII. 52.)	"	5)(5)(4	"	"	"	
1606 bis.	Kuba B.H. 981. Ms.	(11) ZzZz 5. 8,6,8,6,	8)(5)(4	1–8	"	AB^{5}CB$_v$	
1607 a.	Kuhač 837.	(10) ZzZz 5. 8,6,8,6,	5)(2)(b3	VII–5	1. 8, = ♩♩/♩♩/♩♩/♩♩// 2. 8, = ♫♫/♫♫//	ABCD	
b.	" 828.	"	7)(2)(b3	VII–7	"	"	
c.	" 9.	"	4)(2)(b3	VII–5	"	"	
d.	" 829.	(10) 12,12,14,10,	1)(1)(1	bVI–5		AABC	
1608 a.	Kuba B.H. 1030. Ms.	(10) ZzZz 5. 8,6,8,6,	2)(4)(VII	VII–7	1. 8, = ♫♫/♫♫// 2. 8, = ♩♩/♩♩/♩♩/♩♩//	ABCD	
b.	" " 1031. Ms.	"	"	"	"	"	
c.	" " 1032.	"	VII)(4)(4	"	"	"	
d.	" " 1033. Ms.	"	VII)(4)(2	"	"	"	
e.	" " 1034.	"	IV)(1)(VII	"	"	"	
1609.	Kuhač 301.	(11) ZzZz 5. (7.) 8,7,8,7,	#VII)(X)(3	V–5		AB$_4$CB	
1610.	" 326.	ZzZz 5. 8,7,8,7,	V)(VIII)(1	bVI–4		ABCD	text-st.; rimes
1611 a.	Kuba B.H. 22.	ZzZz 5. 8,7,8,7,	1)(1)(1	V–5		ABAB	
b.	" " 21.	"	"	"		"	

X. 8, 7, 8, 7, (5.) 1) ① (1 – 4) ④ (1

Current №	Original edition	Syll.	Last note of sections	Range	Rhythm. structure	Structure	Remark
1612.	Kuba X. 60.	< ZzZz 8, 7, 8, 7, 5.	1) ① (1	VII – 4		ABAC	Slovak. mel. and text var.-s. Text-st.
1613a.	Kuhač 328.	ZzZz 8, 7, 8, 7, 5.	1) ① (1	1 – b6		ABCD	text-st., rimes; urban., sentiment.
b.	Kuba B.H. 131.	(11) ZzZz 8, 7, 8, 7, 5.	1) (VII) (4	VII – b6		"	
1614.	Kačerovski 64.	< ZzZz 8, 7, 8, 7, 5.	1) ① (b3	bVII – b6		ABCD	
1615.	Kuba B.H. 290.	ZzZz 8, 7, 8, 7, 5.	1) ① (4	VII – b6		ABCD	
1616.	Kuba IX. 54.	ZzZz 8, 7, 8, 7, 5.	5) ① (1	VII – 8		ABCD	
1617.	Kuba IX. 48.	ZzZz 8, 7, 8, 7, 5.	1) (b3) (1	bVII – b6		ABCD	
1618a.	Kuba B.H. 862.	(11) ZzZz 8, 7, 8, 7, 5.	1) (b3) (1	VII – 4		ABAB$_v$	Line-inter.: 8, 7, 4–4, 7,
b.	" " 641.	"	"	VII – 5		"	
c.	" " 933.	"	1) (b3) (VII	VII – 4		ABA$_v$C	
d.	" " 261. (= Kuba XII. 2.)	"	VII) (b3) (VII	VII – b5		ABAB$_v$	
e.	Kuba B.H. 204.	"	"	VII – 5		ABAB$_v$	
1619a.	Kuba B.H. 648.	(11) ZzZz r. 8, 7, 8, 7, 5.	1) (b3) (1	VII – 5		ABA$_v$B$_v$	
b.	" " 697.	(r.) "	"	1 – 5		ABCD	
c.	" " 646.	r. "	b3) (b3) (b3	"		ABAB$_v$	word-inter.: 8, 7, 8; 3–4
d.	" " 116.	r. "	"	VII – 5		ABA$_v$C	
e.	" " 117.	r. "	"	"		"	gigo
f.	" " 231.	r. "	"	VII – b6		"	
g.	" " 647.	[not r.!] "	1) ④ (1	VII – 5		ABAB$_v$	
h.	" " 642.	(11) 8, 7, 11,	1) (b3)	VII – 4		AB ?	
1620a.	Bosiljevac 5.	(11) ZzZz 8, 7, 8, 7, 5.	1) (b3) (1	VII – 5		ABAB$_v$	
b.	Đorđević Nar. Rev. p. 6/2	"	b3) ① (b3	VII – 7		ABAB	
1621.	Kuhač 356.	ZzZz 8, 7, 8, 7, 5.	5) ③ (5	1 – 6		ABCD	urban
1622.	Juž. Sib. 414.	(11) ZzZz 8, 7, 8, 7, 5.	VII) ④ (VII	VII – 5		ABCB$_v$	cf. № 915., 1619. Var. Parry 51.
1623.	Kuba B.H. 203.	ZzZz 8, 7, 8, 7, 5.	2) ④ (2	1 – b6		AA$_v$, BA$_{v2}$	
1624.	Kuba B.H. 277	ZzZz 8, 7, 8, 7, 5.	4) ④ (1	1 – 8		ABCD	

X.8,7,8,7,(5.) 1)⑤(1-4)⑤(4; —16,12,16,12, 5,6,5,6,(6.) — 5,7,57(6.)

Current №	Original edition	Syll.	Last note of sections	Range	Rhythm. structure	Structure	Remarks
1625a.)	Kuba XI. 33.	ZzZz 5. 8, 7, 8, 7,	1)⑤(1	VII-8		AB^5AvB_v	Hungar. type ? (5,8,5,8).
b.}	Kuba B.H. 293.	"	"	"		"	
1626a.)	Kuba B.H. 150.	(11) ZzZz 5. 8, 7, 8, 7,	1)⑤(b3	#VII-8		ABCD	
b.}	" " 271.	ZzZz 5. 8, 7, 8, 7,	"	"		"	
c.)	Kačerovski 26.	(11) ZzZz 5. 8, 7, 8, 7,	"	V-8		"	
1627.	Kuba B.H. 142.	ZzZz 5. 8, 7, 8, 7,	b3)⑤(b3	1-7		ABCD	
1628.	Kačerovski 45.	ZzZz 5. < 8, 7, 8, 7,	4)⑤(1	1-9		ABCD	
1629a.)	Bosiljevac 26.	ZzZz 5. 8, 7, 8, 7	4)⑤(4	1-8		ABCD	
b.}	Kuba B.H. 973. Ms. (=Kuba XIII. 30.)	"	4)⑦(4	"		"	
1630.	~~Dordević~~ 2.	(8b) ZzZz 5. r. 8b, 7, 8b, 7,	2)④(2	VII-5		$ABAB_v$	"igra"
1631.	Kuhač 423.	(10) ZzZz 5. r. 10, 4, 10, 4,	b2)(VII)(b2	VII-4		ABAC	
1632.	Kuba B.H. 403.	(10)? ZzZz 5. r.? 10, 5, 10, 5,	4)①(4	1-4		ABAC	two word-interr.: ! 10, 5, 3^2-6^2 1, 5, !
1633.	Kuhač 87.	(10) ZzZz 5. (r.) 10, 5, 10, 5,	b3)(b3)(b3	bVI-4		ABAC	
1634.	Kuhač 1144.	(10) ZzZz 5. r. 10, 6, 10, 6,	VII)②(VII	VII-4	6, = ♫♩/♫♩‖	$ABAB_s$	"kolo"
1635.	Kuhač 62.	ZzZz 5. 10, 6, 10, 6,	6)③(2	1-6	10, = ♫♩/♬♫/♫♩‖	ABCD	text-st., rimes
1636.	Kuhač 201.	ZzZz 5. 10, 9, 10, 9,	5)⑤(5	1-8		ABABv	Italian ? text-st., ‖: 5, 5, 5, 5 :‖ a a b c rimes'
1637.	Kuhač 885.	(11) ZzZz 5. 11, 5, 11, 5,	4)④(4	V-7		ABCD	
1638.	Kuba IX. 53.	ZzZz 5. 16, 12, 16, 12,	1)①(1	VII-5		ABCB	two text-st.-s to one mel. st.! rimes: ‖: a a b b :‖
1639.	Kuhač 937.	zZzZ 6. 5, 6, 5, 6,	1)(VII)(bVII	bVI-4		$ABAB^s$	
1640a.)	Kuhač 933.	zZzZ 6. 5, 6, 5, 6,	1)(b3)(1	VII-4		ABAC	
b.	" 935.	"	"	1-b6		"	
c.}	" 932.	"	3)⑤(3	1-8		"	
d.	" 934.	6,	1)(b3)(1	1-b6		"	
e.)	" 936.	(10) 10, 10, 6,	(b3)(1	VII-4		AAv_1Av_2	
1641.	Kuba B.H. 462.	zZzZ 6. 5, 6, 5, 6,	1)①(1	1-b3	5, = ♩♩/♫♩‖	ABAB	"Kolo"
1642.	Kuhač 265.	zZzZ 6. 5, 7, 5, 7,	3)③(3	#VI-5		ABABv	

X. 6, 8, 6, 8 (6.) – 8, 11, 8, 11, (6); —— zzzZ (9)

Current №	Original edition	Syll.	Last note of sections	Range	Rhythm. structure	Structure	Remark
1643-4.	Đorđević Nar. Pev. p. 29/1	(8) zZzZ 6. 6, 8, 6, 8,	2) ② (2	1–4		ABAB$_v$	
1645.	Đorđević Nar. Pev. p. 71/1	zZzZ 6. 7, 8, 7, 8,	b2) Ⓘⓥ (b2	IX – b2		ABAB$_v$	
1646.	Kuba B. H. 538.	(7) zZzZ 6. < 7, 10, 7, 10,	b3) ① (b3	VII – 4		ABA$_v$B$_v$	
1647.	Kuba B. H. 265.	zZzZ 6. 8, 9, 8, 9,	b3) (b2) (b3	bVI – b6		ABAB$_v$	
1648.	Kuba B. H. 358.	zZzZ 6. 8b, 9, 8b, 9,	3) ③ (3	1–5		ABAB$_v$	
1649.	Kuhač 264.	(10) zZzZ 6. 8, 10, 8, 10,	3) ⑤ (3	1–8		ABCD	< Hungar. urban mel. („Ég a kunyhó")
1650.	Kuhač 177.	(8) zZzZ 6. †. 8, 11, 8, 11,	8) ⑤ (6	1–10		A^{5}B^{5}AB	Hungar. mel.
1651a.	Juž. Srb. 421.	Zzzz 7. < 8, 5, 5, 5,	b3) (b3) (b3	VII – b6		ABBC	
b.	Kuba B. H. 183.	"	b3) ① (b3	1–7		ABB$_v$C	
1652.	Kuhač 825.	Zzzz 7. 8, 6, 6, 6,	b3) (VII) (1	VII – b6		ABB$_v$B$_v$	text-st., rimes
1653.	Đorđević 423.	(10) Zzzz 7. (†.) 8, 6, 6, 6,	2) ① (1	1–4		ABBB	„sedeljka"
1654.	Kuhač 411.	Zzzz 7. 8, 7, 7, 7,	b2) (b3) (1	1–5		ABCC$_v$	
1655a.	Kuba B. H. 558.	(10) Zzzz 7. (†.) 12, 6, 6, 6,	VII) ① (VII	VII – 5		ABCB	Cf. No 781.
b.	" " 559.	"	VII) ① (1	VII – 4		"	
c.	Bosiljevac 11.	"	VII) ④ (VII	"		ABAB$_v$	
d.	Kuba B. H. 689.	"	"	VII – 5		ABCB$_v$	
e.	Đorđević Nar. Pev. p. 167/2	(10) (†.) 11, 6, 5, 6,	VII) (VII) (VII	VII – 4		ABAB$_v$	
f.	Kačerovski 23.	(8) (†.) 15, 10, 8, 11,	VII) ① (1	"		AA$_v$BA$_v$	
1656.	Kuba B. H. 7.	zZZZ 8. 5, 6, 6, 6,	3) ① (3	1–5		ABCD	
1657a.	Kuhač 1444.	(10) zZZZ 8. (†.) 8, 10, 10, 10,	5) ② (5	1–7		ABCC$_v$	
b.	" 1445.	"	"	"		"	
1658a.	Kuhač 1342.	zzzZ 9. 6, 6, 6, 9,	VII) ① (1	VII – 5		ABCC$_v$	
b.	" 1360a)	"	"	"		AA^{3}BB$_v$	
c.	" 119.	"	? *	"		? *	* distorted
d.	" 1343.	"	VII) ② (1	"		AA^{3}BA$_v$	
e.	" 1360b)	"	"	VI – 5		AA^{3}BA^3_v	

Current No	Original edition	Syll.	Last note of sections	Range	Rhythm. structure	Structure	Remarks
f.	" 73.	"	b3)(b3)(b3	VII–5		AABC	
1659a.	Kuhač 862.	(9) zzzZ 9. 6, 6, 6, 9,	1)(1)(1	VI–b5		AABC	
b.	" 861.	"	"	VI–5		"	
c.	Đorđević Nar. Pev. p. 117/2	"	"	IV–4		"	
d.	Kuba B.H. 847.	"	1)(1)(VII	"		"	
e.	Kuba XII. 36.	"	1)(1)(b2	"		AABB$_v$	
f.	Kuba B.H. 288.	"	1)(1)(4	IV–5		AABC	
g.	" " 926.	(9) 6, 6, [ ], 9,	1)(1)[C]			AA[ ]C	
h.	" " 303.	7,	1)(1)(b2	V–5		AABC	
1660.	Kuba B.H. 668.	(10) zzzZ 9. (4.) 7, 7, 7, 10,	5)(1)(VII	VII–5		ABB$_{5v}$C	
1661.	Đorđević Nar. Pev. p. 162/1	(7) zzzZ 9. 4. 7, 7, 7, 10,	5)(1)(4	1–6		ABCD	
1662.	Kuba B.H. 994. (= Kuba XIII. 38.) MS.	(8) zzzZ 9. 4. 8, 8, 8, 9,	1)(1)(1	VI–7		ABCD	
1663.	Đorđević Nar. Pev. p. 48/1	zzzZ 9. 9, 9, 9, 11,	1)(1)(4	VII–5		AABC	
1664a.	Kuhač 109.	ZZZz 10. 6, 6, 6, 4,	VII)(1)(b3	VII–4		AA^{5}A$_v^{55}$B	
b.	Kuba IX. 11.	"	b2)(b3)(b2	VII–7		AA^{5}BC	
c.	Kuhač 1423.	ZZZz 10. 5, 5, 5, 4	VII)(1)(VII	VII–4		AA^{5}AA$_v^5$	
1665.	Kuba B.H. 651.	ZZZz 10. 6, 6, 6, 5,	VII)(VII)(VII	VII–5		AAA$_v$B	
1666.	Kuba B.H. 567.	ZZZz 10. 6, 6, 6, 5,	VII)(VII)(1	VII–4		AABC	
1667.	Kuhač 26.	ZZZz 10. 7, 7, 7, 6,	b6)(1)(b6	1–b6		ABAB$_v$	Italian? (upbeat!!)
1668.	Đorđević 81.	ZZZz 10. 7, 7, 7, 6,	2)(2)(2	1–4		AAAA$_v$	„deca, kad pada kiša"
1669.	Kuhač 1302.	ZZZz 10. 7, 7, 7, 6,	5)(5)(3	#VII–8		ABCD	Hungar. var. (7, 7, 5, 5)
1670.	Kuba IX. 47.	ZZZz 10. 7, 7, 7, 6,	1)(1)(3	VI–5	1.2. 7, = [illegible] 3. 7, = [illegible]	AABC	
1671.	Kuba B.H. 278.	ZZZz 10. 8, 8, 8, 5,	b2)(VII)(b6	V–b6		ABCD	Ruman. var. (8, 8, 8, 8)
1672a.	Kuba B.H. 238.	(8) ZZZz 10. 4. 8, 8, 8, 5,	4)(4)(2	VII–5		AABC	
b.	Bosiljevac 50.	"	"	"		"	
c.	Kuba B.H. 609.	"	4)(4)(4	"		"	„svatovska"

Current No	Original edition	Syll.	Last note of sections	Range	Rhythm. structure	Structure	Remarks
1673a.	Kuhač 212.	ZZZz 10. 8, 8, 8, 6,	1)①(VII	VI-4		AABC	urban text!
b.	" 213.	"	"	"		"	
1674.	Kuhač 269.	(8)ZZZz 10. r. 8, 8, 8, 7,	VII)(VII)(bVI	VI-7		AABC	urban text
1675a.	Kuhač 1422.	ZZZz 10. 8, 8, 8, 7,	b3)①(b3	VII-4		$AA_{sv1}AA_{sv2}$	urban text
b.	Đorđević Nar. Pev. p. 8/2	"	1)(b3)(1	"		"	" "
1676a.	Kuba X. 15.	ZZZz 10. 8, 8, 8, 7,	b2)(b3)(b2	VII-4		$ABAB_v$	
b.	Kuhač 389.	"	b3)(b3)(b3	1-b6		"	urban text
1677.	Kuba IX. 27.	ZZZz 10. 8b, 8b, 8b, 7	1)①(1	VII-b6		AABC	urban text
1678.	Kuba B.H. 709.	(9)ZZZz 10. r. 9, 9, 9, 5,	1)①(1	VI-5		AABC	
1679a.	Đorđević Nar. Pev. p. 136/1	ZZZz 10. 10, 10, 10, 5,	5)⑤(4	1-8	1.2.10, = 5+5	AABC	Slovak var.? Var. Party 53.
b.	Kuba B.H. 1091. (= Kuba XIII. 8.) Ms.	"	5)⑤(3	1-7	" "	"	
c.	Kuba B.H. 963.	"	5)⑤(5	1-b6		"	
1680.	Kuhač 386.	ZZZz 10. *11, 11, 11, 7,	2)③(2	#VI-5		$AA^{s}A^{ss}B$	* partly wrong metrical structure // Hungar. urban m.
1681.	Đorđević Nar. Pev. p. 189/1	ZZZz 10. < 11, 11, 11, 7,	VII)(VII)(4	VII-5	11, = 5+6,	AABC	
1682.	Kuhač 129.	ZZZz 10. 12, 12, 12, 6,	1)①(1	1-b6		$AABA_v$	urban text; text-st., rimes: 6,6 a b / 6,6,6 a a b !
1683.	Kačerovski 19.	ZZZz 10. 14, 14, 14, 12,	2)①(3	1-8		AA_vBB_v	"kolo"
1684.	Kuhač 1286.	ZZZz 10. 14, 14, 14, 13,	2)②(3	1-8		AABC	
1685.	Kuba B.H. 548.	(8)ZZZz 10. r. 16, 16, 16, 10,	1)①(1	VII-4		ABBC	
1686.	Kuba XI. 57.	ZZZ+ZZ 11. 5, 5, 5+5, 5,	1)①(VII	VI-5		$AAB+B_vA_v$	
1687.	Kuhač 168.	(12)ZZZ+ZZ 11. 6, 6, 6+6, 6,	VII)(VII)(VII	bVII-b3		AAB+BC	
1688.	Kuhač 426.	(10)ZZZ+ZZ 11. 6, 6, 6+6, 6,	VII)①(2	VI-5		AA_vB+BC	
1689.	Kuhač 895.	(12)ZZZ+ZZ 11. 6, 6, 6+6, 6,	1)①(1	bVI-4		$AAB+B_vA$	
1690a.	Đorđević 442.	ZZZ+ZZ 11. 8, 8, 8+8, 8,	1)①(VII	VII-4		AAB+BC	
b.	Kuhač 36.	"	"	VII-4		AAB+BA	
c.	" 37.	8,	5)⑤(4	1-8		$AABA_v$	

Current №	Original edition	Syll.	Last note of sections	Range	Rhythm. structure	Structure	Remarks
1691a.	Kuhač 1441.	ZZZ+ZZ 11. 8, 8, 8+8, 8,	b2) ① (1	1–4		$AA_{v1}B+BA_{v2}$	urban text
b.	" 1450	10,	b2) [O C]			AA_v[ ][ ]	
1692a.	Kuhač 1138.	ZZZ+ZZ 11. 8, 8, 8+8, 8,	5) ① (5	VII–b6		ABC+DB	„poskočnica" Hungar. mel.
b.	" 1139.	8,	5) ① (4	1–6		$ABCB_v$	
1693a.	Kuba B. H. 10. (=Kačerovski 68.)	zzZ+Zz 13. 6, 6, 7+8, 6,	5) ⑤ (1	1–8	Perfect } cadence	$ABC+D_E$	
b.	Kuba B. H. 41.	"	4) ④ (2	1–7	Imperfect } cadence	"	
c.	Kuhač 1017.	?	?	?		?	„igra" = fragments of a. b.
1694.	Kuhač 436.	ZZz+zZ 14. 5, 5, 4+4, 5,	D) ① (1	bVI–4		$ABc+cA_v$	urban text
1695.	Juž. Srb. 405.	ZZz+zZ 14. (8b) 8b, 8b, 5+5, 8b,	VII) (VII) (VI	VII–b3		$AA_{B+B}C$	„igra" probably German mel.; Slovakian and Moravian var.-s
1696a.	Kuhač 501a)	ZZz+zZ 14. <8, 8, 6+6, 8,	b2) (b3) (b6	bVI–7		$ABc+c_vD$	
b.	" 501c)	"	"	"		"	
c.	" 501b)	8, 7, 8, 11,	IV) (V) (V	III–3		ABCD	
d.	" 1428.	11,	VII) ① [C]			AB[ ][ ]	
e.	" 1429.						fragment of d. fragment
1697.	Kuhač 100.	[Z] Zz+zZ 14. [8?], 8, 7+7, 8,	[D?] ① (1	1–5		$[A?]A_{B+B}C$	
1698.	Kačerovski 33.	ZZz+zZ 14. 10, 10, 7+7, 10,	4) ① (1	VII–7		$ABc+DB_v$	
1699.	Kuhač 1296.	ZZz+zZ 14. 12, 12, 6+6, 12,	V) ① (4	I–4		ABc+cB	urban text
1700a.	Kuhač 41.	ZZz+zZ 14. 24, 24, 12+12, 24,	D) ① (1	VII–b6		$AA_{B+B}A$	
b.	" 42.	[Z] Zz+zZ 14. [24], 24, 12+12, 24,	D) ① (3	#VII–8		$[A]A_{B+B}A$	
c.	" 43.						3rd section of a.
d.	" 44.						" " "
e.	" 437.						" " "
f.	" 45.						fragments of a.
1701.	~~Đorđević~~ Nar. Pev. p. 96/1	zzZ+Zz 15. 6, 6, 8+8, 5,	5) ⑤ (2	1–7		$AAB+B_c$	
1702a.	Kuhač 1300.	ZZz+zz 15. 7, 7, 6+6, 4,	D) ③ (5	#VII–6		AA^3B+B_bc	
b.	" 1301.	"	1) (b3) (b2	bIII–4		"	

Current №	Original edition	Syll.	Last note of sections	Range	Rhythmic structure	Stucture	Remark
1703.	Kuba B.H. 80 (= Kuba XII. 30.)	ZZZ+Zz 15. 7, 7, 7+7, 4,	VII) (VII) (b3	VII–5		AAB+Bc	
1704.	Đorđević Nar. Pev. p. 62/1	ZZZ+Zz 15. 8, 8, 8+8, 4,	5) (5) (4	1–7		AAB+Bc	
1705.	Kuba X. 49.	ZZZ+Zz 15. 8, 8, 8+8, 6,	3) (3) (5	1–8		AAB+Bc	„igra" Hungar. var.?
1706.	Kuhač 403.	ZZZ+Zz 15. 8, 8, 8+8, 6,	1) (5) (1	1–8		AA^5B+B_vc	urban text. Hungar. mel. var.?
1707a.	Kuhač 202.	(10) ZZz+zz 15. r. 10, 10, 5+5, 5,	VII) (VII) (1	VII–4		$AA_v B+BC$	
b.	" 203.	(10) [Z] Zz+zz 15. r. [10], 10, 5+5, 5,	[ ] (1) (2			[ ] A B+BC	
1708.	Kuhač 325.	ZZz+zz 15. 10, 10, 6+6, 4,	1) (b3) (b3	1–b6		$AA^3A^3_{v_1}+A_{v_2}A_{v_3}$	Slovak. mel. Cf. № 1716.
1709.	Kuba B.H. 831.	(10) ZZz+zz 15. r. 10, 10, 6+6, 4,	b3) (b3) (b3	VII–4		$AAB+\frac{A}{2}C$	„svatovska"
1710.	Kuba B.H. 369.	(8) zzZ+Zz 15. r. 10, 10, 11+13, 6,	2) (2) (3	1–6		$AAB+B_vc$	
1711.	Kuhač 1322.	ZZz+zz 15. 11, 11, 6+6, 5,	3) (3) (5	1–6		$AAB+B_sc$	Slovak. var.?
1712.	Kuba B.H. 696.	(11) ZZz+zz 15. r. 11, 11, 8+8, 3,	1) (1) (VII	VII–5		AAB+Bc	
1713.	Kuhač 622.	ZZz+zz 15. 11, 11, 8*+8*, 3,	2) (2) (1	1–b6		AAB+Bc	* wrong metrical struct. Slovak. var.?
1714.	Kuhač 587.	ZZz+zz 15. 11, 11, 8+8, 3,	3) (3) (4	V–5		AAB+Bc	Slovak., Hungar. var.?
1715.	Kuhač 1384.	ZZz+zz 15. 11, 11, 8+8, 6,	2) (2) (2	VII–5		AAB+Bc	Sloven. var.: Kuhač 1386 [3) (3) (3]; Hungar. var. (simil.)
1716.	Kuhač 1258.	ZZz+zz 15. 12, 12, 6+6, 6,	1) (3) (1	1–6			„svatovska" Slovak. mel.; cf. № 1708
1717.	Kuhač 312.	ZZz+zz 15. 12, 12, 6+6, 4,	2) (2) (4	V–b6		AAB+Bc	Hungar. var.
1718.	Kuhač 1241.	ZZz+zz 15. 12, 12, 8+8, 6,	3) (3) (2	V–6		AAB+Bc	„svatovska" Hungar. var.
1719a.	Kuhač 1408.	ZZz+zz 15. 13, 13, 8+8, 5,	3) (3) (3	V–6		$AAB+B_{sv}c$	
b.	" 1349.	13, 13, 7+7, 14,	"	"		$AAB+B_sA_v$	
1720a.	Kuba B.H. 266. (= Kuba XII. 60.)	zzZ+zZ 16. 5, 5, 6+6, 7,	5) (5) (1	1–8		AAB+CD	
b.	Kuba B.H. 1077. Ms.	"	4) (4) (5	1–7		AA_vB+CD	
1721.	Kuhač 699.	ZZz+zZ 16. 6, 6, 5+5, 10,	4) (VII) (VII	VII–5		AAB+BC	
1722a.	Kuhač 874.	(8b) ZZz+zZ 16. r. 8b, 8b, 6+6, 15,	1) (1) (1	VII–4		$AAB+BA_v$	
b.	" 875.	"	"	VII–5		"	
c.	" 872.	(8b) [Z] Zz+zZ 16. r. [8b] 8b, 6+6, 15,	[ ] (1) (1	"		$[\,]AB+BA_v$	
d.	" 873.						fragment

Current №	Original edition	Syll.	Last note of sections	Range	Rhythm. structure	Structure	Remarks
1723.	Kuhač 1462	(8) Z Z Z+Z Z 16. r.< 8, 8, 8+8, 10,	1)①(1	b VI–4		AAB+B₃C	Ruman. urban var.?
1724.	Kačerovski 20.	(10) Z Z z+z Z 16. r.? 10, 10, 6+6, 7,	4)①(2	1–8		AB c+c D	cf. Parry 52. (3. section similar)
1725.	Đorđević Nar. Pev. p. 157/1*	Z Z z+z Z 16. < 10, 10, 6+7, 14,	VII)①(1	VII–7		ABc+c D	*p. 156 altogether missing
1726.	Kuba IX. 17.	(10) Z Z z+z Z 16. r. 10, 10, 6+6, 18,	2)②(2	VII–7		A AB+B Bv	
1727.	Kuba B.H. 201.	(5) Z Z z+z Z 16. r. 10, 10, 8+8, 12,	1)①(4	VII–b6		AAB+B C	„svatovska"
1728.	Đorđević Nar. Pev. p. 69/1	Z Z z+z Z 16. 11, 11, 8+8, 12,	4)④(2	IV–7		AAv B+c D	some resemblance to a new Hungar. mel.
1729.	Kuhač 1088.	(10) Z Z z+z Z 16. r. 12, 12, 7+7, 13,	VII)(VII)(2	VII–4		AAB+B C	„poskočnica" two part song (Bosnia)
1730.	Kačerovski 74.	Z Z z+z Z 16. 12, 12, 5+7, 14,	3)③(3	1–6		AAB+B C	
1731.	Kuhač 576.	Z Z z+z Z 16. 13, 13, 7+7, 11,	1)①(1	VII–4		AAB+B° C	Slovak., Hungar. text var.
1732.	Kuhač 689.	Z Z z+z Z 16. 16, 16, 5+5, 9,	5)⑤(7	1–9		<ABCD	contamination of Hungar. mel.-s.
1733a.	Kuhač 27.	(8) Z Z [z+z Z] 16 bis. 11, 8, [6+6, 8]	b3)①[(b3]	VII–4		AAv [ ] [ ]	1st half of a German mel.
b.	Kuba IX. 28.	"	"	"		"	
c.	Kuhač 1383.	"	1)①[(1]	"		"	
1734.	Kuhač 1204.	4, 4, 7, 6, 17.	VII)(VII)(VII	VII–5		AABC	„svatovska"
1735.	Kuhač 1439.	6, 6, 8, 5, 17.	b3)(b3)(b3	VII–4		AABC	
1736.	Kačerovski 27.	6, 6, 8, 7, 17.	4)④(2	VII–5		AABC	
1737a.	Kuba B.H. 71.	6, 6, 9, 10, 17.	1)①(VII	VII–8		AABC	
b.	Kuhač 388.	"	4)④(1	1–8		"	
1738–9.	Kuba B.H. 423.	7, 7, 6, 5, 17.	b3)①(1	1–4		AABC	
1740a.	Kačerovski 73.	7, 7, 8, 6, 17.	VII)①(VII	VII–5		ABCD	
b.	" 83.						1st half of a.
1741.	Đorđević Nar. Pev. p. 149/2	7, 7, 8, 6, 17.	1)①(4	VII–7		AABAv	text-st., rimes
1742a.	Kuba B.H. 255.	7, 7, 8, 6, 17.	V)⑤(1*	V–b6		ABCD	x x x * the last tone has a fourth lower var. (prob. later development) this would give: 1)⑧(4!
b.	Kuba X. 28.	"	5)(b3)(b3	1–b6		"	4x rimes
1743.	Kuhač 1414.	8, 8, 5, 7, 17.	VII)(VII)(4	VII–5		AABC	cf. Bartók, Ruman. Folk-music, II. №
1744a.	Kuba B.H. 836.	(8) r. 8, 8, 6, 5, 17.	VII)(VII)(2	VII–4		ABCD	prob. a „bag-pipe" mel.

Current No	Original edition	Syll.	Last note of section	Range	Rhythm. structure	Structure	Remarks
b.	~~Đorđević Nar. Pev.~~ p. 175/2	(8) r. 8, 8, 6, 7,	1) (VII) (b3	IV – 4		ABCBv	
1745–6.	Kuba B.H. 276. (= Kuba XIV. 11. *)	8, 8, 6, 7, 17.	3) (1) (1	1 – b6		AAvBBv	* 2nd half of text refr. differs
1747.	Kuba B.H. 445.	8, 8, 6, 10, 17.	4) (4) (1	1 – b6		AABC	
1748–9.	Kuhač 1415.	8, 8, 7, 6, 17.	VII) (1) (b3	VII – b6		ABCD	var.: Bartók, Ruman. Folk-music, II. No
1750 a.	Kuhač 96.	8, 8, 7, 6, 17.	3) (2) (1	1 – 6		ABCD	Hungar. var.
b.	" 1115a)	"	3) (2) (2	"		"	"poskočnica"
c.	" 95.	"	3) (1) (2	"		"	
1751.	Kuba B.H. 138.	8, 8, 7, 6, 17.	5) (b3) (4	1 – b6		ABCD	
1752.	Kuba B.H. 281.	8, 8, 7, [9,] 17.	5) (VII) (1	VII – b6		AAvB[C]	> new Hungar. (urban?) mel. [Sej haj göndöra babám]
1753 a.	Kuhač 574.	(8) < 8, 8, 7, 10, r. 17.	9) (5) (5	VI – 10		ABCD	Hungar. urban mel.; text of refr.: transla-tion of the Hung. refr.
b.	Kuba IX. 38.	"	"	#VII – 10		"	
1754.	Juž. Srb. 411.	(8) 8, 8, 10, 4, (r.) 17.	4) (1) (1	VII – b6		ABCBv	
1755.	Kuba B. H. 806.	(8b) 8b, 8b, 10, 4, r. 17.	VII) (1) (VII	VII – b2		ABCCv	word inters.: 8, 2–6, 10, 4, "uspavanka"
1755bis.	~~Đorđević Nar. Pev.~~ p. 15/1	(8b) 8b, 8b, 12, 5, r.	2) (2) (1	1 – 4		AAvBC	giga
1756.	Kuhač 319.	(8) 8, 8, 10, 9, r. 17.	1) (2) (1	1 – 5		ABAvBv	
1757.	Kuba B.H. 886.	(8) 8, 8, 15, 10, r. 17.	b3) (VII) (b2	bVI – 4		ABCD	
1758.	Kuba X. 59.	(8b) 8b, 8b, 16, 15, r. 17.	2) (2) (1	1 – 5		AABC	two part song
1759.	Kuba B.H. 835.	(10) (r.) < 9, 9, 10, 6, 17.	VII) (VII) (VII	VII – 4		AAAvB	
1760.	Kuhač 1113.	10, 10, 6, 8, 17.	VII) (VII) (1	VII – 5		AABBv	"poskočnica"
1762.	Kuba XI. 2.	(7) (r.) 10, 10, 8, 6, 17.	1) (1) (VII	VII – 5	10, = ♩♩♩|♩♩♩|♩♩♩|; 6, = ♩♩♩|♩♩♩|	AAvBC	"svatovska"
1761.	Kuba B.H. 373.	(10) 10, 10, 8, 6, 17.	1) (1) (1	1 – 6		AABC	
1763.	Kuba XII. 19.	10, 10, 8, 7, 17.	2) (2) (2	VII – 5		AAAvB	
1764 a.	Kuhač 1291.	(10) r. 10, 10, 8, 11, 17.	1) (1) (1	bVI – 4		AABC	
b.	Kuhač 1292.	"	2) (VII) (1	VI – 4		AA3BC	
c.	" 1290.	(10) r. 10, 10, [ ], 11,	1) (1) [C]			AA[ ]C	
d.	" 1294	?	?			?	contamination

Current No	Original edition	Syll.	Last note of sections	Range	Rhythm. structure	Structure	Remarks
e.	Kuhač 1295.	?	?			?	contamination
1765.	Kuhač 182.	10, 10, 8, 12, 17.	bVI) (bVI) (b3	V–4		$AA_s BC$	german mel.
1766.	Kuba B.H. 86.	< 10, 10, 13, 15, 17.	5) (IV) (IV	IV–7		ABCD	
1767a.	Kuba B.H. 253.	(10) r. 10, 10, 17, 18, 17.	VI) (VII) (1	V–5		AABC	
b.	~~Đorđević~~ Nar. Pev. p. 112/1	(10) r. 10, 10, 16, 18, 17.	VII) (VII) (VII	VII–4		AABC	
1768.	~~Đorđević~~ 80.	(11) (r.) 11, 11, 6, 7, 17.	b3) (b3) (b3	1–7		AABC	„žetvarska"
1769.	~~Đorđević~~ Nar. Pev. p. 182/1	(8) r. 12, 12, 10, 9, 17.	1) (b3) (1	VII–4		AABC	
1770.	Kuhač 351.	12, 12, 13, 9, 17.	2) (1) (2	1–5		ABCD	
1771.	Kuba X. 38.	12, 12, 13, 11, 17.	bIII) (bVI) (4b	bIII–b3		ABCD	
1772-3.	Kuba B.H. 239.	(6) r. 12, 12, 16, 23, 17.	VII) (VI) (4	VI–7		AABC	
1774.	~~Đorđević~~ Nar. Pev. p. 126/1	(6) r. 14, 14, 10, 13, 17.	b3) (1) (1	VII–7		$ABCC_v$	
1775.	Kuhač 1419.	15, 15, 6, 7, 17.	1) (1) (2	V–4		AABC	
1776.	Kuhač 336.	5, 6, 7, 7, 20.	b3) (b3) (1	VI–5		ABCC	
1777.	Kuba XII. 49.	6, 5, 8, 8, 20.	1) (1) (VII	VII–b5		$ABA_v B_v$	
1778a.	Kuba XI. 9.	(10) (r.) 7, 8, 6, 6, 20.	1) (V) (1	V–5		$AA_v BB_v$	Cf. No 956 and Parry No 25.
b.	~~Đorđević~~ Nar. Pev. p. 14/1	(10) (r.) 7, 8, 10, 10, 20.	b3) (bVI) (b2	bVI–4		$AA_{sv} BB_v$	
c.	Kačerovski 1.	"	"	"		"	
1779.	Kuhač 548	(10) r. 8, 6, 5, 5, 20.	4) (1) (b2	1–b6		ABCD	
1780.	Kuba B.H. 635.	(10) (r.) < 8, 6, 7, 7, 20.	2) (VII) (4	VII–5		$ABCB_v$	line interr.: 8, 6, 2–5, 7,
1781.	~~Đorđević~~ Nar. Pev. p. 190/1	8, 6, 7, 7, 20.	b3) (b3) (b3	1–b3		$ABCC_v$	
1782.	Kuhač 481.	(10) 8, 6, 10, 10, 20.	3) (5) (2	1–6		$ABCC_v$	
1783.	Kuhač 1110.	(10) (r.) 8, 6, 10, 10, 20.	4) (8) (3	1–8		$ABCC_v$	„poskočnica"
1784.	Kuhač 948a) b)	(8) r. 8, 7, 5, 5, 20.	IV) (1) (VII	IV–4		ABCD	
1785.	Kuhač 852.	8, 7, 13, 13, 20.	1) (1) (b3	VI–b6		$ABCC_v$	
1786.	Kačerovski 55.	(6) r. 12, 10, 8, 8, 20.	VII) (VI) (2	VII–7		AABC	

Current No	Original edition	Syll.	Last note of sections	Range	Rhythm. structure	Structure	Remarks
1787.	Kuba X. 56.	7, 5, 7, 4, 21.	bIII) (VII) (1	bIII – 4		ABCD	
1788.	Kuhač 796.	7, 8, 7, 6, 21.	VII) (b3) (VII	VII – 5		ABAB$_v$	urban: upbeat!
1789a.	Kuba B.H. 73.	(8) r. 8, 5, 8, 10, 21.	VII) (1) (VII	VII – 5		ABAB$_v$	„kolo"
b.	" " 312. (= Kuba XIII. 17.)	(11) (r.) 8, 5, 8, 10, 21.	1) (1) (1	VII – 4		"	
c.	Kuba B.H. 521.	(8) r. 8, 5, 8, 10, 21.	4) (VII) (4	VII – 4		ABAB$_v$	
d.	" " 815.	(8) r. 8, 5, 8, 8, 21.	1) (1) (1	VII – 4		"	
e.	" " 816.	"	"	"		"	
f.	" " 1120 Ms	"	"	"		"	
1790.	Kuba B.H. 202.	8, 6, 8, 7, 21.	4) (1) (4	VII – b6		ABAB$_v$	
1791.	Kuhač 324.	(10) r. 8, 6, 8, 7, 21.	VII) (2) (2	VII – b6		ABCA$_v$	
1792.	Kuba B.H. 549.	(8) r. 8, 6, 8, 7, 21.	4) (4) (VII	VII – 4		ABCD	
1793.	Kuhač 1011.	(8) r. 8, 7, 8, 5, 21.	2) (VII) (2	VII – 5			„igra"
1794.	Kuhač 598.	(10) r. 10, 16, 10, 5, 21.	1) (1) (1	VII – 5		ABB$_v$, B$_{v_2}$	
1795a.	Kuhač 11. (= Đorđević Nar. Pev. p. 26/2)	(10) r. 8, 6, 6, 7, 21bis.	VII) (2) (VII	VII – 5		ABCD	
b.	" 10.	"	"	"		"	
c.	" 12.	"	VII) (2) (1	"		"	
1796.	Kuba B.H. 584.	8, 6, 6, 10, 21bis.	VII) (VII) (VII	VII – 4		ABBC	
1797.	Kuba B.H. 580.	8, 7, 7, 6, 21bis.	VII) (1) (b3	VII – 4		ABCD	
1798.	Kuhač 1125.	5, 7, 6, 7, 22.	3) (3) (3	1 – 5		ABAB$_v$	„poskočnica"
1799.	Kuhač 1378.	6, 5, 8, 5, 22.	b3) (b3) (b2	VII – 4		AA$_v$ BC	
1800a.	Kuhač 1402.	7, 6, 8, 6, 22.	2) (VII) (VII	VII – 5		ABA$_v$ C	
b.	" 1403.	"	2) (2) (VII	"		"	
c.	" 76.	"	2) (2) (2	1 – 5		AA$_v$ BC	
1801.	Kuba B.H. 658.	7, 6, 8, 6, 22.	VII) (2) (1	VII – 5		ABCD	
1802.	Kuhač 271.	7, 6, 8, 6, 22.	2) (2) (2	1 – 7		AABC	
1803.	Kuhač 1106.	7, 6, 8, 6, 22.	3) (3) (3	1 – 5		ABB$_v$ C	„poskočnica"

Current №	Original edition	Syll.	Last note of sections	Range	Rhythm. structure	Structure	Remarks
1804a.	Kuhač 220 (=Đorđević Nar. Pev. p. 167/1)	7,6,8,6, [22.]	VII) (4) (1	VII-b6		ABCD	
b.	Kuhač 221.	"	"	"		"	
1805.	Kuba B.H. 919.	7,6,8,6, [22.]	4) (4) (4	VII-4		ABA_vC	
1806.	Kuhač 527.	8,5,6,5, [22.]	4) (2) (2	VII-5		ABCD	
1807.	Kuhač 210.	8,6,7,6, [22.]	3) (V) (3	III-4		ABCD	
1808.	Kuba X. 37.	(10) (r.) 8,6,7,6, [22.]	1) (b3) (b2	VII-5		ABCD	
1809a.	Kuba B.H. 20.	(10) (r.) 8,6,10,6, [22.]	1) (4) (V	V-5		ABCD	new Hungar. mel. [6,6,10,6,]
b.	" " 19.						fragment of a.
1810.	Kuhač 613.	(10) r. 10,6,8,6, [22.]	4) (1) (2	1-6		ABCD	
1811.	Kuba 659.	(10) (r.) 10,6,13,10 [22bis.]	2) (b3) (VII	VII-4		AA_vBC	
1812.	Đorđević 523.	(8) r. 14,17,12,14, [22bis.]	1) (VII) (VII	VII-4		ABB_vA_v	
1813-4	Kuba B.H. 333 (=Kuba XIII. 54.)*	(10) (r.) 8,6,13,12,	b2) (1) (1	VII-4		AA_vBC	„kolo" * two unessential differ.
1815a.	Kuba B.H. 342.	(6) r. 9,5,6,7, [23.]	1) (1) (4	VII-b5		AA_vB A_{v2}	
b.	Đorđević Nar. Pev. p. 28/2	"	"	VII-5		"	
c.	Bosiljevac 2.	"	"	1-5			
1816.	Đorđević Nar. Pev. p. 155/1	10,12,14,13, [23.]	1) (1) (1	VII-4		AA_vBB_v	
1817.	Kuba B.H. 513.	(11) (r.) 11,12,6,7, [23.]	b3) (VII) (VII	VII-4		$ABCC_v$	
1818.	Kuhač 368.	11, 12,10,8, [23.]	VII) (VII) (2	VI-4		AABC	
1819.	Kuba B.H. 512.	(8) r. 12,14,9,10 [23.]	b3) (VII) (VII	VII-b3		ABCD	
1820.	Kuba B.H. 717.	(10) (r.) 8,6,5+5,5 [24.]	VII) (1) (VII	VI-5		$ABC+C_vD$	
1821.	Kuba B.H. 561.	(10) (r.) 8,6,5+5,11, [24.]	1) (2) (3	V-5		ABC+CD	
1822.	Kuhač 1022.	8,8,8,8+8, [24.]	1) (1) (b6	VII-b6		$AA_{sv}BC+C_s$	„igra"
1823.	Kuba B.H. 527.	(8) r. 8,7+7,6+5,5 [24.]	1) (VII) (VII	VII-4		AB+B C+DE	
1824.	Iz Levča 54.	(10) r. 10,6,7+7,3, [24.]	b3) (1) (1	VII-4		$ABC+C_sD$	
1825.	Kuhač 1464.	10,6,8+8,6+6, [24.]	b3) (4) (1	VII-5		$ABC+C_vD+D_v$	

135 X. 24.

Current No	Original edition	Syll.	Last note of section	Range	Rhythm. structure	Structure	Remarks
1826.	Kuba B.H. 987. Ms.	(10) r. 10,8,5+5,6, 24.	VII) (VII) (VII	VII − 4		ABC+DE	gigaga
1827.	Kuhač 298.	10,8,7+6,7, 24.	2) (2) (1	VI − 4		ABC+DE	
1828.	Kuhač 49.	(10) r. 11,5+5,8,6, 24.	2) (VII) (VII	VII − 4		AB+BCD	
1829.	Kuba B.H. 626.	8+8,5,7+8,10, 24.	4) (VII) (1	VII − 5		?	
1830.	Kuba B.H. 1011. Ms.	17,13,8+11,7, 24.	1) (1) (1	VII − 5		ABC+DE	

Melodies of children's play type (no definite structure)

No	Original edition	Remarks
1831.	Kuhač 282.	
1832 a.	Kuhač 382.	
b.	" 449.	
1833.	" 401.	
1834 a.	" 1012.	"kolo"
b.	" 1013.	fragment
1835.	" 1077.	"kolo"
1836.	" 1090	"ciganskokolo"
1837.	" 1104.	"poskočnica"
1838.	" 1120.	"poskočnica"
1839.	" 1243	"svatovska"
1840.	" 1285.	
1841.	" 1305.	
1842.	" 1365.	
1843.	" 1375.	
1844.	" 1430.	
1845.	Kuba B.H. 51.	
1846.	" " 371.	
1847.	" " 427.	
1848.	" " 540.	"kolo"
1849.	" " 1012. Ms.	
1850.	Đorđević 339.	"dečja igra"
1851.	" 393.	"slavska"
1852.	" 517.	"slavska"
1853.	" 521.	
1854.	" 591.	
1855.	Kačerovski 84.	

Melodies of confused, undeterminable structure

No	Original edition	Remarks
1856.	Kuhač 46.	
1857.	" 47.	
1858.	" 54.	
1859.	" 72.	
1860.	" 83.	
1861.	" 90.	
1862.	" 97.	
1863 a.	" 171.	
b.	" 172.	
c.	" 173.	
1864.	" 366.	
1865.	" 465.	
1866.	" 490.	
1867.	" 511.	
1868.	" 531.	
1869.	" 857.	
1870.	" 928.	"u vrijeme mesopusta"
1871.	" 1020.	"igra"
1872.	" 1023.	"igra"
1873.	" 1048.	"kolo"
1874.	" 1062.	Cf. Parry No1. !!
1875.	" 1272.	"svatovska"
1876.	" 1406.	
1877.	Kuba B.H. 6.	
1878.	" " 34.	gigaga
1879.	" " 526.	
1880.	" " 634.	
1881.	" " 650.	
1882.	" " 687.	
1883.	" " 691.	
1884.	Kuba B.H. 699.	
1885.	" " 858.	"svatovsko kolo"
1886.	" " 885.	
1887.	" " 992. Ms.	
1888.	" " 997. Ms.	
1889.	" " 1017. Ms.	
1890.	" " 1068. Ms.	
1891.	Kuba IX. 49.	two part song
1892.	Kuba XII. 38.	
1893.	Đorđević 451.	
1894.	Đorđević Nar. Pes. p. 111/1	
1895.	" p. 140/1	
1896.	Iz Levča 9.	"svatovska"

Finished: July 1942.

136

Tabulation of Parry № 1 – 54.

Current №	Record №	Syll.	Last note of sections	Range	Rhythm. structure	Structure	Referring to variants in Tab. of Mat.
1.	553–4	10, 8,		1–b3	Cf. Kuhač 1062.		Var. № 310 (10,) and 146 (8,)
2.	3572–3	8,	(1)	VII–b3		AAv	Var. № 130
3.	3557–9	8,	(b3)	VII–4		AB	Var. № 181
4.	3586	8b,	(2)	1–4		A³Av	Var. № 236.
5.	3074	8b,	(b3)	VII–4		AB	Var. № 243
6a.	3153–5	10,	(VII)	VII–4		AB	Var. № 265
b.	3574–5	"	"	"		AAv	
c.	3071–3	"	"	"		AB	
7.	609	10,	(VII)	VII–4		AB →	New mel.; its place between № 268 and 269 of Tab. of Mat.
8a.	3125–7	10,	(1)	VII–b3		AA	Var. № 284.
b.	3156	"	"	1–b3		AA	
9.	3197–3200	10,	(1)	VII–5		AAv	Var. № 298
10a.	3137–3141	10,	(1)	1–b3		AA	Var. № 303
b.	3128–9, 3133	"	"	"		"	
11.	3109–3112	10,	(b3)	VII–4		AAv	Var. № 365–6
12a.	3180–4, 3187	10,	(b3)	VII–4		AB	Var. № 384
b.	3052–3	10,	"	"		"	
c.	3079–3080	"	"	"		"	
d.	3225–6	"	"	"		"	
e.	3163–4	"	"	"		"	
13.	1547	10,	(1)	VII–7	4+3+3	AB →	New mel.; its place between № 403 and 404 in Tab. of Mat.
14.	3215–6	(7) 11,	(1)	1–4		AA → (Var. № 418.)	Cf. {№ 592a–d., " 679a–d.} in Tab. of Mat.
15.	3213–4	11,	(b3)	1–5		AB	Var. № 432.
16a.	3232–3 st. 1–6, 9, 10, 12.	(8) 12,	(1)	1–b3	4+4+4	A A	Var. № 452.
b.	st. 7, 8, 11.	(8) 8, 12, 8,	1) (1)	VII–b3		A B Bv	Var. № 993. and Parry № 29.

Current No	Record No	Syll.	Last note of section	Range	Rhythm. structure	Structure	Referring to variants in Tab. of Mat.
17.	3123-4	(8) 12,	(1)	1-4	4+4+4	AA_v	Var. No 34. (fragmentary)
18.	3178-9	8,	(b3) (1	VII-5		ABB	→ New mel., its place between No 639-40 and 641 in Tab. of Mat.
19.	3050-1	10,	(b3) (1	1-3		ABB	→ New mel., its place: between No 654 b&b and 655 in Tab. of Mat.
20.	526-8	8,	VII) (VII)	VII-4		AA_vB	→ New mel., its place: between No 682 and 683 of Tab. of Mat.
21a.	3161	8,	b3) (b3)	1-4		AAB	→ New mel., its place between No 693 and 694 in Tab. of Mat.
b.	3576-7	"	4) (4)	VII-b6		"	"
22.	3121	(8b) 8b, 8b, 5, 1)1.	(4) (2	1-5		AA_vB	→ New mel., its place: between No 727 and 728-9 in Tab. of Mat.
23a.	3081-2	8, 6, 6, 1)5.	(1) (4	VII-4		ABC	Var. No 786.
b.	3486	"	"	VII-5		ABC	"
24.	3547-8	(8b) 11, 8b, 8b, 1)5.	(b3) (4	VII-5		AA_{v1}, A_{v2}	Var. No 827.
25.	3131-2, 3130	(10) (4.) 6, 6, 10, 1)2.	1) (1)	1-4		AAB	Var. No 956. Cf. No 1778
26.	3560-1	(10) 10, 6, 10, 1)3.	2) (4)	1-5		AA_vB	Var. No 980.
27a.	3553-6	(10) 10, 6, 10, 1)3.	b3) (b3)	VII-4		AA_vB	Var. No 983. Cf. No 384 and Parry No 12.
b.	3519-22	"	"	"		"	
c.	3116-7	"	3) (3)	"		"	
d.	3211-2	"	b3) (b3)	VII-5		"	
e.	2934	"	"	"		"	
28a.	1538a), 1539-40	(10) 10, 6, 10, 1)3.	b3) (b3)	VII-7		AA_{v1}, A_{v2}	Var. No 984.
b.	524-5	"	"	1-7		•	
c.	532-3	"	"	"		AA'_vB	
29.	3122	(8) 8, [12], 8, 1)4.	1) [(1)]	VII-b2		$A[\ ]A_v$	Var. No 993. and Parry No 16 b.
30.	3206-7	(11) (4.) 8, 6, 5, 3)3.	1) (4)	1-5		ABC	Var. No 1014.
31a.	3509-11	(10) 4, 6, 6, 4,	1) (1) (b3	1-4		ABBA	Var. No 1033.
b.	3086-9	"	1) (1) (4 / 2) (2) (4	1-5		ABB_vA	
c.	3527	(10) 4, 6, 4, 6, 4	1) (2) (2	1-3		ABBC	

Current №	Record №	Syll.	Last note of sections	Range	Rhythm. structure	Structure	Referring to variants in Tab. of Mat.
d.	3190-1	(10) 4, 6, 6, 4,	4) (b3) (b3	1-4		ABBC	
32.	3031-3	(10) 4, 6, [ ], 4	1) (1) [C]	1-b3		AB[ ]A	New mel., its place: between № 1040-1 and 1042 as … in Tab. of Mat.
33.	3019-20	"	VII) (2) [C]	VII-b3		AB[ ]C	New mel., its place: between № 1040-1 and 1042 as … in Tab. of Mat.
34.	606-8	8,	VII) (VII) (VII	VII-4		ABB_vC	Var. № 1208.
35.	855-7	8,	b3) (1) (b3	VII-7		ABCB	New mel., its place: between № 1224 and 1225 in Tab. of Mat.
36.	519-521	8,	b3) (b3) (1	1-7		ABCD	Var. № 1247 cf. № 1268.
37.	3562	(9) 12,	1) (1) (1	1-b3		AA_vAA_v	New mel., its place: between № 1339 and 1340 in Tab. of Mat.
38.	3566	(8b) 6, 5, 6, 5, 5.	1) (1) (1	VII-4		ABAB	Var. № 1469.
39a.	3157	8, 5, 8, 5, 5.	VII) (1) VII	VII-3		ABAC	Var. № 1495.
b.	2938	"	VII) (b2) (VII	"		"	
40.	3075	8, 5, 8, 5, 5.	2) (1) (2	VII-4		ABAB	New mel., its place: between № 1498 and 1499 in Tab. of Mat.
41.	3077-8	8, 5, 8, 5, 5.	4) (b3) (4	VII-5		ABA_vC	Var. № 1502.
42.	529-530	8, 5, 8, 5, 5.	VII) (b2) (VII	VII-5		ABCD	Var. № 1505. Cf. № 1557.
43.	3174-5	8, 5, 8, 5, 5.	1) 2) (2) (1 (2	VII-4		AA_v, AA_{v_2}	New mel., its place: between № 1506 and 1507 in Tab. of Mat.
44a	3034-5	8, 5, 8, 5, 5.	VII) (4) (VII	VII-5		ABA_vC	Var. № 1514
b.	2936	"	VII) (4) (2	VII-7		"	
45.	3541-2	8, 5, 8, 5, 5.	VII) (3) (VII	VII-4		AA_vAB	New mel., its place: between № 1521 and 1522 in Tab. of Mat.
46.	3192-6	8, 6, 8, 6, 5.	1) (2) (VII) (1	VII-4 (1)		$ABAB_v$	Var. № 1561
47.	3170-1	8, 6, 8, 6, 5.	4) (b3) (4	VI-5		$ABAB_v$	New mel., its place: between № 1572 and 1573 in Tab. of Mat.
48.	3568-9, 3567	8, 6, 8, 6, 5.	2) (2) (2	1-5		$ABAB_s$	Var. № 1580.
49.	3505	(11) 8, 7, 8, 7, 5.	1) (1) (1	V-5		ABAB	New mel., its place: between № 1610 and 1611 in Tab. of Mat.
50.	3234	8, 7, 8, 7, 5.	4) (1) (4	VII-3		ABAC	New mel., its place: between № 1615 and 1616 in Tab. of Mat.
51.	3487-8	(11) 8, 7, 8, 7, 5.	VII) (4) (VII	VII-3		ABA_vB_v	Var. № 1622. Cf. № 915 and 1619.
52.	3523-4, 3525-6	(10) (t.) 12, 6, 12, 6, 5.	2) (b3) (2	1-b6		$ABAB_v$	New mel., its place: between № 1637 and 1638 in Tab. of Mat.; Cf. № 1724.
53.	3512-3, 3514-5	10, 10, 10, 5, 10.	5) (5) (5	VII-7		AABC	Var. № 1679.
54.	3224						Cf. № 869

Appendix III. Kuhač

1 L
2 L ———
3 ——— ?
4 = 189.
5a) = 1216 bis.
5b) = 1302.
6 L ———
7 = 655b.
8a) = 655c.
8b) = 655d.
9 = 1607c.
10 = 1795b.
11 = 1795a.
12 = 1795c.
13 = 1006b.
14 = 945.
15 = 1570h.
16 L ———
17 = 1499b.
18 = 1285j.
19 ——— ?
20 = 1545a.
21 = 270c.
22 = 270e.
23 = 270f.
24a) ———
24b) L
25 = 270d.
26 = 1667.
27 = 1733a.
28 L ———
29 = 1193.
30 L ———
31 L ———
32 = 1214b.
33 = 377a.
34 L ———
35 = 863
36 = 1690b.
37 = 1690c.
38 ——— ?
39 L ———
40 L ———

41 = 1700a.
42 = 1700b.
43 = 1700c.
44 = 1700d.
45 = 1700f.
46 = 1856.
47 = 1857.
48 L ———
49 = 1828.
50 = 1481b.
51 = 327a.
52 = 1097b.
53 = 321a.
54 = 1858.
55 = 1555c.
56 = 1115.
57 ——— ?
58 = 846-7.
59 = 887.
60 = 423a.
61 = 423b.
62 = 1635.
63a) = 1255c.
63b) = 1255b.
64 L ———
65 = 1057d.
66 = 1057c.
67 = 330b.
68 = 414c.
69 = 33.
70 = 755f.
71 = 748.
72 = 1859.
73 = 1658f.
74 = 1246c.
75 L ———
76 = 1800c.
77 = 586.
78 = 1370b.
79 L ———
80 L ———

81 L ———
82 = 563a.
83 = 1860.
84 L ———
85 ——— ?
86 = 1363.
87 = 1633.
88 = 524.
89 L ———
90 = 1861.
91 = 1170.
92 = 1474.
93 L ———
94 = 960.
95 = 1750c.
96 = 1750a.
97 = 1862
98 = 1219.
99 = 641.
100 = 1697.
101 = 1592b.
102 L ———
103 L ———
104 L ———
105 L ———
106 = 511b.
107 = 1543.
108 = 983gg.
109 = 1664a.
110 L ———
111. L ———
112 = 1458b.
113 = 1168e.
114 = 1094h.
115 L ———
116 = 852a.
117 = 852b.
118 = 599.
119 = 1658c.
120 L ———

121 L ———
122 = 200a.
123 = 200f.
124 = 200b.
125 = 200c.
126 = 200g.
127 = 200d.
128 = 1271b.
129 = 1682.
130 = 676.
131 = 1166b.
132 = 1005d.
133 = 105e.
134 = 1570f.
135 = 1570i.
136 L ———
137 L ———
138 L ———
139 = 229b.
140 = 1546c.
141 = 1547.
142 = 1117.
143 = 516b.
144 L ———
145 = 1376.
146a) = 126a.
146b) = 126b.
147 = 1541.
148 = 1531c.
149 = 1506c.
150 ——— ?
151 L ———
152 L ———
153 = 1387.
154 ——— ?
155 = 335c.
156 L ———
157 = 134k.
158a) = 1277a.
158b) = 1277b.
159 = 1009.
160 = 848a.

161 = 848b.
162 ——— ?
163 = 1307.
164 = 912.
165 = 1337b.
166 L ———
167 L ———
168 = 1687.
169 = 663.
170 = 43b.
171 = 1863a.
172 = 1863b.
173 = 1863c.
174 = 1415.
175 = 1394.
176 L ———
177 = 1650
178 = 1010c.
179 = 1124c.
180 = 1301b.
181 = 38.
182 = 1765.
183 L ———
184 = 1330b
185 = 113.
186 = 114.
187 = 43e.
188 L ———
189 = 1246k.
190 L ———
191 L ———
192 L ———
193 L ———
194 L ———
195 = 1128b.
196 = 43c.
197 = 24a.
198 = 868b.
199 = 493.
200 = 1565.

2

(Kuhač)

201 = 1636.
202 = 1707a.
203 = 1707b.
204 = 1244.
205 = 1284c.
206 = 1171.
207 = 1409.
208 L ———
209 = 1142a.
210 = 1807.
211 L ———
212 = 1673a.
213 = 1673b.
214 = 548.
215 = 1585f.
216 L ———
217 L ———
218 = 319.
219 = 848c.
220 = 1804a.
221 = 1804b.
222 L ———
223 ——— ?
224 L ———
225 L ———
226 L ———
227 L ———
228 = 350.
229 L ———
230 L ———
231 = 1386.
232 = 1566.
233 = 513a.
234 = 316.
235 = 996.
236 = 942a.
237 = 1017a.
238 L ———
239 = 163.
240 L ———

241 = 983jj.
242 = 43f.
243 = 43g.
244 L ———
245 L ———
246 = 709b.
247 = 1124b.
248 = 1094g.
249 = 173b.
250 = 303b.
251 = 303c.
252 = 1159.
253 L ———
254 = 78a.
255 = 1079b.
256 L ———
257 L ———
258 = 1150a.
259 = 783.
260 L ———
261 = 931.
262 = 330a.
263 L ———
264 = 1649.
265 = 1642
266 = 1011
267 = 1189b.
268 = 1189a.
269 = 1674.
270 = 1435b.
271 = 1802.
272 L ———
273 = 1585a.
274 L ———
275 L ———
276 = 595.
277 L ———
278 ——— ?
279 = 1094d.
280 = 1370a.

281 = 1262.
282 = 1831.
283 = 1226.
284 = 905a.
285 = 1135a.
286 = 1135b.
287 = 327c.
288 L ———
289 L ———
290 = 1192.
291 L ———
292 L ———
293 = 878b.
294 = 878a.
295 L ———
296 ——— ?
297 = 1246b.
298 = 1827.
299 = 1276.
300 = 70a.
301 = 1609.
302 = 876.
303 L ———
304 = 291.
305 = 379a.
306 = 601.
307 = 1546b.
308 = 1155bis a.
309 = 1515b.
310 = 1515g.
311 = 1224.
312 = 1717.
313 L ———
314 = 1121.
315 L ———
316 = 1165a.
317 = 1585g.
318 = 896.
319 = 1756.
320 ——— ?

321 = 917.
322 = 1369.
323 = 1410.
324 = 1791.
325 = 1708.
326 = 1610.
327 = 20.
328 = 1613a.
329 = 69.
330 = 1139a.
331 L ———
332 L ———
333 = 156.
334 = 1508.
335 ——— ?
336 = 1776.
337 = 843.
338 L ———
339 = 1110.
340 = 674.
341 = 1512b.
342 = 1500.
343 = 473a.
344 = 569.
345 = 1408.
346 = 956.
347 = 98b.
348 = 1540g.
349 ——— ?
350 = 331.
351 = 1770.
352 ——— ?
353 = 1186.
354 = 72a.
355 = 1472.
356 = 1621.
357 L ———
358 = 1506d.
359 = 990.
360 = 994.

361 = 984j.
362 L ———
363a) = 892a.
363b) = 892b.
364 = 1099.
365 L ———
366 = 1864.
367 = 1160a.
368 = 1818.
369 L ———
370 = 487.
371 = 971a.
372 = 971b.
373 = 186a.
374 = 881a.
375 = 1592h.
376 = 265k.
377 = 1389.
378 L ———
379 = 943.
380 = 1540e.
381 = 1168d.
382 = 1832a.
383 = 1520.
384 = 1114.
385 = 1129.
386 = 1680.
387 = 1568b.
388 = 1737a.
389 = 1676b.
390 = 354.
391 = 897b.
392 L ———
393 L ———
394 = 942b.
395 L ———
396 = L ———
397 = 1143a.
398 ——— ?
399 = 1273d.
400 = 1250.

3
(Kuhač)

401 = 1833.
402 = 151b.
403 = 1706.
404 L ———
405 = 579-580.
406 = 1246g.
407 = 1246h.
408 = 1591b.
409 = 1204.
410 = 1225.
411 = 1654.
412 = 1163f.
413 = 1166a.
414 L ———
415 L ———
416 L ———
417 = 94a.
418 = 1540k.
419 = 1158a.
420 = 1158b.
421 ——— ?
422 = 892d.
423 = 1631.
424 L ———
425 = 1138.
426 = 1688.
427 = 822.
428 ——— ?
429 = 1478.
430 L ———
431 = 1150e
432, 433 } = 1017b.
434 = 356a.
435 = 105b.
436 = 1694.
437 = 1700e.
438 = 463.
439 L ———
440 = 1602d.

441 = 47a.
442 = 56e.
443 L ———
444 L ———
445 = 333d.
446 = 1104.
447 = 967.
448 = 24b.
449 = 1832b.
450 L ———
451 202.
452 L ———
453 ——— ?
454 = 1095d.
455 L ———
456 = 1128a.
457 = 229a.
458 = 483.
459 = 211a.
460 893.
461 ——— ?
462 = 1124a.
463 = 1105a.
464 = 672a.
465 = 1865.
466 = 672b.
467 L ———
468 L ———
469 = 1306.
470 = 229d.
471 = 1255d.
472 L ———
473 = 194a.
474 = 1483f.
475 ——— ?
476 = 19.
477 L ———
478 = 164a.
479 = 518.
480 = 94c.

481 = 1782.
482 = 1390.
483 L ———
484 L ———
485 = 1282.
486 = 513b.
487 = 66.
488 = 610d.
489 = 112.
490 = 1866.
491 = 755l.
492 = 755c.
493 L ———
494 L ———
495 = 309c.
496 L ———
497 = 1139b.
498 ——— ?
499 ——— ?
500 L ———
501(a) = 1696a.
501(b) = 1696c.
501(c) = 1696b.
502 ——— ?
503 L ———
504 L ———
505 = 408.
506 L ———
507 = 71.
508 = 432c.
509 L ———
510 = 327b.
511 = 1867.
512 = 1348.
513 = 1464.
514 = 280a.
515 } L ———
516 } L ———
517 } L ———
518 = 1160b.
519 = 1054e.
520 = 1439a.

521 = 643.
522 = 721a.
523 L ———
524 = 1240.
525 = 1292a.
526 = 1292c.
527 = 1806.
528 = 1545h.
529 = 135a.
530 L ———
531 = 1868.
532 L ———
533 = 1280f.
534 = 1280g.
535 ——— ?
536 = 1584c.
537 L ———
538 = 1147.
539 ——— ?
540 = 1036d.
541 = 939.
542 = 43a.
543 = 78c.
544 ——— ?
545a) = 904a.
545b) = 904b.
546 = 904c.
547 = 660b.
548 = 1779.
549 = 1146.
550 = 161.
551 ——— ?
552 ——— ?
553 = 183b.
554 = 377b.
555 = 1118.
556 = 1127.
557 = 1246l.
558 L ———
559 = 1246j.
560 = 1297.

561 L ———
562 = 442.
563 L ———
564 L ———
565 L ———
566 L ———
567 = 1246o.
568 = 1061.
569 = 873.
570 = 1377.
571 = 1393.
572 = 525.
573 ——— ?
574 = 1759a.
575 L ———
576 = 1731.
577 L ———
578 = 732a.
579 = 401b.
580 L ———
581 = 1113.
582 = 1090.
583 = 125c.
584 L ———
585 = 412.
586 = 1074.
587 = 1714.
588 L ———
589 ——— ?
590 = 1084.
591 = 458.
592 = 1001f.
593 = 1001g.
594 L ———
595 = 914.
596 = 1559.
597 = 1570b.
598 = 1794.
599 L ———
600 = 728-9.

4
(Kuhač)

601 = 853a.	641 L———	681 = 1479d.	721 = 353b.	761 = 287.
602 = 853c.	642 = 396a.	682 = 1479 e.	722 = 610b.	762 L———
603 = 853e.	643 = 711a.	683 L———	723 = 399.	763 ———
604 = 1213.	644 = 711b.	684 = 1473.	724 = 1179a.	764 = 714.
605 = 898e.	645 = 297b.	685 = 1198–9.	725 = 1179b.	765 L———
606 = 898a.	646 L———	686 = 1246d.	726 = 401a.	766 = 406.
607 = 898d.	647 L———	687 = 1246f.	727 = 1022a.	767 = 680.
608 = 898b.	648 ——— ?	688 = 1246e.	728 = 1022b.	768 L———
609 = 1128c.	649 = 1007.	689 = 1732.	729 = 1545d.	769 = 571.
610 = 1128d.	650 = 345.	690 = 1133.	730 = 377c.	770 = 616b.
611 L———	651 = 652b.	691 = 1005a.	731 = 1545e.	771 = 645.
612 L———	652a) = 1584b. ? 652b) ———	692 = 270a.	732 L———	772 = 800b.
613 = 1810.	653a) = 1002c. 653b) = 1002b.	693 = 1399m.	733 ——— ?	773 = 355.
614 = 1545g.	654 = 1584a.	694 = 1399l.	734 = 1120.	774 L———
615 = 1545f.	655 = 1584d.	695 = 1399f.	735 = 1116.	775 = 1139e.
616 = 242.	656 = 1584e.	696 = 1399o.	736 = 1033g.	776 L———
617 = 1545b.	657 } = 1285g.	697 = 1399n.	737 = 1483a.	777 = 1206b.
618 ——— ?	658 }	698 = 356c.	738 = 405.	778 = 361–2.
619 = 721d.	659 = 1285f.	699 = 1721.	739 = 864.	779 L———
620 ——— ?	660 = 1049.	700 = 1150d.	740 = 721b.	780 = 1335–6.
621 = 1425.	661 L———	701a) = 1150b. 701b) = 1150f.	741 = 713e.	781 = 1001a.
622 = 1713.	662 = 119g.	702 = 866.	742 = 800a.	782 = 1001b.
623 L———	663 = 1141.	703 = 983hh.	743 = 860c.	783 = 1001c.
624 L———	664 L———	704 = 798.	744 = 868a.	784 = 1246i.
625 = 1143b.	665 = 527.	705 = 175.	745 = 270b.	785 = 1246m.
626 = 991.	666 = 531.	706 = 195.	746 L———	786 = 1246p.
627 L———	667 = 655g.	707 = 1271f.	747 L———	787 = 196c.
628 L———	668 = 603a.	708 L———	748 = 232c.	788 L———
629 L———	669 L———	709 L———	749 } 1091.	789 = 1515h.
630 L———	670 L———	710 = 648a.	750 }	790 L———
631 L———	671 = 1271a.	711a) = 1089a. ? 711b) ———	751 = 43d.	791 L———
632 L———	672 L———	712 = 1089b.	752 = 1545c.	792 = 304b.
633 L———	673 L———	713 = 1149a.	753 L———	793 L———
634 L———	674 = 1200.	714 = 1123.	754 = 871.	794 L———
635 = 660a.	675 = 678.	715 = 235.	755 L———	795 = 1024e.
636 = 1001j.	676 = 1462.	716 = 56b.	756 = 868c.	796 = 1788.
637 = 424a.	677 = 905b.	717a) = 334a. 717b) = 334b.	757 = 1076.	797 L———
638 = 830.	678 = 1479b.	718 = 999a.	758 = 1054f.	798 L———
639 L———	679 = 1479c.	719 = 999c.	759 = 1062.	799 = 1168g.
640 L———	680 = 1479a.	720 = 999b.	760 L———	800 = 1252.

5
(Kuhač)

801 = 1208.
802 = 849a.
803 = 849b.
804 = 1380.
805 = 75a.
806 = 81.
807 = 1509.
808 = 758b.
809 L——
810 = 1233.
811 = 1004.
812 = 68.
813 L——
814 = 1272.
815 = 1570e.
816 = 1303d.
817 = 1303c.
818 = 1303a.
819 = 94b.
820 = 825.
821 = 621.
822 = 623b.
823 = 47.
824 = 1153.
825 = 1652.
826 L——
827 = 326.
828 = 1607b.
829 = 1607d.
830 = 983g.
831 = 530b.
832 = 1343.
833 L——
834 = 10.
835 —— ?
836 = 1022c.
837 = 1607a.
838 = 961a.
839 = 961b.
840 = 961c.

841 = 507.
842 = 1164.
843a) = 1513a.
843b) = 1513b.
844 = 1513c.
845 = 1513e.
846 = 1513d.
847 = 1540c.
848 = 1540a.
849 = 1540b.
850 = 1303b.
*851 = 1496
852 = 1785.
853 = 1510.
854 = 1540j
855 = 742.
856 = 74.
857 = 1869.
858 = 73d.
859 L——
860 = 41.
861 = 1659b.
862 = 1659a.
863 = 1058d.
864 = 1058b.
865 = 1058a.
866 = 1058c.
867 —— ?
868 = 761a.
869 = 761c.
870 = 1513f.
*871 = 1496.
872 = 1722c.
873 = 1722d.
874 = 1722a.
875 = 1722b.
876 = 651.
877 = 158g.
878 = 158d.
879 = 1047a.
880 = 1047b.

881 = 1047c.
882 = 313.
883 L——
884 = 1295.
885 = 1637.
886 = 1573a.
887 = 767.
888 = 1570a.
889 L——
890 L——
891 = 1596.
892 = 1033c.
893 = 499.
894 = 1108.
895 = 1689.
896 = 1151.
897 = 1506a.
898 = 1506g.
899 = 1506b.
900 = 1399b.
901 = 1399a.
902 = 1399i.
903 = 1399c.
904 = 1384b.
905 = 1357b.
906 = 1357a.
907 L——
908 = 530a.
909 = 911.
910 = 414d.
911 = 414b.
912 = 414a.
913 = 1289b.
914 = 1602j.
915 = 1602g.
916 = 1602a.
917 = 1602i.
918 = 1602h.
919 = 1602k.
920 = 906a.

921 = 1211.
922 L——
923 = 1300.
924 = 1253.
925 = 1248.
926 = 1430.
927 = 1144bis.
928 = 1870.
929 = 22a.
930 = 1558a
931 = 1558c.
932 = 1640c.
933 = 1640a.
934 = 1640d.
935 = 1640b.
936 = 1640e.
937 = 1639.
938 = 1201b.
939 = 593a.
940 = 593b.
941 = 593c.
942 = 591b.
943 = 593d.
944 = 1142b.
945, 946 } = 1298a.
947 = 1298c.
948a), 948b) } 1784.
949 = 1134.
950 = 1107a.
951 = 1094a.
952 = 1094i.
953 = 1094j.
954 = 933.
955 = 953.
956 = 288a.
957 = 740.
958 = 485b.
959 —— ?
960 —— ?

961 ——
962 = 1094b.
963 = 993f.
964 = 1094c.
965 = 1094f.
966 = 1094e.
967 = 1094k.
968 = 314.
969 = 56a.
970 L——
971 L——
972 = 1094l.
973 L——
974 —— ?
975 = 841b.
976 = 841a.
977 = 835b.
978 = 835e.
979 = 835f.
980 = 835c.
981 = 835d.
982 —— ?
983 = 930a.
984 = 930b.
985 = 930d.
986 = 875a.
987 = 875b.
988 = 1185.
989 L——
990 L——
991 L——
992 = 104.
993 = 352.
994 L——
995 L——
996 L——
997 L——
998 L——
999 L——
1000 L——

* Published twice!

6

(Kuhač)

1001a) = 1588a.
1001b) = 1273e.
1001c) = 1588b.
1002 = 1576c
1003 = 1576d.
1004 = 123a.
1005 = 123f.
1006 = 123e.
1007 = 123c.
1008 = 1598.
1009 = 969.
1010 = 1602e.
1011 = 1793.
1012 = 1834a.
1013 = 1834b.
1014 = 616a.
1015 = 1490a.
1016 = 1490b.
1017 = 1693c.
1018 = 1189c.
1019 = 619.
1020 = 1871.
1021 = 936.
1022 = 1822.
1023 = 1872.
1024 = 1330d.
1025 = 850.
1026 = 2.
1027 = 755e.
1028 = 4.
1029 = 1555d.
1030 = 1555a.
1031 = 1298b.
1032 ———
1033 ———
1034 ——— ?
1035 ———
1036 ———
1037 = 993e.
1038 = 852 bis.
1039 = 1002g.
1040 = 1002h.

1041 = 993d.
1042 = 452e.
1043 = 134i.
1044 = 134h.
1045a) = 130g.
1045b) = 134c.
1046 = 134e.
1047 = 8.
1048 = 1873.
1049 = 18.
1050 = 134m.
1051 = 134l.
1052 = 359b.
1053 = 1001d.
1054 = 172.
1055 = 134f.
1056 = 134j.
1057 = 1260.
1058 = 183h.
1059 = 277.
1060 = 360a.
1061 = 360b.
1062 = 1874b.
1063 = 48a.
1064 = 48b.
1065 = 134b.
1066 = 134d.
1067 = 281d.
1068 = 165i.
1069 = 1050.
1070 = 134g.
1071 = 119a.
1072 = 469–470.
1073 = 222.
1074 = 134a.
1075 = 162.
1076 = 6.
1077 = 1835.
1078 = 1100.
1079 = 9.
1080 = 31.

1081 = 1403c.
1082 = 1447c.
1083 = 1002d.
1084 = 1587b.
1085 = 1587a.
1086 = 1586d.
1087 = 198.
1088 = 1729.
1089 = 258.
1090 = 1836.
1091 = 1447d.
1092 = 390d.
1093 = 1403b.
1094 = 1403a.
1095 = 750a.
1096 = 502.
1097 = 333c.
1098 = 721a.
1099 = 1002f.
1100 = 1484c.
1101 = 905e.
1102 = 1360.
1103 = 889.
1104 = 1837.
1105 = 683.
1106 = 1803.
1107 = 1273c.
1108 = 1575.
1109 = 1344.
1110 = 1783.
1111a) = 1573c.
1111b) = 1591c.
1112 L———
1113 = 1760.
1114 = 1435a.
1115a) = 1750b.
1115b) = 1273b.
1116 = 721e.
1117 = 191a.
1118 = 1482.
1119 = 1140.
1120 = 1838.

1121 1570d.
1122 1355.
1123 1321.
1124 1382.
1125 1798.
1126 335d.
1127 1567a.
1128 ——— ?
1129 1440a.
1130 1257.
1131 1180.
1132a) 335a.
1132b) 1196.
1133 L———
1134 L———
1135 L———
1136 L———
1137 ——— ?
1138 1692a.
1139 1692b.
1140 1418.
1141 1374.
1142 962a.
1143 1128e.
1144 1634.
1145 60a.
1146 ——— ?
1147 L———
1148 L———
1149 18.
1150 ———
1151 ———
1152 ——— ?
1153 ———
1154 ———
1155 ———
1156 1490c.
1157 ———
1158 ——— ?
1159 ———
1160 ———

1161
1162
1163
1164
1165
1166
1167
1168
1169
1170
1171
1172
1173
1174
1175
1176
1177
1178 ?
1179
1180
1181
1182
1183
1184
1185
1186
1187
1188
1189
1190
1191
1192
1193
1194
1195
1196
1197
1198
1199
1200 L———

γ (Kuhač)

1201 = 98a.
1202 = 359a.
1203 = 1466.
1204 = 1734.
1205 = 22b.
1206 = 1540d.
1207 = 1540l.
1208 = 1033h.
1209 = 480c.
1210 = 7c.
1211 = 1214a.
1212 = 1144a.
1213 = 1144b.
1214 = 1144d.
1215 = 1144c.
1216 = 436.
1217 = 480b.
1218 = 147.
1219 = 480a.
1220 = 903.
1221 = 1086.
1222a) = 1480.
1222b) = 290a.
1223 = 1536.
1224 = 262c.
1225 = 755b
1226 L ———
1227 L ———
1228 ——— ⎫
1229 ——— ⎪
1230 ——— ⎬ ?
1231 ——— ⎪
1232 ——— ⎭
1233 = 1340.
1234 = 1571a.
1235 = 216a.
1236 = 216b.
1237 = 216a.
1238 L ———
1239 = 753b.
1240 = 239.

1241 = 1718.
1242 = 1315.
1243 = 1839.
1244 = 391c.
1245 = 452d.
1246 = 1064.
1247 = 1437.
1248 = 1001e.
1249a) = 36b.
1249b) = 1433.
1250 = 56f.
1251 = 555b.
1252 = 934.
1253 L ———
1254 = 237i.
1255 = 492a.
1256 = 1130.
1257 = 241.
1258 = 1716.
1259a) = 238.
1259b) = 1573b.
1260 = 1101.
1261 = 1157.
1262 = 1107c.
1263 = 393a.
1264a) = 39c.
1264b) = 1397.
1265 L ———
1266 = 39b.
1267 = 39a.
1268 = 760b.
1269 = 492e.
1270 = 758a.
1271 = 1051–2.
1272 = 1875.
1273 = 755g.
1274 = 356b.
1275 = 1107d.
1276 = 1161.
1277 = 713d.
1278 = 279.
1279 L ———
1280 L ———

1281 L ———
1282 = 851.
1283 = 1063.
1284 = 36c.
1285 = 1840.
1286 = 1684.
1287 = 1194.
1288 = 717a.
1289 = 717b.
1290 = 1764c.
1291 = 1764a.
1292 = 1764b.
1293 = 1447b.
1294 = 1764d.
1295 = 1764e.
1296 = 1699.
1297 = 1095a.
1298 = 1201a.
1299 = 1201c.
1300 = 1702a.
1301 = 1702b.
1302 = 1669.
1303 = 1483d.
1304 = 1483e.
1305 = 1841.
1306 = 609b.
1307 = 1352b.
1308 = 1352a.
1309 L ———
1310 = 1190.
1311 L ———
1312 L ———
1313a) = 1283c.
1313b) = 1283d.
1314 L ———
1315 = 1345.
1316 = 837.
1317 ——— ?
1318 L ———
1319 = 1081.
1320 L ———

1321 L ———
1322 = 1711.
1323 = 1145c.
1324 = 1145b.
1325 = 1461.
1326 = 1326.
1327 L ———
1328 = 1391.
1329 = 1305.
1330 = 1384a.
1331 = 1422.
1332 = 1460b.
1333 = 1460a.
1334 = 838b.
1335 L ———
1336 L ———
1337 L ———
1338 ——— ?
1339 L ———
1340 = 1481a.
1341 = 1424.
1342 = 1658a.
1343 = 1658d.
1344 L ———
1345 L ———
1346 = 836.
1347 = 1155bis.
1348 = 1452.
1349 = 1719b.
1350 L ———
1351 L ———
1352 L ———
1353 = 944.
1354 = 514.
1355 L ———
1356 L ———
1357 L ———
1358 = 844.
1359 = 1119.
1360a) = 1658b.
1360b) = 1658e.

1361 L ———
1362 = 1582b.
1363 = 1586a.
1364 = 262f.
1365 = 1842.
1366 L ———
1367 L ———
1368 = 1271d.
1369 = 1271c.
1370 L ———
1371 = 1273a.
1372 L ———
1373 ——— ?
1374 = 1426.
1375 = 1843.
1376 = 387.
1377 = 1289a.
1378 = 1799.
1379 = 763.
1380 = 204.
1381 = 1156a.
1382 L ———
1383 = 1733c.
1384 = 1715.
1385 = 1356.
1386 L ———
1387 = 1567b.
1388 L ———
1389 ——— ?
1390 ——— ?
1391 L
1392 L
1393 L
1394 L
1395 L
1396 L
1397 L
1398 L
1399 L
1400 L

8
(Kuhač)

1401 = 1401.
1402 = 1800a.
1403 = 1800b.
1404 = 1453.
1405 = 1337.
1406 = 1876.
1407 = 1188a.
1408 = 1719a.
1409a) L ———
1409b) L ———
1410 = 730-1.
1411 = 1477.
1412 L ———
1413 L ———
1414 = 1743.
1415 = 1748-9.
1416 = 1237.
1417 L ———
1418 ——— ?
1419 = 1775.
1420 L ———
1421 = 1381a.
1422 = 1675a.
1423 = 1664c.
1424 L ———
1425 = 1445.
1426 = 1538.
1427 = 1271e.
1428 = 1696d.
1429 = 1696e.
1430 = 1844.
1431 = 371.
1432 L ———
1433 = 1580.
1434a) L ———
1434b) L ———
1434c) L ———
1435 = 389.
1436 ——— ?
1437 = 1444a.
1438 L ———
1439 = 1735.
1440 = 838a.

1441 = 1691a.
1442 = 1255a.
1443 = 1585b.
1444 = 1657a.
1445 = 1657b.
1446 = 1021c.
1447 L ———
1448 = 1589d.
1449 = 1574.
1450 = 1691b.
1451 = 1537b.
1452 = 845.
1453 = 176.
1454 = 636.
1455 = 1581.
1456 = 516a.
1457 L ———
1458 = 1572.
1459 = 383a.
1460 = 567a.
1461 ——— ?
1462 = 1723.
1463 = 1202.
1464 = 1825.
1465 ——— ?
1466 = 1571c.
1467 = 983kk.
1468 = 1236.
1469 = 1148a.
1470 = 485a
1471 = 1221.
1472 = 1499a.
1473 = 1522.
1474 ———
1475 = 1534.
1476 L ———
1477 = 1228.
1478 ——— ?
1479 = 124.
1480 = 1209a.

1481 = 1227.
1482 = 1181a.
1483 = 1310i.
1484 = 1209b.
1485 = 1209c.
1486 = 1172-3.
1487 = 1209d.
1488 = 1261.
1489 L ———
1490 ——— ?
1491 = 1310f.
1492 = 397.
1493 = 1310r.
1494 = 1310p.
1495 = 1310m.
1496 = 1310a.
1497 = 353a.
1498 = 1310b.
1499 = 1310c.
1500 = 1310h.
1501 = 1310s.
1502 = 329.
1503 = 305c.
1504 = 267b.
1505 L ———
1506 L ———
1507 = 1310t.
1508 = 983ee.
1509 = 983ii.
1510 = 983l.
1511 = 983z.
1512 = 1310d.
1513 L ———
1514 ——— ?
1515 ——— ?
1516 ——— ?
1517 L ———
1518 = 390c.
1519 = 1310n.
1520 = 1310e.

1521 L ———
1522 = 984f.
1523 = 1595.
1524 = 13.
1525 ——— ?
1526 = 59.
1527 = 1589e.
1528 L ———
1529 L ———
1530 L ———
1531 = 433e.
1532 = 1323.
1533 L ———
1534 = 70b.
1535 ——— ?
1536 = 609a.
1537 L ———
1538 L ———
1539 L ———
1540 L ———
1541 = 341.
1542 L ———
1543 L ———
1544 L ———
1545 ———
1546 = 1347.
1547 = 1283b.
1548 L ———
1549 = 1235.
1550 = 1310u.
1551 = 1339a.
1552 = 1350.
1553 = 1339b.
1554 L ———
1555 L ———
1556 L ———
1557 L ———
1558 L ———
1559 L ———
1560 L ———

1561 L
1562 L
1563 L
1564 L
1565 ——— ?
1566 L
1567 L
1568 L
1569 L
1570 L
1571 L
1572 L
1573 L
1574 L
1575 L
1576 L
1577 L
1578 L
1579 L
1580 L
1581 L
1582 L
1583 ——— ?
1584 L
1585 L
1586 L
1587 L
1588 L
1589 L
1590 L
1591 L
1592 L
1593 L
1594 = 127.
1595 L
1596 L
1597 L
1598 L
1599 L
1609 L

Kuba B. ^{9}H.

No.	=	No.	=	No.	=	No.	=	No.	=
1	546.	41	1693b.	81	577b.	121	433c.	161	1314a.
2	310g.	42	997.	82	1444c.	122	433b.	162	455c.
3	869.	43	738a.	83	1444b.	123	1163b.	163	1263.
4	392a.	44	738b.	84	1560.	124	1163e.	164	1537a.(?)
5	1331.	45	1577b.	85	1491.	125	503c.	165	1195a.
6	1877.	46	1258.	86	1766.	126	983a.	166	1195c.
7	1656.	47	1292b.	87	796b.	127	1187.	167	1195b.
8	388.	48	1318.	88	891c.	128	927.	168	1175.
9	600.	49	1535.	89	648c.	129	301b.	169	881b.
10	1693a.	50	958e.	90	433a.	130	1546d.	170	1216.
11	1182b.	51	1845.	91	183a.	131	1613b.	171	987.
12	1353.	52	718.	92	103.	132	1371a.	172	520.
13	1402.	53	880b.	93	957b.	133	244.	173	385.
14	1439b.	54	1184.	94	1266a.	134	186b.	174	259.
15	1168a.	55	1330c.	95*	782b.	135	1516b.	175	177d.
16	1021a.	56	1330a.	96	39e.	136	1470b.	176	1137.
17	1168b.	57	710.	97	623a.	137	372.	177	1098b.
18	1168f.	58	344b.	98	503a.	138	1751.	178	1304.
19	1809b.	59	656a.	99	1188b.	139	988.	179	231a.
20	1809a.	60	1366.	100	1242.	140	1019.	180	231b.
21	1611b.	61	1493b.	101	812c.	141	813.	181	321f.
22	1611a.	62	343.	102	788h.	142	1627.	182	880a.
23	1392a.	63	344a.	103	1540h.	143	840.	183	1651b.
24	1392b.	64	280e.	104	1470a.	144	275.	184	432b.
25	1385a.	65	280f.	105	1525.	145	1540i.	185	1077d.
26	1385b.	66	280g.	106	1444d.	146	1319a.	186	1313 e.
27	240b.	67	725.	107	321e.	147	1571b.	187	656b.
28	247a.	68	1016a.	108	321c.	148	1371b.	188	689a.
29	951a.	69	1016b.	109	321d.	149	1593b.	189	694.
30	951b.	70	344e.	110	1269a.	150	1626a.	190	656c.
31	665a.	71	1737a.	111	384b.	151	260b.	191	440a.
32	665b.	72	578.	112	1558b.	152	572.	192	440b.
33	322.	73	1789a.	113	467b.	153	1311.	193	1033f.
34	1878.	74	823.	114	492d.	154	1554.	194	657.
35	317b.	75	1079c.	115	153.	155	591a.	195	—— ?
36	1287.	76	1332a.	116	1619d.	156	1077b.	196	1217.
37	952.	77	1332.	117	1619e.	157	998.	197	1317.
38	916.	78	1493d.	118	762.	158	363.	198	1191.
39	711d.	79	52bb.	119	1077c.	159	280d.	199	1364.
40	906b.	80	1703.	120	886a.	160	344d.	200	223.

* identical with Kuba B.H. 1025

10

(Kuba B.H.)

201 = 1727.	241 = 1434.	281 = 1752.	321 = 310c.	361 = 1589c.
202 = 1790.	242 = 1378.	282 = 1109.	322 = 416.	362 = 1589a.
203 = 1623.	243 = 963.	283 = 726.	323 = 603b.	363 = 1365.
204 = 1618e.	244 = 271e.	284 = 700.	324 = 1550b.	364 = 1586b.
205 = 1284c.	245 = 984k.	285 = 804a.	325 = 1274.	365 = 937.
206 = 1421.	246 = 872a.	286 = 727a.	326 = 638–640.	366 = 123b.
207 = 909.	247 = 1338c.	287 = 727b.	327 = 754.	367 = 1414.
208 = 1033i.	248 = 1524.	288 = 1659f.	328 = 607b.	368 = 957a.
209 = 685.	249 = 696a.	289 = 983v.	329 = 311a.	369 = 1710.
210 = 819c.	250 = 696b.	290 = 1615.	330 = 311b.	370 = 193a.
211 = 715–6.	251 = 653.	291 = 699.	331 = 55.	371 = 184b.
212 = 395.	252 = 1443.	292 = 907.	332 = 63.	372 = 240a.
213 = 1514c.	253 = 1767a.	293 = 1625b.	333 = 1813–4.	373 = 1761.
214 = 983cc.	254 = 724d.	294 = 465.	334 = 684b.	374 = 196f.
215 = 566a.	255 = 1742a.	295 = 1039h.	335 = 486.	375 = 1169.
216 = 713b.	256 = 1230a.	296 = 397bis.	336 = 794.	376 = 196a.
217 = 1207.	257 = 265d.	297 = 1229b.	337 = 500a.	377 = 196b.
218 = 429b.	258 = 64a.	298 = 1310g.	338 = 500b.	378 = 196c.
219 = 429c.	259 = 1523.	299 = 1229a.	339 = 1037–8.	379 = 1493c.
220 = 1313f.	260 = 1001h.	300 = 736.	340 = 983m.	380 = 92.
221 = 986b.	261 = 1618d.	301 = 764b.	341 = 684a.	381 = 240c.
222 = 301a.	262 = 679d.	302 = 1319b.	342 = 1815a.	382 = 128b.
223 = 985.	263 = 1519a.	303 = 1659h.	343 = 615c.	383 = 1531d.
224 = 1313c.	264 = 260a.	304 = 1325a.	344 = 872b.	384 = 105.
225 = 1313a.	265 = 1647.	305 = 54.	345 = 1515d.	385 = 165j.
226 = 1313b.	266 = 1720a.	306 = 281b.	346 ——— ?	386 = 448m.
227 = 1313d.	267 = 448c.	307 = 479e.	347 = 1603.	387 = 303e.
228 = 431.	268 = 1301a.	308 = 448b.	348 = 636.	388 = 165b.
229 = 654bisc.	269 = 819a.	309 = 392c.	349 = 1042.	389 = 165c.
230 = 656d.	270 = 819d.	310 = 288b.	350 = 21a.	390 = 232e.
231 = 1619f.	271 = 1626b.	311 = 286a.	351 = 1549.	391 = 303a.
232 = 1493a.	272 = 577a.	312 = 1789b.	352 = 1013bis.	392 = 1044.
233 = 185a.	273 = 932b.	313 = 511a.	353 = 615b.	393 = 109.
234 = 984d.	274 = 268.	314 = 563c.	354 = 435e.	394 = 165g.
235 = 1102c.	275 = 1436.	315 = 432d.	355 = 72b.	395 = 462.
236 = 658.	276 = 1745–6.	316 = 786.	356 = 562.	396 = 1517.
237 = 915.	277 = 1624.	317 = 751d.	357 = 193b.	397 = 165d.
238 = 1672a.	278 = 1671.	318 = 310h.	358 = 1648.	398 = 310f.
239 = 1772–3.	279 = 773a.	319 = 310b.	359 = 576.	399 = 492g.
240 = 396b.	280 = 438.	320 = 615a.	360 = 1031–2.	400 = 1469c.

II
(Kuba B. H.)

401 = 21b.
402 = 347.
403 = 1632.
404 = 1358b.
405 = 839.
406 = 1033e.
407 = 566b.
408 = 983bb.
409 = 688.
410 = 596.
411 = 711c.
412 = 709c.
413 = 429a.
414 = 1417a.
415 = 732.
416 = 358.
417 = 713c.
418 = 435d.
419 = 1383a.
420 = 550a.
421 = 1284b.
422 = 1284a.
423 = 1738-9.
424 = 380.
425 = 39g.
426 = 521.
427 = 1847.
428 = 938a.
429 = 1036c.
430 = 317a.
431 = 1163c.
432 = 309a.
433 = 381.
434 = 394a.
435 = 1181b.
436 = 299.
437 = 707.
438 = 413.
439 = 810c.
440 = 320a.

441 = 1379.
442 = 1266b.
443 = 1417b.
444 = 435a.
445 = 1747.
446 = 959a.
447 = 778a.
448 = 926.
449 = 479h.
450 = 212a.
451 = 143c.
452 = 430b.
453 = 143b.
454 = 993b.
455 = 132d.
456 = 283a
457 = 592d.
458 = 130f.
459 = 130a.
460 = 130d.
461 = 130e.
462 = 1641.
463 = 214a.
464 = 132a.
465 = 132c.
466 = 214d.
467 = 214b.
468 = 733.
469 = 824.
470 = 131b.
471 = 978.
472 = 265i.
473 = 265j.
474 = 752c
475 = 1023.
476 = 1013.
477 = 464.
478 = 592c.
479 = 213.
480 = 1045.

481 = 164b.
482 = 1584f.
483 = 574.
484 = 118.
485 = 449.
486 = 12.
487 = 918.
488 = 1465.
489 = 214c.
490 = 214e.
491 = 1388d.
492 = 1469b.
493 = 1027c.
494 = 293.
495 = 1498c.
496 = 533a.
497 = 283b.
498 = 976a.
499 = 1027b.
500 = 220.
501 = 295.
502 = 1177.
503 = 216c.
504 = 137.
505 = 323b.
506 = 1494a.
507 = 1010a.
508 = 910.
509 = 232a.
510 = 690b.
511 = 1375.
512 = 1819.
513 = 1817.
514 = 332.
515 = 488b.
516 = 488a.
517 = 82a.
518 = 82c.
519 } = 339a.
520 }

521 = 1789c.
522 = 1502a.
523 = 679a.
524 = 679b.
525 = 679c.
526 = 1879.
527 = 1823.
528 = 365-6a.
529 = 365-6b.
530 = 775a.
531 = 647.
532 = 257.
533 = 265g.
534 = 775b.
535 = 1502b.
536 = 567b.
537 = 983n.
538 = 1646.
539 = 750b.
540 = 1848.
541 = 265e.
542 = 337-8.
543 = 364b.
544 = 286b.
545 = 265f.
546 = 1054b.
547 = 855a.
548 = 1685.
549 = 1792.
550 = 630.
551 = 925b.
552 = 925c.
553 = 925d.
554 = 1018a.
555 = 1018b.
556 = 835g.
557 = 835h.
558 = 1655a.
559 = 1655b.
560 = 364a.

561 = 1821.
562 = 925e.
563 = 27.
564 = 267a
565 = 390b.
566 —— ?
567 = 1666.
568 = 415.
569 = 770a.
570 = 232i.
571 = 265h.
572 = 274.
573 = 206a.
574 = 1497.
575 = 365-6c.
576 = 1505a.
577 = 390a.
578 = 1440b.
579 = 492b.
580 = 1797.
581 = 158e.
582 = 550b.
583 = 905d.
584 = 1796.
585 = 119f.
586 = 902.
587 = 369a.
588 = 734a.
589 = 1071.
590 = 796a.
591 = 1212b.
592 = 713a.
593 = 713f.
594 = 183g.
595 = 424b.
596 = 339b.
597 = 433d.
598 = 1502d.
599 = 392d.
600 = 1550d.

12

(Kuba B. H.)

601	= 1550c.	641	= 1618b.	681	= 1281b.	721	= 207.	761	= 547a.
602	= 39f.	642	= 1619h.	682	= 370.	722	= 496a.	762	= 538b.
603	= 756.	643	= 1241b.	683	= 1102d.	723	= 1036b.	763	= 1582a.
604	= 435b.	644	= 1241a.	684	= 1281c.	724	= 1036a.	764	= 419.
605	= 590a.	645	= 587.	685	= 490.	725	= 1399g.	765	= 378.
606	= 941.	646	= 1619c.	686	= 248.	726	= 1399h.	766	= 255-6.
607	= 497.	647	= 1619g.	687	= 1882.	727	= 1399k.	767	= 130b.
608	= 803b.	648	= 1619a.	688	= 1010b.	728	= 908.	768	= 778c.
609	= 1672c.	649	= 1601b.	689	= 1655d.	729	= 159b.	769	= 816.
610	= 297c.	650	= 1881.	690	= 1515f.	730	= 271c.	770	= 479c.
611	= 702.	651	= 1665.	691	= 1883.	731	= 271d.	771	= 263a.
612	= 708d.	652	= 724c.	692	= 1178.	732	= 1281a.	772	= 93.
613	= 119d.	653	= 724a.	693	= 879.	733	= 1467b.	773	= 445h.
614	= 724b.	654	= 159d.	694	= 602.	734	= 1467a.	774	= 46a.
615	——— ?	655	= 924.	695	= 1495.	735	= 426a.	775	= 262e.
616	= 1488.	656	= 312c.	696	= 1712.	736	= 426b.	776	= 445c.
617	= 353c.	657	= 995.	697	= 1619b.	737	= 877a.	777	= 445j.
618	= 634.	658	= 1801.	698	= 1505c.	738	= 877b.	778	= 445d.
619	= 637.	659	= 1811.	699	= 1884.	739	= 833c.	779	= 445e.
620	= 772.	660	= 955.	700	= 980.	740	= 833d.	780	= 445i.
621	= 1502c.	661	= 860a.	701	= 428	741	= 833g.	781	= 1056.
622	= 834b.	662	= 1441.	702	= 1027a.	742	= 833b.	782	= 445f.
623	= 983x.	663	= 1152.	703	= 221.	743	= 770c.	783	= 983s.
624	= 206b.	664	= 860b.	704	= 160a.	744	= 771.	784	= 265a.
625	= 206c.	665	= 735.	705	= 513c.	745	= 271a.	785	= 515.
626	= 1829.	666	= 1197b.	706	= 894.	746	= 271b.	786	= 243i.
627	= 812b.	667	= 273	707	= 139.	747	= 1551.	787	= 808.
628	= 294.	668	= 1660.	708	= 1066.	748	= 1550a.	788	= 737.
629	= 581.	669	= 1569a.	709	= 1678.	749	= 357a.	789	= 117b.
630	= 1485.	670	= 272.	710	= 856.	750	= 357b.	790	= 212b.
631	= 1406.	671	= 394b.	711	= 365-6d.	751	= 357c.	791	= 1501.
632	= 340.	672	= 1215.	712	= 510b.	752	= 439a.	792	= 11.
633	= 712.	673	= 435.	713	= 512.	753	= 632.	793	= 455e.
634	= 1880.	674	= 205.	714	= 297a.	754	= 95b.	794	= 870.
635	= 1780.	675	= 95a.	715	= 1583b.	755	= 1015.	795	= 211c
636	= 1579b.	676	= 1281d.	716	= 1034-5.	756	= 796c.	796	= 741.
637	= 1388c.	677	= 1238.	717	= 1820.	757	= 143a.	797	= 899.
638	= 1388b.	678	= 457.	718	= 479i.	758	= 778b.	798	= 283c.
639	= 958d.	679	= 1467c.	719	= 159a.	759	= 37.	799	= 592b.
640	= 958g.	680	= 1556b.	720	= 751.	760	= 538a.	800	= 749c.

(Kuba B. H.)

801	= 749b.	841	= 1569b.	881	= 481a.	921	= 119c.	961	= 1431.
802	= 749a.	842	= 267c.	882	= 582.	922	= 228.	962	= 703.
803	= 289b.	843	= 1383.	883	= 218.	923	= 296a.	963	= 1679c.
804	= 265c.	844	= 125b.	884	= 534c.	924	= 776d.	964	= 689b.
805	= 592a.	845	= 708c.	885	= 1886.	925	= 1446a.	965	—— ?
806	= 1755.	846	= 125a.	886	= 1757.	926	= 1659g.	966	= 435c.
807	= 117a.	847	= 1659d.	887	= 445b.	927	= 190.	967	= 1210.
808	= 752b.	848	= 898c.	888	= 517b.	928	= 1024b.	968	= 1338a.
809	= 479b.	849	= 1a.	889	= 517a.	929	= 622.	969	= 809.
810	= 752a.	850	= 1b.	890	= 882a.	930	= 392b.	970	= 697a.
811	= 265b.	851	= 1167a.	891	= 97.	931	= 788g.	971	= 1519b.
812	= 264a.	852	= 1167b.	892	= 484.	932	= 631.	972	= 697b.
813*	= 417.	853	= 1396b.	893	= 709a.	933	= 1618c.	973	= 1629b.
814	= 570.	854	= 1396c.	894	= 776b.	934	= 1256.	974	= 575.
815	= 1789d.	855	= 1122.	895	= 296b.	935	= 812a	975	= 1249.
816	= 1789b.	856	= 610a.	896	= 148b.	936	= 919.	976	= 1532d.
817	= 810b.	857	= 1515e.	897	= 608.	937	= 1423.	977	= 1604.
818	= 810a.	858	= 1885.	898	= 318.	938	= 776a.	978	= 773b.
819	= 1083.	859	= 684c.	899	= 330b.	939	= 1515c.	979	= 1593.
820	= 638c.	860	= 14.	900	= 1310k.	940	= 82b.	980	= 773c.
821	= 384c.	861	= 692.	901	= 386.	941	= 1163a.	981	= 1606 bis.
822	= 178.	862	= 1618a.	902	= 804b.	942	= 1163g.	982	= 707e.
823	= 479a.	863	= 1407.	903	= 690c.	943	= 556.	983	= 779c.
824	= 890.	864	= 1570g.	904	= 1163d.	944	= 818a.	984	= 885.
825	= 310a.	865	= 986a.	905	= 776e.	945	= 818b.	985	= 1319c.
826	= 561.	866	= 954c.	906	= 776c.	946	= 298.	986	= 132b.
827	= 15.	867	= 135b.	907	= 958c.	947	= 437.	987	= 1826.
828	= 49b.	868	= 64b.	908	= 965.	948	= 492f.	988	= 1606b.
829	= 1553.	869	= 962b.	909	= 290b.	949	= 659.	989	= 468.
830	= 450-1.	870	= 64e.	910	= 788f.	950	= 687.	990	= 123g.
831	= 1709.	871	= 519b.	911	= 49a.	951	= 1096.	991	= 583.
832	= 590b.	872	= 1028-9.	912	= 734b.	952	= 271f.	992	= 1887.
833	= 481b.	873	= 1025b.	913	= 158f.	953	= 200e.	993	= 1492.
834	= 481c.	874	= 826.	914	= 286c.	954	= 787.	994	= 1662.
835	= 1759.	875	= 1040-1.	915	= 286e.	955	= 935.	995	= 1054a.
836	= 1744a.	876	= 1003.	916	= 286d.	956	= 983c.	996	= 526a.
837	= 654bisb.	877	= 278.	917	= 832.	957	= 1446c.	997	= 1888.
838	= 940.	878	= 262a.	918	= 119a.	958	= 321h.	998	= 461.
839	= 323a.	879	= 479f.	919	= 1805.	959	= 224.	999	= 302b.
840	= 445a.	880	= 983ff.	920	= 119b.	960	= 590c.	1000	= 233.

* identical with Kuba B.H. 1121.

(Kuba B.H. 14)

No.	=	No.	=	No.	=	No.	=
1001	116.	1041	130c.	1081	1327a.	1121**	417.
1002	302a.	1042	1254b.	1082	1327b	1122	1512a.
1003	1043.	1043	1254a.	1083	1325b.	1123	196d.
1004	323c.	1044	1243a.	1084	1327c.	1124	1054.
1005	115b.	1045	1243e.	1085	1325e.	1125	1446b.
1006	308.	1046	1243d.	1086	1325f.		
1007	328.	1047	1243f.	1087	1325c.		
1008	628.	1048	1243c.	1088	1327d.		
1009	——— ?	1049	1269b.	1089	1327e.		
1010	1247a.	1050	1203b.	1090	1325d.		
1011	1830.	1051	638b.	1091	1679b.		
1012	1849.	1052	1243b.	1092	286g.		
1013	384d.	1053	761.	1093	1039g.		
1014	1247b.	1054	1514d.	1094	1039c.		
1015	925a.	1055	784b.	1095	1039a.		
1016	149-50	1056	1514b.	1096	1039e.		
1017	1889.	1057	1514e.	1097	983a.		
1018	303f.	1058	784a.	1098	983b.		
1019	285.	1059	1514a.	1099	983c.		
1020	888a.	1060	1532i.	1100	983d.		
1021	344c.	1061	1532c.	1101	983e.		
1022	344f.	1062	1532h.	1102	983f.		
1023	797.	1063	1532k.	1103	983g.		
1024	782e.	1064	1532m.	1104	983h.		
1025*	782b.	1065	1532l.	1105	983i.		
1026	782f.	1066	1532g.	1106	983j.		
1027	782a.	1067	1532j.	1107	983t.		
1028	782d.	1068	1890.	1108	384a.		
1029	782c.	1069	989b.	1109	983ll.		
1030	1608a.	1070	989c.	1110	984a.		
1031	1608b.	1071	989d.	1111	984b.		
1032	1608c.	1072	989h.	1112	984e.		
1033	1608d.	1073	989e.	1113	638a.		
1034	1608e.	1074	989g.	1114	984i.		
1035	648d.	1075	1329a.	1115	984c.		
1036	790c.	1076	1329b.	1116	210c.		
1037	779b.	1077	1720b.	1117	1521b.		
1038	790a.	1078	1267.	1118	1532f.		
1039	790b.	1079	1327g.	1119	1338b.		
1040	695.	1080	1327h.	1120	1891.		

* identical with Kuba B.H.95. ** identical with Kuba B.H.813.

Kuba IX (Croatian) 15

1 L———	14 = 439b.	27 = 1677.	40 = 1602f.	53 = 1638.
2 = 1354.	15 = 1296.	28 = 1733b.	41 = 929.	54 = 1616.
3 = 1002a.	16 = 588.	29 = 467a.	42 = 1458a.	55 = 1145b.
4 = 379c.	17 = 1726.	30 = 1005c.	43 = 1080.	56 = 1246b.
5 = 321g.	18 = 1381a.	31 = 188.	44 = 187.	57 = 1277c.
6 = 897a.	19 = 1546a.	32 = 747.	45 = 1516a.	58 = 1156b.
7 = 1162.	20 = 321b.	33 ——— ?	46 = 610e.	59 = 280b.
8 = 690a.	21 = 473b.	34 L———	47 = 1670.	60 = 226.
9 = 1280b.	22 = 1006a.	35 = 505.	48 = 1617.	61 L———
10 = 183d.	23 = 1373.	36 = 853f.	49 = 1892.	62 L———
11 = 1664b.	24 = 280c.	37 = 1220.	50 = 1132.	63 } ——— ?
12 = 618.	25 = 379b.	38 = 1753b.	51 = 1155.	64 } ——— ?
13 = 655d.	26 = 369b.	39 = 1310c.	52 = 1024a.	

Kuba X (Dalmatian)

1 = 1218.	14 = 249.	27 = 56c.	40 = 835a.	53 = 73c.
2 = 1273f.	15 = 1676.	28 = 1742b.	41 = 801.	54 = 383b.
3 L———	16 L———	29 = 61.	42 = 25.	55 = 1511a.
4 = 1111.	17 = 1125a.	30 = 1150c.	43 = 1486.	56 = 1787.
5 L———	18 = 73a.	31 = 565.	44 = 1125b.	57 ——— ?
6 L———	19 = 1399d.	32 = 73b.	45 = 1093.	58 = 1005b.
7 = 1570c.	20 = 56d.	33 = 229c.	46 = 1103.	59 = 1758.
8 = 201a.	21 = 1299.	34 = 303d.	47 = 455d.	60 = 1612.
9 = 1234.	22 = 743.	35 = 642.	48 = 1154.	61 = 57.
10 L———	23 = 1381c.	36 = 1310j.	49 = 1705.	
11 = 905g.	24 = 227.	37 = 1808.	50 = 503b.	
12 = 624.	25 = 1586e.	38 = 1771.	51 = 1506e.	
13 = 1506f.	26 L———	39 = 993c.	52 = 201b.	

Kuba XI (Montenegrian)

1 = 1036e.	15 = 1259a.	29 = 495.	43 = 610c.	57 = 1686.
2 = 1762.	16 = 814.	30 = 1033a.	44 = 143d.	58 = 1483c.
3 = 1320.	17 = 829.	31 = 1026f.	45 = 539.	59 = 1197.
4 = 1564.	18 = 598.	32 = 795.	46 = 983p.	60 = 1102a.
5 = 446c.	19 = 1396a.	33 = 1625a.	47 = 905c.	61 = 286f.
6 = 320b.	20 = 160b.	34 = 522.	48 = 862.	62a) = 892c. 62b) = 1328.
7 = 755h.	21 = 1395.	35 = 817.	49 = 563b.	63 = 519a.
8 = 1077a.	22 = 993a.	36 = 1039b.	50 = 128a.	64 L———
9 = 1778a.	23 = 324.	37 = 1469d.	51 = 1025a.	65 L———
10 = 755a.	24 = 1511b.	38 = 757.	52 = 834a.	66 L———
11 = 446a.	25 = 633.	39 = 789.	53 = 1001i.	67 L———
12 = 1447a.	26 = 970.	40 = 777.	54 = 29.	68 = 1112.
13 = 1399e.	27 = 1589b.	41 = 460.	55 = 311c.	69 = 232d.
14 = 938b.	28 = 753a.	42 = 803a.	56 = 16.	70 = 1417c.

Kuba XII (Serbian)

1 = 1367a.	13 = 1585a	25 = 1082.	[37] = 268.	49 = 1777.
[2] = 1618d.	14 = 652a.	26 = 1126.	38 = 1893.	50 = 183d.
3 = 905f.	15 = 1527.	27 = 1098a.	39 = 768–9.	51 = 1176.
4 = 185b.	16 = 722–3.	[28] = 1096.	40 = 958b.	52 = 1349.
5 = 1334.	17 = 1085b.	29 = 1593c.	41 = 398.	[53] = 1550d.
6 = 107.	18 = 828.	[30] = 1703	42 = 617.	54 = 1427.
7 = 686.	19 = 1763.	31 = 745	[43] = 1436.	[55] = 932b.
[8] = 1439b.	20 = 827c.	32 = 1310l.	[44] = 919.	[56] = 1229a.
[9] = 648c.	[21] = 1331.	33 = 396c.	45 = 1342.	57 = 424c.
10 = 648b.	22 = 183c.	34 = 1020b.	46 = 1429.	[58] = 1269b.
11 = 1399j.	23 = 1278.	35 = 1585e.	47 = 1308.	59 = 179.
12 = 506.	[24] = 511a.	36 = 1659e.	48 = 1075.	[60] = 1720a.

Kuba XIII (Bosnian-Hercegovinian)

[1] = 1603.	13 = 592a.	[25] = 1332a.	[37] = 1314a.	49 = 654bis a.
[2] = 1242.	[14] = 321c.	[26] = 344a.	[38] = 1662.	[50] = 715–6.
[3] = 1039a.	[15] = 1310g.	[27] = 503a.	[39] = 880a.	[51] = 185a.
[4] = 280g.	[16] = 1292b.	[28] = 797.	40 = 1203a.	[52] = 1606b.
[5] = 963.	[17] = 1789a.	[29] = 659.	[41] = 984k.	[53] = 63.
6 = 550a.	[18] = 578.	[30] = 1629b.	[42] = 1371b.	[54] = 1813–4.
[7] = 1392b.	[19] = 265a.	[31] = 432b.	[43] = 697a.	[55] = 983cc.
[8] = 1679b.	[20] = 433c.	[32] = 1311.	[44] = 1077b.	[56] = 321d.
9 = 247b.	21 = 315.	[33] = 699.	[45] = 1325a.	[57] = 1313d.
10 = 1532e.	[22] = 1444b.	[34] = 1540h.	[46] = 1593a.	[58] = 1327g.
[11] = 684a.	[23] = 344d.	35 = 492c.	[47] = 984i.	[59] = 1327b.
12 = 1333.	[24] = 636.	36 = 557.	48 = 1149f.	[60] = 1327a.

Kuba XIV (Old-Serbian)

1 = 1413.	7 = 842.	13 = 232h.	[19] = 1263.	25 = 1533.
[2] = 455c.	8 = 1073a.	14 = 1420.	[20] = 1448a.	26 = 138.
[3] = 679d.	[9] = 271e.	[15] = 1385b.	21 = 1448b.	27 = 1087b.
4 = 1521c.	10 = 966b.	16 = 1346.	22 = 1518	28 = 1388a.
5 ______ ?	[11] = 1745–6.	[17] = 1364.	23 = 920–1.	29 = 330a.
6 = 1515a.	12 = 1540i.	[18] = 185c.	24 = 1526b.	30a) = 693.
				30b) = 1174.

17
Dordević

1	= 1362.	41	= 1469a.	81	= 1668.	121	= 1576e.	161	= 1324b.
2	= 1630.	42	= 168a.	82	= 922.	122	= 237d.	162	= 1324a.
3	= 739b.	43	= 671a.	83	= 948.	123	= 661b.	163	= 1285b.
4	= 173a.	44	= 243h.	84	= 855b.	124	= 788a.	164	= 123r.
5	= 1442.	45	= 671b.	85	= 1367b.	125	= 788i.	165	= 209.
6a)	= 1275.	46	= 644.	86	= 292a.	126	= 788e.	166	= 237e.
6b)	= 950.								
7	= 1602c.	47	———	87	= 1552.	127	= 123b.	167	= 788c.
8	= 34.	48	———	88	= 719.	128	= 661a.	168	= 146c.
9	= 459.	49	———	89	= 1351.	129	= 489b.	169	= 584c.
10	= 667.	50	———	90	= 780b.	130	= 237g.	170	= 131a.
11	= 677.	51	= 197a.	91	= 1106.	131	= 246b.	171	= 1222.
12	= 624.	52	= 83.	92	= 246a.	132	= 786.	172	= 166-7
13	= 1556a.	53	= 448g.	93	= 191b.	133	= 28.	173	= 123l.
14	= 430a.	54	= 1368.	94	= 654.	134	= 184.	174	= 52.
15	= 554.	55	= 243l.	95	= 1087a.	135	= 606.	175	= 243j.
16	= 261e.	56	= 232g.	96	= 123g.	136	= 199c.	176	= 1291.
17	= 84.	57	= 219a.	97	= 673	137	= 400c.	177	= 67
18	= 739a.	58	= 232f.	98	= 1085a.	138	= 123z.	178	= 148a.
19	= 261d.	59	= 439c.	99	= 992.	139	= 123dd.	179	= 174d.
20	= 243c.	60	= 155a.	100	= 208a.	140	= 788b.	180	= 504.
21	= 129a.	61	= 664a.	101	= 974.	141	= 237c.	181	= 418.
22	= 85.	62	= 664b.	102	= 1136.	142	= 211d.	182	= 947.
23	= 123y.	63	= 183e.	103	= 1404a.	143	= 123x.	183	= 146a.
24	= 305e.	64	= 477.	104	= 1404b.	144	= 928.	184	= 448d.
25	= 307.	65	= 157c.	105	= 251.	145	= 806.	185	= 129b.
26	= 169.	66	= 494.	106	= 232b.	146	= 1067.	186	= 140.
27	= 230.	67	= 1060.	107	= 245	147	= 1324c.	187	= 123h.
28	= 243f.	68	= 325a.	108	= 1285c.	148	= 802e.	188	= 91
29	= 421a.	69	= 180a.	109	= 441.	149	= 375.	189	= 597a.
30	= 87.	70	= 819e.	110	= 1471.	150	= 1286.	190	= 544f.
31	= 236.	71	= 376a.	111	= 208b.	151	= 225.	191	= 1468c.
32	= 44.	72	= 261a.	112	= 312b.	152	= 144-5	192	= 788d.
33	= 334c.	73	= 80b.	113	= 1268.	153	= 123m.	193	= 165e.
34	= 62.	74	= 261c.	114	= 1065.	154	= 545b.	194	= 744.
35	= 123k.	75	= 376b.	115	= 1251a.	155	= 282.	195	———
36	= 47c.	76	= 325b.	116	= 1231.	156	= 649.	196	———
37	= 289a.	77	= 90a.	117	= 564.	157	= 234a.	197	———
38	= 1288.	78	= 174b.	118	= 662.	158	= 509.	198	———
39	= 342.	79	= 284.	119	= 1576a.	159	= 403.	199	= 199b.
40	= 154.	80	= 1768.	120	= 174a.	160	= 545a.	200	= 199a.

18
(Dordević)

201 = 110.
202 = 40.
203 = 831.
204 = 1232.
205 = 542.
206 = 489c.
207 = 446d.
208 = 629.
209 = 1358c.
210 = 402a.
211 = 146b.
212 = 210a.
213 = 115a.
214 = 489a.
215 = 123p.
216 = 305k.
217 = 443b.
218 = 498.
219 = 237f.
220 = 90b.
221 = 807.
222 = 306.
223 = 183i.
224 = 36d.
225 = 443a.
226 = 237h.
227 = 165a.
228 = 42.
229 = 625.
230 = 197b.
231 = 402b.
232 = 448n.
233 = 123bb.
234 = 58.
235 = 65.
236 = 802d.
237 = 815b.
238 = 543b.
239 = 155b.
240 = 708a.

241 = 1044a.
242 = 1070.
243 = 844.
244 = 219b.
245 = 106.
246 = 949.
247 = 24c.
248 = 133.
249 = 243b.
250 = 76.
251 = 446b.
252 = 766a.
253 = 544i.
254 = 7a.
255 = 7b.
256 = 203.
257 = 410.
258 = 123n.
259 = 1561d.
260 = 1432b.
261 = 1432a.
262 = 448a.
263 ————
264 ————
265 ————
266 ————
267 ————
268 ————
269 ————
270 ————
271 ————
272 = 262d.
273 = 100.
274a) = 164c.
274b) = 262c.
275 ————
276 ————
277 ————
278 ————
279 = 1181c.
280 ————

281 = 216e.
282 = 448k.
283 = 448e.
284 = 448h.
285 = 1416a.
286 = 1416b.
287 = 448l.
288 = 123t.
289 = 215.
290 = 276b.
291 = 276a.
292 = 883b.
293 = 883a.
294 = 666b.
295 = 1563e.
296 = 210b.
297 = 1565d.
298 = 1563c.
299 = 1563a.
300 = 80a.
301 = 123o.
302 = 77a.
303 = 264b.
304 = 264c.
305 = 1053.
306 = 152b.
307 = 1048.
308 = 88.
309 = 815e.
310 = 815a.
311 = 243k.
312 = 79b.
313 = 79c.
314 = 35.
315 = 607.
316 = 537.
317 = 349c.
318 = 346b.
319 ————
320 ————

321 ————
322 ————
323 ————
324 ————
325 = 17a.
326 = 17b.
327 = 132h.
328 = 132f.
329 = 129c.
330 = 129d.
331 = 129e.
332 = 243m.
333 = 1021b.
334 = 930c.
335 = 981.
336 = 958f.
337 = 895.
338 = 1605.
339 = 1850.
340 = 402d.
341 = 1465.
342 = 312a.
343 = 1165b.
344 = 886c.
345 = 766b.
346 = 1498a.
347 = 336.
348 = 79a.
349 = 448j.
350 = 237a.
351 = 349a.
352 = 479d.
353 = 760a.
354 = 1000b.
355 = 304a.
356 = 123gg.
357 = 959b.
358 = 132g.
359 = 305a.
360 = 627.

361 = 780a.
362 = 529e.
363 = 374.
364 = 157b.
365 = 1026a.
366 = 613a.
367 = 1498b.
368 = 901.
369 = 523.
370 = 281c.
371 = 281a.
372 = 79d.
373 = 448f.
374 = 448i.
375 = 305d.
376 = 815c.
377 = 533b.
378 = 573b.
379 = 243a.
380 = 181.
381 = 252a.
382 = 252b.
383 = 101.
384 = 123j.
385 = 964.
386 = 585.
387 = 254.
388 = 589.
389 = 541.
390 = 472b.
391 = 611.
392 = 1576b
393 = 1851.
394 = 243g.
395 = 210d.
396 = 456.
397 = 536.
398 = 53.
399 = 553a.
400 = 597b.

19
(Đorđević)

401 = 305f.
402 = 349b.
403 = 152a.
404 = 217.
405 = 407.
406 = 123ff.
407 = 1000d.
408 = 86.
409 = 182.
410 = 400b.
411 = 1484a.
412 = 75b.
413 = 168d.
414 = 373.
415 = 346.
416 = 1542.
417 = 348.
418 = 36a.
419 = 82e.
420 = 1285a.
421 = 123d.
422 = 547b.
423 = 1653.
424 = 261b.
425 = 815d.
426 = 237b.
427 = 620.
428 = 102.
429 = 1563b.
430 = 253.
431 = 670.
432 = 792a.
433 = 533c.
434 = 594.
435 = 391.
436 = 666a.
437 = 1451.
438 = 802c.
439 = 558-9.
440 = 132e.
441 = 30.
442 = 1690a.
443 = 1205.
444 = 421c.
445 = 23.
446 = 555a.
447 = 1057a.
448 = 886a.
449 = 177c.
450 = 1026d.
451 = 1894.
452 = 553b.
453 = 755j.
454 = 411.
455 = 266a.
456 = 549b.
457 = 473c.
458 = 535a.
459 = 1600.
460 = 351.
461 = 472a.
462 = 309b.
463 = 216f.
464 = 584b.
465 = 46b.
466 = 553c.
467 = 833g.
468 = 778d.
469 = 1097a.
470 = 454a.
471 = 49c.
472 = 82d.
473 = 305j.
474 = 402c.
475 = 120b.
476 = 543a.
477 = 1507.
478 = 123u.
479 = 123i.
480 = 534a.
481 = 216e.
482 = 534b.
483 = 1024e.
484 = 553d.
485 = 452c.
486 = 452a.
487 = 535b.
488 = 234b.
489 = 123ee.
490 = 704-5.
491 = 779a.
492 = 584a.
493 = 1012.
494 = 304c.
495 = 701a.
496 = 708e.
497 = 452b.
498 = 1057b.
499 = 544h.
500 = 755i.
501 = 811.
502 = 613b.
503 = 400a.
504 = 691a.
505 = 407a.
506 = 821.
507 = 701b.
508 = 701c.
509 = 45.
510 = 121.
511 = 1562.
512 = 1020c.
513 = 1521a.
514 ——
515 = 781b.
516 = 168e.
517 = 1852.
518 = 402e.
519 = 1398a.
520 = 1398b.
521 = 1853.
522 = 708b.
523 = 1812.
524 = 792.
525 = 5.
526 ——
527 ——
528 = 528.
529 ——
530 ——
531 ——
532 ——
533 ——
534 ——
535 = 802b.
536 = 528c.
537 = 151a.
538 = 755k.
539 = 89b.
540 = 89c.
541 = 50-51.
542 = 96.
543 = 544c.
544 = 528d.
545 = 1472 bis.
546 = 1046.
547 = 573a.
548 = 192.
549 = 802a.
550 = 447.
551 = 77b.
552 = 157a.
553 = 544a.
554 = 141-2
555 = 544b.
556 = 243d.
557 = 833h.
558 = 243e.
559 = 540.
560 = 820.
561 = 650.
562 = 805.
563 = 1285d.
564 = 669
565 = 174c.
566 = 604a.
567 = 263c.
568 = 263b.
569a) = 165h.
569b) = 310i.
570 = 508.
571 = 604b.
572 = 604c.
573 = 604d.
574 = 604e.
575 = 1468b.
576 = 77d.
577 = 476.
578 = 310e.
579 = 305g.
580 = 310d.
581 = 168c.
582 = 781a.
583 = 3.
584 = 305h.
585 = 1544.
586 = 24d.
587 = 269.
588 = 24e.
589 = 168b.
590 = 305i.
591 = 1854.
592 ——
593 = 489d.
594 = 1539.
595 ——
596 ——
597 = 123cc.

Dordević Nar. Pev. [20]

(Page)

- 1/1 = 1489.
- 1/2 = 491.
- 2/1 = 792b.
- 2/2 = 305b.
- 3/1 = 1548.
- 3/2 ——
- 4/1 ——
- 4/2 = 1585c.
- 5/1 = 1577a.
- 5/2 ——
- 6/1 = 1405.
- 6/2 = 1620b.
- 7/1 = 425.
- 7/2 = 566c.
- [8/1] = 511b.
- 8/2 = 1675b.
- 9 ——
- 10/1 = 1247c.
- 10/2 ——
- 11/1 = 77c.
- [11/2] = 886c.
- 12 ——
- [13/1] = 1665.
- 13/2 ——
- 14/1 = 1778b.
- 14/2 = 746.
- 15/1 = 1755bis.
- 15/2 = 159c.
- 16/1 = 655c.
- 16/2 ——
- 17 ——
- [18/1] = 1285b.
- 18/2 = 45.
- 19/1 ——
- 19/2 = 1312.
- 20 ——

- 21/1 ——
- 21/2 = 765.
- 22/1 = 968.
- 22/2 ——
- 23/1 = 954a.
- 23/2 = 954b.
- 24/1 = 177a.
- 24/2 = 234c.
- 25/1 = 1212c.
- 25/2
- 26/1 = 1072a.
- [26/2] = 1795a.
- [27/1] = 1251a.
- 27/2 ——
- 28/1 = 1054d.
- 28/2 = 1815b.
- 29/1 = 1643–4
- 29/2 = 1039d.
- 30/1 ——
- [30/2] = 897a.
- 31 ——
- 32/1 = 1456.
- [32/2] = 326.
- 33/1 ——
- 33/2 = 170.
- 34 ——
- 35/1 = 1526a.
- 35/2 = 496b.
- 36/1 = 1327f.
- 36/2 = 312d.
- 37/1 = 455b.
- 37/2 ——
- 38/1 = 1457
- 38/2 = 99a.
- 39/1 = 171.
- 39/2 ——
- 40/1 = 977.
- 40/2 ——

- 41 ——
- 42/1 = 427.
- 42/2 = 1532b.
- 43 ——
- 44/1 = 854a.
- 44/2 ——
- 45 ——
- 46/1 = 1294.
- [46/2] = 563a.
- 47/1 = 770b.
- 47/2 ——
- 48/1 = 1663.
- 48/2 ——
- 49 ——
- 50 ——
- [51/1] = 983z.
- 51/2 ——
- 52/1 = 1245a.
- 52/2 ——
- 53/1 = 1531a.
- 53/2 ——
- 54 ——
- 55 ——
- 56 ——
- 57 ——
- [58/1] = 620.
- 58/2 ——
- 59 ——
- 60 ——

- 61 ——
- 62/1 = 1704.
- 62/2 ——
- [63/1] = 930c.
- 63/2 ——
- 64 ——
- 65 ——
- 66 ——
- 67 ——
- [68/1] = 1285f.
- 68/2 ——
- 69/1 = 1728.
- 69/2 = 1002e.
- [70/1] = 208a.
- 70/2 ——
- 71/1 = 1645.
- 71/2 ——
- 72 ——
- 73 ——
- 74/1 = 1599b.
- 74/2 ——
- 75/1 = 1055.
- 75/2 ——
- 76/1 = 973b.
- 76/2 ——
- 77/1 ——
- 77/2 = 158a.
- 78/1 = 975.
- 78/2 ——
- [79/1] = 974.
- 79/2 ——
- 80 ——

- [81/1] = 1508.
- 81/2 ——
- [82/1] = 459.
- 82/2 ——
- [83/1] = 208b.
- 83/2 ——
- 84/1 = 1008.
- 84/2 ——
- 85/1 = 292b.
- 85/2 ——
- 86/1 = 867.
- 86/2 ——
- 87 ——
- 88 ——
- 89/1 = 1309.
- 89/2 ——
- 90/1 = 1088.
- 90/2 ——
- [91/1] = 1292c.
- 91/2 ——
- 92 ——
- 93 ——
- 94 ——
- 95/1 ——
- 95/2 = 1468a.
- 96/1 = 1701.
- 96/2 ——
- [97] = 1534.
- 98 ——
- 99 ——
- 100/1 = 764d.
- 100/2 ——

(Dordević Nat. Pev.)[21]; Iz Levča

101/1 = 1341
101/2 ———
102/1 = 1148b.
102/2 ———
103/1 ———
[103/2] = 1165b.
[104/1] = 1540a.
104/2 ———
105/1 = 791a.
105/2 = 1484b.
106/1 = 827a.
106/2 ———
107/1 = 1168c.
107/2 = 60b.
108/1 = 346c.
108/2 = 1026c.
109 ———
110/1 = 1293.
110/2 ———
111/1 = 1895.
111/2 ———
112/1 = 1767b.
112/2 ———
[113/1] = 1054f.
[113/2] = 230.
114/1 = 1448a.
114/2 ———
115 ———
[116/1] = 898a.
116/2 ———
[117/1] = 1001h.
117/2 = 1659c.
[118/1] = 1021b.
118/2 ———

119 ———
120/1 = 382.
120/2 ———
121/1 = 888b.
121/2 ———
122/1 = 1332c.
122/2 ———
123/1 = 1264.
123/2 ———
124 ———
125/1 = 1594.
125/2 ———
126/1 = 1774.
126/2 ———
127 = 1459.
128 ———
129 ———
130/1 = 1454.
130/2 = 444.
131/1 = 1505b.
131/2 ———
132/1 = 983k.
132/2 ———
133 ———
[134/1] = 1404a.
134/2 ———
135 ———
136/1 = 1679a.
136/2

137 ———
138/1 = 983r.
138/2 ———
139/1 = 1279b
139/2 ———
140/1 = 1896
140/2 ———
141/1 = 1280d.
141/2 ———
142/1 = 1290.
142/2 ———
143 ———
144 ———
145 ———
146/1 = 1557b.
146/2 ———
147/1 = 984h.
147/2 = 698.
148 ———
[149/1] = 1095b.
149/2 = 1741.
150/1 = 833e.
150/2 ———
151/1 = 861a.
151/2 = 391a.
152 ———
153/1 = 1270
153/2 ———
154/1 = 1599a.
154/2 = 250

155/1 = 1816.
155/2 = 424d.
156 ———
157/1 = 1725
157/2 ———
158/1 = 1314b.
[158/2] = 884.
159/1 = 861b.
159/2 ———
[160/1] = 1584b.
160/2 ———
161/1 ———
161/2 = 984g.
162/1 = 1661.
162/2 ———
163/1 ———
163/2 = 1279b.
164/1 = 1283a.
164/2 ———
165 ———
[166/1] = 609a.
166/2 ———
[167/1] = 1804a.
167/2 = 1655e.
168/1 = 1606a.
168/2 ———
[169/1] = 1136.
169/2 = 1530b.
170/1 = 681.
170/2 ———
171 ———
172 ———

[173/1] = 958f.
173/2 = 1590.
174 ———
175/1 = 1230b.
175/2 = 1744b.
176 ———
177/1 = 932a.
177/2 = 853b.
178 ———
179/1 = 1068
179/2 ———
180/1 = 989a.
180/2 ———
181 ———
182/1 = 1769.
[182/2] = 1324a.
183/1 ———
183/2 = 1455.
184/1 = 1503-4.
184/2 ———
185/1 = 646.
[185/2] = 1324e.
186/1 = 1322.
186/2 = 1033b.
187 ———
188/1 = 1014.
188/2 = 1072d.
188/3 = 1059.
189/1 = 1681.
189/2 ———
190/1 = 1781.
190/2 ———
191/1 = 1359.
191/2 = 409.

Iz Levča

1 = 472c.
2 = 1069
3a) 3b)} = 529a.
4 = 770d.

5 = 532b.
6 = 475.
7 = 532a.
8 = 1030b.

9 = 1897.
10 = 560.
11 = 528a.
12 = 532c.

13 = 529b.
14 = 120a.
15 = 1030a.
16 = 584e.

17 = 972
18 = 584d.
19 = 1561a.
20 = 691b.

Iz Levča [22]

21 = 122b.	37 = 529d.	53 = 32.	69 = 673.	85 ———
22 = 1358a.	38 = 865.	54 = 1824.	70 = 1285i.	86 ———
23 = 177b.	39 = 544g.	55 = 891a.	71 = 422c.	87 ———
24 = 165f.	40 = 528b.	56 = 194b.	72 = 123v.	88 ———
25 = 549a.	41 = 89a.	57 = 891b.	73 = 568.	
26 = 529c.	42 = 1183.	58 = 1285h.	74 = 404a.	
27 = 1561b.	43 = 454b.	59 = 544d.	75 = 404b.	
28 = 1030d.	44 = 422a.	60 = 1030c.	76 ———	
29 = 1561c.	45 = 420a.	61 = 180b.	77 ———	
30 = 1555b.	46 = 874.	62 = 333e.	78 ———	
31 = 1206a.	47 = 122c.	63 = 422b.	79 ———	
32 = 266b.	48 = 552.	64 = 453a.	80 ———	
33 = 335b.	49 = 923.	65 = 453b.	81 ———	
34 = 1030e.	50 = 1400.	66 = 489f.	82 ———	
35 = 421a.	51 = 857.	67 = 453c.	83 ———	
36 = 1026b.	52 = 489e.	68 = 544e.	84 ———	

Bosiljevac

1 = 983aa.	14 = 420b.	27 = 706a.	40 ——— ?
2 = 1815c.	15 = 958a.	28 = 1428.	[41] = 496b.
3 = 989f.	16 = 1033d.	29 = 858.	42 = 1212a.
4 = 982.	17 = 1578.	30 = 1125c.	43 = 791b.
5 = 1620a.	18 = 1072c.	31 = 833f.	44 = 1532a.
6a) = 563d.	19 = 474.	32 = 655f.	45 = 99b.
6b) ——— 2.			
7 = 720.	20 = 1246n.	33 = 445g.	46 = 983dd.
8 = 466.	21 = 1107b.	34 = 111.	47 = 158c.
9 = 471.	22 = 1165c.	35 = 979.	48 = 854b.
10 = 455a.	23 = 1285e.	36 = 859.	49 = 1505d.
11 = 1655c.	24 = 1316.	37 = 1039f.	50 = 1672b.
12 = 26.	25 = 1490d.	38 = 819b.	
13 = 882b.	26 = 1629a.	39 = 976b.	

Kačerovski

1 = 1778c.	10 = 900.	19 = 1683.	28 ———	37 ———
2 ———	11 ———	20 = 1724.	29 = 1568a.	38 ———
3 = 1531e.	12 = 706b.	21 = 1529.	30a) = 39h.	39 ———
4a) = 1182a.	13 = 482.	22 = 886d.	30b) = 1438.	40a) = 158b.
4b) = 1591a.			31 = 973a.	40b) = 1412.
5 = 1131.	14 ———	23 = 1655f.	32 ———	41 = 312e.
6 = 1361.	15 ———	24 = 1597.	33 = 1698.	42 = 1072b.
7 = 1245b.	16 ———	25 ———	34 ———	43 ———
8 ———	17 ———	26 = 1626c.	35 ———	44 = 1475.
9 = 1476.	18 = 1557a.	27 = 1736.	36 = 1579a.	45 = 1628.

23
(Kačerovski), Juž. Srb., Manojlović, Bartók

46 = 1483b.	54 = 827b.	62 ______	70 = 1569c.	78 ______
47 ______	55 = 1786.	63 ______	71 = 1569c.	79 ______
48 ______	56 = 1531b.	64 = 1614.	72 = 1419.	80 ______
49 = 954d.	57 ______	65 ______	73 = 1740a.	81 = 1528.
50 = 1280e.	58. = 1586c.	66 = 1280a.	74 = 1730.	82 = 946.
51 ______	59 ______	67 ______	75 = 367–8.	83 = 1740b.
52. ______	60 = 853d.	[68] = 1693a.	76 = 1530a.	84 = 1855.
53 ______	61 = 1449–50.	69 = 1540f.	77 = 668.	

Juž. Srb.

399 = 123aa.	405 = 1695.	411 = 1754.	417 = 1601a.	423 = 682.
400 = 1092.	406 = 614.	412 = 271g.	418 = 478.	424 = 759.
401 = 143e.	407 = 1078.	413 = 501.	419 = 300.	425 = 1601c.
402 = 774	408 = 510a.	414 = 1622.	420 = 612.	426 = 533d.
403 = 1411.	409 = 966a.	415 = 1102b.	421 = 1651a.	427 = 479g.
404 = 266c.	410 = 913.	416 = 1073b.	422 = 605.	428 = 799.

Manojlović

3. = 1265.	4 = 1487.	5 = 136.	6 = 305l.	

Bartók

39d.	1020a.	1223.	1259b.	1602b.

Thematic Index of the Tabulated Melodies

The purpose of this computer produced tabulation is to provide a supplemental method of locating individual melody sections[1] in the music examples published in Vols. I and III, or of comparing those melody sections with others published elsewhere.[2]

In order to make comparisons with other folk music materials it is necessary to determine the melodic (that is, intervallic) contour of the melody sections in those materials, as a first step:

(1) Analyze for content structure (A A, A B, A B C, etc.);

(2) For each melody section of different content, and omitting repeated notes from consideration, calculate not more than seven sequential intervals in terms of plus or minus figures, that is, an ascending second is marked +2, a descending one, —2, and so on.[3] (See Fig. 1 for an illustrated example of this procedure.)

Then compare the derived digital sequence with those published below. If a complete match is found (or a significant subset of intervals) or a similar contour, refer to the respective music examples in Vols. I, III, and IV for further comparative analysis.[4]

[1] A melody section is that portion of the melody which overlies one text-line (further denoted, by Bartók, by means of a caesura sign or of the *tonus finalis* of the melody.

[2] This Index was compiled by means of the GRIPHOS programs developed by Professor Jack Heller of the Department of Computer Sciences, State University of New York at Stony Brook.

[3] Chromatic qualities (major, minor, etc.) are also omitted from consideration, lest variant relationships disappear in a mass of too-finely-drawn tonal properties.

[4] The reader interested in more specific details regarding data processing techniques in Bartókian folk song research should refer to the present writer's essays: "Computer Applications to Bartók's Serbo-Croatian Material", *Tempo* (London) No. 80, Spring, 1967; "Computerized Folk Song Research and the Problem of Variants", *Computers and the Humanities* (New York), March, 1968; "Bartók, Ethnomusicology and the Computer", *ICRH Newsletter* (New York University), December, 1968; "Some Problems in Computer-Oriented Bartókian Ethnomusicology", *Ethnomusicology,* September, 1969, also in *Revista de Etnografie şi Folclor* (Bucharest), XIV/5, 1969 and *Muzsika* (Budapest), July and August issues, 1969; "Computer-Oriented Comparative Musicology", in *Music and the Computer* (ed. by H. B. Lincoln), Cornell University Press, 1970; "The Computer and

Thematic Index of the Tabulated Melodies

Fig. 1 Encoded first melody-section of Parry mus. exx. 39b. (upper notation) and 42 (lower), showing the calculation of interval sequence in the form of signed digits

LEXICOGRAPHICAL ORDER OF MELODY SECTIONS

Interval Sequence	Melody No.*
(*Repeated-note* [g¹] *sections only*)	390d, 478:B, 661b:B, 886a:C, 1048:B, 1058c, 1059:D, 1140, 1463:C, 1532k, 1582b:C, 1589c, 1599b:D, 1606bis, 1634:B
+2	1057d:C, 1135a, 1371a, 1371b, 1376:B, 1481a, 1573c:B, 1584e, 1584f, 1589e, 1658c, 1804b:D
+2+2	191a, 948, 951a, 1081, 1115, 1148a, 1148b, 1403a, 1403c, 1511a:B, 1575:B, 1585g:B, 1769:C
+2+2+2	1059, 1128c, 1128d, 1143a:B, 1463:B, 1514a:B, 1646, 1692b:C
+2+2+2+2	1119, 1123, 1129, 1369, 1460a:B, 1483a:B, 1483b:B, 1483d:B, 1586a:B, 1586b:B, 1586d:B, 1587a:B, 1587b:B, 1588a:B, 1588b:B, 1669
+2+2+2+2+2+2−2	1300, 1754:C
+2+2+2+2+2+3−3	301a
+2+2+2+2+2−2	405, 711a, 1008
+2+2+2+2+2−2+2	425, 1715, 1718
+2+2+2+2+2−2−2	442, 844, 1276:B, 1346:B, 1459:B, 1538
+2+2+2+2+2−2−3	1515g
+2+2+2+2+4−3+3	1305d
+2+2+2+2+4−4	1387

* Numbers without capital letter indicate the first melody section (or other melody sections with *A* content-structure).

Bartók Research in America", *Journal of Research in Music Education,* Spring, 1971, also in *Magyar Zenetörténeti Tanulmányok* (ed. by Ferenc Bonís), Editio Musica (Budapest), 1971; *A GRIPHOS Application to Bartók's Turkish Folk Music Material, Spectra* Publication No. 1, Center for Contemporary Arts and Letters, State University of New York at Stony Brook, 1975.

Thematic Index of the Tabulated Melodies

Interval Sequence	Melody No.
+2+2+2+2−2	653, 1047c, 1406
+2+2+2+2−2+2+2	1732:C
+2+2+2+2−2+3−2	1453
+2+2+2+2−2−2	183b, 183f, 183g, 1480
+2+2+2+2−2−2+2	433d, 1310l:B
+2+2+2+2−2−2+3	1445
+2+2+2+2−2−2−2	897a:B, 1659c:C, 1732:D, 1771
+2+2+2+2−2−2−3	138, 396a, 788g, 1009
+2+2+2+2−2−3	126b:B, 1279b
+2+2+2+2−2−3−2	424b, 849a:B
+2+2+2+2−2−4	1628:B
+2+2+2+2−2−5	1278
+2+2+2+2−3	73d, 159d, 623a:B, 1010b, 1090, 1093:B, 1107c, 1133, 1557b:B, 1582a, 1582b, 1627:B
+2+2+2+2−3+2	1243e
+2+2+2+2−3+3+2	1306d
+2+2+2+2−3+3−2	321c:B
+2+2+2+2−3+3−3	882a
+2+2+2+2−3−2	1279a:B
+2+2+2+2−3−2+2	469–470
+2+2+2+2−3−2+3	1338c
+2+2+2+2−3−3	634, 788h, 1529:C, 1533:C
+2+2+2+2−3−3+2	1364:B
+2+2+2+2−4+2	183e
+2+2+2+2−4+3	1555b
+2+2+2+2−4−2	859:B
+2+2+2+2−4−3−3	1587b
+2+2+2+2−5+2+2	1327h
+2+2+2+3−2−2	615b, 615c, 1246c:B
+2+2+2+3−2−2−2	1636
+2+2+2+3−2−2−3	1264:B
+2+2+2+3−2−3	1204, 1546a
+2+2+2+3−2−3−3	300
+2+2+2+3−2−3−4	773b
+2+2+2+3−3	1233
+2+2+2+3−3−2−2	1329b:B
+2+2+2+3−3−2−4	773a

Thematic Index of the Tabulated Melodies

Thematic Index of the Tabulated Melodies

Interval Sequence	Melody No.
+2+2+2−2−2−3	1756, 1810:C
+2+2+2−2−2−3+2	1359, 1439b:C
+2+2+2−2−2−3−3	1229b
+2+2+2−2−2−3−5	1490a
+2+2+2−2−3	264a, 519a, 519b, 638c:C, 759, 765, 786, 1225:B, 1237, 1246b, 1274, 1399h, 1399j, 1406:C, 1505a, 1535, 1550:B, 1551:B, 1569c, 1613b, 1786:B; Parry 23a
+2+2+2−2−3+2	753b, 760a, 1515h
+2+2+2−2−3+2+2	610b:B, 1868
+2+2+2−2−3+2+3	364a
+2+2+2−2−3+2+4	198
+2+2+2−2−3+2−2	684b:C, 684c:C
+2+2+2−2−3+3	888a
+2+2+2−2−3+3+2	432b
+2+2+2−2−3+3−2	414a
+2+2+2−2−3+3−3	910
+2+2+2−2−3+4−2	432a
+2+2+2−2−3−2	599:B, 1593a
+2+2+2−2−3−2+3	355, 414c
+2+2+2−2−4	1601c, 1659d:B
+2+2+2−2−4+3	1246c
+2+2+2−2−4+4−3	780a
+2+2+2−3	283a, 285, 592c, 1039h, 1189a, 1205:B, 1388a, 1388b, 1399m, 1431, 1479d:B, 1490a:B, 1528:B, 1537b, 1592b; Parry 44b:B
+2+2+2−3+2	159a, 582:B, 954c:B
+2+2+2−3+2−2−2	1284b:B
+2+2+2−3+2−3	1399d, 1610:B, 1822
+2+2+2−3+2−3+3	201a
+2+2+2−3+2−3−2	1629a:C
+2+2+2−3+3−4−3	1404b
+2+2+2−3−2	485b, 750b, 1144a, 1144b, 1395:D, 1439a, 1481b:B, 1483e, 1608d:D
+2+2+2−3−2+2	1785:B
+2+2+2−3−2+2+2	610d:B, 652b, 1722c:B
+2+2+2−3−2+2−2	20
+2+2+2−3−2+3−3	156:B

Thematic Index of the Tabulated Melodies

Interval Sequence	Melody No.
+2+2+2−3−2+4−2	265j
+2+2+2−3−2−2	1474:C, 1512b
+2+2+2−3−2−3	227
+2+2+2−3−2−3+2	1287
+2+2+2−3−3	1613b:B, 1689:B
+2+2+2−3−3−2	1242:B
+2+2+2−3−3−2−3	Parry 28a
+2+2+2−4+2+2+2	1705:B
+2+2+2−4+2+2−3	738a:B
+2+2+2−4+2+4−2	708a
+2+2+2−4+2−2−2	321a:B, 321b:B
+2+2+2−4+2−3−2	1280b
+2+2+2−4+3	1597:B
+2+2+2−4+3−2−2	321d:B, 1659d:C
+2+2+2−4+4	1602j
+2+2+2−5	1103
+2+2+2−6	636
+2+2+3+2	1822:B
+2+2+3+2−2	Parry 54
+2+2+3+2−2−3+3	1417c
+2+2+3+2−2−3−2	279:B
+2+2+3+2−3+2	966a
+2+2+3+2−3−3	240c, 782e
+2+2+3+2−5+4−2	693:B
+2+2+3−2	638b, 1128b
+2+2+3−2+2−2−2	1767a, 1865
+2+2+3−2+2−2−3	286d, 1214a:B
+2+2+3−2+2−3	1610:D
+2+2+3−2+2−3−2	136, 286e
+2+2+3−2+3−2−2	Parry 9
+2+2+3−2−2	247a, 762, 1241b, 1648
+2+2+3−2−2+2−3	1296:B, 1439a:C, 1649:C
+2+2+3−2−2+2−4	993f
+2+2+3−2−2+3−2	433c; Parry 15
+2+2+3−2−2−2	240a, 352, 591b, 1265:C, 1314b:B, 1486, 1574, 1626a:B, 1626b:B, 1626c:B, 1741:B

Thematic Index of the Tabulated Melodies

Interval Sequence	Melody No.
+2+2+3−2−2−2−2	903, 968a, 1300:C, 1308, 1348, 1391, 1399e, 1649:D
+2+2+3−2−2−3	632:B, 898a:B
+2+2+3−2−2−3+4	Parry 15:B
+2+2+3−2−3	82b:B, 132b, 240b, 531, 1483d:D, 1574:B, 1740b:B
+2+2+3−2−3+2+2	856
+2+2+3−2−3+3	180b
+2+2+3−2−3+4	924
+2+2+3−2−3−2	1593b
+2+2+3−2−3−2+3	201b
+2+2+3−2−4	1664b:B
+2+2+3−2−4+2−3	1269b:B
+2+2+3−2−4+3−2	1244c:B
+2+2+3−2−4+4+3	286b
+2+2+3−2−6	1662
+2+2+3−3	158f, 193a, 1246g, 1505c:B, 1157a:B; Parry 42:B
+2+2+3−3+2−3+3	420b
+2+2+3−3+2−3−2	481c
+2+2+3−3+3−2−2	433a
+2+2+3−3+3−2−3	414d, 365–366a
+2+2+3−3+3−4+2	1036a, 1036b
+2+2+3−3−2	43g:B, 1235, 1550d:B
+2+2+3−3−2+2	177d
+2+2+3−3−2+2+2	1338b
+2+2+3−3−2−2	1483a, 1483b
+2+2+3−3−2−3−2	1525
+2+2+3−3−3	898c:B
+2+2+3−3−3+2	1729:C
+2+2+3−3−3+2+4	1285c:B
+2+2+3−3−3+4−3	708d:B
+2+2+3−4	812a:C, 1531d:B, 1531e:B, 1571a:D
+2+2+3−4+2	871:B
+2+2+3−4+3+2−3	1216:B
+2+2+3−4−2	898b:B
+2+2+3−4−2+4−2	424c
+2+2+3−4−2+5	393

Thematic Index of the Tabulated Melodies

Interval Sequence	Melody No.
+2+2+3−4−2−2−2	1304d:B
+2+2+4−2	447b, 1460b:B, 1506f:B
+2+2+4−2+2−2−2	724c
+2+2+4−2−2−2	517b:B, 1297:B
+2+2+4−2−2−2+3	435c
+2+2+4−2−2−2−3	773c, 1210
+2+2+4−2−3	1246c
+2+2+4−2−3+2+3	501
+2+2+4−2−3+2−2	271g
+2+2+4−3−2	499, 859, 1224, 1410, 1602e, 1789b
+2+2+4−3−4	1195b:B
+2+2−2	130a, 130b, 262e, 479g:B, 854b, 886a, 959a, 1054d, 1298a, 1298b, 1491:B, 1523:B, 1553, 1571a:B, 1608c:B, 1658f; Parry 44a:B
+2+2−2+2	628, 1126, 1240, 1413, 1513b:B
+2+2−2+2+2	177a, 1607a:C, 1607b:C
+2+2−2+2+2+2−2	1447b:B
+2+2−2+2+2+2−3	353a
+2+2−2+2+2+3−2	1607d:B
+2+2−2+2+2−2−2	132e
+2+2−2+2+2−2−3	364b
+2+2−2+2+2−3	1250
+2+2−2+2+2−3+2	446c
+2+2−2+2+2−3−2	128b
+2+2−2+2−2	11, 68, 164a, 164b, 232e, 795:C, 1625a:B; Parry 51:B
+2+2−2+2−2+2	455c:B, 854a, 864
+2+2−2+2−2+2−3	1685:C
+2+2−2+2−2−2	116
+2+2−2+2−2−2+2	659:B
+2+2−2+2−2−2+3	616b, 1781
+2+2−2+2−2−2−2	123o, 953:C, 1310g:B, 1526b
+2+2−2+2−2−3	1506f:C
+2+2−2+2−2−3+2	Parry 33:B
+2+2−2+2−2−3−2	1327h
+2+2−2+2−3	134m, 1189b, 1272, 1279a:C, 1380, 1693c:B
+2+2−2+2−3+2	328, 1261

Thematic Index of the Tabulated Melodies

Interval Sequence	Melody No.
+2+2−2+2−3+3−4	973a:C
+2+2−2+3+2−3−2	171
+2+2−2+3+3−3−2	1676b
+2+2−2+3−2	953, 1476
+2+2−2+3−2−2+2	152a
+2+2−2+3−2−2−2	1014, 1506a, 1506b, 1506g, 1557b
+2+2−2+3−2−3	1515b, 1599b:C
+2+2−2+3−2−4+2	1399a
+2+2−2+3−3	1784:B
+2+2−2+3−3+3−4	1036c
+2+2−2+3−3−2	1261:B
+2+2−2+3−3−2−2	1506b:C
+2+2−2+4	1585d:B
+2+2−2+4+2−3	190
+2+2−2+4−2	1292a
+2+2−2+4−2+2−2	286g
+2+2−2+4−2+2−3	158a, 158c
+2+2−2+4−3+2−2	158b
+2+2−2+4−3−2	1301a
+2+2−2+4−4+4−2	1028–1029:B
+2+2−2−2	7a, 7b, 36a:B, 43d:B, 56d, 123dd:B, 123gg:B, 144–145, 211a, 492g:B, 496:B, 666b, 749c, 825:C, 862:B, 931, 946, 957a, 958c, 961c, 1021a:C, 1127, 1129:C, 1139a, 1155bis-a, 1160a, 1160b, 1253, 1259b, 1291:B, 1375:B, 1380:D, 1384a, 1385b, 1438, 1602c:D, 1626a, 1658a
+2+2−2−2+2	56e, 554:B, 873:B, 1192, 1310o, 1432a, 1563a:B, 1580:B
+2+2−2−2+2+2	1607c, 1738–1739
+2+2−2−2+2+2+2	507, 1347, 1607a, 1607b
+2+2−2−2+2+2−2	123gg, 131a, 304a, 422c, 448d, 509, 727a, 855b:B, 909, 1095b:B, 1225, 1269a, 1269b, 1416a, 1487, 1561d:B, 1599a, 1752
+2+2−2−2+2+2−3	18, 156, 1521c
+2+2−2−2+2+3−2	1049
+2+2−2−2+2−2	164a:B, 261a, 452d, 963:B, 1385a
+2+2−2−2+2−2+2	1310r
+2+2−2−2+2−2−2	1241a:B, 1260
+2+2−2−2+2−2−5	1397

Thematic Index of the Tabulated Melodies

Interval Sequence	Melody No.
+2+2−2−2+2−3+2	1602b:C
+2+2−2−2+2−3−3	1712:B
+2+2−2−2+2−4−2	1514a
+2+2−2−2+3	66, 373, 1521a
+2+2−2−2+3+2−2	918
+2+2−2−2+3+3−2	925d
+2+2−2−2+3−2	164c, 210a
+2+2−2−2+3−4+3	1514e
+2+2−2−2+4−2	243e
+2+2−2−2+5−2	1001c
+2+2−2−2−2	226, 717a:B, 822:C, 873, 1111, 1121, 1130:D, 1161:C, 1209b, 1380:C, 1610, 1613a:B, 1628:D, 1669:B; Parry 48:B, 49:B
+2+2−2−2−2+2	99b:B, 465, 1483a:C, 1483b:C, 1483c, 1778a
+2+2−2−2−2+2+2	886d, 1764a:C
+2+2−2−2−2+2−2	1728:B
+2+2−2−2−2+2−3	1214b:C, 1280e, 1285d, 1526a
+2+2−2−2−2+3	911:B
+2+2−2−2−2−2	95a:B, 1231:B, 1280d, 1583b:C 1583a:C, 1671, 1724:B, 1802; Parry 51:D
+2+2−2−2−2−2+2	1285j:C, 1836
+2+2−2−2−2−2+4	1513b:C
+2+2−2−2−2−2−2	111, 1506f, 1514d, 1698:B
+2+2−2−2−2−2−3	458
+2+2−2−2−2−3	1483d:C
+2+2−2−2−2−3+2	715–716
+2+2−2−2−3	742:C, 892b:C, 1105a:C, 1165a:B, 1597:D
+2+2−2−2−3+2	973b:C, 1623
+2+2−2−2−3+2+4	654bis-c:B
+2+2−2−2−3−2	202, 651, 1483e:C, 1514b
+2+2−2−2−3−3+5	1438:B
+2+2−2−2−4+2	915:C
+2+2−2−2−4+2−2	1514c
+2+2−2−2−4+8+2	1337a
+2+2−2−2−5	1130
+2+2−2−3	467b:B, 1094g:B, 1172–1173:B, 1865:C
+2+2−2−3+2	217, 1109:C, 1259a, 1656:D

Thematic Index of the Tabulated Melodies

Interval Sequence	Melody No.
+2+2−2−3+3−2	1483c:C
+2+2−2−3+5−2−2	1362:C
+2+2−2−5+2	1136:B
+2+2−2−5+4+2	253, 1191:B
+2+2−3	134c, 620, 660a, 764b:C, 949, 1000a:B, 1054b, 1054c, 1054e, 1054f, 1060, 1108, 1166a, 1202, 1298c, 1464, 1467a:B, 1570c, 1570h, 1571a, 1571b
+2+2−3+2	583:B, 679a:B, 753a, 792b, 954a:B, 954b:B, 1077d, 1486:B, 1494a:B, 1625b:B, 1734:C
+2+2−3+2+2	674, 792a, 864:B, 866:B, 1155bis-b, 1462, 1532g, 1740b
+2+2−3+2+2+2	232g, 961a:B, 961b:B
+2+2−3+2+2+2+2	914, 1635
+2+2−3+2+2+2+2−5	1458a, 1458b
+2+2−3+2+2+2+4−2	517b
+2+2−3+2+2−2	872a, 886b
+2+2−3+2+2−3	811, 1589d, 1820
+2+2−3+2+2−3+2	349c:B, 560, 743
+2+2−3+2+3−2	639–640
+2+2−3+2−2	243j, 1106:B, 1107d:D, 1319c:B, 1740a; Parry 8b, 16b:B
+2+2−3+2−2+2	165g, 933, 1563b
+2+2−3+2−2+2+2	1770:C
+2+2−3+2−2+2+4	737
+2+2−3+2−2+5	1271d:B
+2+2−3+2−2−2	651:B, 770c
+2+2−3+2−2−3	1313d:B
+2+2−3+2−3	868a:C, 1742b:B
+2+2−3+2−3+2	99a:B, 888b:B
+2+2−3+2−3+2−3	1588a
+2+2−3+2−3−2	1629a:D
+2+2−3+2−4	1102b:B
+2+2−3+3	875a, 1503–1504:B, 1602f
+2+2−3+3+2	177b
+2+2−3+3+2+2−3	800a, 1617
+2+2−3+3+2−2	200d, 1230b
+2+2−3+3+2−4	1298c:B
+2+2−3+3+3+2−2	Parry 47

Thematic Index of the Tabulated Melodies

Interval Sequence	Melody No.
+2+2−3+3+3+2−3	496a
+2+2−3+3+3−2−2	286a
+2+2−3+3+3−3	232b
+2+2−3+3+4−2	1198–1199
+2+2−3+3−2+3−2	200b, 200c, 200g
+2+2−3+3−2−2	516a, 676, 1278:B
+2+2−3+3−2−2−2	977:B, 1629b:C
+2+2−3+3−2−3	1609
+2+2−3+3−3	539
+2+2−3+3−3+2+2	1716
+2+2−3+3−3+5	1528
+2+2−3+4+2−3+3	1545c
+2+2−3+4+3−4−3	635
+2+2−3+4+3−5+2	637
+2+2−3+4−2+3−2	1392a
+2+2−3+4−2−2	533d, 1209b:B
+2+2−3+4−2−2−2	32, 128a, 553b
+2+2−3+4−2−3	1179b, 1613a
+2+2−3+4−3	741:B
+2+2−3+4−3+2+2	265h
+2+2−3+4−3−2	117a
+2+2−3+4−4+2	86
+2+2−3+5	1531c:B
+2+2−3+5−2	1000h
+2+2−3+5−2+2−3	158d
+2+2−3+5−2+2−4	1301b
+2+2−3+5−2−2−2	Parry 7
+2+2−3+5−2−3	1370b:B, 1618c
+2+2−3+5−3+2	708c
+2+2−3+5−4+4−3	1895
+2+2−3+6−2−2−3	176
+2+2−3−2	262f, 747:C, 770a:B, 874:C, 881a:C, 913:B, 1139b:B, 1148b:C, 1209a:B, 1379:B, 1506f:D, 1516b:B, 1519b:B, 1520:B, 1586e:D, 1589e:B, 1595:B, 1640d:B, 1825:C
+2+2−3−2+2	1550b:B, 1748–1749:B
+2+2−3−2+2+2−2	1319b:B

Thematic Index of the Tabulated Melodies

Interval Sequence	Melody No.
+2+2−3−2+2+2−3	635:B, 1252:B, 1626a:C, 1626b:C
+2+2−3−2+2+2−5	1626c:C
+2+2−3−2+2−2+2	1729
+2+2−3−2+2−2−2	1039h:B, 1338c:B
+2+2−3−2+2−2−3	1371b:C
+2+2−3−2+3−5	1631c
+2+2−3−2+4	1579a:B
+2+2−3−2−2	1744b:B
+2+2−3−2−2+2	1624:B
+2+2−3−2−2+3−2	1019:B
+2+2−3−2−2+4	1513a:C
+2+2−3−2−2−2	1527:C
+2+2−3−2−2−2−2	1016b:B, 1240:B
+2+2−3−2−3	526a:B, 1188b:B
+2+2−3−2−3+3−2	872a:C
+2+2−3−2−3+5−2	1338b:B
+2+2−3−2−4+4	628:B
+2+2−3−2−4+5−2	725:B
+2+2−3−3	479i:B, 696b:C, 1267:B, 1690c:B
+2+2−3−3+2	126a:B
+2+2−3−3+3+2+2	1690b:B
+2+2−3−3+3−3	696a:C
+2+2−3−3+6−2	1602k
+2+2−3−3−2	685:B
+2+2−3−4−2+2	866:C
+2+2−4+2+2+2−2	Parry 33
+2+2−4+2+2+2−4	774
+2+2−4+2+3−4+2	14
+2+2−4+2−2−2	1620b:B
+2+2−4+2−2−3	1269a:C
+2+2−4+2−3	774:B
+2+2−4+3	757:B
+2+2−4+3−3	1102c:C
+2+2−4+4	1084:B
+2+2−4−2	904c:B, 914:B
+2+2−4−2−4	1616:C

Thematic Index of the Tabulated Melodies

Interval Sequence	Melody No.
+2+2−4−3	1568b:C
+2+2−5+3−3	675:B, 681:B
+2+2−6+5−2−2−3	1269b:C
+2+3	638a, 1020a, 1079c
+2+3+2+2	1596:B
+2+3+2+2+2−2−2	301b
+2+3+2+2−2	1622:B
+2+3+2+2−2−2−2	1672a:B
+2+3+2+2−2−2−3	1378:C
+2+3+2+2−3	1102c:B
+2+3+2+2−3−2	974
+2+3+2+2−3−3	1619g, 1678
+2+3+2+3−2−3−2	1313a:C
+2+3+2+3−4	665a:B
+2+3+2−2	1383
+2+3+2−2−2+2	1619f
+2+3+2−2−2−2	196a, 412
+2+3+2−2−2−2+2	Parry 44b
+2+3+2−2−2−3+5	727a:B
+2+3+2−2−3	119d, 265g:B, 803a
+2+3+2−2−3+2−2	1824
+2+3+2−2−3+2−3	332
+2+3+2−2−3+3	1629b:B
+2+3+2−2−3+3−4	1601a
+2+3+2−2−3+4−2	983n
+2+3+2−2−3−3+4	968:B
+2+3+2−2−4	1375
+2+3+2−2−4+2+4	983p
+2+3+2−2−4+3−2	1314b
+2+3+2−3	193b
+2+3+2−3+2	1619d
+2+3+2−3+2−2−2	607b
+2+3+2−3+3−2−3	1524:C
+2+3+2−3−2	390d:B, 775a, 1408
+2+3+2−3−2+4−3	992:C
+2+3+2−3−2−2+2	1685

Thematic Index of the Tabulated Melodies

Interval Sequence	Melody No.
+2+3+2−3−3+2	775b
+2+3+2−5+2+3−3	1727:C
+2+3+3	1660
+2+3+3−2−2	Parry 35:C
+2+3+3−2−2−2−2	655f
+2+3+3−3−4−2+5	572
+2+3−2	592d
+2+3−2+2+2	1555a, 1555d
+2+3−2+2+2−2	1246b:B
+2+3−2+2−2	522
+2+3−2+2−2+2	839
+2+3−2+2−2−2+2	374
+2+3−2+2−2−2−2	1815b
+2+3−2+2−3	131b, 1274:C
+2+3−2+2−3+4	232i
+2+3−2+2−3−2+2	981, 983ff, 1722a:B
+2+3−2+3−2	1345:B
+2+3−2+3−2−2	183a
+2+3−2+3−2−2−3	1671:B
+2+3−2+3−2−3−2	1532a, 1532b
+2+3−2+3−2−4+4	983x:B
+2+3−2+4−2−2−2	1672b:B
+2+3−2+4−3−2	697b
+2+3−2+4−4+3	113
+2+3−2−2	211d, 749c:C, 888a:B
+2+3−2−2+2+3−3	1319a
+2+3−2−2+2−2−2	452a
+2+3−2−2+2−2−3	452b
+2+3−2−2+2−3+2	977
+2+3−2−2+3−3	899:B
+2+3−2−2+4	1303b:B, 1502a
+2+3−2−2−2	638b:C, 1102a:B, 1532d, 1569b, 1593c, 1610:C, 1797
+2+3−2−2−2+2	607a
+2+3−2−2−2+3−3	545b
+2+3−2−2−2−2+2	736

Thematic Index of the Tabulated Melodies

Interval Sequence	Melody No.
+2+3−2−2−2−2−2	655f:B
+2+3−2−2−2−3−2	1310g
+2+3−2−2−2−4	1229a:B
+2+3−2−3	1010a, 1666, 1801
+2+3−2−3+2	43f:B
+2+3−2−3+2+2−2	232d
+2+3−2−3+2+2−3	610e:B
+2+3−2−3+2+3	870
+2+3−2−3+2+3−2	533c, 1023c, 1811, 1817
+2+3−2−3+2+3−4	526a
+2+3−2−3+4−2−3	784a
+2+3−2−3+8−3	1180:B
+2+3−2−3−2−2+5	1229b:B
+2+3−2−4+2	1118:D
+2+3—3	958e, 1135b, 1388c, 1388d
+2+3—3+2+2−3+2	348
+2+3—3+2+4−2	1672c:B
+2+3—3+2−2	492d:B
+2+3—3+2−2+4	1232:B
+2+3—3+2−2−2	638a:B, 779b
+2+3—3+2−2−2+2	213, 349a
+2+3—3+2−2−3+2	452c
+2+3—3+2−3	522:B
+2+3—3+2−4	665a, 810b
+2+3−3+3−2+2	1619e
+2+3−3+3−3	702; Parry 8a
+2+3−3+3−3+2−3	547b
+2+3−3+3−3+3−3	1830
+2+3−3+3−3−2	880b, 1819:C
+2+3−3−2	130d, 903:C, 999b, 1532c, 1622, 1767b:B
+2+3−3−2+2+3	627
+2+3−3−2+2+3−3	648a
+2+3−3−2+2−2+2	858:B, 1877
+2+3−3−2+2−2−2	880b:B, 1895:C
+2+3−3−2+2−2−3	1333
+2+3−3−2+3+2−3	578

Thematic Index of the Tabulated Melodies

Interval Sequence	Melody No.
+2+3−3−2+4−3−2	1443:B
+2+3−3−2+5+2+3	431
+2+3−3−2−2	804b
+2+3−3−2−2−2+2	1016b:C
+2+3−3−2−2−4	1748–1749
+2+3−3−2−3−2+5	738a:C
+2+3−3−3	643
+2+3−3−4+4	1751:C
+2+3−4	1112, 1521c:B
+2+3−4+2	1695:C
+2+3−4+2+2+2	525
+2+3−4+2+3	1158b
+2+3−4+2+3−3−2	574
+2+3−4+2+3−4+4	278
+2+3−4+2−2−2−2	1726
+2+3−4+4−2−3+2	570
+2+3−4+4−3−2+2	212b, 1722b:B
+2+3−4−2+2+2+3	1319a:B
+2+3−4−2−2−2	1616:B
+2+3−4−3+2−3+5	658
+2+3−4−3+2−3−2	718
+2+3−5+2−2−2−2	872b:B
+2+4	1239, 1570e:B
+2+4+2−2−2+2−3	846–847
+2+4+2−2−4+4−2	441
+2+4+2−3−3−2+2	1829
+2+4+3−2−3+2+3	726, 1334
+2+4+3−3	1292b
+2+4+3−3−2	244
+2+4−2	679c, 1077c, 1106
+2+4−2+2	966b
+2+4−2+2+2−2−2	183d, 1423
+2+4−2+2−2−3	286c, 832
+2+4−2+2−2−3+3	Parry 11
+2+4−2+2−2−3+4	392b, 392c, 983m
+2+4−2+2−4	179:B

Thematic Index of the Tabulated Melodies

Interval Sequence	Melody No.
+2+4−2+3−2−2	124a
+2+4−2+3−2−3−3	983v
+2+4−2+3−2−4+4	983x
+2+4−2−2+2−2+2	983kk
+2+4−2−2+2−2−2	1024c, 1722d
+2+4−2−2+2−3+2	1039d
+2+4−2−2−2	1144a:B, 1164:B
+2+4−2−2−2+2	123e, 1342
+2+4−2−2−2+2−2	690b
+2+4−2−2−2−2	898d:B, 898e:B, 1764d:B
+2+4−2−2−3	1208, 1734:B
+2+4−2−2−3+2	517a, 983gg
+2+4−2−3	776d, 804a, 881b, 885
+2+4−2−3+2+3	1556b
+2+4−2−3+2+3−2	872b
+2+4−2−3+3	177c
+2+4−2−3+3+2−3	1879
+2+4−2−3+3−3	983ff:B
+2+4−2−3+3−3+2	1039g
+2+4−2−3+3−3+4	1039a, 1039c, 1039e, 1039f
+2+4−2−3+3−3−2	563a
+2+4−2−3+3−4+2	567b
+2+4−2−3+4	776e, 1502c; Parry 41
+2+4−2−3+4−2−2	232a
+2+4−2−3+5−2−2	1882
+2+4−2−3−2	1789a
+2+4−2−3−2+2+3	1885
+2+4−3+2−2−2	287
+2+4−3+3−3−2	842
+2+4−3−2	1594, 1603:C
+2+4−4+5−2−2−2	1655d
+2+4−4−3−3	1625b
+2+4−5+4−2+2−4	563b
+2+5−2	677, 1290
+2+5−2+2+2−3−2	654bis-c
+2+5−2−2	1244, 1601a:B

Thematic Index of the Tabulated Melodies

Interval Sequence	Melody No.
+2+5−2−2−3+2−3	1721
+2−2	16, 48b, 56f, 123h, 661a:B, 681, 739a, 750a, 778c:B, 920–921, 954c, 994, 1005b:B, 1049:B, 1054a, 1057c:C, 1058d:C, 1063, 1087a:B, 1105b, 1110, 1188b:C, 1483f, 1604:B, 1631:C, 1658d, 1659f:B, 1744a:C, 1755, 1782:B
+2−2+2	123z:C, 209, 281c, 1206a:B, 1248:C, 1493d, 1597; Parry 16b
+2−2+2+2	93
+2−2+2+2+2−2+2	1356
+2−2+2+2+3+2−3	1340
+2−2+2+2+3−2	983r, 1709
+2−2+2+2−2	261d, 262c, 262d
+2−2+2+2−2+2−2	1310e
+2−2+2+2−2+3−2	446d
+2−2+2+2−2−2+2	129a, 448h, 1053
+2−2+2+2−2−2−2	13
+2−2+2+2−2−3+2	1310e:B, 1878
+2−2+2+2−2−3+3	1884
+2−2+2+2−3+2	730–731
+2−2+2+2−3+2−2	262a
+2−2+2+3	214d, 232f
+2−2+2+3+2−2	638c
+2−2+2+3+2−3	158e
+2−2+2+3−2	323c, 1048
+2−2+2+3−2+2−2	1271e:B
+2−2+2+3−2−2	397bis
+2−2+2+3−3	1042
+2−2+2+3−4	1602a:B
+2−2+2+4−2	243d
+2−2+2+4−2−2−3	550b
+2−2+2−2	80a, 115b:B, 123x, 461, 474, 649:B, 739a:B, 814, 1043, 1292c, 1591c, 1629b, 1840
+2−2+2−2+2	129b, 536, 544f
+2−2+2−2+2+2	1563d
+2−2+2−2+2+2+2	1313f
+2−2+2−2+2−2	302b, 537, 554
+2−2+2−2+2−2+2	1021b

Thematic Index of the Tabulated Melodies

Interval Sequence	Melody No.
+2−2+2−2+2−2−2	1693a:C, 1693b:C; Parry 34:B
+2−2+2−2+2−3	1310h:B
+2−2+2−2+2−3+2	310a
+2−2+2−2+3+3+2	455d
+2−2+2−2+3−2	Parry 29
+2−2+2−2+3−2−2	17a, 276a, 400b
+2−2+2−2+4−4+2	553d
+2−2+2−2+4−4+4	439c
+2−2+2−2−2	246b, 490, 1310m:B
+2−2+2−2−2+2	282, 1432b
+2−2+2−2−2+2+2	1859
+2−2+2−2−2+2−3	1310h
+2−2+2−2−2−2	806, 835b, 1310b:B, 1548; Parry 27a:B
+2−2+2−2−2−2+2	1447d, 1691a
+2−2+2−2−2−2−2	851
+2−2+2−2−2−3+2	123b:B
+2−2+2−2−3	384c:B
+2−2+2−2−3+2+2	961c:C
+2−2+2−2−3+2−2	1321
+2−2+2−2−3+3	377c
+2−2+2−2−3−3+5	851:B
+2−2+2−3+2+2−4	654
+2−2+2−3+2−2−2	310c
+2−2+2−3−2	219a
+2−2+2−3−2+2	1246i:B
+2−2+2−4	1365:B, 1514e:B
+2−2+2−4+3	73c
+2−2+3	1585b:B, 1607c:C
+2−2+3+2+2−3+3	860b
+2−2+3+2−2	243m, 590b
+2−2+3+2−2−3	1212a, 1212c
+2−2+3+2−3−2	19
+2−2+3+2−4+3+2	445d, 445f
+2−2+3+3	1092
+2−2+3+3−2	925a
+2−2+3+3−2+2	860a

Thematic Index of the Tabulated Melodies

Interval Sequence	Melody No.
+2−2+3+3−2−2−2	286f
+2−2+3+3−2−3	894
+2−2+3+3−3+2−3	323b
+2−2+3+3−4+2−2	1036e
+2−2+3−2	216d
+2−2+3−2+2	100
+2−2+3−2+4−3+2	1826
+2−2+3−2−2	132h, 203:B
+2−2+3−2−2+2−2	448k
+2−2+3−2−2−3	223:B
+2−2+3−2−3	770c:B
+2−2+3−2−3−2	874:B
+2−2+3−3	479f, 1101, 1789b:B
+2−2+3−3+2−2+3	1214b
+2−2+3−3+3	445h
+2−2+3−3−2	1283d:B
+2−2+3−3−2+3+3	1283d:C
+2−2+3−3−2+4	1358b
+2−2+4	786:B, 1179a
+2−2+4+2−2−3	1618a
+2−2+4+3−2	590a
+2−2+4−2	94a, 94b, 214b
+2−2+4−2+2−2+2	991:B
+2−2+4−2+2−3−2	383a, 1848
+2−2+4−2−2+2	157b
+2−2+4−2−2+2−3	553a
+2−2+4−2−2−2+2	1034–1035, 1704:B
+2−2+4−2−2−2+3	553c
+2−2+4−2−2−2−2	906b, 1311
+2−2+4−2−3	445g, 1629a
+2−2+4−2−3+2	212a
+2−2+4−2−3+3+2	430a
+2−2+4−2−3+5−3	1016a
+2−2+4−3+2	94c, 232c
+2−2+4−3+2+2−2	265g
+2−2+4−3+3−3−2	265f

Thematic Index of the Tabulated Melodies

Interval Sequence	Melody No.
+2−2+4−3+4−2−2	265e
+2−2+4−3−2	1283d, 1512a
+2−2+4−3−2−3	1443
+2−2+4−4+2−2	1325a, 1827:C
+2−2+4−4+2−2−2	321e:B
+2−2+4−4+4−3−2	344c
+2−2+5+2−3−2−2	1762
+2−2+5+3−4	679d
+2−2+5−2	232h, 679a, 679b, 690c, 1555c, 1558b
+2−2+5−2+2−2−4	1320:B
+2−2+5−2−2−2	287:B
+2−2+5−2−3−2	1024b
+2−2+5−4+2+2−2	365–366b
+2−2+6+2−2−3	1620b
+2−2+6−2−3+4−2	445b
+2−2+8−3	1294
−2−2−2	81, 88, 146a:B, 146b:B, 174b:B, 185a, 502:B, 744:C, 755k:B, 778b:B, 781a:B, 781b:B, 801:B, 854b:C, 855a:C, 889:C, 890:C, 892a:B, 892b:B, 893:C, 925c:B, 1002a, 1030b, 1120, 1148a:C, 1148b:B, 1219, 1226:B, 1365:C, 1378:D, 1398a:B, 1398b:B, 1403a:C, 1479b:B, 1480:B, 1493d:B, 1496:B, 1512b:B, 1530b:B, 1586a:D, 1586b:D, 1589b, 1589c:D, 1638:C, 1654:B, 1658c:B, 1658f:B, 1670:C, 1719a:C, 1744a:D, 1779:C, 1805:C, 1866:B
+2−2−2+2	6, 359b, 624:B, 672b:B, 721a, 755g:C, 998:B, 1160a:B, 1160b:B, 1518:B, 1585f
+2−2−2+2+2+2−3	1309:B
+2−2−2+2+2−2+2	1813–1814:B; Parry 37
+2−2−2+2+2−2−2	305g, 532a, 532b, 610c:B, 755e, 846–847:B, 860c:B, 891c, 1432a:B, 1432b:B, 1602c; Parry 31b:B
+2−2−2+2+2−3	132g:B, 1764b:B
+2−2−2+2+2−3+2	305h, 305i, 346c
+2−2−2+2+2−3+4	432c
+2−2−2+2+3	1484b:B
+2−2−2+2+3+2−2	657
+2−2−2+2+3−3+2	1026d:B
+2−2−2+2+4−3	1285j:B

Thematic Index of the Tabulated Melodies

Interval Sequence	Melody No.
+2−2−2+2−2	115a, 132c:B, 252a, 1236:B, 1585a, 1668; Parry 3:B
+2−2−2+2−2+2	79b, 79c
+2−2−2+2−2+2+2	281a
+2−2−2+2−2+2−2	400c, 709b:B, 719
+2−2−2+2−2+3−2	Parry 51:C
+2−2−2+2−2−2	1211:B, 1280c, 1310c:B
+2−2−2+2−2−2+2	440a:B, 942b, 1310l, 1356:B
+2−2−2+2−2−2−2	183d:B, 270d:B, 1585d
+2−2−2+2−2−2−3	1217:B
+2−2−2+2−2−2−4	1207, 1772–1773:C
+2−2−2+2−2−3	126b, 1795b; Parry 18:B
+2−2−2+2−2−3+2	119d:B, 1363:B
+2−2−2+2−3	485b:B, 713b, 1723, 1830:D
+2−2−2+2−3+2	310c:B, 454a, 1447c
+2−2−2+2−3+3−2	1310c:C
+2−2−2+2−3+3−3	853c:B
+2−2−2+2−3+3−4	313:B
+2−2−2+2−3−2	200b:B, 270c:B, 317b, 864:C, 1310e
+2−2−2+2−3−2+2	566c, 1330a:B
+2−2−2+2−3−2−2	1528:C
+2−2−2+2−3−3	853a:B, 908:B, 1389:B, 1435a
+2−2−2+2−3−3+3	280f:B
+2−2−2+2−3−3−2	1327f
+2−2−2+2−3−4+4	1276
+2−2−2+2−4	1011:B
+2−2−2+2−4−2	1742a:C
+2−2−2+2−5+2+2	1717:B
+2−2−2+3	1795a:B, 1795b:B, 1795c:B
+2−2−2+3+2−2−2	993e
+2−2−2+3+3−2−3	940
+2−2−2+3−2+2−3	990:B
+2−2−2+3−2−2	421c, 926:B, 1045, 1563e:B
+2−2−2+3−2−2−2	1327a, 1551
+2−2−2+3−3	132e:B
+2−2−2+3−3+3−2	1817:B

Thematic Index of the Tabulated Melodies

Interval Sequence	Melody No.
+2−2−2+4	788b:B
+2−2−2+4−2+2−2	305b
+2−2−2+4−2−2+3	12
+2−2−2+4−2−2−2	1568b:D
+2−2−2+4−4+2+2	305a
+2−2−2+4−4−2−2	1802:B
+2−2−2+4−5	1243f
+2−2−2+5	1592a:B
+2−2−2+5−3−2−2	987
+2−2−2−2	39g:B, 118, 123a:B, 663, 697b:B, 762:C, 786:C, 817:C, 887:B, 1022a:C, 1036e:B, 1093:C, 1156b, 1171, 1186, 1231:C, 1248:B, 1280f, 1285c, 1369:B, 1370b:C, 1430, 1515d:C, 1516b:D, 1521c:C, 1540c:D, 1540f:D, 1540i:D, 1540k:C, 1545b:B, 1569c:B, 1640d, 1677:C
+2−2−2−2+2	214b:B, 229c, 679b:B, 679c:B, 820:B, 1226:C, 1466, 1582b:B, 1727:B, 1799:B
+2−2−2−2+2+2−2	418, 1332c, 1866
+2−2−2−2+2+3	1481b:C
+2−2−2−2+2−2	303b
+2−2−2−2+2−2−3	1358a, 1804a:C, 1804b:C
+2−2−2−2+2−3	1381b:B, 1381c:B
+2−2−2−2+2−3+3	1657a:B
+2−2−2−2+2−4+2	1623:B
+2−2−2−2+3	1271d, 1105a:B
+2−2−2−2+3+2−2	833e:B, 840, 860a:B, 867, 1697:B; Parry 32:B
+2−2−2−2+3+3	1657a:C, 1657b:C
+2−2−2−2+3−2−2	834a:B
+2−2−2−2+3−3	1435b
+2−2−2−2+3−4+2	1021c
+2−2−2−2+3−5+2	1523:C
+2−2−2−2+4	1724:D
+2−2−2−2+4−2+2	327c
+2−2−2−2+4−2−2	602:B
+2−2−2−2+8	1807:C
+2−2−2−2−2	159d:B, 225, 401a:B, 492f, 956:B, 993c, 1105b:B, 1163g:B, 1165c:B, 1287:B, 1292a:B, 1327e:B, 1415, 1505c:C, 1771:C, 1795a, 1795c

Thematic Index of the Tabulated Melodies

Interval Sequence	Melody No.
+2−2−2−2−2+2	906b:B
+2−2−2−2−2+2+2	1322:B, 1444b:B, 1444c:B, 1454, 1540c:C, 1540f:C, 1568b
+2−2−2−2−2+2+3	1347:C
+2−2−2−2−2+2−2	853f:B
+2−2−2−2−2+3	886b:B, 886d:B
+2−2−2−2−2+3−2	1863b
+2−2−2−2−2+4	1020a:B
+2−2−2−2−2+4+2	197b, 1340:B, 1714
+2−2−2−2−2−2	767, 787b, 878a, 1182a:C, 1250:B, 1513e, 1513f, 1651a:C, 1661:B, 1802:C
+2−2−2−2−2−2+2	360a, 1791:C
+2−2−2−2−2−2+4	860a:C, 860b:C
+2−2−2−2−2−2+5	835a:B
+2−2−2−2−2−3	1876
+2−2−2−2−2−3+2	1446b:B
+2−2−2−2−3	1494a:C, 1628:C; Parry 42:C
+2−2−2−2−3+3+2	724a:B
+2−2−2−2−3+3−2	280e:B
+2−2−2−2−4+4+2	1718:B
+2−2−2−3	39d, 39e, 39f, 39g, 958g:B, 1064, 1075, 1089b, 1094h, 1377:B, 1476:B, 1658a:C, 1658d:B, 1658e:B, 1659a:B, 1659b:B, 1697, 1761:B, 1820:B
+2−2−2−3+2	1611a:B; Parry 54:B
+2−2−2−3+2+2+2	1442:B
+2−2−2−3+2+2−3	426a:B
+2−2−2−3+2−2	711a:B
+2−2−2−3+2−3	126a
+2−2−2−3+2−3−2	1312:C
+2−2−2−3+3	379b, 985
+2−2−2−3+3+2−3	599, 1887
+2−2−2−3+3+3−2	1434
+2−2−2−3+3−2+2	1566
+2−2−2−3+3−2−2	1357a:B
+2−2−2−3+3−2−3	1638:B
+2−2−2−3+3−3+4	Parry 41:C
+2−2−2−3+3−3−2	207

Thematic Index of the Tabulated Melodies

Interval Sequence	Melody No.
+2−2−2−3+4+2−2	1421:B
+2−2−2−3+4−2−2	1846
+2−2−2−3+5−2−2	413:B
+2−2−2−3−2	1386, 1762:B
+2−2−2−3−2+3−2	280g:B
+2−2−2−4+2	1271c, 1405:D
+2−2−2−4+2+2−2	125a:B
+2−2−2−4+2+4−2	301b:B
+2−2−2−4+3−2	563c:B
+2−2−2−4+3−3+2	511a:B
+2−2−2−4+4−2−3	271a:B
+2−2−2−4+5+2−2	274
+2−2−3	39f:B, 53:B, 471, 732:B, 755g, 803b:B, 905c:B, 974:B, 992:B, 1058a, 1058b, 1073a:C, 1095a, 1095c, 1142b, 1165b, 1268:D, 1367b:B, 1471:D, 1540a:D, 1540h:D, 1540j:D, 1640a, 1640b, 1704:C, 1744a, 1779:B; Parry 20:B
+2−2−3+2	229b, 755a:B, 760a, 905d:B, 919:B, 1212c:B, 1515f:D, 1532i, 1656:C
+2−2−3+2+2	1426
+2−2−3+2+2+2−4	609b:B
+2−2−3+2+2−2−2	299, 850, 990
+2−2−3+2+2−2−3	357c, 1579a
+2−2−3+2+2−3	707
+2−2−3+2+3	1285g:B
+2−2−3+2+3−3	1472:C
+2−2−3+2+3−3−3	513a
+2−2−3+2−2	1204:D, 1503–1504, 1571b:D
+2−2−3+2−2+2	1212b:B
+2−2−3+2−2+2+2	603a:B
+2−2−3+2−2+2−2	1037–1038:B
+2−2−3+2−2+3	245
+2−2−3+2−2+4−2	892a
+2−2−3+2−2−2	1184:D, 1660:B
+2−2−3+2−2−2−2	735:B, 1317:C
+2−2−3+2−3	1720b:C
+2−2−3+2−3+2	81:B
+2−2−3+2−3+4+2	609a:B

Thematic Index of the Tabulated Melodies

Interval Sequence	Melody No.
+2−2−3+2−3+4−3	1733c
+2−2−3+2−3−2	772, 1686:B
+2−2−3+2−3−2+3	888b
+2−2−3+2−3−3−3	1366
+2−2−3+2−5+2+2	1657b:B
+2−2−3+3	755f:B, 1167b:B
+2−2−3+3+2+2−3	577a
+2−2−3+3+2−2	711b, 711d
+2−2−3+3+2−2−2	Parry 31a:B, 32
+2−2−3+3+2−2−3	473b, 616b, 728–729, 1214a, 1694:C, 1808
+2−2−3+3+2−3	1212a:B
+2−2−3+3+2−3+3	549b
+2−2−3+3+3	1169
+2−2−3+3−2	1425:B, 1532e, 1532f, 1602e:B
+2−2−3+3−2−2	1284c:B, 1302:B, 1800a
+2−2−3+3−2−2+2	310b, 549a, 1033a:B
+2−2−3+3−2−3+2	1344
+2−2−3+3−3	304c, 416
+2−2−3+3−3+2−2	981:B
+2−2−3+3−3−3	703:B
+2−2−3+3−4+2	190:B
+2−2−3+3−4+3−2	1681
+2−2−3+4+2+2−2	656d
+2−2−3+4+2+2−3	1747, 1779
+2−2−3+4+2−2−3	732
+2−2−3+4−2+2−2	377b
+2−2−3+4−2−2	174d
+2−2−3+4−2−2+2	1363
+2−2−3+4−2−2−2	424c
+2−2−3+4−2−2−3	294:B
+2−2−3+4−2−3+4	282b:B
+2−2−3+5−2	1285d:B
+2−2−3+5−2−2−2	1277b:B
+2−2−3−2	3, 930a
+2−2−3−2+2+2	1540a:C, 1540e:B
+2−2−3−2+2+2+2	196f:B, 1352a

Thematic Index of the Tabulated Melodies

Interval Sequence	Melody No.
+2−2−3−2+3−2+3	850:B
+2−2−3−2+4	1540h:C, 1540i:C
+2−2−3−2+4+2+4	197a
+2−2−3−2−3+2+4	397bis:B
+2−2−3−3	1606a
+2−2−3−3+2	687
+2−2−3−3+2+2	1178, 1265
+2−2−3−3+2+2−3	636:B
+2−2−3−3+3−2−2	1662:B
+2−2−3−3+4−2−2	954b:C
+2−2−3−3−4+2+3	984e
+2−2−3−4+3−2−3	696b:B
+2−2−4	954b, 1485, 1795c:C
+2−2−4+2	1163d:B
+2−2−4+2+2−4	1375:C
+2−2−4+2+4	1579b:B
+2−2−4+3	1620a:B
+2−2−4+3+2−2−2	270a, 317a, 357b:B, 382
+2−2−4+3+2−4−2	270b
+2−2−4+3+3−5	689b:B
+2−2−4+3−2	1568a:D, 1602e:D
+2−2−4+4+2+2	104
+2−2−4+4+2−2+5	796a
+2−2−4+6+3	1872
+2−2−4+6−2−3+3	1663:B
+2−2−4−2+5	1054f:B
+2−2−5+2+3	1618b:B
+2−2−5+5−2−2	1310b
+2−2−5−3+3	696a:B
+2−3	132a:B, 402c:B, 958d, 1045:C, 1055:B, 1082:B, 1162:B, 1371a:B, 1371b:B, 1377, 1567a, 1586c:D, 1589b:C, 1664a:B, 1863a:C; Parry 39b:B
+2−3+2	585:B, 610c:B, 1077d:B, 1266b, 1298a:C, 1384a:B, 1384b:B, 1432a:C, 1510:D, 1513d:B, 1524:B, 1687:C, 1703, 1753b:D, 1803:B
+2−3+2+2−3	89c, 141–142, 303d, 752a, 778b, 833f:B, 833h, 1298b:B, 1403c:B, 1602f:B, 1750b:C, 1750c:C
+2−3+2+2−3+2+2	261e

Thematic Index of the Tabulated Melodies

Interval Sequence	Melody No.
+2−3+2+2−3+2−3	391a
+2−3+2+2−3+3−2	597b:B
+2−3+2+2−3+5−3	438:B
+2−3+2+2−4	1046
+2−3+2+2−4−2	675:C
+2−3+2+3−2	1004:B
+2−3+2+3−2+2	860c
+2−3+2+3−2+3−2	1025b:B
+2−3+2+3−3+2−3	989f
+2−3+2+3−3+3−3	989g
+2−3+2+4−4−2	681:C
+2−3+2−2	89b, 143b, 151a:B, 168c, 402b:B, 552:B
+2−3+2−2+2	110
+2−3+2−2+2+2−2	839:B
+2−3+2−2+2−2	173a
+2−3+2−2+2−3	974:C, 1435a:B
+2−3+2−2+3	1266b:B
+2−3+2−2+3−3+2	540
+2−3+2−2−2	770a, 1505d:C
+2−3+2−2−2+2−2	266b
+2−3+2−2−2+3+2	1350:B
+2−3+2−2−2+3−3	1435b:B
+2−3+2−2−2−2	1242
+2−3+2−2−3	1327e
+2−3+2−3	74:B, 147, 1110:B, 1283b:B, 1460b:C, 1505b:C, 1540c, 1806:C
+2−3+2−3+2	1022a:B, 1565
+2−3+2−3+2+4−2	1770
+2−3+2−3+2−2−2	1638
+2−3+2−3+2−3+2	843
+2−3+2−3+2−3−2	251:B
+2−3+2−3+3	1005a:B
+2−3+2−3+3−2−4	201a:B, 201b:B
+2−3+2−3+3−3−2	853d:B, 853e:B
+2−3+2−3+3−4	425:B, 724c
+2−3+2−3−2	125c, 678:B, 906a, 1303a:B

Thematic Index of the Tabulated Melodies

Interval Sequence	Melody No.
+2−3+2−3−2+2	391c
+2−3+2−3−2+2+2	1005a
+2−3+2−3−2+3	1585b
+2−3+2−3−2−2	628:C
+2−3+2−3−2−2+5	1772–1773:B
+2−3+2−3−3+2+3	853b:B
+2−3+2−3−5+6	1440a:B
+2−3+2−4	1896
+2−3+3	1499b:B
+2−3+3+2−3+2−2	701a:B
+2−3+3+4−5	944
+2−3+3−2+3−3−2	407b
+2−3+3−2−2+2−4	983hh:B
+2−3+3−2−2−2	1013bis
+2−3+3−2−2−2−2	1619b:C
+2−3+3−2−3	41
+2−3+3−3	168b, 1690a:C
+2−3+3−3+2	265h:B
+2−3+3−3−2−3+2	983aa:B
+2−3+3−3−3+5+2	1427:B
+2−3+4	1655d:B
+2−3+4−2	1285f:B
+2−3+4−2−2−3	1269a:B
+2−3+4−3	824:B, 1006b:C
+2−3+4−3−2	117b
+2−3+4−4+2	561:B
+2−3+5−2	1283b:C
+2−3−2	39c:B, 75a, 357c:B, 473b:B, 925e:B, 938a:B, 1089a, 1163e:C, 1384a:C, 1415:B, 1495:B, 1513a:D, 1513b:D, 1513f:B, 1526b:D, 1580:C, 1632:B, 1703:C, 1870:B, 1875:B
+2−3−2+2	510a, 936, 1426:B, 1614:B, 1626a:D
+2−3−2+2+2	1753a:D
+2−3−2+2+2+2+2	1033g
+2−3−2+2+2−5+3	345:B
+2−3−2+2+4−2	1285i:B
+2−3−2+2−2−2−2	273

Thematic Index of the Tabulated Melodies

Interval Sequence	Melody No.
+2−3−2+3+2−3−2	848c, 1040–1041, 1324b:B, 1499a
+2−3−2+3+2−3−3	391b
+2−3−2+3+3−2	98a
+2−3−2+3−2+2+3	939
+2−3−2+3−2−2−3	955:B
+2−3−2+4	1062:B
+2−3−2+4−2−3+2	827c
+2−3−2+5−2−2−2	1277c:B
+2−3−2−2	249:B, 798:B, 892d:B, 1213:B, 1388b:C, 1494b:B, 1545a:B
+2−3−2−2+2+2−3	1308:B
+2−3−2−2+2+5−2	1332c:B
+2−3−2−2+2−2−3	1679a:B
+2−3−2−2+2−2−5	1279b:C
+2−3−2−2+3	886a:B
+2−3−2−2+3−2	135b:B
+2−3−2−2+4+2−3	270d
+2−3−2−2+4+2−4	610d
+2−3−2−2+5−3+2	925e
+2−3−2−2−2	73c:B
+2−3−2−2−2+3−4	600:B
+2−3−2−2−2−2+2	989g:B
+2−3−2−3	321h, 782c
+2−3−2−3+4−2−2	1324a:B
+2−3−3	688, 1144d, 1197b, 1268:C, 1388a:C, 1789a:B
+2−3−3+2	510a:B, 1736:C
+2−3−3+2+2	783:B
+2−3−3+2+2−2−2	713e:B
+2−3−3+2+2−6+4	835g:B
+2−3−3+2+3	1790
+2−3−3+2+3+2−3	610b
+2−3−3+2+3−2+2	1663:C
+2−3−3+2+3−2−3	193b:B, 1245a:C
+2−3−3+2+3−3−2	267b
+2−3−3+3+2+2−3	833b:B
+2−3−3+3+2−2−2	1311:B

Thematic Index of the Tabulated Melodies

Interval Sequence	Melody No.
+2−3−3+3+2−3−3	1033d:B
+2−3−3+3−2+2−3	Parry 31c:B
+2−3−3+3−2+3	1399k:B
+2−3−3+4+2−3−3	Parry 31c
+2−3−3+4−3−2	575:B
+2−3−3+4−3−3	1674:B
+2−3−3+5−2−2	606
+2−3−3−2	1058c:B
+2−3−3−2+5+2−2	431:B
+2−3−4+5−2−3−3	Parry 53:B
+2−3−4−2+2+2	1328:B
+2−4	126a:B, 1033h:B, 1515e:C, 1532e:B, 1532f:B
+2−4+2	753b:B, 1148a:B, 1271c:B
+2−4+2+2+2−4+3	421a
+2−4+2+2+3−2−3	314:B
+2−4+2−2	755e:B
+2−4+2−3	1500:B
+2−4+2−3+4−2−2	1024a:B
+2−4+3+2	1058c:C
+2−4+3+2−2	179, 1014:B
+2−4+3+2−2+2−3	265a:B
+2−4+3+2−2−2	868c
+2−4+3+2−2−2−2	904a, 904b, 1255b:B
+2−4+3+2−4+2	173b
+2−4+3−2−2−2	1791
+2−4+3−2−2−2−2	1881
+2−4+4+2−3	709c
+2−4+4+2−3−3	1579b
+2−4+4−2−2−2−2	984f
+2−4−2	947:B
+2−4−2+2−2	1511a
+2−4−2+3+3−2+2	333c
+2−5+2+4−2	Parry 5
+2−5+2−2+2+2+2	388:B
+2−5+3+2−2−2−2	94a:B
+2−5+5−2−4+3−2	435e

Thematic Index of the Tabulated Melodies

Thematic Index of the Tabulated Melodies

Interval Sequence	Melody No.
−2+2+2+2−4+2−3	1258:B
−2+2+2+2−6	1153:C
−2+2+2+3−2	1735
−2+2+2+3−2−2	159c, 1047a
−2+2+2+3−2−2−2	137, 162:B
−2+2+2+3−2−3	783, 1570a
−2+2+2+3−2−3+2	1673b
−2+2+2+3−2−3+3	1731
−2+2+2+3−3−3+2	1176:C, 1659h:C
−2+2+2+3−5	1131:B
−2+2+2+4−3−3+2	1673a
−2+2+2−2	210d, 281d, 479d:B, 672b, 809:C, 1116:B, 1131, 1168c:B, 1658e
−2+2+2−2+2+2−2	1764b
−2+2+2−2+2+2−4	563c
−2+2+2−2+2+3−2	1346
−2+2+2−2+2−2	532c
−2+2+2−2+3−2−3	780b
−2+2+2−2+3−3+2	281b
−2+2+2−2+4	1630:B
−2+2+2−2+5−4	1888
−2+2+2−2−2	7c, 66:B, 80b, 123ee, 132f, 132g, 701a, 701b, 701c, 802d:B, 1270:B, 1602g:B, 1743:C, 1862:C; Parry 16a
−2+2+2−2−2+2	475
−2+2+2−2−2+2+2	410, 1602a, 1699:C
−2+2+2−2−2+2−2	305f, 448e, 1289b, 1310a:B
−2+2+2−2−2+2−3	1352b:B, 1457:B
−2+2+2−2−2−2	194b, 203, 1010b:B, 1303c, 1198–1199:C
−2+2+2−2−2−2+2	1303a, 1303b
−2+2+2−2−2−2+3	1289b:B
−2+2+2−2−2−2−2	321f:B, 1205
−2+2+2−2−2−2−4	1352a:B, 1568a
−2+2+2−2−2−3	224
−2+2+2−2−2−3+2	1456:C
−2+2+2−2−3	1094c; Parry 48
−2+2+2−2−3+2−2	1719b:B

Thematic Index of the Tabulated Melodies

Interval Sequence	Melody No.
−2+2+2−2−3−2	1474
−2+2+2−2−3−2+2	1630
−2+2+2−3	56c, 163, 822:B, 1001i:B, 1635:D
−2+2+2−3+2+2+2	1332b:B
−2+2+2−3+2−2+2	1838
−2+2+2−3+2−2−2	1635:C
−2+2+2−3+2−3	1804a, 1804b
−2+2+2−3+2−3+2	229a
−2+2+2−3+2−3−2	1440b:B
−2+2+2−3+3	1570b:B
−2+2+2−3+3−2−2	444, 852a:B
−2+2+2−3+3−4	938b:B
−2+2+2−3+3−4+2	743:C
−2+2+2−3+4	1585f:B
−2+2+2−3+4−2−2	444:B
−2+2+2−3+4−3−2	1770
−2+2+2−3−2	480a, 480b, 835f
−2+2+2−3−2+2	1621:B
−2+2+2−3−2+2+2	835e:B, 1540f
−2+2+2−3−2+2−2	677:B
−2+2+2−3−2−2−2	123aa
−2+2+2−3−2−2−4	1506a:C
−2+2+2−3−3	652a, 823
−2+2+2−3−3+2+3	434:B
−2+2+2−3−3+5−3	1830:B
−2+2+2−4	1061:C
−2+2+2−4+2	1111:D, 1834b
−2+2+2−4−2+4−4	393:B
−2+2+2−5	954a
−2+2+3	1168g:B, 1514c:B, 1589b:B
−2+2+3+2−2−2−2	342:B, 1364, 1778c:B
−2+2+3+2−2−3	938a
−2+2+3+2−3	70a
−2+2+3+2−3−2−2	1778b:B
−2+2+3+2−3−4+2	1811:C
−2+2+3+3−2−2+2	452e

Thematic Index of the Tabulated Melodies

Interval Sequence	Melody No.
−2+2+3−2	1128e, 1540a:B, 1540b:B, 1540i:B, 1664b, 1676b:B, 1867
−2+2+3−2+2	1595, 1804a:B, 1804b:B
−2+2+3−2+2−2−2	383b:B
−2+2+3−2+2−3+2	1659a:C
−2+2+3−2−2+2−2	375:B
−2+2+3−2−2+3	1012
−2+2+3−2−2−2	593d, 594, 930b:B, 1399g
−2+2+3−2−2−2+2	648b, 1680
−2+2+3−2−2−2−2	694, 842:B
−2+2+3−2−2−2−3	438
−2+2+3−2−3+2	1505d
−2+2+3−2−3+2−2	857:B
−2+2+3−3+2−2+3	989a
−2+2+3−3+2−3+2	1890
−2+2+3−3+3−3−2	1632
−2+2+3−3−2	1409:B, 1410:B
−2+2+3−3−2+2+3	21b
−2+2+3−3−3+2+2	194a
−2+2+3−4+2+2	1002g
−2+2+3−4−2+2+2	983y
−2+2+4+2−3−3	809
−2+2+4+2−3−3+4	1502d
−2+2+4−2	692, 1077c:B, 1568a:B
−2+2+4−2+2−3−2	344e
−2+2+4−2−2	1692a:C
−2+2+4−2−3	775b:C, 1111:C
−2+2+4−2−3+2+3	1556a
−2+2+4−2−4−2−3	1491, 1524
−2+2+4−3−2−2	1827:D
−2+2−2	46b:B, 100:B, 123r, 182, 191b, 318:B, 448b, 461:B, 476:B, 509:B, 545a:B, 752c:B, 789, 802e, 815b:B, 821:B, 886d:C, 1027b, 1222:C, 1280f:B, 1465:B, 1468b, 1498c, 1520, 1534, 1602i:B, 1605:B, 1768:B, 1793:D, 1824:B, 1874
−2+2−2+2	755l:B, 853e:C, 972:B, 1581
−2+2−2+2+2	65, 123ff, 1581:C
−2+2−2+2+2+2	1472

Thematic Index of the Tabulated Melodies

Interval Sequence	Melody No.
−2+2−2+2+2+2−4	1835
−2+2−2+2+2−2−2	312a
−2+2−2+2+3	989h, 1185
−2+2−2+2−2	49a:B, 68:B, 1179a:B, 1275; Parry 31d
−2+2−2+2−2+2	123n:B
−2+2−2+2−2+2−2	1862
−2+2−2+2−2+4	1667
−2+2−2+2−2−2	1310m, 1659h:B; Parry 1, 37:B
−2+2−2+2−2−2+2	448n
−2+2−2+2−2−2−2	269, 1655f:B
−2+2−2+2−2−3	1441
−2+2−2+2−2−3−3	1257:B
−2+2−2+2−3	165j, 1243d
−2+2−2+2−3+2	162, 165c
−2+2−2+2−3+2−2	538b
−2+2−2+2−3−2	34, 1310d
−2+2−2+3	1468b:B
−2+2−2+3−2	123s:B
−2+2−2+3−2−2	17b, 246a, 1176:B
−2+2−2+3−2−2+2	448l
−2+2−2+3−2−2−2	659
−2+2−2+4−3	743:B
−2+2−2+4−3−2−2	1313b
−2+2−2+4−5	1203a, 1254:B
−2+2−2−2	36d:B, 49b, 91:B, 168a:B, 376a:B, 778d:B, 802a:B, 802b:B, 925a:B, 928:C, 940:B, 1069:B, 1129:B, 1195a:B, 1279a, 1310t, 1466:B, 1483c:D, 1539:B, 1542:B, 1563c:B, 1705c, 1735:C
−2+2−2−2+2	130b:B, 796c:B, 800b:B, 819d:B, 1101:D, 1283d:D
−2+2−2−2+2+2	1600
−2+2−2−2+2+2+2	241; Parry 52
−2+2−2−2+2+2−2	315:B
−2+2−2−2+2+2−3	448j
−2+2−2−2+2+3−3	860b:B
−2+2−2−2+2−2	992, 1126:B, 1310f:B
−2+2−2−2+2−2−2	882a:B, 1310d:B, 1326:B, 1889

Thematic Index of the Tabulated Melodies

Interval Sequence	Melody No.
−2+2−2−2+3−2	85
−2+2−2−2+3−2+3	342
−2+2−2−2+3−2−2	129d, 1769:B
−2+2−2−2+4	77c, 243h, 1583a:B
−2+2−2−2+4−2	181, 1544
−2+2−2−2+4−4	1388a:B
−2+2−2−2−2	49c, 123k, 125c:B, 174a, 174b, 178:B, 403, 810c:B, 1000b:B, 1210:B, 1310o:B, 1327a:B, 1544:B, 1545e:B, 1607a:B, 1613a:D, 1639:B, 1659c:B
−2+2−2−2−2+2	169, 215
−2+2−2−2−2+2−2	1853
−2+2−2−2−2+3	476
−2+2−2−2−2+4	199a, 199b
−2+2−2−2−2+4−2	1659g:B
−2+2−2−2−2−2	1310j
−2+2−2−2−3	39h, 782f, 1591c:C, 1667:B
−2+2−2−2−3+2	Parry 12e:B
−2+2−2−2−3+2+3	904a:B
−2+2−2−2−3+2+4	1417b
−2+2−2−2−3+3+2	595:B
−2+2−2−3	36b, 39c, 865:B, 1737a, 1737b, 1599b:B; Parry 45:B
−2+2−2−3+2	123y
−2+2−2−3+2+2	453a, 453c
−2+2−2−3+2+2−2	833a:B
−2+2−2−3+2+2−3	904c; Parry 31d:B
−2+2−2−3+2+3−2	592d:B
−2+2−2−3+2−2	310i
−2+2−2−3+2−2+2	310h
−2+2−2−3+3	1618c:B
−2+2−2−3+3−2−2	1760
−2+2−2−3+3−2−3	604b, 604c, 604e
−2+2−2−3+3−3−2	604a, 604d
−2+2−2−3+4−2−2	231a
−2+2−2−3+5−5+3	611
−2+2−2−3−2	713f:B, 819a:B, 1513d, 1576a, 1577a

Thematic Index of the Tabulated Melodies

Interval Sequence	Melody No.
−2+2−2−4	654bis-b
−2+2−2−4+2	Parry 12a:B
−2+2−2−4+2+3−2	288b:B, 726:B, 1334:B
−2+2−3	796b:B, 1070, 1075:B, 1095d:B, 1145a:B, 1145b:B, 1150e:B, 1156b:C, 1179b:B, 1367a, 1399n:B, 1409, 1462:B, 1472bis:B, 1521a:C, 1540a, 1540g:D, 1570d, 1581:D, 1588b, 1589a:C, 1602f:C, 1635:B, 1694:B
−2+2−3+2	39a, 46a:B, 264a:B, 481c:B, 701c:B, 739b:B, 777:B, 1209d:B, 1469d:B
−2+2−3+2+2	1618a:B
−2+2−3+2+2+2−2	459
−2+2−3+2+2+2−4	1714:B
−2+2−3+2+2−2+2	1590
−2+2−3+2+2−3−3	989b:B
−2+2−3+2−2	216c, 808:B
−2+2−3+2−2+2	1476:C
−2+2−3+2−2+3	646
−2+2−3+2−2−2	746
−2+2−3+2−2−2+2	310f
−2+2−3+2−2−2−2	802b, 1860
−2+2−3+2−2−3+2	1535:C; Parry 12b:B
−2+2−3+2−2−3+5	854a:B
−2+2−3+2−2−3−2	513c
−2+2−3+2−3	1092:B, 1854
−2+2−3+2−3+2	959b
−2+2−3+2−3+2+2	310g, 1813–1814:C
−2+2−3+2−3+4−2	793
−2+2−3+2−3−2	805
−2+2−3+2−3−3	1490a:C
−2+2−3+2−4+2+2	865
−2+2−3+3	1540j
−2+2−3+3+2−2−2	312c, 312e, 400a, 535a
−2+2−3+3+2−3	875b
−2+2−3+3+3−2+2	893
−2+2−3+3−2	123x:B
−2+2−3+3−2+2−2	296b
−2+2−3+3−2+2−3	158a:B, 303a, 1649, 1691a:B, 1730:B; Parry 4

Thematic Index of the Tabulated Melodies

Interval Sequence	Melody No.
−2+2−3+3−2−2+2	312d
−2+2−3+3−2−2−3	1487:B
−2+2−3+3−2−3+3	335c, 335d
−2+2−3+3−3−2	513a:B
−2+2−3+3−3−3+5	298:B
−2+2−3+3−4	818a:B
−2+2−3+3−4+2	780a:B
−2+2−3+3−4+2−3	513b
−2+2−3+4	77b, 792b:B
−2+2−3+5−3−2−2	654bis-a
−2+2−3−2	473a:B, 621, 713d:B, 804b:B, 812c, 983gg:B, 1088:B, 1483a:D, 1483b:D, 1514a:C, 1613b:D, 1639, 1764b:C
−2+2−3−2+2	96, 523, 678, 1022c:B, 1282:B, 1461, 1540d
−2+2−3−2+2+2+2	1352b
−2+2−3−2+2+3	1182a:B, 1182b:B
−2+2−3−2+2−5+2	1706:B
−2+2−3−2+3	957b, 1181c
−2+2−3−2+3−2−2	120b
−2+2−3−2+4	199c
−2+2−3−2+5−2−2	984h
−2+2−3−2−2	758a, 958a, 958b
−2+2−3−2−2+2	1175
−2+2−3−2−2+2−2	878b:B
−2+2−3−2−2+4	1232
−2+2−3−2−3	1571a:C
−2+2−3−2−3+4−2	852b:C
−2+2−3−2−4+2+2	1892:B
−2+2−3−3+2+2+2	1428:B
−2+2−3−3+2+2−3	1263:B, 1449–1450, 1740a:C
−2+2−3−3+2+4	390c
−2+2−3−3+2−2−2	1039d:B
−2+2−3−3+3	975
−2+2−3−3+3+3−2	852bis:C
−2+2−4	1019:C, 1172–1173, 1538:B
−2+2−4+2+3−2+2	1033c:B
−2+2−4+2−2−2	1483d

Thematic Index of the Tabulated Melodies

Interval Sequence	Melody No.
−2+2−4+2−2−2+2	1452
−2+2−4+2−3	1113
−2+2−4+2−3+5−2	1833
−2+2−4+3+2−4	648a:B
−2+2−4+3−2−2−2	1597:C
−2+2−4+3−2−3+3	1851
−2+2−4+3−4+2	983h:B
−2+2−4+4+2+2+3	1389
−2+2−4+4−2+2+2	Parry 28c
−2+2−4+4−2+2−2	311a
−2+2−4+4−2+2−3	1766
−2+2−4+4−2+2−4	1033c
−2+2−4+4−2−2−2	1660:C
−2+2−5+2+2+2−2	1655c
−2+2−5+3+3−3−2	971a:B
−2+2−5+3−2	1377:C
−2+3	1128a, 1196, 1805:B
−2+3+2−2−2	132c, 993d
−2+3+2−3+2−2−2	1419:B
−2+3+2−3+2−3	1441:C
−2+3+2−3+2−3−2	770b
−2+3+2−3−2	770b:B, 1002d:C
−2+3+2−3−2+3+2	21a
−2+3−2	78c, 216b, 464:B, 479a:B, 479c:B, 675, 802e:B, 1005c:B, 1221:C, 1230a, 1283a:C, 1515b:B, 1540f:B, 1540j:B, 1540k, 1576d:B, 1585g
−2+3−2+2	673
−2+3−2+2−2	129c, 129e
−2+3−2+2−2−2	164b:B
−2+3−2+2−3	46a
−2+3−2+2−3+2−2	7d, 1828
−2+3−2+3−2−2	1631
−2+3−2+3−2−2	926
−2+3−2−2	123a:B, 302a, 912:B, 945, 959b:B, 963, 1221:B, 1511a:C, 1515b:B, 1515f:B, 1878:C
−2+3−2−2+2−2	1037–1038
−2+3−2−2+2−2−2	722–723

Thematic Index of the Tabulated Melodies

Interval Sequence	Melody No.
−2+3−2−2+2−3	Parry 6b:B
−2+3−2−2+2−3+4	1696a:C, 1696b:C
−2+3−2−2+2−4−2	467a
−2+3−2−2+3−2	35, 448a, 1021a
−2+3−2−2+3−2−2	252b, 262b, 448f, 468
−2+3−2−2−2	755j, 779a:B, 805:B, 825:B, 1022c:C, 1801:B
−2+3−2−2−2+2−2	340
−2+3−2−2−2+2−3	321h:B, 1891
−2+3−2−2−2−2	322:B, 1329b, 1606b, 1614:D, 1894
−2+3−2−2−2−2+4	1342:B
−2+3−2−2−2−3	1720a:B
−2+3−2−2−3	1777
−2+3−2−2−3+2+3	886c:B
−2+3−2−2−3+2−2	1815a
−2+3−2−2−3+3	1618d:B
−2+3−2−2−3−2	1576d
−2+3−2−2−4+3+2	1429:B
−2+3−2−3	1532a:B, 1532b:B, 1599b, 1791:B
−2+3−2−3+2	380, 1418:B
−2−3−2−3+3	1005c
−2+3−2−3−3	1651b:B
−2+3−2−4−2	1795a:C
−2+3−2−5+2+3	1618e:B
−2+3−3	1594:C, 1664a, 1806:D
−2+3−3+2	455e, 1473:B
−2+3−3+2−2	89a, 1181c:B, 1197b:B
−2+3−3+2−2+2	503c
−2+3−3+2−2+3−2	266a
−2+3−3+2−2+3−3	1561b, 1561c
−2+3−3+2−2−2	923:B
−2+3−3+2−3+4−3	411
−2+3−3+4−2−2−2	1811:B
−2+3−3−2	103, 624:C, 672a:C, 672b:C, 906b:C, 1022b:C, 1230a:B, 1461:B
−2+3−3−2+2+3−3	480b:B
−2+3−3−2+3−2	1026f:B

Thematic Index of the Tabulated Melodies

Interval Sequence	Melody No.
−2+3−3−2−3+2	1611b:B
−2+3−4+2+2+3−3	1026c:B
−2+3−4+2−2	78c:B
−2+3−4+2−2−3+2	1532c:C
−2+3−4+2−3	777
−2+3−4+3−2	480a:B
−2+3−4+5−3+2−3	1036d
−2+3−4−2+4−4+2	647c
−2+3−5+2+4	1583b:B
−2+3−6+4−3	53
−2+4	749c:B
−2+4+2+2	1671:C
−2+4+2−2	1184:C
−2+4+2−2−3−2−2	1349
−2+4+2−2−3−3	322
−2+4+2−4−2+2−3	1016a:B
−2+4−2+2−3	46b
−2+4−2+3−2	1815a:B, 1815b:B, 1815c:B
−2+4−2−2	135a:B, 1826:D
−2+4−2−2+2+2	369b
−2+4−2−2−2	881a, 1474:B
−2+4−2−2−2+2−2	655a:C, 655d:C, 655e:C
−2+4−2−2−2−2−2	1005b:C
−2+4−2−2−3+2	881b:B
−2+4−2−3	1102d
−2+4−2−3+2−3	713a:C
−2+4−2−4+2+2−3	1206b:B
−2+4−3	1246n:B
−2+4−3+2	766a:B
−2+4−3+2−2−2	779c, 1758
−2+4−3+2−3+2	784a:C
−2+4−3−2	82d, 305e
−2+4−3−2+3−3	523:B
−2+4−3−2+4−3	1392b
−2+4−3−2−2+2	758b, 1522
−2+4−3−3−3	782d

Thematic Index of the Tabulated Melodies

Interval Sequence	Melody No.
−2+4−4+2−2−2−2	1362:B, 1774:B
−2+4−4+4−5	1203b
−2+4−4−2−2	1088:C
−2+4−4−2−3	950:C
−2+4−4−2−4	1275:B
−2+4−6+3−3	621:C
−2+5−2−2	1244:B
−2+5−2−2−2−2+4	989b
−2+5−2−3	55:B
−2+5−5+6−3	1598:B
−2−2	36b:B, 38:B, 40:B, 62:B, 123d:B, 305l, 462:B, 473c:B, 500a:B, 508, 527:B, 545b:B, 641, 645, 664a, 748:B, 776b:B, 778a:B, 790b:B, 803a:B, 837:C, 853b:C, 853d:C, 875b:C, 886c:C, 911:C, 1005d, 1026f, 1070:B, 1073b:C, 1095a:B, 1095c:C, 1096, 1107:D, 1109:D, 1110:D, 1115:D, 1145a:C, 1145b:C, 1148a:D, 1148b:D, 1161, 1168e:C, 1221, 1260:C, 1368:C, 1482, 1506a:D, 1506g:C, 1508:B, 1518:C, 1521b:B, 1532i:B, 1533:D, 1541:B, 1543, 1554:C, 1561d, 1566:B, 1570g, 1570i, 1573a:B, 1573c, 1575:C, 1548d:C, 1587a:C, 1587b:C, 1602d:C, 1602f:D, 1631:B, 1640a:C, 1640b:C, 1640c:C, 1640d:C, 1659e:B, 1701, 1702a:C, 1711:C, 1713:C, 1714:C, 1717:C, 1750a:D, 1750b:D, 1750c:D, 1784:D, 1820:D, 1869:B, 1863a:D
−2−2+2	40, 72a, 83, 165b, 472c:B, 746:B, 750a:B, 994:B, 1002f:B, 1003, 1005b, 1022b:B, 1059:C, 1074:B, 1143a, 1143b, 1152:B, 1283c:D, 1400, 1403b:B, 1563b:B, 1743:B
−2−2+2+2	800a:B, 928:B, 1134:B, 1154:C, 1157:B, 1509:B, 1591b
−2−2+2+2+2−2	1246k
−2−2+2+2+2−2−2	557, 1302:C
−2−2+2+2+2−3−2	326, 1711:B
−2−2+2+2−2	234a, 234c, 1577b:B, 1687
−2−2+2+2−2−2	155a:B, 180b:B, 348:B, 1200:C, 1298a:D, 1298b:D, 1298c:D, 1423:B, 1532j, 1602:B, 1608b
−2−2+2+2−2−2+2	152b, 346a, 836:B, 979:B, 1026b, 1583a, 1583b, 1654, 1681:B, 1818:B
−2−2+2+2−2−2−2	266c, 642, 1327d, 1458a:B, 1458b:B, 1720b, 1753a:B, 1753b:B
−2−2+2+2−2−2−3	782a, 1313b.B, 1608d, 1624:C

Thematic Index of the Tabulated Melodies

Interval Sequence	Melody No.
−2−2+2+2−3	78a:B, 588:B, 1094e:B, 1094f:B, 1101:B, 1155:B, 1372, 1591a
−2−2+2+2−3+2	698
−2−2+2+2−3+2−3	544e
−2−2+2+2−3−2	148b, 237i, 1267
−2−2+2+2−3−2−3	1613a:C
−2−2+2+2−4	239, 1105b:C
−2−2+2+2−4+4	1515f:C
−2−2+2+2−5	1111:B
−2−2+2+2−6+4−2	1516a:C
−2−2+2+3	951a:B
−2−2+2+3−2	922
−2−2+2+3−2+2−2	292a, 351
−2−2+2+3−2−2+3	Parry 22
−2−2+2+3−2−2−2	1325b
−2−2+2+3−3−2	755a
−2−2+2+3−4+2	257:B
−2−2+2+3−4+3−3	292b
−2−2+2+4−2−2	656b
−2−2+2+4−2−2−2	1674
−2−2+2+4−2−3−2	1313a
−2−2+2+4−4	721e:C
−2−2+2−2	59:B, 94c:B, 134f, 143d, 166–167:B, 232c:B, 232g:B, 243k, 303e, 448c, 501:B, 905f:B, 1044:B, 1141, 1484a, 1563d:B, 1592a:C, 1655b:B, 1655e:B; Parry 30:C
−2−2+2−2+2	165a, 815c
−2−2+2−2+2+2	448g
−2−2+2−2+2+2−3	544i
−2−2+2−2+2−2	448m
−2−2+2−2+3	704–705
−2−2+2−2+3−2−2	304b, 833g:B, 833h:B
−2−2+2−2+3−3+2	234b
−2−2+2−2+3−5+4	983g:B
−2−2+2−2+4	773c:B, 815d:B, 1576b:B
−2−2+2−2+4−2+2	243c
−2−2+2−2+4−2−2	123cc:B, 1025a:B

Thematic Index of the Tabulated Melodies

Interval Sequence	Melody No.
−2−2+2−2+5−3−2	1026b:B
−2−2+2−2−2	42, 70a:B, 120a, 171:B, 543b, 607a:B, 781a, 837:B, 871:C, 929:C, 954a:C, 970, 1107d:C, 1142b:B, 1161:B, 1235:B, 1301b:B, 1409:C, 1595:C, 1618c:C, 1750b:B; Parry 46
−2−2+2−2−2+2	123bb, 134g, 155b:B, 1498a
−2−2+2−2−2+2+2	721a:B
−2−2+2−2−2+2−2	690b:B, 929:B
−2−2+2−2−2+2−3	983r:B
−2−2+2−2−2+3−3	1755bis:B
−2−2+2−2−2+4−2	721b:B
−2−2+2−2−2−2	123v, 648c:B, 648d:B, 873:C, 1220:B, 1310c, 1562d, 1692a:B, 1692b:B, 1783:C
−2−2+2−2−2−2+3	1446a:B, 1783:B
−2−2+2−2−2−2−2	771
−2−2+2−2−2−3	1569a:C
−2−2+2−2−3	721d:C, 745:C, 1139b, 1516b:C; Parry 28c:B
−2−2+2−2−3+2	597a, 1317:B
−2−2+2−2−3+2+2	948:C
−2−2+2−2−3+3+2	721d:B, 721e:B
−2−2+2−2−3+4−2	615c:B
−2−2+2−2−3+5−2	1353b
−2−2+2−2−4+2	958f:B
−2−2+2−3	50–51, 71, 243f:B, 493:B, 765:B, 1005d:B, 1094k:B, 1395:C, 1483f:B, 1545c:B, 1651a:B, 1674:C, 1723:C, 1829:B
−2−2+2−3+2	132d:B, 177b:B, 462, 472a, 472b, 613a
−2−2+2−3+2+2−2	653:B, 1816
−2−2+2−3+2+3	243g, 1288:B
−2−2+2−3+2+4	646:B
−2−2+2−3+2+4−2	243a
−2−2+2−3+2−2−2	297b:B
−2−2+2−3+2−3	248:B, 721b:C, 1602c:C, 1722d:B
−2−2+2−3+3−2−2	967:B
−2−2+2−3+3−2−4	297a:B
−2−2+2−3+4−2−2	1721:B
−2−2+2−3+4−2−3	952:B
−2−2+2−3−2	159a:B, 465, 721a:C, 1001a:B, 1089a:B, 1243e:B, 1408:B, 1472:B, 1578:C

Thematic Index of the Tabulated Melodies

Interval Sequence	Melody No.
−2−2+2−3−2+2	614, 1192:B
−2−2+2−3−2−2	1604:C
−2−2+2−3−4	1164:C
−2−2+2−4	958d:B, 1077d:D, 1082:C, 1096:B, 1118:B, 1800b:C
−2−2+2−4+2	359a
−2−2+2−4+3+2−2	356a:B
−2−2+2−4+4	772:B
−2−2+2−4−2	1091:B
−2−2+2−4−2+5−4	983u:B
−2−2+2−5+2+3+3	1725:D
−2−2+3	755h:B, 784a:B, 947, 962a, 1139c:B, 1400:B, 1561c:B
−2−2+3+2+2	1253:B
−2−2+3+2+2−2	134j
−2−2+3+2−2	134k, 1608d:B
−2−2+3+2−4+2−2	1033d
−2−2+3+3−2	1545b
−2−2+3+3−2+2−3	27
−2−2+3+3−2−2	333a, 333b
−2−2+3+3−2−2−2	1310n
−2−2+3+3−2−3	119f, 934
−2−2+3+4−3+3−2	288b
−2−2+3−2	98b:B, 918:B, 1008:B, 1022b, 1097a, 1246a:B, 1546c:B, 1555d:B
−2−2+3−2+2−2	346b
−2−2+3−2+2−3+2	571
−2−2+3−2+2−3−2	279
−2−2+3−2+3−2	200a
−2−2+3−2−2	123e:B, 123i:B, 123m, 123ee:B, 135a, 143e, 158b:B, 168d, 180a:B, 183f:B, 216a, 473a, 479g, 487, 492e:B, 585, 649, 794:B, 815a:B, 816:B, 828:B, 836, 853a:C, 900:B, 949:B, 983a:B, 1107d:B, 1222, 1247c:B, 1383:B, 1467c, 1468a, 1496, 1510:C, 1540i, 1575, 1599a:B, 1602h:C, 1750a:C, 1775:B; Parry 5:B
−2−2+3−2−2+2	1780
−2−2+3−2−2+2−2	1343; Parry 10b
−2−2+3−2−2+2−3	220, 989a:B

Thematic Index of the Tabulated Melodies

Interval Sequence	Melody No.
−2−2+3−2−2+3−2	123o:B
−2−2+3−2−2+3−3	303f
−2−2+3−2−2+5−2	1823:C
−2−2+3−2−2−2	247a:B, 597a:B, 802c, 833e, 1094l, 1256:B
−2−2+3−2−2−2+2	833c:B
−2−2+3−2−2−2+4	1420
−2−2+3−2−2−2−2	348b:B, 1707a; Parry 19:B
−2−2+3−2−2−2−3	1220
−2−2+3−2−2−3	713c:B, 1521b:C, 1624:D
−2−2+3−2−2−3+2	Parry 6a:B
−2−2+3−2−3+2	1684:C
−2−2+3−2−3	1453:B, 1492, 1541:C, 1800c:B; Parry 30
−2−2+3−2−3+2	158d:B, 1301a:C
−2−2+3−2−3+2−3	1532h:C
−2−2+3−3	55, 153:B, 666b:B, 1540l, 1675b
−2−2+3−3+2−2−3	935
−2−2+3−3+2−3	310d, 684b:B, 1406:B
−2−2+3−3+3−3+2	306:B
−2−2+3−3+4	200f
−2−2+3−3−2	1197a
−2−2+3−3−2+4−2	1785:C
−2−2+3−3−4	984k
−2−2+3−4+2	755f
−2−2+3−4−3	1094d:B
−2−2+3−5	1751:D
−2−2+4	77a, 671b, 1143b:B, 1570f:B, 1578:B, 1585c:B
−2−2+4+2−2	1137:B
−2−2+4+2−2−2−2	855a:B
−2−2+4+2−2−3	1246a:D
−2−2+4+4	764d:B
−2−2+4−2	98b, 613b
−2−2+4−2+2−2−2	709a
−2−2+4−2−2	113:B, 168a, 1005e, 1246g:B, 1472:D
−2−2+4−2−2+2	1022c
−2−2+4−2−2−2	1381a:B, 1800b
−2−2+4−2−2−2+2	1362, 1774

Thematic Index of the Tabulated Melodies

Interval Sequence	Melody No.
−2−2+4−2−2−2−2	394a, 833c
−2−2+4−2−3	690c:B, 1842
−2−2+4−2−3+3−2	978:C, 1659f:C
−2−2+4−2−3+3−3	394a:B
−2−2+4−2−3+4−3	550a
−2−2+4−2−3−2	1621:D
−2−2+4−3	1545d, 1633:C, 1771:D
−2−2+4−3−2	1027b:B
−2−2+4−3−3	1696c:C, 1800a:B
−2−2+4−4	1502b:B
−2−2+4−4+2	606:B
−2−2+5+2−2	929
−2−2+5−2	1246j:B, 1585e:B
−2−2+5−2+2−3	1445:B
−2−2+5−2+2−3−2	706a, 706b
−2−2+5−2+2−3−3	223
−2−2+5−2+2−5+2	1284a, 1284b
−2−2+5−2−2	1170:C
−2−2+5−2−2+2−3	1246k:B
−2−2+5−2−2−2	514:B, 1277a:B
−2−2+5−2−2−2−2	835d:C
−2−2+5−2−3	1122:C, 1149b:B, 1246d:B, 1246e:B, 1800b:B
−2−2+6−2	1559
−2−2+6−2−2−2−2	1661:D
−2−2+8	1824:D
−2−2+8−2	930a:C
−2−2+8−2−2	930b:C, 930c:C
−2−2−2	36a, 36c, 47b:B, 52:B, 54:B, 174a:B, 478, 747:B, 751:C, 759:B, 767:B, 788c, 788d, 881a:B, 883b:B, 892c:B, 892d:C, 1002h:B, 1045:B, 1094a, 1115:B, 1118:C, 1120:B, 1132:B, 1138:B, 1139a:B, 1139c:C, 1144c:B, 1144d:B, 1188b:D, 1222:B, 1259b:C, 1328:C, 1370a, 1370b, 1379:C, 1388b:B, 1388d:C, 1397:B, 1399a:B, 1399b:B, 1399c:B, 1399e:B, 1399f:B, 1399h:B, 1399i:B, 1399j:B, 1399l:B, 1399m:B, 1401, 1479c:C, 1493c:B, 1499a:B, 1506e:B, 1519a:B, 1530a:B, 1532c:B, 1540l:B, 1543:B, 1545f:B, 1591b:C, 1607c:B, 1649:B, 1654:C, 1672a:C, 1672b:C, 1720a, 1728:C, 1789c:B, 1800c:C, 1865:B; Parry 40:B

Thematic Index of the Tabulated Melodies

Interval Sequence	Melody No.
−2−2−2+2	134d:B, 481a:B, 589, 666a:B, 755b:B, 755c:B, 867:B, 953:B, 1123:C, 1159:B, 1165b:B, 1193:C, 1280a, 1289a, 1460a:C, 1529:D, 1570f, 1655a:B, 1738–1739:C, 1799:C, 1803, 1821:B, 1823:D
−2−2−2+2+2	498, 776e:B, 1107c:C, 1273a:B, 1273b:B, 1273f:B, 1540k:B, 1642:B
−2−2−2+2+2+2	524, 1270
−2−2−2+2+2+2+2	1289a:B
−2−2−2+2+2+2−2	353b, 1332a:B
−2−2−2+2+2+2−4	321c
−2−2−2+2+2−2	545a
−2−2−2+2+2−2−2	356b:B
−2−2−2+2+2−3	997:C, 1249
−2−2−2+2+2−3+2	230, 719:B
−2−2−2+2+2−4+2	1177:B
−2−2−2+2+2+3	64b, 64c, 796a; Parry 47:B
−2−2−2+2+3+2−2	1027c:B
−2−2−2+2+3−2−2	237a, 1448b:B
−2−2−2+2+3−3−2	966a:B
−2−2−2+2+4	1655c:B
−2−2−2+2−2	104:B, 790c:B, 1097b:B
−2−2−2+2−2+2	1155bis-b:B
−2−2−2+2−2+3−2	530a
−2−2−2+2−2−2+3	318, 1446c:B
−2−2−2+2−2−2−2	26, 240a:B, 1337a:B, 1427
−2−2−2+2−2−2−3	656b:B
−2−2−2+2−2−3	510b, 680:C, 1677:B
−2−2−2+2−2−3+2	969:B
−2−2−2+2−2−3−3	1526a:B
−2−2−2+2−2−4	Parry 13
−2−2−2+2−3	70b:B, 196e:B, 660b:C, 869:C, 1227:C
−2−2−2+2−3+2	123g:B, 1209b:C
−2−2−2+2−3+2−2	353c
−2−2−2+2−3+2−3	951a:C
−2−2−2+2−3+4−2	615a:B
−2−2−2+2−3−2	1603
−2−2−2+2−3−2+4	1259a:B

Thematic Index of the Tabulated Melodies

Interval Sequence	Melody No.
−2−2−2+2−3−2−2	915:B
−2−2−2+2−3−3−2	1532e:C, 1532f:C
−2−2−2+3	596, 995:B, 1404a:B, 1776:B, 1798:B
−2−2−2+3+2	890:B
−2−2−2+3+2+3	645:B
−2−2−2+3+2−2−2	Parry 31a, 31b
−2−2−2+3+2−5+2	364b:B
−2−2−2+3+3	1576a:B
−2−2−2+3+3+4	1228:C
−2−2−2+3+3−2−2	1700a:B
−2−2−2+3+3−4	1677
−2−2−2+3−2	1093, 1125b, 1301b:C
−2−2−2+3−2+3−2	834b:B
−2−2−2+3−2−2	23, 123s, 174c, 246b:B, 861b:C, 863:C, 1174:B
−2−2−2+3−2−2−2	597b, 1281b:B, 1310a, 1818
−2−2−2+3−2−3	563a:B, 1224:B, 1483f:C
−2−2−2+3−3	237e, 237g, 768–769, 1117:B, 1505a:C
−2−2−2+3−3+2−3	684a:B
−2−2−2+3−3+3−2	592a:B
−2−2−2+3−3+4−2	385:B
−2−2−2+3−3−2	937:C; Parry 50:B
−2−2−2+3−3−3	240b:B
−2−2−2+3−4	1478:B
−2−2−2+3−4+2+2	1733a, 1733b
−2−2−2+4	788d:B, 1020c, 1825:B
−2−2−2+4+2+2	1302
−2−2−2+4+2+2−2	686
−2−2−2+4+2+3−2	Parry 53
−2−2−2+4+2−2	186b
−2−2−2+4+2−3−2	610e
−2−2−2+4+3−2−2	Parry 18
−2−2−2+4−2	1094j:B, 1273b
−2−2−2+4−2+2−3	529e, 958c:B
−2−2−2+4−2−2	326:B, 1251:B, 1382
−2−2−2+4−2−2−2	24d, 154, 614:B, 684c:B, 803b, 818b:B, 1493a, 1608e, 1754:B

Thematic Index of the Tabulated Melodies

Interval Sequence	Melody No.
−2−2−2+4−3	1190:B
−2−2−2+4−3+3−2	592c:B
−2−2−2+4−3−2	107
−2−2−2+4−3−3+2	208b:B, 797
−2−2−2+4−4+2	445e:B
−2−2−2+4−4+2+3	592b:B
−2−2−2+4−4+5−2	392a:B, 392d:B
−2−2−2+5	817:B, 1131:C, 1310u:B, 1590:B
−2−2−2+5−2+2−2	280d:B, 367–368
−2−2−2+5−2−2	690a; Parry 40
−2−2−2+5−2−3	184, 1618
−2−2−2+5−3−3+2	1699:B
−2−2−2+9−2+4−5	1456:B
−2−2−2+10−2	112:B
−2−2−2−2	73a:B, 73b:B, 124, 193a:B, 406:B, 490:B, 569:B, 643:C, 674:C, 736:C, 763:B, 891c:B, 948:B, 1001c:B, 1001d:B, 1015:B, 1058a:B, 1058b:B, 1058d:B, 1071, 1079a:B, 1099:B, 1113:C, 1146:B, 1150a:B, 1150c:B, 1160a:C, 1160b:C, 1163c:B, 1171:B, 1194:D, 1204:C, 1330d:B, 1370a:C, 1399d:B, 1399g:B, 1399k:C, 1399o:B, 1405:B, 1467c:B, 1470a:B, 1478:D, 1493b:B, 1506a:B, 1506b:B, 1506g:B, 1511a:D, 1513e:B, 1516a:D, 1519b:C, 1537b:B, 1585e, 1591b:D, 1671:D, 1697:C, 1710:C, 1786:C, 1800a:C, 1807:B, 1873; Parry 39a:C, 44a:C, 53:C
−2−2−2−2+2	232i:B, 713d, 776a:B
−2−2−2−2+2+2+2	827a, 1223, 1295:B
−2−2−2−2+2+2+3	827b, 966b:B
−2−2−2−2+2+2+4	1389:C
−2−2−2−2+2+2−2	1310n:B, 1436:B, 1761, 1830:C
−2−2−2−2+2−2−2	240c:B, 1195b:C, 1195c:C
−2−2−2−2+2−3+3	1434:B
−2−2−2−2+2−3−3	372:B, 1217
−2−2−2−2+2−4+5	440b:B
−2−2−2−2+2−4−2	718:B
−2−2−2−2+3	228, 1562d:B
−2−2−2−2+3+2−2	835c:B
−2−2−2−2+3+3−2	15, 270c, 270e, 270f
−2−2−2−2+3−2	881b:C, 1330b:B

Thematic Index of the Tabulated Melodies

Interval Sequence	Melody No.
−2−2−2−2+3−3	1387:B
−2−2−2−2+4	1020c:B
−2−2−2−2+4−2−2	339a, 1325c:B, 1455:B
−2−2−2−2+5−2	Parry 24
−2−2−2−2−2	951b:B, 1091, 1147:B, 1273f:C, 1511b:C
−2−2−2−2−2+2+2	1313e:B
−2−2−2−2−2+2−3	989c:B
−2−2−2−2−2+2−4	396c:B
−2−2−2−2−2+5−2	851:C
−2−2−2−2−2−2	1335–1336:B, 1619f:C
−2−2−2−2−2−2+2	Parry 44b:C
−2−2−2−2−2−2+7	1765:C
−2−2−2−2−2−2−2	989f:B, 1341, 1354b:B, 1390:C, 1698
−2−2−2−2−3	1430:B, 1598
−2−2−2−2−3+2+2	1306d:C
−2−2−2−2−3+3−3	432b:B
−2−2−2−2−3+4−3	1348:B
−2−2−2−2−3−2	1526b:C
−2−2−2−2−4	1460a, 1460b
−2−2−2−3	745:B, 1108:B, 1109:B, 1552:B, 1571b:C, 1679b:C
−2−2−2−3+2	198:B, 1316:B, 1721:C
−2−2−2−3+3−2	563d:B
−2−2−2−3−2+2+2	1540g:C, 1894:B
−2−2−2−4+2+3−2	989e:B
−2−2−2−5+2+2+2	158g:B
−2−2−3	785, 819e, 880b:C, 1054a:B, 1054b:B, 1054c:B, 1066:B, 1144bis:B, 1248:D, 1367a:B, 1396:B, 1403a:B, 1470b:B, 1592b:C, 1601c:C, 1608a:D, 1627:D, 1679c:C, 1750c:B; Parry 22:B, 36
−2−2−3+2	57, 123f:B, 487:B, 518:B, 908:C, 1172–1173:C, 1268:B, 1329a:B, 1578:D, 1818:C
−2−2−3+2+2	1249:B
−2−2−3+2+2+2	1771:B
−2−2−3+2+2+2−2	958a:B
−2−2−3+2+2+3−2	423a, 1512a:C
−2−2−3+2+2+3−4	556:B
−2−2−3+2+2−2	639–640:B, 1307:B

Thematic Index of the Tabulated Melodies

Interval Sequence	Melody No.
−2−2−3+2+2−2−2	Parry 26:B
−2−2−3+2+2−3	176:B, 1246m:B, 1417c:B
−2−2−3+2+2−3+2	987:B
−2−2−3+2+3	1007:B, 1180
−2−2−3+2+3−2	1214b:B
−2−2−3+2+3−2−3	958g:C
−2−2−3+2+3−3−2	405:B
−2−2−3+2+4	1417a
−2−2−3+2+4+2	1325c
−2−2−3+2−2	503a:B, 1166b:B, 1865:D
−2−2−3+2−3	795:B
−2−2−3+2−3+3−2	983v:B
−2−2−3+3+2+2−2	654bis-a:B, 1313c:B
−2−2−3+3+2−2−2	353b:B, 717b:B
−2−2−3+3+2−2−3	353a:B
−2−2−3+3+2−3−2	183b:B
−2−2−3+3+3−2−2	1327b
−2−2−3+3−2	1558b:B
−2−2−3+3−2+2−3	356c:B
−2−2−3+3−2+3−2	429c:B
−2−2−3+3−2+3−3	1033h
−2−2−3+3−2−2	159c:B, 526b:B
−2−2−3+3−2−2−2	715–716:B, 1195a:C
−2−2−3+3−2−3+4	429b:B
−2−2−3+3−3	78b:B, 380:B, 880a:C, 1727
−2−2−3+3−3+2+2	618:B
−2−2−3+3−3+2+3	424b:B
−2−2−3+3−3+5−2	260b:B
−2−2−3+3−3−3+3	1679b:B
−2−2−3+3−3−3−2	1313a:B
−2−2−3+4+2−3−2	283b
−2−2−3+4−2−2	280b:B, 524:B, 1619b:D
−2−2−3+4−3	1546a:B, 1546d:B
−2−2−3+4−3−2	159b:B
−2−2−3+4−3−2−2	196a:B
−2−2−3+4−3−3	196d:B

Thematic Index of the Tabulated Melodies

Thematic Index of the Tabulated Melodies

Interval Sequence	Melody No.
−2−3+2+2+2−3+2	1351:B
−2−3+2+2+2−3−2	321d
−2−3+2+2+3−2−3	1304d, 1407
−2−3+2+2−2−2	900:C, 1747:C
−2−3+2+2−2−3	1365
−2−3+2+2−2−3+2	1646:B
−2−3+2+2−2−3+3	721c:B
−2−3+2+2−3	97:B
−2−3+2+2−3+2−3	989h:B
−2−3+2+2−3−2	835e
−2−3+2+2−3−2+2	334c
−2−3+2+3	1570a:B
−2−3+2+3+2−2	1007
−2−3+2+3−2	386
−2−3+2+3−2−2	1648:B
−2−3+2+3−2−2−2	1281c:B, 1327c
−2−3+2+3−2−3+2	609b, 735:C, 755b
−2−3+2+3−3+2−3	544h
−2−3+2+3−3−2	319:B
−2−3+2+3−4	812a:B
−2−3+2+3−4+2	177c:B
−2−3+2+3−4+2−3	335c:B
−2−3+2+4−2−2+2	330a:B, 343:B
−2−3+2−2	134c:B, 503c:B, 519b:B, 810a:B, 1163f:B, 1331:B, 1616:D
−2−3+2−2+2	1079b:B; Parry 43
−2−3+2−2+2+2+2	655d:B, 655e:B, 1710:B
−2−3+2−2+2+2−2	655b:B
−2−3+2−2+2−2	295:B
−2−3+2−2+2−3	875b:B, 1281d:B
−2−3+2−2+3−2+2	543a
−2−3+2−2+4−3	655a:B
−2−3+2−2−2	226, 1395:B, 1680:B; Parry 20
−2−3+2−2−2−2	946:C
−2−3+2−2−2−2−2	963:C
−2−3+2−2−3	149–150, 946:B

Thematic Index of the Tabulated Melodies

Interval Sequence	Melody No.
−2−3+2−3	73d:B, 954d:B, 1090:B, 1107c:B, 1608c:D, 1608e:D
−2−3+2−3+2	1422:B, 1612:C, 1741
−2−3+2−3+3−3	1793:B
−2−3+2−3+5	1133:B
−2−3+2−3+5−2−3	Parry 51
−2−3+2−3−2−2+2	1345
−2−3+2−4+2+4	1294:B
−2−3+2−4+5+4−3	344f:B
−2−3+3	379c, 1570g:B; Parry 52:B
−2−3+3+2	1101:C
−2−3+3+2+2−2−4	819a
−2−3+3+2−2	24c
−2−3+3+2−2−2	356b, 356c
−2−3+3+2−2−2−2	962b:B
−2−3+3+2−2−2−3	321g:B
−2−3+3+3−3−3	205
−2−3+3+3−3−3+2	983o:B
−2−3+3−2	772:C, 791a:B, 791b:B, 1806:B
−2−3+3−2+2−2−2	340:B
−2−3+3−2+2−3	882b:B
−2−3+3−2+2−3−2	319
−2−3+3−2+3−2−2	852b:B
−2−3+3−2−2	4, 638b:B, 710:B, 788i, 802a, 885:B, 1274:B, 1310k:B, 1662:D, 1755bis:C
−2−3+3−2−2+2	165h, 1382:B, 1800c
−2−3+3−2−2−2	709c:B, 713b:B
−2−3+3−2−2−2+2	1782:C
−2−3+3−2−2−3+2	1663
−2−3+3−2−3	507:B, 1060:B, 1107b:B, 1589c:C
−2−3+3−2−3+2−2	1357a
−2−3+3−2−3+4−2	615b:B
−2−3+3−2−3−4+5	1357:B
−2−3+3−3	132b:B, 183e:B, 237d, 237f, 237h, 603a, 638c:B, 1163a:B, 1747:B; Parry 35:B
−2−3+3−3+2−2	562:B, 1033b
−2−3+3−3+4−4	255–256:B

Thematic Index of the Tabulated Melodies

Interval Sequence	Melody No.
−2−3+3−3+5−3−2	488b
−2−3+3−3−2	123i, 123u, 692:C, 755i, 1609
−2−3+3−3−2+2	1315
−2−3+3−4	108:B, 125b, 1608b:D
−2−3+3−4−2	1629b:D
−2−3+4	788e:B, 1094k, 1576e:B
−2−3+4+2−2−2−2	330b
−2−3+4−2	63, 531:B, 785
−2−3+4−2−2	138:B, 243i, 484:B, 519a:B, 1246o:B, 1468c, 1613b:C
−2−3+4−2−2+3−2	265i:B, 858
−2−3+4−2−2−2	24e, 1690b
−2−3+4−2−2−2+2	130e:B
−2−3+4−2−2−2+3	1767a:B
−2−3+4−2−2−2−2	Parry 44a
−2−3+4−2−3	123l, 419, 863:B, 1511b:B
−2−3+4−2−3+2+3	265j:B
−2−3+4−2−3+3−2	416:B
−2−3+4−2−3+3−3	555b
−2−3+4−2−3+4−3	384d:B
−2−3+4−2−4−2+4	426a
−2−3+4−3−2	1185:B
−2−3+4−3−3	125a, 1440b
−2−3+4−3−3+2	1303c:B
−2−3+4−4	799:B
−2−3+4−4+2−2−2	1786
−2−3+5−2	588
−2−3+5−2−2+2−2	Parry 6c:B
−2−3+5−2−2−3	1245b:C
−2−3+5−2−3	773a:C, 1216bis
−2−3+5−3−2	1195c
−2−3+5−3−3	183c:B
−2−3+5−4	764a:C
−2−3−2	1001b:B, 1054e:B, 1393:C, 1493d:D, 1664b:C, 1679a:C, 1751:B, 1784:C
−2−3−2+2	163:B, 471:B, 608
−2−3−2+2+2−3−2	1349:C

Thematic Index of the Tabulated Melodies

Interval Sequence	Melody No.
−2−3−2+2+3−2−2	1766:B
−2−3−2+2+3−2−3	312c:B
−2−3−2+2+4−2−3	841a
−2−3−2+2−3−3+3	657:B
−2−3−2+3	1555b:B
−2−3−2+3−2	1669:D, 1878:B
−2−3−2+3−3+2+4	1437:B
−2−3−2+4−3	1678:B
−2−3−2+4−3−2−2	196b:B
−2−3−3	45, 1291, 1489:B, 1745–1746:B
−2−3−3+2	1526a:C
−2−3−3+2+5−2−3	958d:C
−2−3−3+3+3	1254a:B
−2−3−3+4+2+2−3	271e
−2−3−3+4−3	1681:C
−2−3−3+5−2+2−2	271c, 271d
−2−3−3+6−2−4+4	271f
−2−3−3−3+3+4−2	1821:D
−2−4	46b:B, 102c:D, 447:B, 1521b:D
−2−4+2	1087a:C, 1163b:B, 1264:D, 1490a:D, 1589d:C
−2−4+2+3	73b, 1085a:B, 1167a:B
−2−4+2+3−2	1145c:C
−2−4+2+4	1109, 1158a:B
−2−3+2+4−2	1602e:C
−2−4+2+4−2+3−2	1033i
−2−4+2+4−2−4+2	429a
−2−4+2+4−2−4+5	429c
−2−4+2−2	1089b:B
−2−4+2−3+4−4+2	712:C
−2−4+3	1515e:B, 1658c:C
−2−4+3+2−3−3+2	983y:B
−2−4+3+3−2−2−3	337–338
−2−4+3+3−2−3+4	311b
−2−4+3−2	983d:B, 1394:B, 1479b:C
−2−4+3−2+2+2−4	905f
−2−4+3−2−3	1145c:B, 1780:B

Thematic Index of the Tabulated Melodies

Interval Sequence	Melody No.
−2−4+3−3+2	935:B
−2−4+4−2	1057b
−2−4+4−2+2−2−2	832:B
−2−4+4−2−3+2−2	650
−2−4+4−3−2	1507
−2−4+4−3−2+2	664a
−2−4+5−2+2−3−2	295
−2−4+5−2−2−3	576:B
−2−4+5−3+2−3	139:B
−2−5+2	1033i:B
−2−5+4	1742a:D
−2−5+4+3−2−5+4	693
−2−5+5−2	1809b:C
+3	500a, 500b, 1061, 1536:B, 1875
+3+2	1073, 1132:C
+3+2+2+2−2−2+2	1326
+3+2+2+2−2−2−2	1317
+3+2+2+2−3+2+2	941
+3+2+2+2−3+2−2	1532h
+3+2+2+4−2−2−2	343:B
+3+2+2−2	1110:C, 1619e:B
+3+2+2−2+2−2−3	1325e
+3+2+2−2−2	153
+3+2+2−2−2−2−2	324
+3+2+2−2−3	713f:C
+3+2+2−2−3+3−3	598:B
+3+2+2−2−4	631
+3+2+2−3	950, 1694
+3+2+2−3+2−4+3	268
+3+2+2−3−2	775a:B
+3+2+3−3−2+2−2	601:B
+3+2−2	1174, 1257, 1403, 1571b:B, 1571c, 1736, 1778b
+3+2−2+2−2	684a, 1246m
+3+2−2+2−2+4−2	1730
+3+2−2+2−2−3	492d, 1330c
+3+2−2+2−3+2−3	486

Thematic Index of the Tabulated Melodies

Interval Sequence	Melody No.
+3+2−2+2−3−2−3	344b
+3+2−2+3−2−2−2	25
+3+2−2+3−2−2−3	123c
+3+2−2+3−5	1393
+3+2−2+4−2−2−2	280e, 280f
+3+2−2+4−4−2−3	1330a:C
+3+2−2+4−6+2−3	1330c:B
+3+2−2−2	800b:C, 1492:B, 1536, 1550c:B
+3+2−2−2+2+2−2	1266a
+3+2−2−2+2−2	165f; Parry 2
+3+2−2−2+2−2−2	896
+3+2−2−2+2−3	383a:B, 1288, 1736:B
+3+2−2−2+2−3−2	1355
+3+2−2−2+2−3−3	482, 689b
+3+2−2−2+3−2−2	442:B
+3+2−2−2+3−2−3	566:B
+3+2−2−2+5−2−2	280g
+3+2−2−2−2	480c, 489d, 810a, 826, 1088, 1094i, 1256:C, 1271a, 1271b, 1300:B, 1320, 1655a:C
+3+2−2−2−2+2+2	1449–1450:B
+3+2−2−2−2+2−2	1203b:B
+3+2−2−2−2+3+2	1794:B
+3+2−2−2−2−2	686:B, 706b:B, 1178:B, 1740a:B
+3+2−2−2−2−2+3	1325f
+3+2−2−2−2−2−2	398:B, 894:B, 1324b:C
+3+2−2−2−3	891c:C, 1150c, 1550b, 1658b:B
+3+2−2−2−3+3	229d
+3+2−2−2−3−2−2	1324c:C
+3+2−2−2−3−5+4	1490b
+3+2−2−2−4	1655d:C
+3+2−2−3	486:B, 492c:B, 868b:B, 1087b, 1150d, 1150e, 1162, 1212b, 1517
+3+2−2−3+2	494
+3+2−2−3+2+2−2	22b
+3+2−2−3+2−2	965
+3+2−2−3+2−3	954c:C
+3+2−2−3+2−3+4	603b:B

Thematic Index of the Tabulated Melodies

Interval Sequence	Melody No.
+3+2−2−3+2−3−2	1312:B
+3+2−2−3+3+2	503a, 503b, 794
+3+2−2−3+3+2−2	576, 795, 1312, 1330b, 1637, 1688:B, 1819:D
+3+2−2−3+3−2	791a
+3+2−2−3+3−3	1537a:B
+3+2−2−3−2	706a:B, 1163c
+3+2−2−3−3	689a
+3+2−2−3−3+2−2	1330b:C
+3+2−2−4+2+3−4	395:B
+3+2−3	1095c:B, 1602g, 1789d, 1789e, 1789f
+3+2−3+2	58, 1298b:C, 1513a:B
+3+2−3+2+2	1501
+3+2−3+2−2	123c:B
+3+2−3+2−2−2	489e, 489f, 770c
+3+2−3+2−3	800a:C
+3+2−3+2−3+3−3	579–580
+3+2−3+2−5+3+2	860c:C
+3+2−3+3−3−3	983dd:B
+3+2−3+3−4	433e:B
+3+2−3−2	887, 1150a, 1151, 1480:C, 1742b:D, 1828:D
+3+2−3−2+2−3	629:B
+3+2−3−2+2−3−2	1493b:C
+3+2−3−2+3	1473
+3+2−3−2+3+2−3	409, 1685:B
+3+2−3−2+4−2	445i
+3+2−3−2−2	1796:B
+3+2−3−3	1388c:B, 1493a:B
+3+2−3−3+3−2−2	1341:B
+3+2−3−3+3−3	983cc:B
+3+2−3−3+3−4+2	587:B
+3+2−3−3−2	621:B
+3+2−4+2+2+3−3	1030d:B, 1030e:B
+3+2−4+2−2	496b:B
+3+2−4+2−2+3−3	1030c:B
+3+2−4+2−4+5−2	1431:B
+3+2−4+3+2−4+3	291, 633

Thematic Index of the Tabulated Melodies

Interval Sequence	Melody No.
+3+2−4+3−2−2	900
+3+2−4+3−2−2−2	1284a:B
+3+2−4+3−2−2−4	1033f:B
+3+2−4+3−3	1560:B
+3+2−4+3−3+3+2	1031–1032
+3+2−4+3−3+4	983s
+3+2−4−2+2	172
+3+2−4−2−2−2−2	872a:B
+3+2−5	601
+3+3	1531a:B, 1589a:B
+3+3+2	1554
+3+3+2+2−2−2−2	361–362
+3+3+2+2−2−2−4	618
+3+3+2+3−3	656a
+3+3+2−2	563d, 1077b, 1138, 1144c, 1200:B, 1244b, 1246a, 1255a, 1255d, 1602h, 1778c
+3+3+2−2+2−2−2	260b, 1246p
+3+3+2−2−2+2−2−3	1837
+3+3+2−2+2−4	1244c
+3+3+2−2−2	99a, 99b, 855b, 1546d, 1578
+3+3+2−2−2+2−2	297a, 297c, 818b
+3+3+2−2−2+2−3	908, 982, 1794
+3+3+2−2−2+2−4	852bis
+3+3+2−2−2−2	196b, 1246d, 1251, 1509
+3+3+2−2−2−2+2	1444b, 1444c
+3+3+2−2−2−2+4	398
+3+3+2−2−2−3	1490d; Parry 23b, 27d:B
+3+3+2−2−2−3+3	396b
+3+3+2−2−3	196c, 196d, 196f, 967, 1246f, 1246n, 1602i, 1605, 1750b, 1793
+3+3+2−2−3+2	1825
+3+3+2−2−3+3	1633
+3+3+2−2−3+3+2	1857
+3+3+2−2−3+3−4	1390
+3+3+2−2−3−3+4	384b
+3+3+2−2−4	43d, 139
+3+3+2−2−4+3−2	1424

Thematic Index of the Tabulated Melodies

Interval Sequence	Melody No.
+3+3+2−3	1226
+3+3+2−3+2	1742a:B
+3+3+2−3−2	159b
+3+3+2−3−2+4	Parry 27e
+3+3+2−3−2+4−3	455a, 455c
+3+3+2−3−3+3	713f
+3+3+3+2−2+2−3	1280b:B
+3+3+4−2+2−3−2	280d
+3+3+4−2+2−3−3	817
+3+3+4−3−2+2−2	280c
+3+3+4−3−2−2−2	1252, 1314a
+3+3+4−3−2−3	280a, 280b, 514, 1228
+3+3−2	897b:B, 905a:B, 1002b, 1002c, 1477, 1584a, 1584b, 1584d
+3+3−2+2	1805
+3+3−2+2+2	189
+3+3−2+2+2+2−5	902
+3+3−2+2+2−2−3	1330a
+3+3−2+2−2	1117
+3+3−2+2−3	1116
+3+3−2+2−3+2−2	1767
+3+3−2+2−3+3−2	983k; Parry 27b
+3+3−2+2−3−2	983l
+3+3−2+2−3−2−2	527
+3+3−2+2−3−3	9, 1550d
+3+3−2+2−4	591a
+3+3−2+3−2	958f, 1193
+3+3−2+3−2−2+2	818a
+3+3−2+3−2−2−2	958b:B, 1020b
+3+3−2+3−2−3+2	298
+3+3−2−2	1071:B, 1150b, 1515d:B, 1541:D, 1601b:B, 1619b:B
+3+3−2−2+2−3	714:B
+3+3−2−2+3	1184; Parry 50
+3+3−2−2+3−2	Parry 27c
+3+3−2−2+3−3+2	455b
+3+3−2−2−2	114, 1102d:B

Thematic Index of the Tabulated Melodies

Interval Sequence	Melody No.
+3+3−2−2−2+2+2	1444a
+3+3−2−2−2+2+3	Parry 12b
+3+3−2−2−2−2	855a, 1768
+3+3−2−2−2−2+2	325b, 983z:B, 983ee:B
+3+3−2−2−3	72b, 1515d, 1548:B
+3+3−2−2−3+2+3	1847
+3+3−2−2−3+4	983b
+3+3−2−3	892a:C, 1479d
+3+3−2−3+2	1316
+3+3−2−3+2+2	384c, 983f
+3+3−2−3+2+2+2	1716:B
+3+3−2−3+2−2−2	325a, 1229a:C, 1763:B
+3+3−2−3+2−3	Parry 39a
+3+3−2−3+3−2−3	917
+3+3−2−3+4−2	734b
+3+3−2−3+5−2−3	265k:B
+3+3−2−3−2	1164:D, 1240:C
+3+3−2−3−2+3+3	869
+3+3−3	1082, 1750a, 1750c
+3+3−3+2−2	790a
+3+3−3+2−2−2+2	877a
+3+3−3+2−3	877b
+3+3−3+2−3+2	1183
+3+3−3+2−3+2−3	932b
+3+3−3+3+2−2−3	483, 1546b
+3+3−3+3+2−3	1246l
+3+3−3+3−2+2−3	297b
+3+3−3+3−2−2	790b
+3+3−3+3−2−2+3	979
+3+3−3+3−2−2−3	492c
+3+3−3+3−2−3+2	1451
+3+3−3+3−3+2−2	370
+3+3−3+3−3+2−3	530b
+3+3−3+3−3−2−2	189:B
+3+3−3+3−4	1234:B
+3+3−3−2	983ii:B, 1795a:D, 1795b:D, 1804a:D; Parry 39a:B

Thematic Index of the Tabulated Melodies

Interval Sequence	Melody No.
+3+3−3−2+2−3	932a:B
+3+3−3−2−3+4−3	1203a:C
+3+3−3−3	119a, 119b, 119c, 1100
+3+3−3−3+2+2+2	1832b
+3+3−3−3+2+2+3	1655b
+3+3−3−3+3+3−3	581
+3+3−3−3−2+2+3	384a:B
+3+3−4	43e
+3+3−4+3	983u
+3+3−4+3−2	1619d:B
+3+3−4+3−2−2	856:C
+3+3−4+5	1592b:B
+3+3−4−2+2−2+2	1021b:B
+3+3−5+2	699:B, 1795c:D
+3+3−5+3+3	1765:B
+3+3−5+3+3+2−4	1765
+3+4−2−2	1124a
+3+4−2−2−2−2	833b
+3+4−2−2−3−2	1234:C
+3+4−3−2−3	1166b
+3+5−3−3	1778a:B
+3+5−4−2	1619f:B
+3−2	38, 479b:B, 479e:B, 751:B, 808:C, 816, 868a:B, 993a, 1002d:B, 1006a:B, 1006b:B, 1021c:B, 1056, 1124c, 1481a:C, 1486, 1569a:B, 1584c, 1589a, 1615
+3−2+2	502, 733, 866, 889:B, 905b:B, 1260:B, 1506e, 1862:B
+3−2+2+2	825
+3−2+2+2−2+2+2	1764a, 1764c
+3−2+2+2−2−2+2	261c, 323a, 401b
+3−2+2+2−2−3+3	844:B
+3−2+2+2−3	1211
+3−2+2+2−3+3−2	999a:C
+3−2+2+2−3−2	1821
+3−2+2+2−4	8
+3−2+2+3−4	518

Thematic Index of the Tabulated Melodies

Interval Sequence	Melody No.
+3−2+2+3−4+3	242
+3−2+2−2	778c, 808, 1869
+3−2+2−2+2+2	1563c
+3−2+2−2−2	485a, 491:B, 815a, 815e, 1181a:B, 1542
+3−2+2−2−2+3−2	347
+3−2+2−2−2−3+3	1767b:C
+3−2+2−2−3	909:B
+3−2+2−2−3+2−2	1018a
+3−2+2−2−4	1665
+3−2+2−2−4+2	1310d:B
+3−2+2−3	485a:B, 707:B, 954d, 1050, 1227, 1484c:B
+3−2+2−3+2−2+2	443a:B
+3−2+2−3+2−2−2	361–362:B
+3−2+2−3+2−3−2	123b, 1634
+3−2+2−3+3−2	464
+3−2+2−3+3−2+2	5
+3−2+2−3+3−2−2	1755:C
+3−2+2−3+3−3	479b, 479c, 479e; Parry 4:B
+3−2+2−3+5−2	654:B
+3−2+2−3−2	175, 183h, 488a:B, 627:B, 629, 1227:B, 1573a, 1760:B
+3−2+2−3−2+2	996
+3−2+2−3−2+2+2	841b:B
+3−2+2−3−2+2+2+3	838b:B, 841a
+3−2+2−3−2+4−2	848a:B
+3−2+2−3−3	1828:C
+3−2+2−3−3+2	954d:C
+3−2+2−3−3+2+4	1892:C
+3−2+2−4	904b:B, 1483e:B
+3−2+2−4+2	232b:B, 708e:B, 973:B
+3−2+2−5+2	270e:B
+3−2+3	978:B, 1506c, 1506d
+3−2+3−2	830, 853a, 853b, 853c, 853d, 853e, 853f, 874
+3−2+3−2+2−3−3	1870
+3−2+3−2−2−2	303c
+3−2+3−2−2−2−2	1764e:B

Thematic Index of the Tabulated Melodies

Interval Sequence	Melody No.
+3−2+3−2−3	1655e
+3−2+3−2−3+3−2	1391:B
+3−2+3−2−5	1743
+3−2+3−3+4−3	1001j
+3−2+3−3−2+4	1285e:B
+3−2+3−4+2+3−2	479h
+3−2+3−5+3−2	930d:C
+3−2+4+2+3−3−3	710
+3−2+4−2	1001d
+3−2+4−2+2−3−2	265k
+3−2+4−2−2−2	593b, 593c
+3−2+4−2−2−2−2	1058a:C
+3−2+4−2−3+4−2	445a
+3−2+4−5+4−2	1285h:B
+3−2−2	96:B, 140, 146c:B, 185c, 261b, 660b, 721e, 775b:B, 821:C, 861a:B, 868c:B, 964, 1000a, 1043:B, 1072a, 1089a:C, 1100:B, 1150f, 1168d:B, 1230a:C, 1399l, 1526b:B, 1568a:C, 1602b:B, 1658b, 1688, 1696a:B, 1696c:B
+3−2−2+2	228:B, 999c, 1002e, 1676a:B, 1753a, 1753b; Parry 46:B
+3−2−2+2+2+3−2	1766:C
+3−2−2+2+2−2+2	305j
+3−2−2+2+2−2−2	1327f:B, 1422
+3−2−2+2+2−2−3	422b
+3−2−2+2+2−3	479a
+3−2−2+2+3	1484a:B
+3−2−2+2+4	1582a:B
+3−2−2+2−2	132f:B, 211d:B, 214e:B, 926:C, 1500:C, 1563e
+3−2−2+2−2+2	455a:B
+3−2−2+2−2+2−2	1849
+2−2−2+2−2+3−2	305d, 835f:C, 1432b:C
+3−2−2+2−2−2	95b:B, 1051–1052, 1209a, 1241:B, 1416a:B, 1416b
+3−2−2+2−2−2+2	534a
+3−2−2+2−2−2−2	186b:B, 630:B
+3−2−2+2−2−2−3	617:B
+3−2−2+2−2−3	1313e
+3−2−2+2−3	79a, 183a:B, 1191:C; Parry 25

Thematic Index of the Tabulated Melodies

Interval Sequence	Melody No.
+3−2−2+2−3+2−3	654bis-b:C
+3−2−2+2−3−2	682, 1619b
+3−2−2+2−5	1645:B
+3−2−2+3	962b, 1057a:C
+3−2−2+3+2+2	1545h
+3−2−2+3+2+2+2	1810
+3−2−2+3+2−2	1645
+3−2−2+3+2−2−3	134b, 331
+3−2−2+3+2−3+2	341, 446b, 1022a
+3−2−2+3+3	798, 1545g
+3−2−2+3+3−2	925b, 1545f
+3−2−2+3+3−2+2	976b
+3−2−2+3+3−2−2	800b
+3−2−2+3+3−3−2	1386:B
+3−2−2+3−2	33, 233, 276b, 515, 745, 863, 896:B, 937, 1469c, 1469d, 1545e, 1573b, 1813–1814
+3−2−2+3−2+2−2	421b
+3−2−2+3−2−2	115b, 123n, 123t, 305k, 479d, 534b, 722–723:B, 778d, 779a, 861b:B, 1325d, 1513c, 1561a, 1587a
+3−2−2+3−2−2+2	868a
+3−2−2+3−2−2+3	1730:C
+3−2−2+3−2−2−2	312a:B, 349b, 834a, 868b, 995:C
+3−2−2+3−2−2−4	1696d:B
+3−2−2+3−2−3+2	427
+3−2−2+3−2−4+3	422a
+3−2−2+3−3	210b, 623b, 877a
+3−2−2+3−3+2−3	913
+3−2−2+3−3+3	1388d:B
+3−2−2+3−3+3−2	1451:B
+3−2−2+3−3−2+2	878a:B
+3−2−2+3−4	277
+3−2−2+4	788f:B
+3−2−2+4−2	243l, 1563a, 1797:C
+3−2−2+4−2−2	1271f
+3−2−2+4−2−2−2	123cc, 889
+3−2−2+4−3	708c:B, 1602d:D
+3−2−2+4−3−2	749b

Thematic Index of the Tabulated Melodies

Interval Sequence	Melody No.
+3−2−2+5+2−2	1545a
+3−2−2+5−2+2+4	1783
+3−2−2−2	206c:B, 488b:B, 868b:C, 883a:B, 896:C, 925d:B, 930a:B, 930c:B, 956, 983kk:B, 1010b:B, 1026e:B, 1054b:C, 1168a:B, 1219:B, 1231, 1310u, 1325b:B, 1414:B, 1469a, 1479e, 1531a:C, 1531d:C, 1531e:C, 1549, 1588a:C, 1588b:C, 1591c:D, 1607b:D, 1607c:D, 1626c:D, 1655b:C, 1665:B, 1720a:C, 1801:C, 1864
+3−2−2−2+2	284
+3−2−2−2+2+2−2	829:B, 1028–1029
+3−2−2−2+2+3	1330d
+3−2−2−2+2+3−2	1285b:B, 1353b:B
+3−2−2−2+2−2	1856
+3−2−2−2+2−3	893:B, 1484c
+3−2−2−2+3+2−3	835h
+3−2−2−2+3−2−2	232f:B, 1652; Parry 17
+3−2−2−2+4−3	130e
+3−2−2−2+4−4+2	1310i:B
+3−2−2−2−2	39e:B, 43e:B, 188, 668:C, 768–769:B, 994:C, 1190, 1481b:D, 1696a:D, 1696b:B, 1718:C
+3−2−2−2−2+2	1626b:D, 1658f:C
+3−2−2−2−2+2+2	648b:B, 1323
+3−2−2−2−2+2−2	316, 1725
+3−2−2−2−2+3+3	1767a:C
+3−2−2−2−2+4−2	1788:B
+3−2−2−2−2−2	1327b:B, 1327d:B
+3−2−2−2−2−2+4	1720b:B
+3−2−2−2−3	1130:C
+3−2−2−2−4+4	1310i
+3−2−2−3	623a:C, 1065:B, 1098b, 1483f:D, 1515b:C, 1651b
+3−2−2−3+2	272:B, 1107b:C
+3−2−2−3+2+2	440a
+3−2−2−3+2+2+2	440b
+3−2−2−3+2+2−3	1322
+3−2−2−3+2+3−2	1358c
+3−2−2−3+2−2	1292b:B
+3−2−2−3+2−3−2	1280g

Thematic Index of the Tabulated Melodies

Interval Sequence	Melody No.
+3−2−2−3+3+2+3	724d:B
+3−2−2−3+3+3−2	852bis:B
+3−2−2−3+3−2	127:B
+3−2−2−3+3−2+2	565
+3−2−2−3−2	54
+3−2−2−3−2+3−2	689a:B
+3−2−2−3−2+4−2	1027a:B
+3−2−2−3−2−2+2	1354b
+3−2−2−4	1387:D, 1531d, 1531e, 1787
+3−2−2−4+4+2	250
+3−2−2−4+9−2	249
+3−2−3	43a, 642:B, 677:C, 679d:B, 875a:C, 879:B, 925b:B, 999c:B, 1002e:B, 1076:B, 1089b:C, 1165a, 1368:B, 1394, 1491:C, 1506d:C, 1549:B, 1658a:B, 1664c, 1701:C, 1787:C; Parry 38
+3−2−3+2	207:B, 1054c:C, 1086:B, 1375:D, 1384b:C, 1487:C
+3−2−3+2+2	1112
+3−2−3+2+2−2	111:B
+3−2−3+2+2−2−2	1000a:C
+3−2−3+2+3	62
+3−2−3+2+3−2+2	320a:B
+3−2−3+2+3−2−3	354:B, 390b, 460, 1298a:B
+3−2−3+2+3−4+3	1034–1035:B
+3−2−3+2+4	1792:B
+3−2−3+2−2+2−2	1792:C
+3−2−3+2−2+2−3	734a
+3−2−3+2−2−2+2	28
+3−2−3+2−2−2−3	396b:B
+3−2−3+2−3	955
+3−2−3+2−3	1744a:B
+3−2−3+2−3+2	1018b
+3−2−3+2−3−2+2	335d:B
+3−2−3+2−3−3+2	712:B
+3−2−3+2−4	1384b, 1436
+3−2−3+3	1506c:C, 1521b
+3−2−3+3−2	862

Thematic Index of the Tabulated Melodies

Interval Sequence	Melody No.
+3−2−3+3−2+3−2	1715:B
+3−2−3+3−3	1560:D
+3−2−3+3−3+2−2	121:B
+3−2−3+4	1083:B
+3−2−3+4−2+2−2	1366:B
+3−2−3+4−2−2	654bis-b:B, 1006a:C
+3−2−3+4−2−2−2	999b:C
+3−2−3+4−3−2	1024c:B
+3−2−3+5−2+2−2	1774:C
+3−2−3−2	1024b:B, 1808:D, 1817:C; Parry 45
+3−2−3−2+2	324:B, 1079c:C, 1483e:D
+3−2−3−3+6−2−2	1636:B
+3−2−4	665b, 1098a
+3−2−4+2	123ff:B, 1087b:C, 1524:D, 1532h:D
+3−2−4+2+4−4	399:B
+3−2−4+3−2−2	1759
+3−2−4+4−2−3+2	267a
+3−2−5+2+2+2−3	1490b:B
+3−2−5+4+3−2−5	1523
+3−2−5+4−2−3+2	161
+3−3	47b, 165i, 480c:B, 688:B, 788c:B, 809:B, 895:B, 916:C, 1030a, 1097b, 1099, 1139c, 1168e:B, 1191, 1468c:B, 1479a, 1501:B, 1650, 1797:B
+3−3+2	92, 905e:B, 1257:C
+3−3+2+2+3−2	Parry 3
+3−3+2+2−2−2	999a, 1215:B
+3−3+2+2−2−2−2	1318:B
+3−3+2+2−3	973a
+3−3+2+2−3+2+2	439b
+3−3+2+2−3+3−3	1821:C
+3−3+2+3	1776
+3−3+2+3+2−2−3	567a
+3−3+2+3−2−2	1263
+3−3+2+3−3	493
+3−3+2+4	1058b:C, 1087b:B
+3−3+2+4−3+3−4	238

Thematic Index of the Tabulated Melodies

Interval Sequence	Melody No.
+3−3+2−2	102:B, 116:B, 130c, 508:B, 669:B, 755i, 790a:B, 790c, 1072b, 1072c, 1072d, 1541, 1602c:B, 1777:B, 1789d:B, 1789f:B, 1797:B
+3−3+2−2+2	516a:B
+3−3+2−2+2−2	402a:B
+3−3+2−2+2−2−2	1420:B
+3−3+2−2+3−2−2	1033b:B
+3−3+2−2+3−3	1286:B
+3−3+2−2+3−3+2	192, 542, 835f:B
+3−3+2−2−2	891a:B, 891b:B, 1209c
+3−3+2−2−2+2	1484b
+3−3+2−2−2+2+2	1412:B
+3−3+2−2−2+4	1385b:B
+3−3+2−2−2−2	815b
+3−3+2−2−2−2+2	1447c:B
+3−3+2−3+2	691b
+3−3+2−3+2+3−3	1687:B
+3−3+2−3+2+4−2	854b:B
+3−3+2−3+2−2	309b
+3−3+2−3+3−3	253:B
+3−3+2−3+3−3+2	838a:B
+3−3+2−3+4−2−2	1279b:B
+3−3+2−3−2+3−2	912
+3−3+2−4+3	1114
+3−3+3	763, 1511b, 1602d
+3−3+3+2	505
+3−3+3+2+2−2−2	401a
+3−3+3+2−2	186a, 1827
+3−3+3+2−2−2	1339b
+3−3+3+2−2−3	1678:C
+3−3+3+2−3	132a
+3−3+3+2−3+2−2	833g
+3−3+3+3	1478
+3−3+3+3−2−2−2	1339a
+3−3+3+3−2−3+2	1757:C
+3−3+3+3−3−2	345

Thematic Index of the Tabulated Melodies

Interval Sequence	Melody No.
+3−3+3+3−4+3−3	1700c
+3−3+3+4−3−2−2	1537a
+3−3+3+4−3−3	265d:B
+3−3+3−2	791b, 1433, 1700e
+3−3+3−2−2	350, 528c, 528d
+3−3+3−2−2−2	650:B
+3−3+3−2−3	905b
+3−3+3−2−3+2	930d:B, 1182a, 1182b, 1475
+3−3+3−2−3+2+3	1845, 1892
+3−3+3−2−3+3−3	1700b:B
+3−3+3−2−3−2	1560:C
+3−3+3−3	48a, 75b, 1246j, 1510, 1586e
+3−3+3−3+2	1104
+3−3+3−3+2+2+2	439a
+3−3+3−3+2+3	1360:B
+3−3+3−3+2−2−2	408
+3−3+3−3+3−2	210c
+3−3+3−3+3−2−2	538a
+3−3+3−3−2	270f:B
+3−3+3−3−2+2	105
+3−3+3−3−2+3−2	305c
+3−3+3−3−2−2+4	397
+3−3+3−4	1094g
+3−3+4	788a:B
+3−3+4−2+2−3+2	1013
+3−3+4−2+4−2−2	1696c:D
+3−3+4−2−2−2	183g:B
+3−3+4−2−2−3+2	290a
+3−3+4−2−3	354, 592a
+3−2+4−3	741:C
+3−3+4−3+3−3+2	546
+3−3+4−3+3−4+2	265a
+3−3+4−3−2	1187
+3−3+4−3−2+3−2	265b, 265c
+3−3+4−4+2−2−3	275:B
+3−3+4−4+3	741

Thematic Index of the Tabulated Melodies

Interval Sequence	Melody No.
+3−3+5	1531b:B
+3−3+5+2−3	1748–1749:C
+3−3+5+2−3+3−2	408:B
+3−3−2	758b:B, 905g:B, 939:B, 1123:B, 1283c:B, 1403b:C, 1506c:B, 1506d:B, 1640b:B, 1707a:C
+3−3−2+2	931:B, 1522:B
+3−3−2+2+3−3−2	1729:B
+3−3−2+2−2−2+2	1684:B
+3−3−2+2−3	695, 1243a, 1243b, 1243c
+3−3−2+2−3+2	Parry 13:B
+3−3−2+2−4−2+2	1276:C
+3−3−2+3+4	1283c:C
+3−3−2+3−2	1793:C
+3−3−2+3−2−3−2	930b
+3−3−2+3−3	1567b
+3−3−2+3−5	1531a, 1531b
+3−3−2+4	1585a:B
+3−3−2+4−3−2	224:B
+3−3−2+4−6	1216bis:B
+3−3−2−2	Parry 35, 36:C
+3−3−2−2+3+3−3	1324c:B
+3−3−2−2+3−2	876
+3−3−2−2−2+2	637:B
+3−3−2−2−3	952, 1313c
+3−3−2−3	813:B, 1061:B, 1554:B
+3−3−2−3+2+2+2	1682:B
+3−3−2−3+3−2−2	962a:B
+3−3−2−3−3	1493c:C
+3−3−2−4+2	942a
+3−3−3	1367b, 1796
+3−3−3+2	892c:C, 1054a:C
+3−3−3+2+3−2−4	457:B
+3−3−3+2−2	1545h:B
+3−3−3+4−2−2+3	1008:C
+3−3+4−2−4+4	424d:B
+3−3−3+4−2−4+5	424a:B

Thematic Index of the Tabulated Melodies

Interval Sequence	Melody No.
+3−3−3−3	1247c
+3−3−3−3+5−5+2	828
+3−3−4+4−2−3−2	196c:B
+3−3−5+6+2−3	600
+3−4	74, 1047b:B, 1047c:B, 1299, 1592b:D, 1627:C
+3−4+2	558–559:B, 749b:C
+3−4+2+2−2−2+2	999c:C, 1002e:C
+3−4+2+2−4+2	755k
+3−4+2+3	101
+3−4+2+3−2−2−2	309a; Parry 27b:B
+3−4+2+3−4	1025b
+3−4+2+4	762:B
+3−4+2−2	137:B, 577b:B
+3−4+2−2−2−2	1327c:B
+3−4+2−4+2+4−4	1292c:B
+3−4+3+2−3+2−3	1758:B
+3−4+3−2+2−2−2	907
+3−4+3−2−3−2	930d
+3−4+3−4+3−2	1193:B
+3−4+4−2	1047b
+3−4−2+2	835g:C, 1077b:B
+3−4−2+3+3−2	925c
+3−4−2+3−2	1197a:B, 1413:B
+3−4−3	1299:C
+3−4−3+2−2+2+2	655b:C, 655c:C
+3−4−3+2−3+2+3	1683:B
+3−4−3+2−3+4−2	280a:B
+3−4−4+2	1602h:B
+3−5+2	1369:D, 1531b:C
+3−5+2+2	1513c:B
+3−5+2+2+2−2−2	1236
+3−5+3+2−3+2−2	447
+3−5+3+3−5	1673a:B, 1673b:B
+3−5−3+5−2−3+3	300:B
+3−6+3+3−2−2−2	1650:B
+3−6+5−2−2	37

Thematic Index of the Tabulated Melodies

Interval Sequence	Melody No.
+3−7+3+2	1531c:C
−3	39a:B, 39d:B, 635:C, 638a:C, 661b:C, 664b, 1195b, 1479b, 1494b:C, 1535:B, 1640c, 1672c:C
−3+2	1002g:B, 1085b, 1090:C, 1147, 1469a:B, 1476:D, 1505b:B, 1584f:B, 1607a:D, 1744b:C, 1863a
−3+2+2	73a, 1085a, 1273c:B, 1799
−3+2+2+2+2	910:B
−3+2+2+2−2+2−2	1282
−3+2+2+2−2−3−2	971b:B
−3+2+2+2−2−4+2	1700d
−3+2+2+2−3	1105a
−3+2+2+2−3+2−3	544a, 544b, 544c, 544g
−3+2+2+2−3−2−2	1702a:B
−3+2+2−2	1396a:C
−3+2+2−2+2−2−2	238:B
−3+2+2−2+2−3−3	989d
−3+2+2−2+3−3+2	573a
−3+2+2−2−2	143a
−3+2+2−2−2+2	1693c
−3+2+2−2−2+2+2	1709:B
−3+2+2−2−3	875a:B
−3+2+2−2−4+2	709a:B
−3+2+2−3	143c, 1213, 1472bis, 1540b, 1540g, 1642
−3+2+2−3+2	123p, 154:B, 1437, 1447a:B, 1564
−3+2+2−3+2+2−2	1839
−3+2+2−3+2−3	148a, 880a
−3+2+2−3+2−3+2	529d
−3+2+2−3+3	1600:B
−3+2+2−3−2	1329a
−3+2+2−3−2+2+3	1621
−3+2+2−3−2+2−2	Parry 25:B
−3+2+2−3−2+4−2	204
−3+2+2−3−2+6−2	856:B
−3+2+2−3−3	660a:B
−3+2+2−4+2+4−2	708b
−3+2+2−4+2−3	1770:D
−3+2+3	1078:B, 1570c:B, 1570h:B

Thematic Index of the Tabulated Melodies

Interval Sequence	Melody No.
−3+2+3+2	764a:B
−3+2+3+2−2+2−2	1863c
−3+2+3+2−2+2−4	434
−3+2+3+2−2−3	938b
−3+2+3+2−3−2	119g
−3+2+3−2	1177, 1181b, 1246h:B, 1255d:B, 1540c:B, 1540d:B, 1540g:B, 1572:B
−3+2+3−2−2	755h
−3+2+3−2−2+2−3	943
−3+2+3−2−2−2	557:B, 1381b, 1381c
−3+2+3−2−2−3	1490c
−3+2+3−2−2−3−2	1577b
−3+2+3−2−3	Parry 23a:C, 23b:C
−3+2+3−3+2−2	216e
−3+2+3−3+2−2−3	394b
−3+2+3−3−2	1413:C
−3+2+3−4+2−2	812b:B
−3+2+4−2+2−3−2	293
−3+2+4−2−2−2+4	965:B
−3+2+4−3+2−3+2	216f
−3+2−2	79d, 130a:B, 134b:B, 283a:B, 498:B, 662a:B, 733:B, 737:B, 770d:B, 779c:B, 780b:B, 1056:B, 1069, 1073a:B, 1073b:B, 1121:C, 1247b:C, 1330d:C, 1498a:B, 1498b:B, 1515c:C, 1556a:B, 1576d:C, 1641, 1789e:B, 1798
−3+2−2+2	766b:B, 1181a
−3+2−2+2+2−2−2	1447b, 1764e
−3+2−2+2−2	165d:B, 347:B, 404a
−3+2−2+2−2+3−3	547a
−3+2−2+2−2−2	311c
−3+2−3+2−3+2	237b, 691a
−3+2−2+2−3+4−2	835d:B
−3+2−2+3	802c:B, 807:B, 1781:B
−3+2−2+3+2−3	1755:B
−3+2−2+3−2+3−3	133
−3+2−2+3−3	477, 1643–1644
−3+2−2+3−3+2−2	158c:B, 169:B, 336, 453b, 466, 682:B, 1026a, 1033e, 1044

Thematic Index of the Tabulated Melodies

Interval Sequence	Melody No.
−3+2−2+3−3+3−2	504
−3+2−2+3−4+2	634:B
−3+2−2+4	792a:B
−3+2−2+4−2	625
−3+2−2+4−3	824:C
−3+2−2−2	77d, 123j:B, 660a:C, 744:B, 924:B, 1532m:B, 1693b:D
−3+2−2−2+2	776c:B, 778a, 1498b
−3+2−2−2+2+3−3	1012:B
−3+2−2−2+2−2	168e, 402e
−3+2−2−2+2−2−2	566a
−3+2−2−2+3−2−2	30, 456
−3+2−2−2+3−3	122c
−3+2−2−2+4−2−2	1686
−3+2−2−2+4−3	445c:B
−3+2−2−2+4−3+2	1026a:B, 1852
−3+2−2−2−2	802d, 1001e:B, 1171c, 1206a, 1417b:B
−3+2−2−2−2+2	766a, 983m:B
−3+2−2−2−2+2−2	713a:B
−3+2−2−3	804a:B, 1212a:C, 1301a:B
−3+2−2−3+2	60b, 513c:B, 972
−3+2−2−3+2+2	472c
−3+2−2−3+2+3−2	1796
−3+2−2−3+5−2+2	394b:B
−3+2−3	58:B, 1057a, 1152, 1440a, 1463, 1464:B, 1506f:C, 1586c:C, 1586b:C, 1586d:C
−3+2−3+2	376b:B, 670, 753a:B, 755j:B, 961a, 1183:B, 1532h:B, 1557a:C, 1612:B
−3+2−3+2+2	76, 1564:B
−3+2−3+2+2+2−4	121
−3+2−3+2+2−2−2	831:B, 1026d, 1237:B
−3+2−3+2+2−3+2	448i
−3+2−3+2+3	669
−3+2−3+2+3−4	563b:B
−3+2−3+2+4−2	243b
−3+2−3+2+4−4	1305d:B
−3+2−3+2−2	436:B

Thematic Index of the Tabulated Melodies

Interval Sequence	Melody No.
−3+2−3+2−2+2	170
−3+2−3+2−2+3−2	820
−3+2−3+2−2−2	513b:B
−3+2−3+2−3	1119:B
−3+2−3+2−3+2+2	335b, 905c
−3+2−3+2−3+2+3	905d
−3+2−3+2−3+2−2	923
−3+2−3+2−4	103:B
−3+2−3+3	378
−3+2−3+3+3+2−3	496b
−3+2−3+3+3−2+2	335a
−3+2−3+3−2	483:B
−3+2−3+3−2−2−2	1576b, 1893
−3+2−3+3−2−3+2	177a:B
−3+2−3+3−3+3	1719a:B
−3+2−3+4	643:B
−3+2−3+4−2	793:B
−3+2−3+4−2−2−2	261b:B, 1690c
−3+2−3+4−3+2	1357b:B
−3+2−3+4−3+2−2	529b, 535b, 573b
−3+2−3+4−3+2−3	529a, 529c, 970:B, 1695:B, 1828:B
−3+2−3+4−3−2	905a
−3+2−3+4−3−2−2	390a
−3+2−3+5−2−2−3	1820:C
−3+2−3+6+3−3−3	344b:B
−3+2−3+6−2+4−3	344c:B
−3+2−3−2	72a:B, 481b, 1107a:B
−3+2−3−2+2	64a:B, 64c:B, 1163e:B
−3+2−3−2+2+2	1273d:B
−3+2−3−2+2+2−2	1036d:B
−3+2−3−2+2−2−2	1589e:C
−3+2−3−2+3+2−4	1030d
−3+2−3−3−2	958e:B
−3+2−3−3−2−2	1809b:B
−3+2−4	1202:B
−3+2−4+2+2+2−4	454b

Thematic Index of the Tabulated Melodies

Interval Sequence	Melody No.
−3+2−4+2+3−2−2	941:B
−3+2−4+3	1532k:B
−3+2−4+3+2−3	810b:B
−3+2−4+3−2	983i:B, 983j:B
−3+2−4+4−4+2	555a:B
−3+3	69, 749a:B, 755g:B
−3+3+2+2−3	1827:B
−3+3+2+2−3+2−3	714:B
−3+3+2−2	684c, 1094j, 1675a
−3+3+2−2+2−2−2	569
−3+3+2−2−2	327b
−3+3+2−2−2+2−3	379a
−3+3+2−2−2−2	308; Parry 26
−3+3+2−2−2−2+3	377a
−3+3+2−2−2−2−2	1702b:B
−3+3+2−2−2−3	1707b, 1788
−3+3+2−2−3+3−3	289b
−3+3+2−2−3+4−2	852b
−3+3+2−2−4+2	2
−3+3+2−3	822
−3+3+2−3+2	157a
−3+3+2−4	158e:B, 1500
−3+3+2−4+2	983s:B
−3+3+3	1586c:B
−3+3+3+2−2−5+3	1861
−3+3+3−2	Parry 30:B
−3+3+3−2+2−4+3	1002f
−3+3+3−2−2−3+2	289a, 1385a:B
−3+3+3−2−3	999a:B
−3+3+3−2−3	999b:B
−3+3+3−2−3+2−2	152a:B
−3+3+3−3−3+2	858:C
−3+3+3−4+4	937:B
−3+3+3−5+2+5	1809b
−3+3+4−2−2−2−2	1331
−3+3+4−3−2+2−3	259

Thematic Index of the Tabulated Melodies

Interval Sequence	Melody No.
−3+3−2	56b, 327a, 1468a:B, 1506d:D, 1555a:B, 1571c:C, 1709:C, 1762:C
−3+3−2+2	151a
−3+3−2+2+3−2−2	903:B
−3+3−2+2−2	739b
−3+3−2+2−3	109, 512:B, 548
−3+3−2+2−3+2−2	349c, 871
−3+3−2+2−3+3−2	1754
−3+3−2+3−3+3−2	1558c
−3+3−2−2	36c:B, 87, 123k:B, 661b, 788i:B, 806:B, 1026e, 1170:B, 1515h:C, 1532l:B, 1540e
−3+3−2−2+2	134h
−3+3−2−2+2−3	983k:B
−3+3−2−2+3+2−4	1030c
−3+3−2−2+3−2−2	1418
−3+3−2−2−2	200c:B, 200d:B, 200g:B, 214c:B, 833f, 1021a:B, 1230b:B, 1281a:B, 1602a:C
−3+3−2−2−2+2+3	24b
−3+3−2−2−2+5−2	1094b
−3+3−2−2−2−2	481a, 1198–1199:B
−3+3−2−3	1787:B
−3+3−2−3+3	1679c:B, 1753a:C, 1753e:C
−3+3−2−3+3−2−3	1424:B
−3+3−2−4+2	64b:B, 983ll:B
−3+3−3	47c, 123y:B, 149–150:B, 185b, 755c, 755l, 997, 1122:B, 1149a, 1156a, 1466c, 1502c:B, 1540h, 1570e, 1608a, 1782, 1790:B; Parry 21a:B, 41:D, 42:D
−3+3−3+2	1643–1644:B
−3+3−3+2+2−2	210c:B
−3+3−3+2+2−3+2	1855
−3+3−3+2+3	1094d
−3+3−3+2+3+2−3	1858
−3+3−3+2−2	503b, 667:B, 892c; Parry 10a
−3+3−3+2−2+2	1539
−3+3−3+2−2+2+2	1764d, 1843
−3+3−3+2−3	43b
−3+3−3+2−3+2	130g, 1411

Thematic Index of the Tabulated Melodies

Interval Sequence	Melody No.
−3+3−3+2−3+2+3	989c
−3+3−3+3	1489
−3+3−3+3+2+2	97
−3+3−3+3+2+2−2	577b
−3+3−3+3−3	123v:B
−3+3−3+3−3+3−3	263a, 263b, 443b, 833d:B, 969
−3+3−3+3−3+3−4	415, 598
−3+3−3+3−3−2	43c
−3+3−3+4+2−2	134l
−3+3−3+5−5−3	1203a:B
−3+3−3−2	263c, 275, 582, 584d
−3+3−3−2+2	47a, 134i:B
−3+3−3−2+2+2−3	835a
−3+3−3−2+2−2	652a:B
−3+3−3−2+2−2+2	404b
−3+3−3−2−2	788e
−3+3−3−3+2	1265:B
−3+3−3−3+2+2	84
−3+3−3−3+2−2−2	1039c:B, 1039e:B
−3+3−3−3+3	1369:C
−3+3−3−3+4−2−3	1039f:B
−3+3−3−4+4−2−2	1039b:B
−3+3−3−4+4−2−4	1039a:B
−3+3−4+2	541
−3+3−4+2+4−2−2	1036b:B, 1036c:B
−3+3−4+2−2	520:B
−3+3−4+2−2+2	1834a
−3+3−4+2−3+2−3	1822:C
−3+3−4+3−3+2	29
−3+3−4+3−3+2−2	429a:B
−3+3−4+5−2−3−2	1036a:B
−3+3−4−2+3−2−2	1039g:B
−3+3−5+3−3+2+2	195
−3+4	1122
−3+4+2+2−4−3	703
−3+4+2−2	78a

Thematic Index of the Tabulated Melodies

Interval Sequence	Melody No.
−3+4+2−2−2−2+3	1700f
−3+4+2−2−2−3+4	986b
−3+4+2−3−2	492b:B
−3+4+3−4	371
−3+4−2	78b, 1094e, 1149b, 1165c, 1167a, 1167b, 1502d:B, 1576c:B, 1640e; Parry 41:B
−3+4−2+2	206b, 782a:B
−3+4−2+2−3+2+3	654bis-c:C
−3+4−2−2	56a, 782f:B, 1165a:C
−3+4−2−2+2−3+2	983b:B, 1691b
−3+4−2−2−2	504:B, 1102b, 1181b:B, 1374, 1689
−3+4−2−2−2+4−2	983t
−3+4−2−2−2−2+4	567a:B
−3+4−2−2−2−2−2	1841
−3+4−2−2−3	1154:B, 1204:B
−3+4−2−3	623a, 782b:B, 1102a, 1552, 1612
−3+4−2−3+2	983f:B, 1696c
−3+4−2−3+2−3+5	396c
−3+4−2−3+3−3	307
−3+4−2−3+4	1374:B
−3+4−2−3−2	1216
−3+4−2−3−2+2	983t:B
−3+4−2−3−2+3+3	457
−3+4−2−3−2−2+2	370:B
−3+4−2−4+2−2+2	989e
−3+4−2−4+3−2	1239:B
−3+4−2−4−2	1576c
−3+4−3+2−5	1795b:C
−3+4−3−2	1187:B
−3+4−3−2+2	698:C
−3+4−3−2−2	756
−3+4−4	1067:B
−3+4−4+2−3	551:B
−3+4−4+4−2	1592a
−3+4−4+4−4−3	1254b:B
−3+4−5	1596:C

Thematic Index of the Tabulated Melodies

Interval Sequence	Melody No.
−3+5	1149a:B
−3+5−2+2−2−2−2	327c:B
−3+5−2+2−2−3+3	450–451
−3+5−2+2−3+2	206c
−3+5−2+2−3+2−3	1018b:B
−3+5−2+4−2−2−2	1313d
−3+5−2−2−2	1168f:B, 1407:B
−3+5−2−2−2−2+4	593b:B, 593c:B
−3+5−2−2−3	782c:B, 782d:B, 943:B
−3+5−2−3+4−2−3	1031–1032:B
−3+5−2−3−2	782e:B
−3+5−2−4	1126:C
−3+5−3+2−2	1619a:B
−3+5−3+2−2−2−2	194a:B
−3+5−3−2	1715:C
−3+5−3−3	1102c
−3+5−3−3+3	1619c:B
−3+5−3−3+4	1619g:B
−3+6−2+2−3−2	383b
−3+6−2−2	869:B, 1074
−3+6−3+2+2−3−2	321a, 892d
−3+6−3+4−2−2−2	321b
−3+6−3−2−3+2+3	578:B
−3+6−3−2−3+3−3	1785
−3+6−4−2−2+5	698:B
−3−2	740:B, 776d:B, 922:B, 1002a:B, 1057a:B, 1171:D, 1477:B, 1490d:B, 1506c:D, 1514c:C, 1521a:B, 1584e:B, 1586d:D, 1707b:C
−3−2+2	626, 670:B, 1072c:B, 1151:B, 1512a:D, 1558a:B
−3−2+2+2	157c, 1374:C
−3−2+2+2+2−3−2	897b
−3−2+2+2−2	1166a:B, 1705
−3−2+2+2−2−2	652b:B
−3−2+2+2−2−2−2	616a:B
−3−2+2+2−2−3	1628
−3−2+2+2−2−3+5	1076:C
−3−2+2+2−3	1194:C

Thematic Index of the Tabulated Melodies

Interval Sequence	Melody No.
−3−2+2+3+2−2−4	1601a:C
−3−2+2+3−2−2	555b:B
−3−2+2+3−2−2−2	242:B, 488a
−3−2+2+3−2−3	Parry 7:B
−3−2+2+3−3	584e
−3−2+2+3−3+2−3	544d
−3−2+2+3−3−2	158f:B
−3−2+2+3−3−2+2	1303d:B
−3−2+2+3−3−2−2	1347:D, 1516b
−3−2+2−2	119c:B, 1086, 1107a:C
−3−2+2−2+3−4+2	1026c
−3−2+2−2−2	910:C, 1810:D
−3−2+2−3	1234, 1293:B; Parry 34
−3−2+2−3+2−2	247b:B
−3−2+2−3−2+3	1315:B
−3−2+2−3−3+3	177d:B
−3−2+2−3−3+5−2	656a:B
−3−2+2−4	1607b:B
−3−2+3	626:B, 960, 1809a:B
−3−2+3+2	1108
−3−2+3+2+2+2−2	1679a
−3−2+3+2−2−3+2	516b
−3−2+3+2−3−2	473c, 1033a, 1033f
−3−2+3+3−2−3−2	841b
−3−2+3−2	1195a, 1546b:B
−3−2+3−2−2	237c, 489b, 779b:B, 1601b:C
−3−2+3−2−2+2+3	1757:D
−3−2+3−2−3	1169:B
−3−2+3−3	1502a:B
−3−2+3−3+2−2−2	568
−3−2+4	1584a:B, 1584b:B, 1584c:B
−3−2+4+2+3−2+2	251
−3−2+4+3−2+2	796c
−3−2+4+3−2+4	796b
−3−2+4+3−2−3	160b
−3−2+4−2+2+3−2	1780:C

Thematic Index of the Tabulated Melodies

Interval Sequence	Melody No.
−3−2+4−2+2−3−2	313
−3−2+4−2+2−5+2	257
−3−2+4−2−2	130f:B, 130k:B
−3−2+4−2−2−2	1b
−3−2+4−3	123u:B, 754:B
−3−2+4−3+2−2	1a
−3−2+4−3−2	123z:B, 787, 1707a:B
−3−2+4−3−2−2	1033e:B
−3−2+5	1589c:B
−3−2+5+2−2+2−2	1883
−3−2+5+2−2−3	160a
−3−2+5−2−2−2+3	983b:B
−3−2+5−2−2−2−2	833d
−3−2+5−2−3	445b:B, 1246f:B
−3−2+5−2−3−2+2	983c:B
−3−2+6−2	1290:B
−3−2+6−2−2−2−2	112
−3−2+6−3−4	1618d
−3−2+7−2−2−2	1189a:B
−3−2+8−2−2−3	1611b
−3−2+8−3−3	1611a
−3−2−2	920–921:C, 1002c:B, 1247a, 1247b, 1366:C, 1525:C, 1532j:B, 1582a:C, 1693a:D
−3−2−2+2	664b:B, 1306d:B
−3−2−2+2+3−3−2	830:B
−3−2−2+2−2	1001f:B, 1556b:B
−3−2−2+2−2+5−4	1001f
−3−2−2+2−2−2	525:B
−3−2−2+2−2−2+2	907:B
−3−2−2+2−3	927:B
−3−2−2+3+2−4+2	1030e
−3−2−2+3+3	92:B
−3−2−2+3−2−2	1220:C
−3−2−2+3−4+2	1392a:B
−3−2−2+4−2−2−2	397:B
−3−2−2+5−3−2−2	1024a

Thematic Index of the Tabulated Melodies

Interval Sequence	Melody No.
−3−2−2+6−2−2−3	1620a
−3−2−2−2	186a:B, 674:B, 1259b:B
−3−2−2−2+3+2+2	231a:B
−3−2−2−2−2+2+2	1540d:C
−3−2−2−3	1291:C, 1405:C
−3−2−2−3+4−2	916:B
−3−2−2−4+8+2	506
−3−2−3	499:B
−3−2−3+3+2−2−2	1005c:C
−3−2−3+4−2−2−2	989d:B
−3−2−3+4−2−3−2	1267:C
−3−2−3+8−4+4−3	344d:B
−3−2−4+3	656c:B
−3−3	39b, 789:B, 1058c:D, 1059:B, 1535:D
−3−3+2	474:B, 895:C, 1001h:B, 1057c, 1057d, 1555c:B, 1584d:B, 1673a:C, 1673b:C
−3−3+2+2	95a, 387
−3−3+2+2+2−2−2	964:B
−3−3+2+2+3−3−3	976a
−3−3+2+2+3−4	423b
−3−3+2+2−2	119a:B, 119b:B
−3−3+2+2−2+3−2	1655a
−3−3+2+3	1404a:C
−3−3+2+3−2−2	208a:B
−3−3+2+3−2−2−2	958e:C
−3−3+2+3−2−3+2	738b
−3−3+2−2−2−2	1313f:B
−3−3+2−2−4+2+2	736:B
−3−3+3+2−3	1545d:B
−3−3+3+3	787:B
−3−3+3+3+2−4+3	633:B
−3−3+3+3−2+2−3	898b, 898d, 898e
−3−3+3+3−2−2−2	971b, 983o
−3−3+3+3−2−2−3	897a
−3−3+3+3−2−3−2	898a
−3−3+3+3−3−2	358

Thematic Index of the Tabulated Melodies

Interval Sequence	Melody No.
−3−3+3+3−3−3+2	898c
−3−3+3+3−3−3+3	696a, 696b
−3−3+3+4−2−2	1696a
−3−3+3−2−2	1310k, 1776:C, 1810:B
−3−3+3−2−2−3	1264:C
−3−3+3−3	185a:B, 505:B
−3−3+3−3−3	Parry 36:B
−3−3+4+3−3	1170:D
−3−3+4−2	583
−3−3+4−2−2−2	1659b:C
−3−3+4−2−3	185b:B
−3−3+4−3	1669:C
−3−3+4−3−3	1586a:C, 1586e:C
−3−3+5+3−2−2	699
−3−3+5+4−3−2+4	363
−3−3+5−3	671a
−3−3+5−3+2−3+2	980
−3−3+5−3+3−3−2	365–366d
−3−3+5−3−3	455d:B, 463, 1206b
−3−3+5−4	63:B
−3−3+6−2	1238
−3−3+7−2−2−2	1189c:B
−3−3−3+5	797:B
−3−3−4+2+4+2+2	1679b
−3−3−4+4+2+2	95b
−3−4+3+3	1404b:B
−3−4+3−2	1001j:B
+4	1002h
+4+2+2+2+2	1481b
+4+2+2−2	1405
+4+2+2−2−2	1247a:B
+4+2+2−3+2	1264
+4+2+2−3−4	1247b:B
+4+2+3−3−2+4−3	1831
+4+2+3−3−2−4	1784
+4+2−2	1256

Thematic Index of the Tabulated Melodies

Interval Sequence	Melody No.
+4+2−2+2+2−2	1661
+4+2−2+2−3	742
+4+2−2−2	433e, 1125a, 1515c:B
+4+2−2−2+2−3+2	619, 1084
+4+2−2−2+2−4+2	713e
+4+2−2−2−3	829, 1163b, 1163g, 1515c
+4+2−2−2−3+4	1871
+4+2−2−2−4	622
+4+2−2−2−4+2−2	1421
+4+2−2−3+3+2−2	1332b
+4+2−2−3+3−2−3	819b
+4+2−2−3−2	1243b:B
+4+2−2−4−3+2+2	441:B
+4+2−3+2−2−2−2	695:B
+4+2−3+2−2−3	757, 891a
+4+2−3+2−3	771:B
+4+2−3+2−4+3−3	1515a
+4+2−3−2+2−4+2	605
+4+2−3−2−2	1519a, 1530a, 1530b, 1577b:C, 1624
+4+2−3−2−2+2−2	919
+4+2−3−2−3+4−3	1243c:B
+4+2−4	1027c
+4+2−4+2+2+2	812b
+4+2−4−2	776a
+4+2−5+2	1467a
+4+2−5+2+2−2−5	1492:C
+4+2−5+4+2−2−2	1243a:B
+4+3−2	1510:B
+4+3−2−2	1516a:B
+4+3−2−2−2−4+2	727b
+4+3−2−2−4	930c
+4+3−2−3	1010b, 1125c
+4+3−3	108, 587, 1200
+4+3−3−2−2	1619e:C
+4+3−3−3	1619a
+4+3−4−3	1601b

Thematic Index of the Tabulated Melodies

Interval Sequence	Melody No.
+4+4−2−2−2−4	1335–1336
+4+5−3−3−2	1195c:B
+4+5−4+2	756:B
+4+5−5	1170
+4−2	243f, 590c, 1079b, 1188a, 1319c, 1540h:B, 1569b:B, 1656
+4−2+2	1073a, 1471:B
+4−2+2+2+2+3−2	1223:B
+4−2+2+2+2−2	248
+4−2+2+2+2−2−2	1456
+4−2+2+2−2	983a, 1168g
+4−2+2+2−2−2−2	329, 495
+4−2+2+2−3	709b
+4−2+2+3−5+2	1745–1746
+4−2+2−2	102, 1285g, 1285i, 1285j, 1693b; Parry 21a
+4−2+2−2+2+2	799
+4−2+2−2+2+2−2	1457
+4−2+2−2+2−2	376a, 376b, 1285h
+3−2+2−2+2−2−3	1812:B
+4−2+2−2+2−3	1285a
+4−2+2−2+2−3+2	443a
+4−2+2−2+2−3−2	219b
+4−2+2−2+2−4	1258
+4−2+2−2+3+2−4	700
+4−2+2−2−2	861a, 861b, 1095b, 1653
+4−2+2−2−2+2	928
+4−2+2−2−2+2−2	236
+4−2+2−2−2+2−3	1816:B
+4−2+2−2−2−2	883a, 883b; Parry 6b
+4−2+2−2−2−2+2	1444d
+4−2+2−2−2−2+3	1769
+4−2+2−2−2−3+4	381
+4−2+2−2−3	749a
+4−2+2−2−3−2	123a
+4−2+2−2−3−2+4	1812
+4−2+2−2−4+2+2	564
+4−2+2−3+2+2−2	708e

Thematic Index of the Tabulated Melodies

Interval Sequence	Melody No.
+4−2+2−3+2−2+2	1824:C
+4−2+2−3+2−2−2	310e, 402a, 402b, 402c
+4−2+2−3+2−3	123dd
+4−2+2−3+4−2−2	813
+4−2+2−3+4−3	1285a:B
+4−2+2−3−2	1137, 1505b, 1617:B
+4−2+2−3−2+2+3	385
+4−2+2−3−2+3−2	558–559
+4−2+2−3−2−3	1617:C
+4−2+2−4	692:B, 1593a:B
+4−2+2−4+2−2	Parry 6c
+4−2+2−4+3−3	Parry 6a
+4−2+2−4+4−2	740
+4−2+2−4+5−2−3	1283a
+4−2+3	1670:B
+4−2+3+2−2−3+2	1414
+4−2+3−2	1189c
+4−2+3−2−2	158g, 1619c
+4−2+3−2−2+3−2	433b
+4−2+3−2−2−2	Parry 12d:B
+4−2+3−2−2−2+4	738a
+4−2+3−2−2−2−2	491
+4−2+3−2−2−3	1515f
+4−2+3−2−2−3+2	1016b
+4−2+3−2−4	497:B
+4−2+3−2−4+4−2	725
+4−2+3−3+2−2−2	1338a
+4−2+3−3+2−4	1690a
+4−2+3−3−2+2+2	258
+4−2+3−3−3	781b
+4−2+4−2	1693a
+4−2+4−2−2−2+2	339a
+4−2+4−3+2−3−3	339b
+4−2−2	91, 132d, 211b, 661a:C, 1080, 1124b, 1156a:C, 1188b, 1465, 1479a:B, 1481a:D, 1570d:B, 1572:C, 1577a:B, 1596, 1755bis, 1787:D
+4−2−2+2	180a, 668, 1515a:B

Thematic Index of the Tabulated Melodies

Interval Sequence	Melody No.
+4−2−2+2+2−2−2	435d
+4−2−2+2+3−2−3	214e
+4−2−2+2−2	123z, 165e
+4−2−2+2−2+2−2	838a
+4−2−2+2−2−2+2	1310s
+4−2−2+2−2−2−2	1513b, 1690a:B
+4−2−2+2−2−3−2	1737a:C
+4−2−2+2−3+3−2	610a:B
+4−2−2+2−3+4	106
+4−2−2+2−3−2	1513a
+4−2−2+2−4	44
+4−2−2+3	1470a, 1470b
+4−2−2+3−2−2	612
+4−2−2+3−2−3	520, 761
+4−2−2+3−2−3+3	562
+4−2−2+3−3+2−2	22a
+4−2−2+3−3+3	445e
+4−2−2+4	1490c:B
+4−2−2+4+2−2−2	1017b
+4−2−2+4−2−2−2	609a, 655g:B
+4−2−2+4−4	983j
+4−2−2−2	49a, 52, 82e:B, 146a, 146b, 146c, 306, 831, 884:B, 1062, 1077a:B, 1146, 1163a, 1163d, 1168b:B, 1245b:B, 1262, 1271e, 1280a:B, 1653:B, 1688:C, 1693a:B, 1693b:B, 1738–1739:B
+4−2−2−2+2	155a, 344f, 766b
+4−2−2−2+2+2−2	183i
+4−2−2−2+2−2	36d, 770e
+4−2−2−2+2−2−2	1700a
+4−2−2−2+2−3+2	1428
+4−2−2−2+3−2−2	407a
+4−2−2−2+3−3	667
+4−2−2−2+4−2	375, 648c, 648d
+4−2−2−2+4−2−2	130f, 533a, 1444a:B, 1732:B
+4−2−2−2+4−2−3	449
+4−2−2−2+4−3+2	533b
+4−2−2−2+5	978

Thematic Index of the Tabulated Melodies

Interval Sequence	Melody No.
+4−2−2−2+5−3−2	575
+4−2−2−2−2	492a:B, 748, 821, 1378:B
+4−2−2−2−2+2	1752:B
+4−2−2−2−2+2+2	1540b:C
+4−2−2−2−2+2+3	1347:B
+4−2−2−2−2+2−3	1285b, 1894:C
+4−2−2−2−2−2+3	1608c:C
+4−2−2−2−2−2−2	711d:B
+4−2−2−2−2−2−3	1608b:C
+4−2−2−2−2−3+3	1448a:B
+4−2−2−2−3	1245a:B
+4−2−2−2−3+2	1353b
+4−2−2−2−3+3−2	1700b
+4−2−2−2−4+2−3	1439b:B
+4−2−2−3	82a, 82b, 1559:B
+4−2−2−3+2	622:B
+4−2−2−3+3	1594:B
+4−2−2−3−5+8−2	1337b:B
+4−2−3	135b, 728–729:B, 861a:C, 1163f, 1515g:C, 1532l, 1540b:D
+4−2−3+2	123g, 155b, 756:C, 983e:B, 983jj:B
+4−2−3+2+3−3−2	1819:B
+4−2−3+2+3−4	526b:B
+4−2−3+2−2	1815c
+4−2−3+2−2+4−2	1725:C
+4−2−3+2−2−2−2	1447a
+4−2−3+2−3	595
+4−2−3+3	807
+4−2−3+3+2−2	735
+4−2−3+3+2−2−2	417
+4−2−3+3+2−2−3	1488
+4−2−3+3−2	214a
+4−2−3+3−2−2	489c, 1165a:D
+4−2−3+3−3+2	927
+4−2−3+3−3+2−2	877b:C
+4−2−3+3−3+4	1039b
+4−2−3+4	788g:B, 788h:B, 983e; Parry 23b:B

Thematic Index of the Tabulated Melodies

Interval Sequence	Melody No.
+4−2−3+4+2−2+3	1679c
+4−2−3+4+2−2−2	312b
+4−2−3+4−2	214c, 879, 1469b, 1471
+4−2−3+4−2+2−3	290b, 430b
+4−2−3+4−2+3−2	309c
+4−2−3+4−2−3	484, 754, 983hh
+4−2−3+4−2−3+2	916
+4−2−3+4−2−3+4	555a
+4−2−3+4−3+2−3	901
+4−2−3+4−3+4−2	280c:B
+4−2−3−2+2+2	1540j:C
+4−2−3−2+2+4−2	603b
+4−2−3−2+2−2−2	1338a:B
+4−2−3−4	1560
+4−2−4	467a:B
+4−2−4+2	1547:B
+4−2−4+2+2−2−3	1307
+4−2−4+2+3−4+2	915
+4−2−4+2+4	455b:B, 773b:B; Parry 23a:B
+4−2−4+3−2	82a:B
+4−2−4+3−2−3	1283a:B
+4−2−4+4+2−2−3	610a
+4−2−4+4−3+2−2	1327g:B
+4−3	151b, 661a, 1023:B, 1150b:B, 1150d:B
+4−3+2	134i, 1079c:B, 1512a:B
+4−3+2+2−2	1285f
+4−3+2+2−3	584c
+4−3+2+2−3+2−2	446a
+4−3+2+2−3+3−3	1280d:B, 1280e:B
+4−3+2+2−3−2	265i
+4−3+2+2−4−2	647
+4−3+2−2	496a:B, 854a:C, 993b
+4−3+2−2+2−2	1013b
+4−3+2−2−2	90a, 90b, 1175:B
+4−3+2−2−2+2+3	1025a
+4−3+2−2−2+3−2	552

Thematic Index of the Tabulated Melodies

Interval Sequence	Melody No.
+4−3+2−2−2−2	1004
+4−3+2−3	481b:B
+4−3+2−3+4−3+2	479i, 528a, 824
+4−3+3	749b:B
+4−3+3+2+2−2−2	Parry 27e:B
+4−3+3−3−2	776b
+4−3+3−3−2+2	283c
+4−3+3−4	265d
+4−3+3−4+2	666a
+4−3+3−4+4−5	647:B
+4−3+4+2−2−2+2	1017a
+4−3−2	187, 543b:B, 744, 788b, 788f, 1006a, 1006b, 1083, 1283b, 1283c, 1572, 1737b:C
+4−3−2+2+2−2−3	884
+4−3−2+2−2−2	1519b
+4−3−2+2−3−2+3	845
+4−3−2+2−3−3	880a:B
+4−3−2+2−4	1608d:C
+4−3−2+3+3−2+2	1419
+4−3−2+3−3	1547
+4−3−2+4−3	1602a:D
+4−3−2+4−3+2−2	528b
+4−3−2+4−3−2	697a, 1604
+4−3−2+4−3−2+4	445c
+4−3−2+4−3−2−2	372
+4−3−2+4−3−3	984d
+4−3−2−2+3−2+2	835b:B
+4−3−2−2−2	1285e
+4−3−2−2−2−2	738b:B
+4−3−2−2−2−3	1608a:C, 1608e:C
+4−3−2−2−3	668:B, 985:C, 988
+4−3−2−2−4	1737b:B
+4−3−2−3+2+2−3	1371a:C
+4−3−2−3+3+4−3	848a
+4−3−2−3−3	1493a:C
+4−3−2−4+4−2−2	738b:C

Thematic Index of the Tabulated Melodies

Interval Sequence	Melody No.
+4−3−2−5+2+4+2	986b:B
+4−3−3	902:B, 1077d:C
+4−3−3+2+4	773a:B
+4−3−3+4−3−2+3	988:B
+4−3−3+5−2−2−3	720:B
+4−3−3−3+5−2	984i
+4−3−4+2+2−4+2	1011
+4−4	1076
+4−4+2	749a:C
+4−4+2+2	680
+4−4+2+2+2−2−2	402d
+4−4+2+2−2−2−2	1314a:C
+4−4+2+3−3−2	211c
+4−4+2+3−4	218
+4−4+2+4−3+2	708d
+4−4+2−2−2−2	761:B
+4−4+2−3+2−3−3	363:B
+4−4+2−3−2+4−2	1647:B
+4−4+2−3−3−2+5	984b
+4−4+3	1079a
+4−4+3+2−4−2	764c
+4−4+3+3−2	711c
+4−4+3+3−3+2−3	1829:D
+4−4+3−2	445j, 1554:D
+4−4+3−2+2−2−3	122a
+4−4+3−2−2	1241a:C
+4−4+3−2−2+3−2	901:B
+4−4+3−2−2−2	764a, 764d
+4−4+3−2−3	43f, 43g
+4−4+3−2−3−3+4	1766:D
+4−4+4+2+3−3+2	1360
+4−4+4+3+3−3	1609:C
+4−4+4+4−5+2−3	344e:B
+4−4+4−2−2−2+2	123j, 815d
+4−4+4−2−3	592b, 1019
+4−4+4−2−3+2+3	1819

Thematic Index of the Tabulated Melodies

Interval Sequence	Melody No.
+4−4+4−3−2	231b
+4−4+4−3−2−3	344a
+4−4+4−4	1439b, 1602d:B
+4−4+4−4+2−2	752b
+4−4+4−4+4−4+2	1731:B
+4−4+4−4−3+3+4	1361
+4−4+5+2−3+2−5	271a
+4−4+5−2−4	271b
+4−4+5−3−2−3	399
+4−4−2+2−2	1233:B
+4−4−2+3+2−2−2	892b
+4−4−2+3−2	134e
+4−4−2+3−2−2+2	1280c:C
+4−4−2−2	1540d:D
+4−4−3+2−2+2+2	655a, 655b, 655c, 655d, 655e
+4−4−3+2−3+4−2	852a
+4−4−3+3−2−2+2	655g
+4−4−3+3−2−2−2	1277a, 1277b, 1277c
+4−4−3+4−2−2+2	966:B, 1280b:C, 1280d:C, 1280e:C
+4−4−3+4−2−4+3	1314b:C
+4−4−3−3+5−2−2	1696d
+4−5+4−2	166–167
+4−5−2	1123:D
+4−5−2−2+2	1585c
+4−6+2	1392b:B
+4−6+3+2−2	1246a:C
+4−6+3−2−2	961b
−4	586, 1145a, 1145b, 1145c, 1387:C, 1469b:B
−4+2	1712:C
−4+2+2	1268, 1514d:B, 1809a:D
−4+2+2+2	1168f
−4+2+2+2+3	1168b
−4+2+2+2−2−2−2	641:B, 694:B
−4+2+2+2−3+3−2	1218
−4+2+2+2−4+2+2	24a, 1444b:C, 1444c:C, 1444d:B
−4+2+2+3−2	1168a, 1168c, 1168d, 1168e

Thematic Index of the Tabulated Melodies

Interval Sequence	Melody No.
—4+2+2+3—2—3	294
—4+2+2—2—2	823:B, 1381a, 1545b:C
—4+2+2—2—2+2—2	1310p:B
—4+2+2—2—2—3	782b
—4+2+2—2—3	317c
—4+2+2—3	489a, 1248
—4+2+2—3+2	1602j:B
—4+2+2—3+2—3+2	971a
—4+2+2—4+3+2—3	721c:C
—4+2+3	1154
—4+2+3+3—2—2—3	1027a
—4+2+3+3—3	1098b:B
—4+2+3—2—2—2	770e:B
—4+2+3—2—2—2+4	840:B
—4+2+3—4+2	1707b:B
—4+2+3—4—3	1254a
—4+2+4+2—2—2—3	834b
—4+2+4—2—2—2	377b:B
—4+2+4—2—2—3+2	983p:B
—4+2+5—2+2—3—2	1284c
—4+2—2	94b:B, 500b:C, 1134
—4+2—2+2+2—2—2	701b:B
—4+2—2+2+2—3+2	333e
—4+2—2+2+3—2—2	1007:C
—4+2—2+3—3—3	1243f:B
—4+2—2—2	39h:B, 1155, 1228:B
—4+2—2—2—2	1144b:B
—4+2—2—2—2+3+2	1701:B
—4+2—3	1637:D, 1670
—4+2—3+2—2	222:B
—4+2—3+3+3+2—2	321g
—4+2—3+3+3—3+2	333d
—4+2—3+3+3—3—2	365–366c
—4+2—3+4—2+2+3	857
—4+2—3+4—2—2+2	369a
—4+2—3+4—2—2+3	267c

Thematic Index of the Tabulated Melodies

Interval Sequence	Melody No.
−4+2−3+5−2−3+4	296a
−4+2−3+5−4+2−3	1713:B
−4+3	1085b:B, 1661:C
−4+3+2	1402:C
−4+3+2−2−2	60a
−4+3+2−2−3+4	1158a
−4+3+2−2−3−2	1606bis:C
−4+3+2−2−4+2	1722b
−4+3+2−3+2−2−2	1722a
−4+3+2−3−2	711c:B, 1722c
−4+3+2−3−3	835h:B
−4+3−2	1507:B
−4+3−2−2	1632:C
−4+3−2−2+2	1398a, 1398b
−4+3−2−2+2−2−2	1895:B
−4+3−3	584a, 584b
−4+3−3−2	711b:B, 1656:B
−4+3−3−3−2	482:B
−4+4	1144bis
−4+4+2	764b:B, 1293
−4+4+2+2	1107b
−4+4+2+2+2−3−2	1494b
−4+4+2+2+3−2	406
−4+4+2+2−2	1176, 1659c, 1659d, 1659f, 1659g, 1659h
−4+4+2+2−2+2+2	1429, 1719a, 1719b
−4+4+2+2−2−2+2	835c, 835d
−4+4+2+2−3+2−5	1337b
−4+4+2+2−3+3+2	511b
−4+4+2+2−3−4	1742a
−4+4+2+2−3−4+4	835g
−4+4+2+3	764c:B
−4+4+2+3−2−2−2	511a
−4+4+2+3−3	1494a, 1744b
−4+4+2−2−4+4+2	1404a
−4+4+3	1807
−4+4+3+2−2−3	1651a

Thematic Index of the Tabulated Melodies

Interval Sequence	Melody No.
−4+4+3+3−2−2	196e, 1378
−4+4+3+3−3−2	127
−4+4+3−2	466:B, 1659e
−4+4+3−2+2−3	1626c
−4+4+3−3	1153
−4+4+4−4	665b:B, 1098a:B
−4+4+5−2−2−2+2	1446c
−4+4+5−2−2−2−2	1446a, 1446b
−4+4+5−2−3+2−3	1455
−4+4−2+3−2−2−2	321e
−4+4−2−2	492f:B
−4+4−2−2+4−2−4	784b:B
−4+4−2−2−3+5−2	429b
−4+4−2−3	511b:B, 572:B; Parry 21b:B
−4+4−2−3+2	130d:B
−4+4−4	685:C, 895, 1586a, 1586b, 1586c, 1586d
−4+4−4+2−2	206a
−4+4−4+4+2+2	436, 1702b
−4+4−4+4+2+2−2	1717
−4+4−4+4−4+4−4	1850
−4+4−4+5−2−2−2	984g
−4+5+2+2−2−2+2	1728
−4+5−2−3+2−2−2	1417a:B
−4+5−5	1826:B
−4+5−5+2+3−3−2	1826:C
−4+6	1616, 1751
−4+6+2+2−2−2	1844
−4+6+3+2−2−3−3	1015
−4+6−2+2	1809a
−4+6−2+2−3−4	1297
−4+6−2−2−2	1164
−4+6−3	837
−4+7−2−2−2	1121:B
−4+7−2−3	1493c
−4+7−3−2−2+2	1200:D, 1775:C
−4+8−2−2−2	1296

Thematic Index of the Tabulated Melodies

Interval Sequence	Melody No.
−4+8−4+5−2−5+2	632
−4−2	1652:B
−4−2+2+2+2+2	905g
−4−2+2+2+2−3+5	1390:B
−4−2+2+3	1001b
−4−2+2+5−2−3+3	437
−4−2+2−2	984j, 1001g:B
−4−2+2−2+5−4	1001g
−4−2+3+2−3	905e
−4−2+3+3−4−2	1493b
−4−2+3+3−4−2+3	1447d:B
−4−2+3−2−2	1254a:C
−4−2+3−3+2	577a:B
−4−2+5−2	1000i, 1001a
−4−2+5−4	1606bis:B
−4−2+6−2+2−6	1618e
−4−2−2	1132:D
−4−2−2+2	1142a
−4−2−2+2+2	1273e
−4−2−2+2−2	187:B
−4−2−2+2−2−2	1605:C
−4−2−2+3−3	1571c:B
−4−2−2+4−2	1273a, 1273f
−4−2−2+5+4−3−3	344a:B
−4−2−2−2+2−2	1439a:B
−4−2−3	1247a:C
−4−3	1734
−4−3+2+2	1273d
−4−3+2+2+4+3−2	1021b:C
−4−3+2−3−2	1538:C
−4−3+2−4+5−2	984c
−4−3+4−2	1273c
−4−3−3+6−2+3+2	1699
+5	958g, 1379, 1742b
+5+2	1153:D
+5+2−2	61, 1529, 1533, 1692b

Thematic Index of the Tabulated Melodies

Interval Sequence	Melody No.
+5+2−2+2−2−3	1467b
+5+2−2−2	497, 1077c:C, 1402
+5+2−2−2+2	721c
+5+2−2−2+2−3	1763
+5+2−2−2+2−3−2	1713
+5+2−2−2+2−5+3	1425
+5+2−2−2−2	995
+5+2−2−2−2+2+2	1459
+5+2−2−2−2+3−2	983aa
+5+2−2−2−2−2	833a
+5+2−2−2−2−3	751, 1493d:C
+5+2−2−2−3+4−2	384a
+5+2−2−3	388, 1246e
+5+2−2−3+3−3	721d
+5+2−2−3−3+4−2	384d, 1725:B
+5+2−3+2−3+3−2	Parry 27d
+5+2−3−2+2−3−2	1325a:B
+5+2−3−2−3+5−2	Parry 12e
+5+3−2−2−2	1229a
+5+3−4	1525:B
+5+3−5+3	1395
+5+4−3−2−3	998, 1518
+5+4−3−2−3+3−2	983l
+5−2	178, 1066
+5−2+2	1118
+5−2+2+2−2−2−3	724a
+5−2+2−2	1672a; Parry 21b
+5−2+2−2+2−2+2	1880
+5−2+2−2−2	713c; Parry 19
+5−2+2−2−2−2	713a, 1216bis:C, 1281a
+5−2+2−2−2−3	810c
+5−2+2−2−3	1823
+5−2+2−2−3−2	512
+5−2+2−3	983z, 1157
+5−2+2−3−2	1182b:C
+5−2+2−3−2−2	1448a

Thematic Index of the Tabulated Melodies

Interval Sequence	Melody No.
+5−2+2−3−3	1569a
+5−2+2−3−3+5−2	983g
+5−2+2−4	1593b:B
+5−2+2−4−2	1602b:D
+5−2+2−4−2+2	Parry 12c:B
+5−2+2−4−2+5−2	Parry 12c
+5−2+2−5	983ii
+5−2+3−2−2−3	1495
+5−2+3−2−3−3	320a
+5−2+4	656c
+5−2+4−2−2−2−2	1442
+5−2+4−2−2−3+3	983ee
+5−2−2	1065, 1368
+5−2−2+2+2+2−2	1309
+5−2−2+2+2−2−2	330a
+5−2−2+2+2−3	1281c
+5−2−2+2+2−3−2	1332a
+5−2−2+2−2+2−3	891b
+5−2−2+2−3−4	1550
+5−2−2+2−3	1246l:B
+5−2−2+2−3+2	10
+5−2−2+3	1478:C
+5−2−2+3−2−3	986a:B
+5−2−2+3−2−3−2	819c
+5−2−2+4−2−3−3	1886
+5−2−2−2	890, 911, 1005e:B, 1158b:B, 1371b:D, 1527:B, 1593c:B
+5−2−2−2+2+3−2	1325d:B
+5−2−2−2+3−3	616a
+5−2−2−2+4	392a
+5−2−2−2−2+5−2	983dd
+5−2−2−3	623b:B, 1087a, 1396a, 1606b:B; Parry 49
+5−2−2−3+2	1617:D
+5−2−2−3+2+3−2	1499b
+5−2−2−3+3−2	983ll
+5−2−2−3+4	Parry 27a
+5−2−2−3+4−2	105:B

Thematic Index of the Tabulated Melodies

Interval Sequence	Melody No.
+5−2−2−3+5−2	983d; Parry 12d
+5−2−2−3+5−2−2	1499a:C
+5−2−2−4+2	1606a:B
+5−2−3	494:B, 1061:D, 1371a:D, 1485:B, 1497:B, 1515e, 1759:B
+5−2−3+2+2−2+3	581:B
+5−2−3+2−2	1629a:B
+5−2−3+2−2−2	31
+5−2−3+2−3+4−2	265f:B
+5−2−3+3+2−2−2	724d, 1712
+5−2−3+3−2−3+2	1095d
+5−2−3+3−3	713b:C, 1801:D
+5−2−3+4	1502b, 1792
+5−2−3+4−2	1757
+5−2−3+4−2−2−2	1448b
+5−2−3−2	1757:B
+5−2−3−2	1467b:B
+5−2−3−2+5−2	Parry 12a
+5−2−3−3	1068
+5−2−3−3−3−2+3	1016a:C
+5−2−4+3+2−2−3	357a:B
+5−2−4+3+3−2−3	714
+5−2−4+3−3+5−2	983c
+5−3	985:B, 1107a
+5−3+2+3−2−3+3	435a
+5−3+2−2+2−2−2	122b
+5−3+2−2−3	320b
+5−3+2−2−3+4	392d
+5−3+2−3	1619h
+5−3+2−4+4−3−2	700:B
+5−3+3−2−2−2	Parry 27c:B
+5−3+3−2−2−3	82c, 1550c
+5−3+3−3−2	1497
+5−3−2	119e, 1054d:B, 1481a:B
+5−3−3	315, 819d
+5−3−3−2+4−3	Parry 28b
+5−4+3+2−4−2	764b

Thematic Index of the Tabulated Melodies

Interval Sequence	Melody No.
+5−4+3−4+5−2	983h
+5−4−3+2−4−2	1737a:B
+5−5	1231:D
+5−5+2+2+3−4	556
+5−5+2+3+2−2−2	724b
+5−5+3−3	1532g:B
+5−5−2−2−2+5−2	984a
−5+2+2+2+2	1657a
−5+2+2+3−3−2	849b
−5+2+2+3−3−2+4	849a
−5+2+3+2	1657b
−5+2+3−3	1748–1749:D
−5+2+3−3+3−3	244:B
−5+2−2+4−4+3−3	983i, 983j
−5+2−2+5−2	1001e
−5+3+3−2−2−2	676:B
−5+3+3−5+3	1516a
−5+3+3−5+3+3	1532m
−5+3−2+4−4+2−3	617
−5+3−2−2	907:C
−5+3−2−2−2−2−2	1809a:C
−5+4	1619h:B
−5+4−2−2	983n:B
−5+4−5+4−3+2	1731:C
−5+5−2−2−3+2	1208:B
−5+5−3+2−3−2	944:B
−5−2+2+2+2	1807:D
−5−2−2−2	914:C
−5−4+4+3−2	1255a:B
+6+2+3−2−2−2+3	1314a:B
+6+2−2−2	1704
+6+2−2−2+2	1692a
+6+2−2−2−3	1373:B
+6+3−2−3+2−3−2	1324a
+6−2	1132
+6−2+2+2+2−3−2	1318

Thematic Index of the Tabulated Melodies

Interval Sequence	Melody No.
+6−2+2+2−3−3	1627
+6−2+2−2	951b, 1672b, 1672c
+6−2+2−2+2−2+2	395
+6−2+2−2+2−5+2	1281b
+6−2+2−2−2−3	260a
+6−2+2−2−2−3−2	208a, 1324b
+6−2+2−2−3+2−3	1710
+6−2+2−2−3+3+2	551
+6−2+2−3+3−2+2	1703:B
+6−2+2−3−2−3	1212b:C
+6−2+2−3−3	1215
+6−2+2−3−3+5−2	435b
+6−2+3−2−2−3	1527
+6−2+4−3−4−3	1772–1773
+6−2+4−4−2−2−2	1324c
+6−2−2+2+2−2−3	720
+6−2−2+2−2+2−3	1723:B
+6−2−2+2−2−2−2	1327g
+6−2−2+2−5+2+3	1310p
+6−2−2+3−3	712
+6−2−2−2	1147:C
+6−2−2−2+3	1621:C
+6−2−2−2+3−4−2	272
+6−2−2−2−2+2+2	713f:D
+6−2−2−2−2−2	208b
+6−2−2−2−2−2+2	360b
+6−2−2−2−3	1163e, 1508
+6−2−2−2−3+5−3	341:B
+6−2−3+2−2+2+2	655c:B
+6−2−3+2−3	1401:B
+6−2−3+3−3−2	221
+6−2−3+4−2−2−2	1441:B
+6−2−5+3−2	1559:D
+6−3	1603:B
+6−3+2−3	1742b:C
+6−3+2−4−2+4−3	1829:C

Thematic Index of the Tabulated Melodies

Interval Sequence	Melody No.
+6−3−2−2	1467c:C
+6−3−4+2+2+2	1615:C
+6−4	1886:B
+6−6+5−2−2−2	1619d:C
+7−2−2+2−3	983cc
+8−3+2+2−3+3−3	1280c:B
+8−3−2	1614:C
+8−4−5	1009:B
+8−5+5	1136

General Index

(Arabic Figures are "Tab. of Mat." Current Nos.)

General Index

General Index